When I'm Sixty-Four

When I'm Sixty-Four

The Plot against Pensions and the Plan to Save Them

Teresa Ghilarducci

PRINCETON UNIVERSITY PRESS   *Princeton and Oxford*

Published by Princeton University Press, 41 William Street, Princeton, New Jersey 08540

In the United Kingdom: Princeton University Press, 6 Oxford Street, Woodstock, Oxfordshire OX20 1TR

Cover design by Tracy Baldwin

First paperback printing, 2018
Paper ISBN 978-0-691-17802-8

The Library of Congress has cataloged the cloth edition of this book as follows:

Ghilarducci, Teresa.
    When I'm sixty-four : the plot against pensions and the plan to save them / Teresa Ghilarducci.
        p.cm.
    Includes bibliographical references and index.
    ISBN 978-0-691-11431-6 (hbk. : alk. paper)   1. Pensions—United States.
2. Social security—United States.   I. Title.
    HD7125.G465   2008
    331.25'20973—dc22   2007045942

British Library Cataloging-in-Publication Data is available

This book has been composed in Minion Pro

Printed on acid-free paper.   ∞

press.princeton.edu

Printed in the United States of America

For William O'Rourke

_____

Contents

Part II
What Is Good about America's Retirement Income Security System

Chapter 6
The Short History of Old Age Leisure in America   *181*

Chapter 7
The Distribution of Retirement Time: Who Really Gets to Retire?   *197*

Chapter 8
Working: The New Retirement's Effect on the Economy   *217*

When I'm Sixty-Four

Introduction

In the mid-1960s, when the first wave of American baby boomers—the 76 million people born between 1946 and 1962—tripled college enrollments and Medicare legislation was adopted, the Beatles' song "When I'm Sixty-Four," could not, in retrospect, have been more forward-looking.

Since the first Social Security check was sent sixty years ago, Americans losing their hair have been receiving "pension valentines." Today, as the Beatles' first fans are approaching age sixty-four, American workers wonder if the promised pensions, Social Security, and medical care, will materialize in their old age.

In the face of a crumbling pension system, a badly functioning medical insurance system for the aged, and soaring national deficits, policymakers and leaders can find a way to save retirement—a necessary, if now threatened, feature of all civilized democracies—by combining the appropriate governmental, economic, and social ingredients into a new, and newly imagined, retirement system. By mustering the political will and economic intelligence to do this, leaders will not only spare society the travails of the currently damaged system, but will provide generations present and future a new blueprint for maximizing the well-being and social contribution of elderly people—a win-win formula. This book explains how.

Categorically, everyone admits that Social Security has been stunningly successful at halving the elderly's poverty rate and enabling the middle class to retire. The entire pension system, including employer pensions, has been even more successful. Europeans are often surprised that Americans have any guaranteed income programs at all. Even more surprisingly, given this nation's reputation for "do-it-yourself" financial lives, there is widespread acceptance that older Americans, even those who are healthy and still able to work, deserve to retire.

In 1950, a working man could look forward to seven years of retirement time before he died; for women it was about thirteen and a half years. By 2000, on average, men retired for almost fourteen years and women eighteen. Overall, as a nation, we have constructed steady improvements in a very valuable resource—retirement time—and it should be a cause of celebration (see figure 0.1). Nevertheless, powerful forces threaten this vital addition to the quality of workers' lives.

Although most of us value our "leisure," while doing research for this book I discovered revulsion for that word. Friends, reporters, and politicians recoiled from my phrase, "retirement-leisure." Defending retirement-leisure—the kind of retirement where older people can afford to not work—was more challenging than I expected. The financial ability to withdraw voluntarily from the labor force, the ability to rest, and, even to recuperate before dying, is, to workers, a fundamental part of dignified living and a marker for achieving middle-class status. And, if pressed, most economists would admit to expecting that, as civilized societies grow richer, they will create institutions that permit able-bodied people to retire.

Figure 0.1
Number of Years in Retirement, by Birth Year (1885–1938)

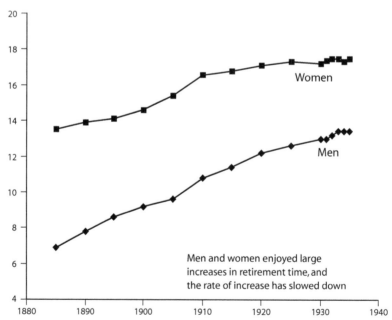

Note: Retirement time = leisure rate x number of years to live = ((100–lfp)/100) × life expectancy in years after age 65.

Sources: 1950, 1960, 1970–2000: *Health, United States 2002*, at http://www.cdc.gov/nchs/data/hus/tables/2002/02hus028.pdf; 1955: *Vital Statistics of the United States, 1955*, vol. I, introduction, 1957; *Vital Statistics of the United States, 1965*, vol. 2, sec 5, 1968.

However, all people seemed defensive about the notion of retirement, quickly asserting that they wanted to be productive, not shrivel up and die. Nevertheless, the notion that retirement was a last chance to do what one wanted grew sweeter as one contemplated it coming at the time when life is filled with nothing but last chances. Time before death has special proprieties. Chief among them is scarcity, and scarcity always increases value. In Saul Bellow's novel *Ravelstein*, an older writer reflects on his life-threatening illness; he wants very much for his much younger wife to understand how valuable time is before death:

> And Ivan Ilyich also mentions the slow rise of a stone thrown into the air. When it returns to earth it accelerates thirty-two feet per second. You are controlled by gravitational magnetism and the whole universe is involved in this speeding up of your end.—Art is one rescue from this chaotic acceleration. Meter in poetry, tempo in music, form, and color in painting. Nevertheless, we do feel that we are speeding earthward, crashing into our graves. (Bellow, 192)

I used to include this quotation on birthday cards—but very few were amused.

We are deep in a national bargaining session over "socially optimal" retirement. I wrote this book to articulate what is at stake: that the needless fear that retirement is not deserved, nor affordable, is framing the debate and distorting the analysis.

As I was finishing this book in the summer of 2006, a retired United Airline pilot called me, apologetic for taking my time. He told me he lost 68.3% (he rounded to one decimal point!) of his pension after flying thirty-five years for one company. He said, "Except the military, I worked for United about my whole life." He said he made "pretty good" money and "they" told him to put his money toward his retirement. "And now it's gone. How can they do that?" At sixty-one, he needed to find a way to keep his house. Taking retraining classes at the local high school, he created a website as a project for his computer class. He still does not have a job; but he has a website dedicated to "not letting what happened to me happen to other people." He used his much smaller pension to buy the domain name www.protectpensions.org.

This book aims to explain these kinds of pension losses with the hope that they never happen in the future.

- Part I explores the undermining of the U.S. retirement income security system, which, despite popular belief, is not caused by Social Security collapsing, but by work-based pensions tottering badly, as many financial risks that workers cannot control are no longer shared by employers and the government, but shifted entirely to workers.

- Part II addresses the break from the forty-year trend of older men withdrawing from the labor force. Older workers are being partly pulled into the labor force by more job opportunities, and partly because of their diminishing pensions and health insurance.

- Part III identifies who benefits when older people work more. Human-resource consultants warn clients that the supply of teenagers, housewives, and immigrants will dry up,[1] raising workers' bargaining power and causing upward pressure and a squeeze on profits.[2]

The book concludes with proposals for a retirement income policy that finances retirement and distributes it more evenly across workers.

Part 1

The Attack on Retirement

Chapter 1

Hope for Retirement's Future

Until the 1950s, only the wealthy could expect to retire. In 1951, less than 5% of men said they retired because they wanted to rest and have some time off, and these were the men with the highest incomes.[1] In that same year, over half of older men were working and most of the others were unemployed or unemployable. Today, over 60% of older Americans, not working, actually chose to retire because they prefer free time to paid work. Making retirement available to almost all workers, that is, "democratizing" retirement, is one of the greatest achievements of robust market economies. Nonetheless, even in rich societies, conflict persists about who is entitled to pensions and how generous they should be. Reflecting on the debate over Americans' new social insurance programs—Social Security, unemployment insurance, and poor relief programs—philosopher Bertrand Russell wrote in 1935:

> The idea that the poor should have leisure has always been shocking to the rich. . . . When I was a child, shortly after urban working men had acquired the vote, a number of public holidays were established. I remember hearing an old Duchess say, "What do the poor want with holidays? They ought to work."[2]

The nineteenth-century duchess reflects a twenty-first-century conviction, deeply held in some circles, that because people are living longer, instead of society shoring up pensions, the elderly ought to work more. Indeed, if trends continue, sixty-five-year-olds in 2010 on average will live longer than sixty-five-year-olds ever lived before; however, perplexingly, the expected months in retirement will fall by 14%. People will live longer but they will work a whole lot more.

This book explores the basis of the belief that the elderly have too much retirement leisure; and asks the question, Who loses and who wins if and when pension income becomes less secure and the elderly work more as a consequence?

Older people, who must work longer than they want to make ends meet, lose. Employers, who avoid raising wages as older workers stay in the labor pool, win. Financial managers, eager to manage individual retirement accounts, defined contribution or 401(k)-type plans, which could be newly created from converted traditional company pensions (defined benefit plans) and privatized Social Security, also win.

This book also covers the sources of retirement income, the distribution of retirement time, and ways to rescue the pension system.

This opening chapter argues several issues:

- that civilized societies enable people to retire;

- that the United States has achieved much toward ensuring entitlement to retirement for ordinary workers; and

- that moves toward individual retirement accounts—defined contribution pension plans, 401(k)-type pension plans, and Social Security commercial personal accounts—are flawed responses to pension troubles and to the decreasing ratio of workers to retirees.

The financial industry and political groups, devoted to making government smaller, promote the replacement of employer pensions and Social Security accounts with individual accounts—while ignoring what public policy has accomplished for retirement security. Their vision of a reformed U.S. retirement income system moves away from what good reform should do—that is, make the system more fair, enhance productivity, and be more efficient. No pension system should waste people's money.

Principles for a Pension Rescue Plan

In 1960, half of the nation's private sector workforce and almost all of the public sector were covered by a traditional pension plan, commonly referred to as a defined benefit pension plan. Forty-seven years later at the beginning of the twenty-first century, the same share of the private sector workforce is offered a pension plan at work. But the type of plan they are offered has changed dramatically: the defined contribution 401(k)-type individual-account plan is now dominant. Public sector workers still have defined benefit plans.

There are many differences between defined benefit and defined contribution plans. One is particularly stark: In defined benefit plans, employers make all the investment decisions and must pay the pension regardless of the pension fund's investment earnings. In a defined contribution plan, the employee makes all the decisions and accepts the risk that the accumulations in her account could be lower than expected. Here is how the plans work.

A defined benefit (DB) pension plan credits every year of service with a certain percentage of salary earned, which is usually some average of the salary over the final years on the job. For example, a typical defined benefit plan pays a retiree an annual benefit equal to 2% for every year of service multiplied by an average of the last three years of salary. Therefore an employee who earned, on average, $40,000 in his last three years of his twenty-year service would have an annual pension of $16,000, calculated as follows: 2% of $40,000 is $800; twenty years at $800 per year of service is $16,000. That annual pension payment comes to 40% of the $40,000 average of the last three years' annual earnings. (Keep in mind that 40%!) The employer contributes annually to a fund to pay for these defined benefit pensions as they come due, according to federal regulations.

In a defined contribution (DC) plan, the employee and most employers pay a defined amount into the employee's individual retirement account. Whatever the account accumulates and earns on its investments is what is available. A savings account and an individual retirement account are fairly similar, except an individual is advised to invest the retirement account in many different investment vehicles and there are certain rules about withdrawing money from it. A worker can borrow against or withdraw funds from her or his retirement account before age fifty-seven-and-a-half, but must pay a tax penalty—a 10% tax rate is added to the employee's ordinary federal tax rate—on the amount of funds withdrawn. Many employees do withdraw their money and pay the tax penalty. Until the 1990s, defined contribution plans were mostly used as supplements to defined benefit plans. Now, many companies have replaced their traditional pension plans with defined contribution plans.

As 401(k) plans overtook traditional company pensions, Social Security emerged as the only reliable source of income for the elderly. During the same time period, wage income emerged as the elderly's fastest-growing source of income. As you will see, this means that more of the elderly will be poor, and many more of those who don't fall into poverty will experience a significant fall in living standards after they retire

Making people work longer and look for work at older ages to augment inadequate pensions may be a reasonable proposition. But to ensure that older people freely choose work over retirement and that future generations are not downwardly mobile, facing a retirement future as bleak as retirement was before the 1970s, the following needs to happen:

- Workers must be required to save 5% of their salary (up to the Social Security earnings cap) in a guaranteed retirement account. The accumulations in these accounts should become available after age sixty-five; the government must guarantee the rate of return; and a government agency, not a commercial money manager, must administer the accounts.

- Tax subsidies for 401(k) plans must be replaced with a $600 refundable tax credit for each worker, to help offset the financial sacrifice of having to save 5% of earnings. The replacement will equalize government tax subsidies between high- and low-income earners.

- Social Security payroll tax increases must be scheduled for 2020 and general revenues—from the estate tax particularly—used to eliminate old-age poverty.

- Worker representation on employers' pension boards should be mandatory. This will help workers save because they will be engaged in the management of their money; worker representation will also inhibit employers from managing the company's pension plan to serve their own interests.

These policies could make it easier and less costly for anyone, especially low- and middle-income workers, to save for retirement. More importantly, these changes would avoid the problems of the narrow interests of the financial industry and having employers steering pension reform. Historically, workers have better pensions when both their political influence and their bargaining power are strong, and when workers feel entitled to income and leisure after a lifetime of hard work.

The Successes of the U.S. Retirement System

So far, at the beginning of the twenty-first century, Americans expect time off at the end of their working lives. Americans consider that it is reasonable to expect paid retirement time—a concept that has evolved, just as the entitlement to any time off has evolved, as implicit in overtime, the eight-hour day, and "the weekend." These entitlements resulted from compromises between workers, organized labor, firms, and federal and state governments. Workers throughout the post–World War II period have continued to want, and to pay for, holidays and vacations, paying in the form of forgone increases in cash wages and/or increased productivity. The New York City transit workers risked public ire and severe consequences when they stranded millions of commuters in chilly December 2005 in a strike over a proposed cutback in their pension benefits. Not only is entitlement to paid time off important, American workers and their unions have come to regard pension plans as a way for ordinary workers, many of whom are and were immigrants, to achieve middle-class status by obtaining some of the same kinds of income security arranged for their managers and bosses.

Gains in retirement time were quite large before the start of the twentieth century (before the year 1900). Men born after the Civil War lived much longer—their average time in retirement leaped approximately 9% compared to men born five years earlier (these calculations are explained in chapter 2). From 1900 to 1999, the largest gains in retirement time were for those people born around 1911; women enjoyed a more than 12% boost in retirement time compared to women five years older, and men an 8.2% boost. This age group retired in the mid-1970s, when Social Security benefits increased rapidly and company-provided pension plan coverage was growing. The rates of increase in retirement time for each successive group of people born five years later gradually fell; the increases may have gotten smaller, but they nevertheless were increases! Not until the late 1990s did the growth in retirement time begin to turn downward. Both men and women retiring around 1999 could expect less retirement time (about 1% fewer years) than people just a few years older. Clearly, people are living longer, but they seem to be using the longevity increases to engage in paid work, not to experience retirement leisure (figure 1.1).

Perhaps workers are freely choosing to use their longer lives to work more. Or it could be that people increasingly feel forced to work longer because their retirement income has become less adequate and secure. The reality is somewhere in between. And because the gap in retirement leisure between different groups is growing as middle-class retirees and lower-income retirees suffer from less secure and smaller pensions, the changes are hurting some groups and helping others.

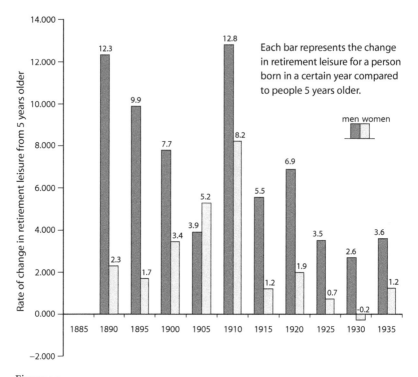

Figure 1.1

Men and Women Stopped Getting Improvements in Retirement Leisure in the Late 1990s: Longevity Improvements Went to Paid Work

Sources: See data in Appendix 3.1.

Origins of Retirement Time

There are three ways a person can obtain more time in retirement—retiring younger, living longer, or both. Retirement time for Americans had, until recently, grown—at different rates, for different reasons, for different people, at different times. In 1960, 66% of men over age sixty-five retired, which was more than the 54% of the men over sixty-five who retired in 1950. Men working in 1960 expected to live 12.8 years beyond age sixty-five, which was about the same life expectancy for men working in 1950. Nevertheless, retired men in 1960 got more retirement time than retired men in 1950—the younger men experienced, on average, a 28% increase in retirement time. They enjoyed this increase from retiring at earlier ages rather than living longer.[3] Moreover, even younger men, those turning sixty-five between 1965 and 1980, lived longer and retired at earlier ages.

A reversal occurred beginning in the mid 1980s; older men continued to live longer, but their longevity improvements—additional years of life after age sixty-five—did not make up for the increase in their work effort. Recently, between 1998 and 2000, life expectancy for a sixty-five-year-old male was up 2% (see Appendix 3.1 and figure 1.1). Nevertheless, in the same period, the share of men older than age sixty-five who continued in the work force was up 6%. During the same period, older women's life expectancy did not increase but older women's work effort was up 2%. Unquestionably, when increases in life expectancy begin to lag behind increases in labor force participation, years and months spent in retirement will shrink.

In the 1970s, a higher percentage of workers over age fifty who retired did so at younger ages, and lived longer. At that time, there were no complaints that the rise in "old-age leisure" was inappropriate, undeserved, unaffordable, or would impede economic growth by causing labor shortages.

The Positive—but Subtle—Aspects of the U.S. Retirement System

Giving people more free time near the end of their lives is a good reason to celebrate, defend, and even expand particular aspects of the American pension and Social Security system. However, there are three other, more subtle, positive aspects of the current American pension system: the system has "democratized" retirement time, meaning that people of different socioeconomic groups and races came to expect that they will retire for about the same amount of time; employer pensions, together with Social Security, help promote worker productivity and economic stability over the business cycle; and the American retirement system is, for the most part, remarkably affordable and efficient.

There are three reasons why it is affordable and efficient. One reason is that the current pension system distributes retirement leisure fairly equally across socioeconomic classes. This fact is remarkable given the increase in inequality in almost every other aspect of American economic life: wealth, income, access to health care and a college education. The distribution of retirement time is somewhat equal because, relative to the lifespan of average workers, the workers who die earlier than average (workers laboring under worse working conditions, with lower incomes, and more likely to be non-white) are actually able to withdraw from the labor force at younger ages.[4] At the same time, the system encourages higher-income workers, who tend to start their careers at older ages, to retire at older ages. A simple example makes this point: a lower-educated worker who enters the paid workforce at age eighteen can retire with early retirement Social Security benefits at age sixty-two, and may die at age seventy-five. A higher-income worker may likely enter the labor force at age twenty-four, retire from a professional job at sixty-eight, and die eighty-one, having had more health insurance, a better diet, and a physically easier job. Yet both work forty-four years and are in retirement for thirteen years.

This equity in retirement time comes about because of the particular characteristics of employer-based defined benefit pension plans and the structure of Social Security. Both systems are flexible and well designed to allow workers to retire at approximately the same real ages. The idea that chronological and real ages are different has evolved into cliché: "fifty is the new thirty," "sixty is the new forty." (The cliché seems to change depending on the chronological age of the pundit.) Computing anyone's real age is an elaborate exercise in assessing vitality and, ultimately, life expectancy—the number of years from your birth matters less than the number of years until your death. Compare the real age of a forty-year-old in 1950—more likely someone whose physical well-being has been sorely affected by smoking and lack of exercise—to a forty-year-old in 2007—someone who avoids tobacco and bounds up the stairs. A popular self-help book[5] shows how to compute a real age, taking into consideration factors such as hereditary and lifestyle choices. Good genes and choices earn months deducted from your real age. (People who roam bookstores—surely more likely leafy-vegetable eaters and non-smokers, among other healthy choices—predictably have real ages, according to the calculator, far younger than their actual age, and are presumably happy to spend $20 in the self-improvement section.) Yet many bleak factors negatively impacting longevity are not made explicit—bad housing, inadequate health care, and brutish jobs make a fifty-year-old poor person effectively "older" than a fifty-year-old rich person who lives in a nice house, has no difficulty getting physical checkups, and can handle work stress. Socioeconomic factors mean that, if we all retired at sixty-five, some of us would have much less retirement leisure than others.

A system that allows workers who are likely to die earlier to retire earlier promotes equity in retirement time. Because defined benefit pension plans are more equally distributed across occupations than 401(k) plans and are more likely connected to physically and mentally difficult jobs (you will see why in chapter 7), for example in steel-making and mining, they serve as social "levelers," meaning they help abolish social inequity in the distribution of free time among older people from different socioeconomic classes. That is, pensions, together with Social Security, allow people to retire at approximately the same real age.

The shift from defined benefit plans to defined contribution plans, which are individual account plans like 401(k)-type plans, may increase social inequality by encouraging people with high real ages to keep on working, because the size of a defined contribution pension depends on each individual's disciplined savings, good investment returns, lower investment fees, and successful use of annuities. Higher-income individuals do better in all four areas.

As the use of individual retirement account plans (defined contribution plans or 401(k)-type plans) increases, an opposite and perverse relationship could begin to develop between work and death: people with the lowest levels of education and income would work the longest, while higher-income workers who live longer would retire earlier. The gap in retirement time by class would grow, reversing a remarkable achievement of the U.S. retirement system that, despite the increasing gaps in income, wealth, housing, and health, retirement time was converging between people in different socioeconomic classes.

The second reason the American pension system is affordable and efficient is that the employer system enhances productivity; there is little reason for employers to sponsor pensions if they did not promote productivity. Pensions are part of the production system. A move away from company pensions in favor of pensions that rely on a workers' taking a "do-it-yourself" approach will fail. Such an approach relies on individuals to save for retirement from each pay check—regardless of a child's need, financial urgency, or tempting vacation. No developed or developing nation requires its citizens to make long-term plans to secure their retirement income without a great deal of institutional support.

Employers offer pensions to attract and retain loyal and skilled workers. Employer pensions also pay for "used-up" labor—that is, workers whose skills cannot keep up with the technology or the image of youth a company uses or wants to exhibit. In either sense, employer pensions are analogous to depreciation allowances for physical capital that wears out. Viewing pensions as labor depreciation payments or deferred wages has different connotations (explored in chapter 9), but both perceptions clearly identify employers' obligation to redeem pension promises, and also identify the value employers obtain from providing pensions. At the same time, pensions are efficient savings vehicles for workers; they help workers defer consumption and boost overall levels of household wealth.

The American pension system also has an underappreciated effect in keeping consumer spending from falling too far during economic stress and difficulty. This "parachute" on dips in spending helps businesses recover faster than they otherwise would in recessions. In such bad times, workers who are eligible to receive defined benefits and Social Security benefits are far more likely to leave the labor force rather than look for jobs when they are laid off. This reduces the number of people looking for work and thus stabilizes unemployment rates and economic decline. If defined benefit pensions are transformed into individual retirement accounts, whose value is based on financial assets, this source of economic stabilization disappears. Consider this: When pension income is solely based on the health of financial markets, its value falls during economic downturns, which impels and obligates older workers to stay in their jobs, if they can keep their jobs, or to seek work—precisely the opposite behavior wanted when unemployment is growing.

And third, employer pensions and Social Security, despite common beliefs, are affordable, partly because the benefits from each are relatively low, and partly because the system is quite efficient and immune to costly conflicts of interests.

Compared to other industrialized nations, the United States has a young workforce and low Social Security benefits. The United States's projected spending on Social Security in 2050 is 7%, measured as a share of the size of the economy, commonly referred to as gross domestic product (GDP), which is the value of all the final products produced in an economy. Other Organization for Economic Cooperation and Development (OECD) nations—the thirty economically developed nations in the world—expect to spend between 8% and 20% of their GDP on their public pension systems. Because Social Security is mandatory for almost all employers, its administrative costs are less than 0.1% of its revenue. In addition, state and local pension plans for their employees are united into one system, which helps achieve economies of scale—that is, the cost per person falls as the size of the system grows. (In the same way as fixed costs, like the cost of the computers, land costs, etc., are spread over more production, which lowers costs.) The costs are lower than for commercial 401(k) accounts because the government pension plans are managed on a not-for-profit basis. (In January 2006, Michigan Governor Jennifer Granholm proposed that her state's pension administrative structure help small private businesses set up pension plans through the state system precisely because the state fund is so well managed without costly retail fees.)

Many private-sector pensions are efficient and managed with integrity. Despite that, defined benefit employer pension fees are larger than Social Security's centralized and not-for-profit administrative fees, although the DB fees are much smaller than fees charged for managing 401(k)-type plans.[6] If employers switched to 401(k)-type plans exclusively, administration, advertising, and regulation fees would be much higher.[7] If employers wanted to keep the same level of benefits provided in a defined benefit plan in a new individual account, that is, in a defined contribution plan, they would have to contribute far more than they did to the DB plan. We may be headed in the direction of eliminating pension security precisely because what is commonly "known" about pension security is wrong.

Three Beliefs That Threaten the Pension System

Americans seem to believe these three ideas:

1) Life expectancy is increasing, so we should work longer.

2) The United States will suffer labor shortages as the population ages.

3) Pensions are unaffordable.

These three propositions are invalid, and for these reasons: People retiring earlier could be the reason for increased life expectancy; a lower future rate of growth in the labor force will increase wages, not cause labor shortages; and there are other ways (besides shifting tax breaks away from high-income employees, who would save without the subsidy, to middle- and lower-income workers who would benefit from them) in which governments and employers play a strong role in a functioning pension system.

Let us consider each proposition.

First false proposition: Americans should work longer because they are living longer. Using almost every measure—entry into the labor force at young ages, longer hours of work, relatively later retirement ages, and higher labor force participation of parents with young children—Americans work more than workers in most developed nations. Societies in different nations deal in different ways with the scarcity of time—time for work and time for leisure. Mothers with small children in the United States work more than mothers in France, the United Kingdom, Germany, and Japan. French and German workers have on average fewer years of education than U.S. workers, suggesting that French and German citizens start work sooner, but they also end their work careers at much younger ages (table 1.1). If Americans work longer and reduce their time in retirement, they will be pulling even further away from other nations in valuing leisure.

However, in the United States, as in any nation, not all groups are able to retire. Not everyone has enough pension savings. Not everyone lives to the same age. Here is the problem: life expectancy is increasing, yes—but not for everyone. There is a growing gap in longevity between those with college educations and those without.[8]

Although large amounts of retirement leisure, through better pensions and longer lives, is a sign of a rich economy, the recent increases in the United States in the expected time in retirement resulted from longer lives, not from more valuable pensions. The largest leap in longevity rates came after 1965: when Medicare extended health insurance coverage to almost all the elderly; larger Social Security benefits reduced the adverse health effects of low income; and traditional pension plans let workers who wanted to, especially those in physically demanding jobs, retire before age sixty-five. People living longer is a flimsy justification for weakening pensions and compelling older people to work more. It is an anemic course of reasoning because the argument is based on the assumptions that (a) workers do not value free time as

Table 1.1
Americans' Work Effort Tops That of Most Nations

	Average Hours Worked per Year, 1997–98[c]	Average Education (in Years)[a]	Labor Force Participation of Mothers[b]
United States	1,966	12.7	68%
Japan	1,889	13.5	54%
Britain	1,731	13.2	62%
Germany	1,560	12.2	41%
France	1,634	10.7	68%

Notes:
[a] Using data from the International Labor Organization and the OECD for 1990–98 (Phillips 2002, 163).
[b] Computed by weighting the percentage of the population having attained certain levels of education (*Statistical Abstract of the United States*, 2000).
[c] Mothers are defined as women with either husbands or partners, and child(ren) under the age of six (Kamerman 2000).

they age, and (b) older people can do the new jobs, and (c) people are not living longer because they are improving their health by retiring sooner.

Assumption (a) is false because, as the nation grew richer, work hours fell and vacation time soared. Assumption (b) is false because there is little evidence that the ability of older people to work longer has improved. Since 1981, the share of older workers reporting limitations in the ability to work stayed steady at between 15% and 18%. Jobs demanding heavy lifting, stooping and kneeling, and overall physical effort are declining, especially for men. However, older workers report a 17% increase in jobs involving a lot of stress and intense concentration. Older women report a 17% increase in jobs requiring require good eyesight. As to whether the computer has made jobs easier for older workers, the jury is out (table 1.2.)

As for why assumption (c) is false, consider this: Retirement time itself boosts longevity. Retired men do not age as fast—their health deteriorates at a slower pace than for men who are still working, but both are alike in many other ways. Retired women are in better health than they would have been had they still been working.[9] This evidence suggests that longevity itself improved because people retired! If older people are compelled to stay in the labor force longer, this could reverse the progress society has made in increasing life expectancy for American people over age sixty-five. This is unfortunate for the less obvious reason that the impressive longevity improvements have shrunk what would otherwise have been a severe decrease in average retirement time. In short, as older people work more and experience more unemployment, they will likely encounter health difficulties, especially if they experience downward mobility in their status at work. They will become less able to do a job well, and they will have less time to care for themselves—sleeping, exercising, preparing and eating meals. So, instead of improved longevity being a reason why older people should work more, it is a fact that older people who worked less improved their longevity.

Second false proposition: The United States will soon suffer labor shortages as the population ages. This proposition implies that there is a labor shortage and older people have to help solve it. This is false for several reasons.

One reason is that labor shortages simply do not exist. What is called a "shortage" in any market merely describes any situation where demand exceeds supply. Reasonably, employers reckon labor supply will meet labor demand only when wages increase or the job offer is made more attractive. To paraphrase Wharton Business School economist Peter Cappelli, this is unlikely to be a problem for public policy.[10] Should pensions be made more

Table 1.2
Jobs Now Require Less Brawn, but Better Eyesight,
Plus Tolerance for Stress and Intensity
Working people (aged 55–60) report on age-related requirements of their jobs

	Men		Women	
	2002	*Change since 1992*	2002	*Change since 1992*
Good for older people				
Hardly any lifting of heavy loads required	56.8	8.6%	81.2	17.1%
Hardly any stooping or kneeling required	42.1	6.9%	39.2	0%
Hardly any physical effort	38.7	26%	36.5	2.9%
Difficult for older people				
Always or almost always requires good eyesight	62.2	8%	71.3	17.7%
Always or almost always requires intense concentration	52.9	17.8%	56.3	15.1%
Strongly agree that job involves a lot of stress	18.3	18.1%	23.2	17.8%

Source: Johnson 2004, table 3, 52.

insecure because the generation coming after the boomers (in 2008, the oldest baby boomer turns sixty-two and the youngest boomer turns forty-five) is smaller and employers would rather not raise wages? There are three ways pension income will become more insecure, thus making older workers more likely to work:

- the erosion of employment-linked defined benefit pension plans and development of a system of commercial, individual-based pensions (401(k) type plans) to replace them;

- the projected decline in Social Security benefits; and

- upward pressure on noninsured health care costs.

Third false proposition: Pensions are unaffordable. Many argue that the greatest threat to pensions is the enormity of their expense, implying that pensions must shrink because they are not affordable. For example, Boston University's Laurence Kotlikoff and coauthor Scott Burns argue just that in their brisk-selling book, *The Coming Generational Storm* (2004), a title that announces the boomers' retirement as if it will be a disaster as severe as a tsunami. The truth is that the money now spent on pensions is largely wasted and could be used to extend pension coverage to millions more Americans.

Yes, the government does spend a great deal on pensions—above the expense for Social Security programs and Medicare. The expense is through the system of tax breaks for voluntary employer and individual retirement plans: defined benefit plans, all defined contribution plans (including 401(k) plans), individual retirement accounts (IRAs), and other retirement savings vehicles. Contributions to these plans and investment earnings on the contributions are not taxed; only the pensions paid out at retirement are taxed, but commonly at a much lower tax rate than when the employee was working. The tax-favored treatment for retirement plans has been, until 2006, the largest of all categories of federal government tax expenditures. In 2009, taxes not collected on pension funds and contributions will be the federal government's second-to-largest tax expenditure. The government's largest tax expenditure will be employer contributions for medical health insurance premiums. Employers' contributions are government tax expenditures because the contributions are exempted from income tax. This means the government forgoes revenue and "spends" that forgone revenue on the tax break.

What remains puzzling is why, despite the huge and growing tax subsidy for pensions, pension coverage has stagnated. The puzzle is explained by the changing structure of the tax subsidy. The tax subsidy for 401(k) plans mostly benefits higher-income workers. Higher-income workers (and indirectly their employers) pay higher income tax rates under the progressive income tax structure; so a tax break is worth more to higher-income workers relative to the same tax break for lower-income workers. This means that workers at different earnings levels, say each contributing 10% of their salary to a pension plan, receive widely different tax breaks from the federal government.

DATA TO DIGEST   *A worker earning $20,000 per year is at the 15% tax bracket and receives a federal tax break, that is, a pension subsidy, worth 15% of his or her $2,000 pension contribution, equal to $300. In contrast, a worker earning $200,000 per year is at the 36% tax bracket, and therefore receives 36% of her pension contribution of $20,000, worth $7,200.*

If a worker does not participate in a pension plan, of course, he gets nothing from the federal program subsidizing pensions. For reasons described in later chapters, among workers with pensions, it is the lower- and middle-income workers who are less likely to participate in 401(k) plans than in defined benefit plans. Thus, as 401(k) plans overtake defined benefit pensions, tax subsidies grow because pension coverage shifts to high earners, while overall pension coverage does not improve. This is a waste of taxpayers' money because tax policy toward employee benefits aims to meet public goals for retirement security. The tax breaks do not help households save more, increasing the nation's savings in proportion to national income. The $115 billion of tax expenditures for all retirement accounts in 2004 was equal to one-fourth of Social Security contributions. Rather than increasing savings, research suggests that tax breaks mostly induce high-income households to shift savings they already have in financial assets that are taxed to tax-favored accounts.[11]

> DATA TO DIGEST   *The amount of tax subsidy to retirement accounts is perversely larger than all household's personal savings of $103 billion, which includes contributions to retirement plans.[12] Moreover, tax expenditures for 401(k) plans are expected to grow 28% by 2009, while tax expenditures for traditional pensions are expected to fall by 2%.[13]*

In direct contrast to the common belief that pensions are not affordable is the idea that the money spent for pensions has to be redistributed away from the highest-income earners to the middle- and lower-income earners rather than drastically cut.

> Bottom Line   *More than $115 billion dollars per year is spent on pensions. That money could be better spent to cover lower- and middle-income workers who need pensions the most.*

The economic reality of pensions is a political reality, which is not reflected in the title of Kotlikoff's book, but it is reflected in Brookings Institution economists Aaron, Bosworth, and Burtless's 1980 book title, *Can We Afford to Retire?* The rhetorical question produces a considered answer: "We" can afford pensions if we want to. The authors beg the political economy questions: Who is "we"? And do "we" have common or opposing interests?

Individual Retirement Accounts: Current Reform Ideas Fall
Short of a Vision to Successfully Preserve Retirement

Although these three propositions—people living longer should work
longer, labor shortages will hurt the economy, and pensions are unaffordable
for employers and government—are false, they nevertheless result in a cock-
tail of solutions that reduces pension security: raising the retirement age for
Social Security, which reduces benefits; allowing defined benefit plans to collapse; and promoting defined contribution, 401(k)-type retirement accounts.
These solutions fall short of what should be an efficient and low-cost retirement system that delivers adequate levels of pensions for workers at all income levels and for different life expectancies.

Instead, the political groundwork is being laid for turning Social Security
into individual retirement pension accounts and collapsing all retirement
savings vehicles into comprehensive types of individual retirement savings
accounts (RSAs), which were advanced by the White House in 2004.[14] Two
things primarily characterize individual retirement accounts: they are based
on financial market assets rather than an annuity as found in defined benefit
pensions and in Social Security; and the employer has no responsibility for
retirement income. Both add up to one result—that the elderly, when retired,
will not be able to rely on pension income and will need other sources of reliable income. Neither the kindness of strangers' charitable contributions nor
financial support from relatives provides an elderly person with control over
the source of income. More reliable is work. Alas, finding work depends considerably on the employer. But at least an elderly person can decide to look or
not to look for work. What an individual retirement account system does is
promote a "save or work" policy. Anyone who has to work more to reach the
same income suffers a decline in living standards. Moreover, a person who
suffers an income loss, such as a loss in pension, experiences a decrease in her
"reservation wage"—that is, the minimum wage that an employer has to pay
to get her to the workplace. When this reservation wage falls, that worker's
individual bargaining power falls. When reservation wages fall, and nothing
else changes, employers can pay workers less, boosting their profits. Thus, the
loss in secure pensions shifts market power from workers to employers. And
that means that the value of the reduction in workers' wages is shifted to an
increased value in employers' profits!

Employers achieve significant amounts of work from the elderly—not by inducing the elderly to work with flexible schedules, better pay, and improved working conditions—by cutting their pensions.

Individual Retirement Accounts Represent a Wrong Vision for Retirement

To begin to discuss why it is a wrong vision, let us first consider what comprises a right vision for retirement. Mandatory retirement pension systems make workers save and insure themselves against "superannuation"—a rarely used word of many syllables that simply and sadly refers to the awkward stage of life when people either cannot work or no one wants them to work. Saving and insuring, which are mandatory in Social Security and employer pensions, shift risks efficiently from individuals to larger entities, such as the government and employers, which spread pension risks over time and among different kinds of people. Mandating participation means that firms providing these insurance-based pension systems are prevented from competing against other firms by not providing pensions or reneging on promises to pay pensions by terminating or freezing a pension plan. In addition, mandatory pension insurance benefits all workers, except perhaps those who start rich and end rich enough to self-insure their own pensions. And pensions give older workers some economic bargaining power when they are looking for work past an age when most people are retired. None of these features are anywhere in the framework of an individual-based pension system. As we shall see in chapter 10, Guaranteed Retirement Accounts that supplement Social Security provide the right pension reform framework.

In a 401(k)-type individual retirement account system, the employer is entirely out of the business of providing pensions. To see what that means, consider that, while the government is not in the business of providing pensions above and beyond Social Security (except for its own employees), the government's tax expenditures—government revenue losses from the tax rules that allow contributions to and earnings in retirement accounts to defer tax until the money is withdrawn—will mushroom over time. The tax revenue losses have and will grow increasingly because the wealthy will continue to transfer their assets in taxable accounts to these tax-favored 401(k)-type accounts.[15] This means that overall savings do not rise; higher-income workers—those in the top 5%—enrich themselves by paying fewer taxes, and government debt rises to make up for that shortfall. Continuing to use tax policy to boost workers' demand for pensions is off target. It's like providing yacht subsidies for housing a special category of Hurricane Katrina victims—those having incomes over $100,000 per year.[16]

The so-called tax incentives' lack of ability or means to achieve social goals suggests that a sea change is needed in pension engineering.

Conclusion: Retirement's Future

Since there is no evidence—in any nation, across any time period—nor any reasonable set of assumptions to suggest that typical workers alone can accumulate enough assets to fund a comfortable retirement, it is unlikely that retirement savings accounts will do better then our current pension system. Specifically, retirement savings accounts will not do better than Social Security and defined benefit pensions. The opposite is more likely, that a national system based on individual retirement accounts is expected to create smaller and less predictable pensions for almost all workers, while those at the top will have more wealth.

Retirement is a result of economic prosperity. And the choice to retire should be an achievable goal of everyone's financial life. A fundamental desire of everyone is to be able to make choices about how to spend our time. As we grow older time grows more precious. Making our pensions secure is the only way to secure the capacity to choose what to do with the time remaining to us.

Chapter 2

The Collapse of Retirement Income

Retirement income is falling.

It is less secure.

And it is distributed more unevenly across income, class, and gender lines.

What is the inevitable result? For most of the elderly, the material standard of living will fall when they are retired because their retirement income will replace much less of their pre-retirement income. To maintain their standard of living when they do retire, the elderly will likely delay retirement, continue working if possible, or look for work.

This chapter begins by considering retirement income needs, the sources of retirement income, and what is predicted to happen to retirement income in the United States. We will examine the special retirement income needs of women and why their needs remain unmet by the American pension system; regarding men, this chapter will explain why and how men are more adversely affected by the decline in secure sources of retirement income. We will see why low-income workers are facing bleak prospects in retirement, despite the gains in their retirement income made in the recent past.

What People Need in Retirement

It has been commonly accepted that the income needed in retirement is between 60% and 85% of preretirement income, depending on how high or low that income is. (People having lower incomes need the higher percentage.) During the years when people work, they need to: maintain a reliable car and pay for commuting expenses; maintain a wardrobe suitable for work; pay for meals away from home; pay Social Security taxes; and, besides other work-related expenses, they need to save for retirement. People who are retired no longer have these expenses to pay nor obligations to save. Moreover, that rule of thumb, 60% to 80% of preretirement income, assumes that retirees have already paid for their children's college expenses, have no debt, and have paid off a mortgage.

While all this may be true, that percentage range of preretirement income no longer works as an appropriate goal for retirement income. Projected health care costs, inflation, longer lives, and higher property and sales taxes, all together, have boosted the income needed during retirement to nearer 100% of preretirement income for the average earner and more than 100% for low-income workers. Many older people have debt, and may be part of the "sandwich" generation—adult children are the underside slice of bread who need help with down payments for mortgages or cash to smooth over a divorce; their own parents are the upperside slice of bread who need financial help. What's beginning to happen is that lifelong low- and medium-wage workers will need more than 100% of their income—while still working, and surely after retirement. The working poor will need more income in retirement than they were earning just to stay above the poverty level.

Consider a household with the median amount of preretirement working income of $45,000 per year. Guaranteeing that same flow of income by purchasing an annuity at retirement would cost a sixty-five-year-old more than twenty times as much as $45,000, or well over $900,000, according to experts who earn their living doing this kind of math. This household needs a cool $1 million (a low estimate) at age sixty-five. Giving up the daily lattes at Starbucks and the premium cable channel will not cut it.

Now, say you earn today's average income, about $45,000 per year, and you start saving at your current age, forty years old, and you earn 3% per year above inflation on your investments—an optimistic estimate. Those numbers mean you need to save nearly $27,000 each year, or 60% of your income every pay period, to have enough cash at retirement to purchase an annuity paying $45,000 every year. But, if you start saving at age thirty, you only need to save $16,000 per year, or 36% of your income, to have accumulated enough to buy an annuity paying $45,000 annually during retirement.

The average value of Social Security income is over $13,000 per year, adjusted for inflation. That income lessens the amount a person must save during working years to obtain $45,000 per year of income in retirement. Also, if people's optimistic assumptions are correct, for example, that their investments will earn a hefty rate of return, that they will borrow equity from their home when retired, that they will not incur any debt, then their savings goals could be smaller and their retirement readiness picture much rosier. Many scholars believe that most people in the boomer generation have not accumulated enough money to retire and maintain their standard of living during retirement. One of the more dire estimates is that one in five Americans could be poor in old age (the elderly poverty rate is now about one out of seventeen).[1]

What People Think They Know:
Retirement Income Expectations

The sources for American retirement income are becoming fewer and more unstable, and more and more workers are becoming aware of that. The share of workers responding to a survey that they are "not too confident" and "not at all confident" of having enough money to live comfortably throughout their retirement years increased from 25% in 1993 to 31% in 2006. The percentage of workers responding that they are "somewhat confident" or "very confident" of having enough money to take care of basic expenses in retirement dropped, from 73% in 1993[2] to 68% in 2006.[3] The decline in confidence that a person will have enough retirement income is particularly acute among middle-aged workers between forty-five and fifty-four years of age. Now, if confidence levels were falling just because younger workers were becoming more pessimistic, the change would hardly be worth mentioning. Indeed, that might even be good news if the young were goaded by their pessimism to save more. Alas, that is not the case. Confidence about retirement income among older, and presumably more informed, workers is lower than their counterparts' confidence ten years ago.

Losing reliable and steady sources of income—like traditional defined benefit plans, and Social Security benefits eroded by Medicare premiums[4]—means relying on sources such as personal savings, family members, charity, public assistance, and whatever unreliable employment may be available from time to time. Losing confidence that they will have sufficient retirement income could explain why, in 2002, one-quarter of workers age forty-five and older decided to postpone their retirement.[5] However, the people who were able to postpone their retirement were the lucky ones! Among those who did retire, 40% were forced to stop work at younger ages than they had planned—nearly half stopped working due to health problems and almost as many because they lost their jobs. The less a person's wealth and earnings, the greater the risk of being forced to retire.[6]

The pessimism about future retirement income is not irrational. Retirement anxiety comes from the familiar fear of having to face and finance old age alone: divorced persons and widow(er)s face two to three times more risk than married couples of suffering poverty.[7] New anxieties stem from three sources: (1) the unprecedented levels of debt among older workers[8]; (2) the political elites—the top political office holders and others—questioning the future of Social Security; and (3) the failures of long-standing pension plans and retiree health plans to prevent poverty risk. In addition, since earnings are becoming a much more important source of "retirement" income, the risk of losing a job or suffering a decrease in wages and hours worked is a new risk, a risk not faced to the same degree by boomers' parents. The difference between older generations and the boomer generation is that the older generation enjoyed the initiation of the Medicare program in 1965, which provided broad access to doctors and hospital care, and increases in real estate values; whereas the current and younger generations will likely experience rising health-care costs, and the home equity loans that followed the increase in real estate values but resulted in no real increase in housing wealth.

Irrationally low expectations about one area of retirement income—Social Security—can explain some of the pessimism. Most preretirees are unaware that Social Security is their most secure source of retirement income. Retirees are five times more likely to rely on Social Security than on their personal assets for most of their old-age income.[9] Yet, when asked where they expect to obtain most of their retirement income, three times as many workers say from personal assets.

Compared to what retirees actually experience, workers overrate what they can do for themselves. In particular, workers tend to exaggerate their abilities to provide for their own retirement. They underrate the importance of employer pensions and Social Security. They sense that the Social Security replacement rate—that is the fraction of preretirement income that Social Security replaces in retirement (for example, workers earning minimum wage their entire career would have Social Security replacing 56% of their incomes)—is falling, and that employer pensions are diminishing, especially for future middle-class retirees.

The actual importance of each source of income workers receive in retirement does not look anything like what young people expect.[10] Young workers think like rich people; they expect that their retirement income will come from the same sources as the income of the top 20% among the elderly. The elderly in the top 20% of the income distribution have earnings from the paid labor force, for example, earnings from surgeon's fees, or from college teaching, or CEO pay, making up 34.2% of their retirement income—which is why they have more income—and 19.5% of their income comes from Social Security. The elderly in the bottom 40% of the income distribution receive more than 89% of their retirement income from Social Security.[11] Anyone not at the top will be shocked and disappointed to learn about the prospects for their own retirement income.

Predictions of Retirement Readiness

As of 2007, retirement incomes are not expected to rise at the same rate that earnings will increase. In other words, the increase in a future retiree's standard of living is not expected to keep up with the expected increases in workers' income net of key expenses. Extensive analysis of Federal Reserve data on the population's wealth holdings—the data set called the Survey of Consumer Finances—and other data sets reviewed by the Congressional Budget Office in 2003 show that the average person's accumulation of assets is not making up for rising health care costs and the decline in Social Security and traditional pensions. The Securities Industry Association predicts that 45% of boomers (in this analysis "boomers" are people born between 1946 and 1965) will not have reached a 60% replacement rate—meaning retirement income will replace less than 60% of their preretirement income—while 20% of boomers will be below the poverty level in retirement! In addition, for all groups of retirees, retirement income will come from sources less secure than the sources of income to retirees in the past—for example, income from Social Security and traditional pensions. Economists Christian Weller and Ed Wolff in a 2005 study use the 2001 Federal Reserve data to show that the accumulation of retirement wealth for the average and median near-retiree household is falling. Most of this decline is due to the change in pensions, from traditional pensions—which are the defined benefit plans that provided income for the retired lifetime of a worker—to 401(k) plans—which are individual accounts that employees, and some employers, contribute to—providing the newly retired employee with a lump sum that can be used up before the death of that retiree.

Economists from the Urban Institute, a Washington, D.C., think tank, estimated that when "late boomers" (workers born between 1956 and 1963) retire, they will have more income and wealth than their parents had in retirement, which is good news. The bad news is that they will not do as well as their parents did in replacing their preretirement income.

DATA TO DIGEST   *In 2003, retired married men, aged sixty-seven, replaced 90% of their preretirement earnings; those who are now in their forties are expected to replace only 81% when they are sixty-seven.*

The decreases in replacement rates are worse for retired married women and unmarried men: the replacement rates for each fall thirteen percentage points to 79% and 83%, respectively.

Retired nonmarried women aged sixty-seven replaced almost all of their income in 2003, but their counterparts in the mid-2020s are expected to replace only 83%.[12]

There has been an increase in older people working, so that retirees have more income from paid work while they are retired—allowing for a bit of illogical identity! But the earnings from work by retirees, which helps offset the fall in preretirement income replacement rates, is not enough to make up for losses from pension income and Social Security income. Table 2.1 shows the average level of income from each source of retirement income and the predicted levels in 2023.

DATA TO DIGEST   *In 2003, earnings to retired elderly households constituted 13% of their retirement income; earnings are expected to make up 18% in 2023 (line 3, table 2.1). Between those same years, the share of retirement income from defined benefit pensions is projected to fall from 21% to 9% (line 2).*

The average preretirement income—or, more specifically, the income during the year immediately preceding retirement for married men who will be age sixty-seven in 2027 (calculated in 2003)—is predicted to rise by 69%. Preretirement income is a good-enough measure of an accustomed standard of living for most researchers.[13] However, the retirement income of those retiring in 2027 is expected to be only 52% higher than the retirement income of those who retired at age sixty-seven in 2003.

Late-boomer women (born 1956–1963), who are not married at age sixty-seven, will have the most difficulty keeping their standard of living in retirement. Their preretirement income is expected to rise by 60%, but their retirement income will increase by only 37%.[14] Women are making improvements in obtaining employer pensions of their own, although the improvements are small, and women over age sixty-five will still suffer higher rates of poverty than men.

The Five Parts of a Retirement Wealth Portfolio: Four Are Failing

A person's portfolio of retirement wealth is not unlike any financial portfolio, although the dimensions of its components may differ in amounts and some sources of total wealth and income—most apparently, the value of a person's human capital and retiree health insurance—which are difficult to measure concretely. A comprehensive accounting of Americans' retirement wealth portfolios must take into account five components of wealth from which a retiree household can derive income. These five are Social Security, pensions, personal wealth, earnings, and kinship and community (including entitlement to "welfare"—income assistance). The only source of wealth not failing is the ability to earn wages and salaries.

Table 2.1

Present and Future Income Sources for the Elderly

Share of income and sources of income, for retired families whose income is the median 10% of all income-recipients, for 2003, and projected for 2023 (in 2003 dollars)

	Median income for those born 1929–35 (2003)	Projected median income of late boomers born 1956–65 (projected for 2023)	Shares of income for those born 1929–35 (2003)	Shares of expected income of late boomers born 1956–65 (projected for 2023)
Social Security benefits	$9,000	$14,000	38%	41%
Defined benefit plans	$5,000	$3,000	21%	9%
Earnings	$3,000	$6,000	13%	18%
Retirement accounts (all defined contributions type)	$1,000	$3,000	4%	9%
Income from assets	$3,000	$4,000	13%	12%
Imputed housing value	$3,000	$4,000	13%	12%
Total	$24,000	$34,000	100%	100%

Source: Butrica, Iams, and Smith 2003, table 5.3; appendix table 5.

Social Security

The main source of elderly income is provided by government—Social Security and income-preserving sources, such as Medicare, housing subsidies, and food stamps. According to economists Ed Wolff and Christian Weller,[15] in 2001, the median household (the *median*, in this case, is the amount where half of elderly households have wealth below and half have wealth above) is entitled to $127,000 from Social Security (the *average* wealth from Social Security is higher, $146,600). Social Security wealth is the present value of the expected stream of income coming from Social Security discounted for interest rates and inflation. In addition, although the share of earnings right before retirement replaced by Social Security is declining, income from this source has decreased less than the fall in the replacement rate from pensions and other assets. Social Security income for retired households with the median—not average—incomes decreased by 4.3%, compared to the income received from employer pensions, which fell by a large 69.3% between 1983 and 2001.[16] For workers with median incomes, aged 47–55, the growth rate for their projected Social Security wealth was positive; between 1983 and 2001, it was 24.3 %; the growth rate for their pension wealth was 18.4%; and for their assets, the growth rate was only 3.4%.[17]

Social Security wealth is decreasing for two reasons:

- the scheduled increases in Medicare premiums, which will come out of income from Social Security to retirees; and

- the increase in the age at which full benefits can be collected.

Both reasons mean that benefits collected at the same age will be lower for future generations than for today's retirees and near-retirees. The effect will be a decrease in Social Security income replacement rate for the worker who earns the *average wage* during his entire working life, from 38.5 in 2000 to 32.5% in 2030,[18] and a decline in replacement rate for the worker earning the *median wage* his entire career, from 41% to 40% (table 2.1).

Employer Pensions

Employer-provided pensions—including defined benefit pensions and defined contribution plans, which come in several varieties but are all similar to the main type, the 401(k)—are the second most important source of retirement income.

The simplest definition of a defined benefit plan is that the benefits payable to participants are predetermined by the plan's formula, and are based on years of service and earnings. Types of DB plans include cash balance plans. The employer contribution to a DB plan is mandatory.

In defined contribution plans, the contributions into an individual account are predetermined. Types of DC plans include money purchase, thrift, and profit sharing, 403(b), 457 (which are basically 401(k) plans for people who work for governments and not-for-profit employers), and the largest category, the 401(k) plan. The employer contribution is optional.

The best way of differentiating between defined benefit and defined contribution pension schemes is by determining where the risks are. In a DB plan, it is the employer that underwrites the vast majority of costs, so that if investment returns are poor or costs increase because people are living longer or more people retire than expected, et cetera, the employer needs either to cut benefits for future workers and service or to increase the employer's contributions. In a DC plan, the contributions are paid at a fixed level. If investment returns are poor or costs increase, workers' retirement benefits will be lower than they had planned for.

Among households with members over age sixty-five in 2001, the *median*—not *average*—present value of the future pension income stream, which we refer to as pension wealth, was only $10,700, having decreased by 69.3% from 1983. Since the distribution of retirement wealth is very skewed toward the top, the *average* present value of pension wealth is $105,400, and the *average* is also increasing by 69%, which eerily mirrors the rate of decline in the pension wealth for the lower-paid median worker.[19]

Pension Coverage

There is no optimistic picture of the future of pension plans—not for workers and their prospective income from pensions. The *share* of all workers between the ages of twenty-five and sixty-four who participated in a pension plan, or worked for an employer with a pension plan in the private sector, fell from 50% in 1999 to 46.7% in 2003. The *number* of workers covered by an employer-sponsored retirement plan fell from 54 million in 1999 to 53.3 million in 2003, representing a fall from 60.7% to 57.3%. Among workers over thirty-five and under fifty-five—the so-called prime-aged workers, in the full-time labor force—the number of workers having employer-sponsored retirement plans, also fell, from 66.8% in 1999 to 62.7% in 2003.[20] The largest rates of coverage—workers in jobs where employers sponsor pension plans—are among public sector employers and they have not fallen as much; over two-thirds of the fifteen million workers in the public sector are covered. Note that *coverage rates* and *participation rates* are different. People who work for an employer who provides a defined benefit plan or a defined contribution pension plan are considered *covered*. But the actual participation rate is smaller—many workers are not included in the pension plan, that is, they are not *participating*, either because they may not have met the threshold for eligibility—over twenty hours per week or tenure, which is usually one year—or because they choose not to contribute to the defined contribution plan, most likely a 401(k).

Why Workers Do Not Have Pensions

Department of Labor economists John A. Turner and Richard Hinz[21] probed why employers may not sponsor pension plans for their workers. Their study indicated two reasons why employers may not provide pension plans:

- Workers do not want pensions.

- Workers want pensions, but their employers do not provide them because pensions do not enhance profits or productivity.

The first reason—workers choosing not to have pensions—does not seem a likely scenario. However, if many workers do not have pensions but want them, there will be a pension crisis. Employers do not have to provide pensions and are under considerably less pressure to do so due to the decline in unions representing workers since the 1970s. Nevertheless, whether a worker has pension coverage or not is not entirely due to employers. Workers influence whether they will have pension coverage and to what extent, as a result of the increase in defined contribution plans and the decline of collective bargaining. Together, both have led to pensions being voluntary. Employers offering a 401(k) do not make participation mandatory—the Pension Protection Act allows firms to provide an opt-out procedure (but does not require it) whereby employees are automatically enrolled in a pension but can opt out if they choose.

Minority, female, and low-income workers are more likely to voluntarily decline coverage in a pension plan when it is offered. Workers at or near the top management ranks of a large firm are likely covered. This differential is an obvious clue that pensions were originally intended for higher-income workers, and the coverage trickled down to workers at the bottom because of the IRS "antidiscrimination rules." IRS antidiscrimination rules are regulations that have existed almost since the beginning of the income tax itself. The IRS will give tax breaks for employee benefits, including pensions, only if all workers receive a reasonable share of what the executives themselves obtain from the benefit. The intention is to take advantage of executives wanting these appealing benefits for themselves, forcing them to extend benefits to all workers—else the higher-paid workers will not get the benefits. These rules could be viewed as "accidental coverage" for workers who may prefer to have more cash wages than to have pension coverage.

Policymakers may not be too concerned about workers who decide not to work for firms that offer pensions. It could be that workers who do not want pensions, all else being equal, gravitate toward firms that offer higher pay instead. There is a flaw in this premise; many researchers have concluded that not many such tradeoffs exist because high earnings tend to be accompanied with very desirable fringe benefits, such as pensions. Most researchers find few tradeoffs between pensions and wages. Rather, it is the opposite—high-paying jobs have better pensions.[22]

To see the weakness in the explanation that the decline in employers' pension coverage is due to workers choosing not to opt for it, consider this: As male workers are getting older, they are moving into ages where pensions would seem to become more valuable to them. Yet pension coverage for full-time male workers declined from 54% in 1972 to 49% in 1988, sixteen years later.[23] Instead of a decrease, we should have expected male pension coverage rates to increase as the male workforce aged. Perhaps employers are less apt to provide pensions as part of the decline in employers' commitment to male workers. Over the past twenty years there has been a steep drop in the number of years men have been employed by the same employer. For men aged forty to forty-four, the proportion who had worked for the same employer at least ten years was 51.1% in 1983, dropping to 36.2% in 2004. For men aged twenty-five to sixty-five and over, the proportion who had worked for the same employer at least ten years fell by an average of 9.4% in each five-year age group from 1983 to 2004.[24]

The opposite is true for women workers. As women workers gained higher pension coverage rates, they earned more and stayed longer with their employers. In 2004 28.6% of women aged twenty-five to thirty-four had worked ten years or more for their current employer, compared to 24.9% in

January 1983. The trend toward rising proportions of women working longer for the same employer occurred mainly among forty- to fifty-four-year-olds. Women in industries where females dominate, such as retail and services, and female-dominated occupations, such as clerical and sales, are less likely to be covered by pensions than men in the same industries and jobs. Women moving into traditionally male jobs are getting the same pension coverage as the men were getting, thereby expanding pension coverage for women.

Whether these trends are caused by workers' choices (male or female) or employer policies cannot be proven. But a common sense conclusion is that both forces together—worker choice and employer policy—explain the difference. Nevertheless, it is also reasonable to conclude that low-income workers probably prefer pensions *and* pay and have few opportunities to choose to trade off one for the other

The second reason given that workers do not have pension coverage is because their employers do not provide it. In the post–World War II economy, many large and small American firms have learned to live with and appreciate pension plans and employee benefits, especially defined benefit plans. Employers recognized the effects pensions and benefits have on worker loyalty and their boost in productivity, no matter that the pension plans were negotiated and won by workers' unions.[25] Even some nonunion firms came to realize that a high-performing firm has paternalistic elements, such as flexible working hours, health insurance, vacations, and pensions.

That employers recognized the effects on worker loyalty and productivity brought about traditional defined benefit pension plans for almost half of the working population. And, doubtless, productivity motivations are behind the growth in defined contribution plans. What also helped was that most of the DB plans were not costly when first implemented. The low cost resulted from negotiated employer-union settings where workers gave up cash wages to have a pension, and was also because the average age of the workforce was young ("young" is referred to as "immature" in actuarial-speak!). Now, various worker groups are mature (older, alas!). Among thirty-one major companies, each has a projected pension liability—that's the value of what each of those companies is obligated to pay to its employees in pension benefits—larger than the worth of the company. But, of course, the pension assets in many companies are worth more than their pension liabilities.[26] Economic pressures on companies, to be sure, contribute to their moving away from defined benefit pensions. So also does the increasing allure of "do-it-yourself" pension planning.

Even if a firm offers pension coverage, it may restrict participation to full-time workers and workers who are permanent employees, leaving out temporary workers or independent contractors. Microsoft and AOL Time Warner workers, for example, complain that their firms avoid paying pensions by inaccurately defining them as temporary workers although they do the work of full-time permanent employees. It is not legal for a firm to classify workers as independent contractors when they have the same everyday relationship to the firm as do employees. If the employer determines a worker's pace of work, determines the process used to get that work done, and provides the tools to get that work done, then that worker is an employee according to national labor law. But to invoke the law and get it enforced, an "independent" contractor-worker must complain to the appropriate government agency, which certainly jeopardizes his "contract" to do the job, and perhaps further, adversely affects his opportunities to work in the industry.

Employer-Provided Retiree Health Insurance

Until recently, close to a majority of workers retiring from large companies was promised and received retiree health coverage. A human-resource consulting firm, Mercer Associates, found that in 1993 46% of large private sector employers (those with over 500 employees) offered retirement benefits to people who retired and were not yet eligible for Medicare; by 2006 that share dropped to 29%.[27] In 2004, 10% of the companies that provided retiree health care coverage dropped it completely, and an increasing number of companies are leaving it up to retirees themselves to pay the entire monthly premium for health care. For retirees without employer-paid retiree health benefits, medical costs are likely to consume an amount equal to 20% of their preretirement income.

Medicare's 2005 prescription drug benefit program, Part D, will likely cause private firms to eliminate or reduce company-paid drug coverage for 2.7 to 3.8 million retirees now receiving prescription drug coverage—the federal government will now pay the tab for that coverage. If the firms had not intended to drop drug coverage for their retirees anyway, Part D will save employers $70 billion between the years 2006 and 2013.[28]

It is not clear what the impact will be of the combination of employer cutbacks in health-care coverage for retirees and the rapidly rising health costs to future retirees. Whatever happens, it will be generally detrimental in the following ways:

- government spending for elderly health care could increase, forcing the federal government to reduce other forms of health-care spending;

- employer cutbacks on health care for retirees and rising health costs to retirees will force the federal government to cut its contributions to state budgets for Medicaid (the health care for the poor);

- the elderly could spend more "out of pocket" for health care, reducing their standard of living; and/or,

- the elderly will spend less on health care to the detriment of their health.

Personal Assets

Personal assets—including home equity, savings net of debt, lottery winnings, gifts from perfect strangers (it is possible that people receive gifts from strangers), even assets from bank robberies, or the in-kind support from a government agency, such as a jail—could be resources. (October 2006: Timothy Bowers, age sixty-two, robbed an Ohio bank and then handed the money to a guard and waited for the police to arrive. He told a judge he wanted to be sent to jail until he turned sixty-five so he could collect his pension.)[29] Any sort of asset can become a source of income in old age.

Among middle-class (the 60% who have income in the mid-range of income distribution) older workers (aged forty-seven to fifty-five in 2001), the average value of assets (including home equity and excluding pensions) is large—it is $185,600, but it has increased by only 1% since 1983 (to 2001). The distribution of assets is quite skewed. The wealthiest have large amounts of wealth and a large share of total wealth—the rate of increase in wealth for the top 20% is in the double digits, and the average level of assets among the wealthiest is $438,000. By comparison, Social Security wealth is much more equally distributed. For workers aged forty-seven to fifty-five, Social Security wealth totals an average $164,100, and has increased 42% since 1983. Pension wealth at $112,700, has increased 55.2% from 1983 to 2002.

Because assets are becoming more unequal and growing at a high rate relative to the more equally distributed sources of income for the elderly, the distribution of income among the elderly will be more unequal over time.

Family Ties

An important source of retirement income for an older person is her or his partner—it may or may not be surprising that adult children provide very little financial assistance to parents. Survivor's benefits and divorced women's benefits in employer pension plans and the Social Security system extend income to many older women.

The married partner, living or dead, can provide income. However, the Social Security spousal benefits may have the unintended consequence of financially burdening the surviving spouse. Upon the death of a spouse, whether the wife or the husband, the survivor receives the benefits deriving from whichever of the couple was the "main worker"—that's the spouse who paid more lifetime Social Security taxes—and no longer receives the benefits due as spouse to that "main worker." While both were living, that spouse had been receiving 50% of the main worker's Social Security benefits and the main worker had been receiving 100% benefits; as a couple, they were receiving 150% benefits. When the main worker dies, the benefits to the household comprising only the surviving spouse fall by one-third, dropping from 150% benefits as a married couple to 100% of the main worker's benefit. Yet, that sole spouse's household consumption probably only falls by 20% because many costs do not vary by the household's size. For example, shelter costs do not vary, while food consumption costs fall by less than one-third.

In the preceding paragraph, insert "woman" everywhere you see "surviving spouse" and you will begin to realize why those survivor benefit rules may contribute to the poverty rate for women. Nevertheless, these rules can be very helpful for many women, though the lack of such benefits explains why[30] women without husbands have much higher rates of poverty. Never-married and divorced women have limited, if any, access to these spousal benefits; it is the reason widowed women have more income than other single older women. Any divorced woman's access to her ex-husband's pension depends heavily on the prowess of her lawyer and the state where she got her divorce—only 27% of divorced women collect pensions from their former husband.

The poverty rate for single older men, although high at 14%, is far lower than the 23% poverty rate for an older woman without a husband.

Except in a few industrialized nations, including Denmark and the Netherlands, a woman's access to old-age income mainly comes from (a) government and employer earnings-related pensions programs—either her own or her husband's; (b) government welfare programs; (c) her own wealth; and (b) primarily in developing nations, her children.[31]

Community kinship networks provide help to old retirees through public assistance, which is income from government programs to help the very poor. Welfare provides very small amounts of retirement income. Needs-based income support, which most people think of as "welfare," is a small part of retirement income—less than 2% for nonmarried women and less than one-half of 1% for married couples.

Earnings

Human capital comprises all the skills a person has, and therefore it is the potential to earn money by working. That makes human capital a form of potential retirement wealth. If a new retiree today worked at double the minimum wage for one thousand hours per year for twenty years, the present value of that person's human capital is something over $135,000 at the start of retirement, at about age sixty-five.[32]

In the United States, men and women over age forty have some protection against age discrimination in employment. Moreover, work in old age is encouraged by a modern American culture that promotes youth and vitality; it is also encouraged by low pensions, and by a growing economy hungry for part-time, low-wage labor. As a consequence, a significant source of income to the U.S. elderly is earnings from paid work, particularly for men.

The role of work in retirement is a major paradox this book explores. Older people are working more hours, postponing retirement, and going back to work after being retired, mainly because of the collapse of the pension system. Whatever favorable and healthful effects elderly people obtain from work, many retirees and older workers are in the labor market because they have either lost their pensions and their health insurance or lost confidence in the security of their retirement income. The Government Accountability Office[33] identifies as "overemployed" those older workers who postpone retirement or leave retirement to find work because of diminishing pensions. The idea that a certain group of people can be overemployed makes perfect sense in a context where people complain about having to work and are disappointed that they do not have enough money to retire on, especially if they had expected to retire. It is the economist who is puzzled why adults would find themselves "involuntarily" employed. After all, economists reason that, with the prohibition of slavery, working for pay is voluntary.[34] If a ninety-year-old works or returns to work, so long as no one is holding a gun to her head to do so, the economist deems her action "voluntary"—even if she lacks rent money, her choice to work is freely made!

Distribution of Retirement Income and Distribution of Retirement Readiness

Another way we can view the collapse of retirement income is through the rising income inequality among the elderly. Among current retirees, the ratio of the average income of the richest 20% of sixty-seven-year-olds to the average income of the bottom 20% is almost double—the average person at the top has nearly 200% more income than the average person at the bottom. By the time the late boomers (born between 1956 and 1963) are sixty-seven, the ratio of income for the top 20% to that of the bottom 20% will be 3.35 to 1, or 335%, or the top 20% will have three and one-third times more income.[35]

Lower-income workers have experienced the steepest decline in employer pension coverage rates.

DATA TO DIGEST   *Men in the bottom third of the income scale in 1996 faced a whopping 21% lower rate of pension coverage than men in the bottom third in 1979. In simpler words, 21% fewer men in the bottom income group had pension coverage in 1996 than did the men in the that group in 1979. Over the same years, 12% fewer men in the middle-income group had pension coverage. Women in the top third of the income distribution in 1996 had 6% less pension coverage than women who were in the top third in 1979. Men in the top third of the income group had 7% less coverage in 1996. See table 2.2.*

Women who were in the middle third of the income distribution in 1996 had a 13% lower rate of coverage than women in the middle third in 1979 (table 2.2). The rate of decrease for men's pension coverage rates has, since the late 1980s, leveled off; during the same years, women's increase in pension coverage has leveled off.

One of the reasons Social Security and pensions are important sources of income for most people—rather than income from their assets—is that these two sources of income cover a large share of the workforce. In 2001, 93% of elderly households received Social Security, 62% received income from employer pensions, and 59% received income from assets; the distribution of income from assets is very skewed. And, 22% of the elderly retired received

Table 2.2

Employer-Provided Pension Coverage, 1979–2005, for Men and Women

Position in the Income Distribution Range	Percent with Pensions 1979	Percent with Pensions 2005	Percent Change in Coverage Rate, 1979–2005
Women in top third	65%	76%	17%
Women in middle third	46%	55%	20%
Women in bottom third	17%	21%	24%
Men in top third	76%	76%	0%
Men in middle third	60%	57%	−5%
Men in bottom third	24%	22%	−8%

Note: The data for 2005 is slightly inflated because of the 20 hours restriction.

Source: Ellwood 1998; author's calculation from CPS data for all workers over age 18 working more than 20 hours.

income from earnings on earnings, while the remainder of their income came from veteran's benefits and public assistance.[36]

Poverty

Compared to the bad news on replacement rates (replacement rate is the part of income before retirement that is replaced by income during retirement), the predictions are mixed for the poverty rate (poverty rate is the proportion of retirees whose income falls below the poverty level). Large increases in the benefits from Social Security in the 1960s and 1970s helped elevate elderly households (households containing those aged sixty-seven and older) out of poverty—from 19% below the poverty level in the 1960s to 8% in 2003. An Urban Institute study predicts that for all workers in their late forties in 2003, the predicted poverty rate when they reach age 67 will be lower at 4%, but the 2006 study by the Securities Industry Association, mentioned above, predicts the poverty rate will be above 20%, not below 4%.

The difference between these two studies and their predictions is in how the analysts treat work. The 2003 Urban Institute study includes earnings from work at age sixty-seven, as "retirement" income. In the past, increases in Social Security benefits were responsible for reducing poverty rates. The Urban

Institute predicts more earnings from work at age sixty-seven will reduce the poverty risk because the Institute study presumes boomers will be working for pay in their retirement. This is a startling finding—that barely adequate retirement income requires working for pay, which, of course, degrades the meaning of retirement, and ignores the fact that workers with lower income and wealth are much more vulnerable to being forced to retire because of lay-offs and health limitations. Despite the controversy over the predictions, no study disputes that the poverty rates are persistently high for nonmarried women.[37] No other industrialized nation puts their older women at such high risk of poverty; in other words, having a greater probability of having incomes below the poverty level than do men.

Women Face Special Pension Circumstances

Women's retirement needs require a special focus because old-age income policy disproportionately affects women: 58.8% of people aged sixty-five or older are women; and very old women (post–age eighty) outnumber men by 2.2 to 1.[38] Women's lives are getting better in one sense, worse in another. Women's emergence as independent economic actors has been unstoppable. Yet women have been enduring high rates of poverty in old age—why?

The answer lies primarily in the labor market and secondarily in marriage. Although economist Theresa Devine emphasizes an essential point—there is no such thing as a bundle of reforms that is good for "women" or bad for "women" because there is no such thing as a composite woman; women on average do have different economic lives than men. To get a sense of what that means, consider that 86% of men have never taken any years out of the labor force since the age of twenty-five, whereas only 46% of women can say they haven't taken time out to raise children or keep house since the age of twenty-five.[39]

The good news is that the average income of the elderly compared to the average income for the rest of the American population is improving, and the comparative status of elderly women, in particular, is also improving. The bad news is that women's poverty rates were higher in 2007 than they were in the 1970s, and older women's share of poverty far exceeds their proportion, women to men, in the elderly population. To make that startlingly clear, consider this: While 11% of the elderly are poor, 75% of the poor are women. Only the United Kingdom's elderly women's poverty rates are anywhere near the poverty rates of women in the United States.[40] This is a relatively new phenomenon attributed to the decrease in pension income as a consequence of Margaret Thatcher's privatization of the United Kingdom's national state-supported social security system in the 1980s (an earnings-related occupational pension scheme). Privatizing the social security system lowered the pension income of many low-income households.

The good news in the United States regarding the income of elderly married couples is that it improved considerably since 1969, from 49% of the median household income to a whopping 83% two decades later.[41] The bad news is that, despite these trends, nearly one out of five elderly women is poor, and every elderly woman's chances of falling into poverty increases by 470% if she does not have a husband. That's 22.8 % of nonmarried women falling below poverty level compared to about 4% of the married women. Poverty rates for married women are predicted to be a low 2% in the mid-2020s. The predictions for never-married and divorced women in the mid-2020s are 11% and 15%, respectively.[42]

> **DATA TO DIGEST**   *Despite the 20.4% rate of poverty among single older women in 2003, it was even higher in households headed by single women with young children, an appalling 36.7% in 2003 (see table 2.3, third and last rows in column 2). Moreover, though both single older women and single women heads of households experienced an increase in real income between 1969 and 2003, the single women over 65 did much better, obtaining a 96% increase in income compared to the much smaller 53% increase for unmarried women with young children (see table 2.3, third row, last column). The bleakness of the economic status of single mothers when they are young seems to follow them throughout their lifetime into old-age poverty, where they subsist on small pensions.*

Source of Retirement Income Affects Women Differently from Men

The U.S. Social Security system, like the social security systems in most other nations, is progressive. It provides higher income replacement rates for lower-income workers. The income from Social Security to someone who had a high income while working will replace a small part of that person's preretirement income, whereas the same or nearly the same amount of income from Social Security to a person earning a low income while working will replace a larger part of that person's preretirement income. People in high-paying

Table 2.3

Older Women Overcame Poverty

Poverty rates in 2003 and change in income from 1969 to 2003
for elderly and nonelderly families

Households	Poverty Rate (%)	Percentage Change in Real Income between 1969 and 2003
Elderly families		
Couples over age 65	5.4	91.0
Single men over 65	13.6	92.0
Single women over 65	20.4	96.0
Nonelderly families		
Couples with children under 18	7.7	61.0
Unmarried women with children under 18	36.7	53.0

Source: Population Resource Center 2005; and U.S. Census Bureau, Housing and Household Economic Statistics Division 2005.

jobs and people in low-paying jobs, both working approximately the same number of years and paying approximately the same amount in Social Security "contributions" over those years, each get similar retirement benefits due to proportional adjustments, no matter that those in higher-paying jobs will have much larger amounts of wealth.

Most retirement income to single women comes from Social Security; only 16.5% comes from employer pensions (private employers and government pensions), less than 15% comes from assets (savings and home equity), and 13% comes from earnings (see table 2.4, last column). Three features of Social Security—its progressive benefits to retirees (the same benefit amount replaces a greater proportion of a low-wage earner's working income than of a higher-wage earner's working income), the subsidy to dependents, and the cost-of-living annual adjustments—help those people who live longer than the average beneficiary. Social Security's progressive structure helps women because they are more likely to be low-income workers than male workers and are more likely to be dependents collecting survivor or spousal Social Security benefits.

Retired couples received less than 38% of their income from Social Security in 1996 and 37.4% in 2003. Less than one-half of American workers, both

Table 2.4

Earnings Swamp Pensions as Source of "Retirement" Income

(Percentage distribution, by marital status and sex, of nonmarried persons)

Source of Income	All Units (%)	Married Couples (%)	Nonmarried Persons		
			Men and Women (%)	Men (%)	Women (%)
Income from all sources	100	100	100	100	100
Social Security[a]	39.4	34.7	46.7	37.6	51.6
Earnings	24.9	30.1	16.8	23.4	13.2
Income from assets	13.6	12.9	14.6	15.2	14.3
Private pensions or annuities	9.9	10.5	8.8	10.9	7.7
Government employee pensions	8.8	8.8	8.7	8.7	8.8
Railroad retirement	0.3	0.3	0.4	0.5	0.4
Public assistance	0.7	0.4	1.2	0.8	1.4
Other	2.4	2.3	2.7	3	2.6
Amount per househould	$26,219	$10,412	$15,806	$4,187	$11,620

[a] Includes retired-worker benefits, dependents' or survivors' benefits, and disability benefits.

Source: Table 7.2 from the Social Security Administration (2004), available online at http://www.ssa.gov/policy/docs/statcomps/income_pop55/2002/sect7.html#table7.2.

men and women, have employer-provided pensions. But women's pensions—approximately $2,500 per year—are half the value of men's. In 2003, almost 20% of married couples' income came from employer-provided voluntary pensions, while only 15.6% of single women's income came from the same kind of pensions. Because retirement income is based mainly on work history and a record of wages, women's pensions are smaller (there is no doubt that, on average, women earn less and enter the workplace later than men).[43]

The Surprising Pension Gender Gap: Women Have More Than Men

Before 2003 women's pension coverage was inferior to men's. Remarkably, by 2005, full-time women workers were more likely to work for an employer who sponsors a pension plan than men—64.0% of women and 61.8%

of men at that time had pension coverage; a considerable change from the early 1980s![44]

In 2003, average income from defined benefit pension for a retired, married sixty-seven-year-old woman was $1,000 per year, while the average income from all her other retirement coverage was less than $1,000 per year. The average retired, married man's income from a defined benefit pension was $4,000 per year, and $1,000 per year from all his other retirement coverage.[45]

Although there is not a clear pattern of female-male differences with regard to pension coverage, it can be easily inferred that employers spend less on women's pensions than on men's. There is no data base that directly compares employers' pension spending on workers by sex. Instead of accepting the lack of data, I calculated the differences in pension spending by sex indirectly, using a data base that reports pension spending by firms. I grouped the firms by industry and classified the industries as female or male by calculating the percentage of female workers and the percentage of male workers employed in each industry. Industries that had a majority of women workers were classified as female-majority industries and those with more men than female workers were considered male-majority industries. Pension spending in male industries was 40% higher than in female industries in the late 1990s.

Only one piece of federal legislation regulating pensions was aimed at improving conditions for women. The 1984 Retirement Equity Act, sponsored by the only woman to be nominated by a major party to run for vice-president, Congressional member Geraldine Ferraro, gave surviving and divorced spouses more rights to claim from their deceased or ex-spouse's pension by requiring all employees to obtain a notarized statement from the worker's spouse stating that the spouse wanted to waive the spousal benefits.

Assets are the third source of income for older Americans, more so for single older women than for elderly couples. Elderly married couples obtained 16.6% of their retirement income from assets in 1996, dropping to 13.9% in 2003, whereas unmarried women received 18.9% of retirement income from assets in 1996, dropping to 16.2% in 2003.

The growth in the work-based share of old-age income for men and women is important because, unlike retired people in other nations, if older retired Americans want to work or need income, they can remain in the labor force. (Although Americans do not want to be forced to retire because of age, they may find that having the option to work, ironically, eases political pressure for, and social approval of, higher Social Security benefits and employer-based pensions.)

> **DATA TO DIGEST**   *Although the labor force participation of American women has increased rapidly, the labor force participation rate for women over sixty-five has remained low. In 1996, 22.9% of income to elderly retired couples came from earnings; in 2003 it was higher, at 25.3%. In contrast, only 8.8% of income to single older retired women came from earnings in 1996; but a much larger share, 15.7%, came from earnings in 2003.[46]*

Sex and Gender Differences Play Out in Retirement

The importance of Social Security in retirement is not the subject of this chapter, but clearly the interaction between the Social Security system and employer pensions must be addressed. Men and women are two different sexes, and there is nothing about the biological differences that would predict different economic outcomes except, perhaps, some aspects of longevity. There are biological reasons women live longer, but as men smoke less[47] and retire more, what looked like a sex-based longevity gap is shrinking. Gender is socially determined, and much of the economic gap between men and women—women have lower wages and spend less time in the labor market—is the gender gap. These factors work together to bring about uncertain and inadequate pensions. Table 2.5 indicates in brief the four main factors, which are based on work, longevity, and marriage, why women have less income from Social Security, and less income from employer pensions.

Women's pay is so much lower than men's because they are paid less and work fewer hours per week and fewer years per lifetime. For example, a woman, on average, is nearly forty before she has forty quarters of credited work under Social Security. Men are covered by age thirty. The difference has to do with the labor force participation of men and women during their prime working years, age thirty to thirty-four. In 2004, 74% of thirty- to thirty-four-year-old females were working or looking for work, whereas 93%, or nearly all men in their primary working years, were in the labor force.[48]

Though women are working and earning more, they still earn far less than men; women's median annual earnings were only 80.4% of men's in 2004.[49] Also, because women live longer than men, they need pension income for more months and years than do men. In 2000, women aged sixty-five were expected to live another 19.4 years, while men were expected to live 16.4

Table 2.5

Why Men Have More Retirement Income Than Women

The gender gap in factors that determine ultimate private pension earnings

Factors	Women	Men
Women work less		
The labor force participation rate of a 30–34-year-old in 2003 (reflects attachment to labor force)[a]	74%	93%
Age at which workers become fully insured under Social Security (reflects attachment to paid work)[b]	38.9 years	30 years
Women are paid less		
Half of men/women earned less than this annual amount in 1999[c]	$18,957	$29,458
Women need pensions over longer time		
Life expectancy for 65-year-olds in 2000[d]	19.1 years	15.8 years
Predicted life expectancy for 65-year-olds in 2030[e]	20.4 years	17.5 years
Husbands matter		
Poverty rate when living alone after age 65 (the penalty for not being married)[f]	20.4%	13.6%

Sources:

[a] U.S. Department of Labor, *Women in the Labor Force: A Databook* (2005), table 1.

[b] Levine, Mitchell, and Phillips (2000), table 1.

[c] U.S. Census Bureau (2000), Summary File 3, table P85.

[d] Anzick and Weaver (2001).

[e] Anzick and Weaver (2001).

[f] U.S. Census Bureau Data (2003), table POV1.

more years, a difference of over 18%. A pension paid in a lump sum is a considerable disadvantage to anyone who expects to live many years after retirement and wants a pension for life. Defined contribution pension plans almost always pay out in a lump sum. People who want to use that lump sum to buy an annuity—a contract that pays a monthly benefit for life—face high prices in the private market. An insurance company (or any other financial entity that will promise income for life for a payment up front) worries, reasonably, that only people in good health would voluntarily seek to buy an annuity. Such a long-lived person will collect for more years than a person with average longevity. The insurance companies will therefore charge everyone wanting to buy an annuity as if they will live longer than the average length of life for people their age. If annuities were mandated, the insurance companies would presume the group contains both people who will die young and those who live longer than average and thus charge for annuities based on average life expectancy.

How Economic Theory Explains the Gender Differences in Pension Benefits

Different economists have different theories about why older women have low incomes both during their work years and then again during their retirement years. Some economists (the neoclassical economists, who have dominated economic scholarship on labor markets since the 1960s) borrow from the classical economists (principally, from the Cambridge, England economist Alfred Marshall's writing in the 1900s), to explain how firms and people make decisions. Neoclassical economists give primary attention to individuals making decisions in a market when explaining labor market outcomes—wages, fringe benefits, hours of work, unemployment—and they pay little attention to the role of government, or culture, or differences in economic bargaining power due to the distribution of wealth and income. These factors are viewed mostly as the side effects of market forces. That is, the neoclassical economists regard whether a person is unemployed, or poorly or highly paid, as a result of continual cost-benefit decisions that a person makes while acting rationally, making decisions on ways to make himself or herself better off. The emphasis is on the individual's choices—choices outside of family considerations or cultural influences, and a psychology that differs from that of a rational actor who is motivated to maximize her or his level of well-being.

Neoclassical theory explains that women have lower pensions because they give unpaid work in the home a higher priority than paid work in the marketplace, and therefore they "most likely trade off wages and other benefits for those benefits, which are of use in household production."[50] This trade-off depends highly on the assumption that pensions and wages are substitutes for one another. The idea is that if women trade away pensions, they get something for it—such as, "family-friendly" flexibility where they work or, if they are working in the marketplace, they get higher pay from employers but no or little pension coverage. However, pensions and wages are complements, not substitutes. The higher-paid the job, the more likely it will have fringe benefits attached.[51]

Other economists, the institutional economists, are viewed as the main rivals to neoclassical economists. Institutional economists emerged to challenge neoclassical economics assumptions about how individuals act. They also flipped the way economic research is conducted. Instead of a heavy emphasis on presuming that individuals and firms act in particular optimizing ways, as the neoclassical economists presumed, the institutionalists are data driven. The institutionalists examine patterns in data and relationships to infer motivations and constraints. Institutionalists emphasize constraints that come from social norms, customs, and from power relationships—where "power relationship" implies the ability of one party simply to walk away from what could be an agreement because it would cost that party more than the other party. In this balance-of-power view, labor is always at a disadvantage because workers can only walk away from management by paying a high cost. Labor is a perishable good. Labor not used today or tomorrow or for however long it is not used, can never be recovered. The value of capital is more durable! In the institutional view, women are paid less and have fewer pensions because of the choices they make due to cultural norms, and because females have less bargaining power than males.

When employers developed pension plans, many excluded women. For example, excluded were the women Sears Roebuck and Kodak used as "buffer" workers (workers are considered buffers if they come into the firm's labor force when there is high demand and drop out when labor demand falls). Buffer workers have little, if any, bargaining power. They are less likely to participate in an employer benefit that encourages loyalty and long-term attachments. In the early part of the twentieth century, social reformers attacked the large retail company, Sears, for paying women wages so low that it forced them into poverty and then into prostitution. In response to this bad publicity, Sears created "one of the nations most generous and public profit-sharing plans."[52] But, because only full-time workers with one year of service could participate, "the plan's prime beneficiaries were not women but men."[53] Sears's only concession to women was that women who were covered under the company's pension plan and left their jobs to get married could have the company contributions in a cash payment after five years of service, rather than the ten years all other employees had to complete.[54]

The labor economists, especially the feminists among them, see family dynamics and employer behavior as intertwined. That is, they see women's labor used as a less costly substitute for men's labor.[55] Bus driving, residential real estate sales, bank clerking, and bartending are examples of occupations that changed from majority-male jobs when they were filled by lower-paid women. Feminist economists blame patriarchy, in its many forms, such as social insurance (for example, Social Security, pensions based on long-term service with an employer) for older women's low economic status relative to men's. (Feminist economists consider patriarchy as comprising the systems of culture and politics that create and maintain men's superior status in the respect that men get first choice in jobs, have better access to financial capital and the confidence and respect of potential business partners, have political power, and have the dominant role in relationships, endowing them with more sway in decisions affecting both men and women.) Furthermore, feminist economist Nancy Folbre argues that men struggled for "retirement" by striking and exerting political pressure to be able to acquire pensions at the workplace and by forming political coalitions around the goal of increasing Social Security benefits. The result was a bias toward men that made it possible for fathers to abandon their children, yet collect a decent Social Security benefit.[56] The Social Security system provides a "housewife bonus," which subsidizes nonworking wives (not employed for pay, although they do unpaid work in the home); wives who do not work can, after ten years of marriage, collect half of their husband's Social Security benefit when he retires and 100% of it when he dies. Feminists argue that this "subsidy" strengthens patriarchal systems by making women's income dependent on their relationships with men.[57] When working wives receive Social Security benefits based on their husband's record of contributions, which is likely given that men's pay is so much higher, they are unfairly receiving a "zero return" on their own contributions to Social Security, it is argued by economists Barbara Bergmann and Barbara Holden. Recent studies suggest that women's earnings would have to increase substantially (over 20%) for a woman to "earn a benefit of her own" under Social Security.[58]

Pension Futures for Workers with Moderate Incomes

The less workers earn, the less likely they are to be covered by their employer's defined benefit pension, and it is just as unlikely that they will participate, when eligible, in their firm's 401(k) pension plan.

> **DATA TO DIGEST**   *In 2001, 9.6% of workers aged fifty to fifty-nine who were eligible to participate in a 401(k) plan and who had earnings over $80,000 chose to participate, while only 68.4% of those earning less than $20,000 chose to participate in a 401(k). This difference is more than 27%. The difference is worse at younger ages. Among thirty- to thirty-nine-year-olds, almost 50% of lower-income workers participated in the 401(k) plan offered by their employer, but over 81% of higher-income workers participated.[59]*

Defined benefit plans provided better coverage for lower-income workers because participation in these plans is not voluntary. Still, fewer than 30% of low-income workers have any kind of pension plan.

Tax Policy Bias Away from Low-Income Earners

Explanations for the pension coverage gap between highly paid and low-wage workers, and whether policymakers believe in the facts of these explanations, seriously demonstrate the need and urgency to fix policy affecting pensions for all. For example, if lower levels of participation by low-income workers are explained by age, then we do not have to worry about the poor coverage because young workers always get older. And when they get older, the presumption is that they will eventually be covered by a pension. Furthermore, if low-income workers are less likely to be covered by a pension because they are working in small firms, then an effective pension policy would be to aim tax incentives at expanding pension plans at small firms. However, since low-income workers and low-profit firms already face lower rates of federal taxes, such a reform of tax policy would not be very effective.

Another policy change would be to mandate that workers and employers supplement Social Security with a defined contribution pension "add-on" through which low-income workers would get a tax credit. This idea is recycled from President Clinton's plan, which was recycled from President Carter's plan. Carter's 1978 plan was called Mandatory Universal Pension Savings (MUPS), and Clinton's 1998 plan was called the Universal Savings Account (USA). I propose a variant called the Guaranteed Retirement Account, discussed in chapter 10.

The U.S. Treasury Department's Internal Revenue Service aimed to prevent firms from obtaining favorable tax treatment to benefit pension coverage that would apply only to their executives. (Chapter 3 discusses ways that executives today are still ensuring their own pension plans at the expense of ordinary workers.)[60] Tax breaks disappear for pension plans that do not include large numbers of low-income workers relative to the number of highly paid employees. Highly paid employees, including management, are limited in how much they can enjoy the tax break because the maximum they can contribute to their pension is based on a specified proportion (according to a complicated set of rules) of low-income workers not participating in the same pension plan. The aim of these tax rules is to make it difficult for highly paid owners to set up pensions for themselves and their executives and not include low-income employees. This indirect approach to encouraging firms to provide their workers with pension plans that supplement Social Security has worked somewhat, especially in large firms or firms that have a large number of highly paid workers.[61] But a tax break is not very compelling when federal tax rates fall. A study covered the tax cuts under President Reagan in the 1980s and found that a 10% decrease in the federal tax rate lowers pension coverage by 4%.[62] More significantly, there is little evidence that these tax breaks increase pension coverage or savings.

Federal pension policy is biased toward 401(k) plans. Despite the well-documented problems of defined contribution plans, Congress expanded the tax breaks for these plans in the Pension Protection Act of 2006, allowing individuals to shelter up to $20,000 from taxes in a retirement account. While expanding tax breaks for DC plans, Congress has imposed additional burdens on DB plans.[63] Participants are not allowed to contribute a single dollar to their DB plans, let alone an extra $20,000; and new funding rules make employer contributions more unpredictable, spurring employers to abandon their defined benefit pension coverage.

Tax breaks mostly benefit high-income workers. The IRS allows 401(k) participants to invest pretax income, deferring taxes until retirement. The tax subsidy is equal to the investment earnings on the deferred taxes, which depends on the marginal tax rate paid by a household. A wealthy family in the 35% tax bracket gets a tax break three-and-a-half times more valuable than a lower-income family in the 10% tax bracket, even if each family contributes the same dollar amount to a 401(k) plan. This is extremely biased, since it is much harder for a low-income household to save than it is for a wealthy household.

Another key reason low-income workers are not covered by a pension plan at work is because either they are not in a union or they work in industries where workers have little or no power to market their labor.[64] Workers with power to market their labor can bargain for employee benefits. For example, no Wal-Mart workers are unionized; only half are covered by employee health benefits; and less than half of those are covered by a 401(k) plan. In contrast, all low-income grocery workers and retail workers who are represented by a union have pensions and health insurance.

In most, if not all, nations, social spending programs aim to prevent poverty and enable workers to retire, even if a worker is still capable of working. Governmental policymakers and economists recognize that people are unable to make, or hopelessly ineffective at making, decisions affecting their lives over a long time horizon.

> **DATA TO DIGEST**   *Without Social Security and employer-provided pensions, a worker who chooses to be, or must be, a "do-it-yourself pension" planner, needs to save about 20% of every paycheck in an account earning at least 4% after inflation and investment fees for an entire working life.[65] It is a tall order to fill; most people don't fill it and couldn't fill it without being forced to save.*

Conclusion: Failures of the Current U.S. Retirement Income Security System

The U.S. retirement income security system fails to provide adequate and guaranteed retirement income for most workers. If current trends continue, the early baby boomers (born between 1946 and 1955) will be the last generation with more retirement security than their parents.[66] Almost 30% of households approaching retirement age have expected retirement incomes below twice the poverty level, or $19,000 per year in 2006 dollars. This includes over 60% of unmarried women and more than 56% of African Americans and Hispanics.[67]

In addition to retirement prospects becoming grimmer for workers earning average wages, inequality in retirement income is growing as Social Security benefits decrease and individual retirement accounts replace traditional pensions.[68] Certain groups are especially hard hit, including divorced women, low-wage workers, and retirees with long-term care needs and medical expenses.

Workers are taking on more risks for no gain. The shift from defined benefit to defined contribution plans and the decline in income replacement rates from Social Security have required workers to shoulder more risk. Workers already bear the risk of being too old to work, being laid off, or being disabled. Inflation, longevity, financial and employment risks, once pooled by larger entities, are now borne by the individual. These risks include payout risk—that's the risk that an individual will not manage a lump sum at retirement to protect against inflation—and the financial risk in living a long life.

Firms have an incentive to persuade workers to favor defined contribution plans over defined benefit plans. The incentive is twofold: workers typically bear more than half of the cost of DC plans, and the firm does not have to pay its share of defined contribution pensions for workers who do not participate. (Despite the convenience of payroll deduction and expensive campaigns to educate workers about these plans, the participation rate for 401(k)-eligible workers has stagnated at about 80%, and is much lower for workers under age forty.)[69]

One reason Americans may have willingly accepted this increased risk is that older Americans have a safety valve, an income source of last resort—the labor market. The share of "retirement income" from work (I am conscious of the irony) is predicted to increase[70] from 14% to 18% as the elderly increasingly postpone retirement or take part-time jobs while retired.

The collapse of retirement income means that elderly people will be worse off in the future in terms of their physical standard of living, and most likely also in terms of their mental well-being. The elderly will be worse off because pensions will less likely be paid in an annuity, and they will be working more for someone else. They will lose free time, and there is no way around the fact that losing free time—having to take a cashier's job because your pension dollars ran out—makes you worse off. Taking a cashier's job because you choose to—it is fun, sociable, and you want extra money—does not make you worse off.

Nations construct retirement systems to provide income from various sources, and the proportions from each source vary widely among nations. In the United States, retirement income, in order of magnitude, comes from Social Security; employer-provided pensions—defined benefit and defined contribution; personal savings and assets; earnings; and to a very small extent, family networks and welfare. Employer plans and programs are a key element in securing enough income in retirement.[71]

Examining the future of retirement income requires special focus on the powerful forces that affect employer-provided pensions, because of the reliance in the United States on this source of retirement income. Employer pensions are the subject of the next chapter.

Chapter 3

When Bad Things Happen to Good Pensions—Promises Get Broken

"I feel like I was kicked in the stomach."

That's what a salaried Verizon Communications employee said to a reporter in December 2005 when her company announced it was freezing its defined benefit pension plan. Her defined benefit pension benefit, as is the case for most DB plans, was based on salary at the time of retirement and total years of service. But, since Verizon froze the plan, she will not earn any more years of service credits and her pension will be based on her salary at the time the plan was frozen, not the higher salary at the time she retires. She figured that as a result of the freeze she would lose $400,000 in total retirement benefits.[1] Surely, you can relate to how she felt. Think about how you would feel if you lost what you thought was yours, if what you lost was a big chunk of your pension and, as a result of that loss, you had to plan to work more years than you expected. Your retirement future is busted. You feel conned, like a chump. Betrayal hurts, right in the gut. The traditional defined benefit pension was at the heart of the pension system of all employers, including Verizon. Defined benefit pension plans covered about half of all private-sector workers in the United States in the 1960s, and almost all employees in the largest companies.

Curiously, fundamental trends—such as an aging work force and companies keen to attract and retain skilled workers—should have made defined benefit pensions expand instead of shrink. This chapter describes how defined contribution type pensions—the most common are the 401(k) plans—once supplemented defined benefit pensions but are now displacing them. Starting in the mid-1990s, workers all over the United States were facing pension losses, not only workers who lost pensions because they were employed by companies that went bankrupt, but also workers who lost pensions because they were employed by healthy firms engaged in profitable restructuring.

Boston College economists calculated that between 2004 and 2006 seventeen "healthy" companies froze their pension plans. (Freezing pension plans means the companies close their plans to new employees, stop pension accrual for all employees, or partially freeze by stopping accrual for some employees.) These companies were healthy, in the sense that they were growing, profitable, and far from bankruptcy. Among these companies were Verizon, IBM, and Sears Holding—three companies that affected a staggering 280,000 employees; and, the pension fund of each company was over 92% funded. The other fourteen companies together affected more than 220,000 employees. Financially troubled firms, such as GM, which froze pension accruals for its salaried workers, were not included in these calculations. Most of the salaried workers were offered 401(k) plans as replacement for what would have been continued accruals, but for most workers the replacement plans do not restore the benefits lost from the freeze.[2]

Three reasons for the decline in workers' pensions were: misguided government policy, growth in the kinds of firms that don't maximize profits by providing secure pensions, and the lack of workers' pension protection. Although older employees with many years of service receive more from a DB plan than younger workers, DB plans are most often better sources of retirement income for younger workers than DC, 401(k)-type plans.

In this chapter, you will first be introduced to the numbers characterizing defined benefit pensions. Then you will see the reasons for the decline in these kinds of pensions.

Defined Benefit Pensions and the Road to a Middle-Class Retirement

As explained in chapter 2, retirement income comes from Social Security; voluntary employer-sponsored defined benefit plans and defined contribution 401(k)-type plans (which commonly make income available to retirees in a lump sum, not as an annuity); personal assets; charity and government-provided welfare; adult children; credit card debt; and senior discounts. At any point in time, less than half of all workers are working for an employer who sponsors some type of employer pension. However, most workers eventually accumulate funds in some kind of individual retirement account or earn a right to collect pensions from a defined benefit plan and retire with a pension supplementing their Social Security income. Employer pension income supplementing Social Security income is the only hope a middle-class worker has to be a middle-class retiree. Income from Social Security replaces about 47.6% to 67.5% of the preretirement income for middle-income workers (shown in the third and fourth quintiles, row 1 in table 3.1). Middle-class retirees receive about 14% to 20% of their total retirement income[3] from employer pensions; this is their most important source of income after Social Security, which provides 47.5% to 47.6% of retirement income to the third and fourth quintiles (see the fourth and fifth columns in table 3.1). If the source of supplemental pension income comes from a DB plan, then a retiree receives a steady stream of modest income for life.

In contrast, workers at the top of the preretirement earnings scale rely on earnings from paid work and income from wealth for over 57% of their retirement income, and 20.4% from pensions.[4] (See table 3.1, fifth quintile, row 3 "earnings" and row 4 "income from assets.")

Diminished Defined Benefit Plans

Defined benefit pension coverage—that's the proportion of full-time workers working year round whose employers sponsor a pension plan—has been falling for years, recently from 62.7% in 2003, to 61.8% in 2004, to 59.7% in 2005. Pension participation—that's the proportion of full-time, year-round, workers who were actually included in their employers' pension plans and who contributed to or were credited with pension benefits—also fell from 54.1% to 53.4% from 2003 to 2004, and to 51.6% in 2005.[5] The share of workers "covered" by employer pensions is greater than the share of workers who "participate," because employers, even if they offer a pension plan, can exempt employees from participating. There are many ways that employees can be excluded from their employer's pension plan—workers who have too few years of service or hours of work per week are not required to be included in the plan. The gap between coverage and participation is worse in defined contribution plans, such as 401(k) plans, because participation in defined contribution pension plans is voluntary. In addition to the fall in coverage by all types of pension plans, the type of pension covering workers is changing. If the change were represented graphically, you might expect to see the succession of years on the horizontal axis and the number of DB and DC pension plans (or participants) on the vertical axis. Looking at such a graph, you would

Table 3.1

Employer Pensions Are Important for Middle-Class Retirees

Percentages of income to each economic quintile of household units with member over age 55, by source

	First quintile	Second quintile	Third quintile	Fourth quintile	Fifth quintile
Social Security (including railroad retirement)	82.9%	84.5%	67.5%	47.6%	19.9%
Government and private employee pensions	3.2%	6.3%	14.5%	24.9%	20.4%
Earnings	1.1%	2.3%	7.0%	14.7%	38.4%
Income from assets (including savings from retirement accounts)	2.4%	3.6%	7.4%	9.8%	18.9%
Public assistance and other sources	10.4%	3.3%	3.7%	3.1%	2.5%
Number (thousands)	5,244	5,244	5,241	5,245	5,244

Note: Quintile upper limits are: $9,721; $15,181; $23,880; $40,982.

Source: Table 7.5, "Percentage distribution, by marital status, and quintiles of total money income," at www.ssa.gov/policy/docs/statcomps/income_pop55/2002.

expect to see the line representing DB going down over successive years, the line representing DC plans going up over the same years, and the lines crossing in about the mid-1990s. A picture is worth a thousand "impressions" and evokes as many feelings; yet it only illustrates a muddle. If the decline of DB plans and increase in DC plans were depicted graphically, as just described, it would look something like the graph shown in figure 3.1. From what you see there, it would be easy for you to infer that defined contribution pensions are *replacing* defined benefit pensions *because* new firms and new workers prefer the one over the other. Alas, experts make the same inference. And, alas again, you and the experts would be making an incorrect inference. The graph is not wrong, but the inference is. Here's why: Almost all workers who have defined benefit plans also have a defined contribution supplement.

In my own survey of large firms that existed from 1983 through 1998, I could distinguish (a) firms that sponsored DB plans but not DC plans; (b) firms that sponsored DC but not DB plans; and (c) firms that sponsored both. A detailed description of the research in my survey comes in chapter 4. But here is the gist: Among 724 firms, the most popular kind of company pension program was a DB plan standing alone—that is, 43.9%, or 320 of the firms surveyed, sponsored only DB plans in 1981. Only 13.8% of firms sponsored only DC pension plans, and 42% of firms sponsored both DB and DC plans. My follow-up survey in 1998 showed that, among the same 724 firms, only 11.2% offered a stand-alone DB plan, and only 17.1% offered a DC plan. Overwhelmingly, the most common pension offering was a combination of a defined benefit and defined contribution—71.7% of firms

Figure 3.1
The Usual Story: The End of Defined Benefit Plans
Percentage of full-time employees in medium and large private establishments, 1983–2003

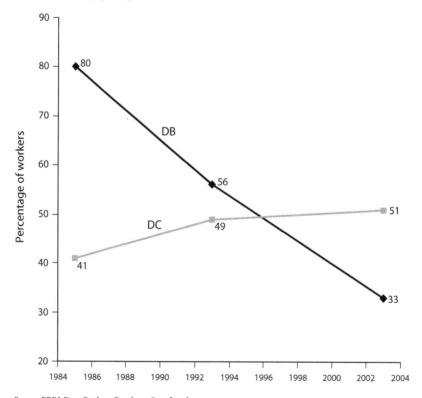

Source: EBRI *Data Book on Employee Benefits*, chapter 10.

in 1998 sponsored both types, compared to 42% of firms that offered both types in 1981.[6] The data from these two surveys showed that a DC plan has become increasingly a supplement to DB pension coverage. Therefore, inhibiting the growth of DB pension plans inhibits the expansion of pension coverage.

DB Plans Help Boost Pension Coverage among Workers; DC Pension Plans Do Not

Here's another way to interpret what is graphically represented in that "cross-over" graph, figure 3.1. Looking to the right of the point where the defined benefit curve and the defined contribution curve cross, someone could conclude that defined benefit pensions started to fail as firms with defined benefit pensions in dying unionized industries were replaced by diverse, dynamic, nonunion firms with defined contribution pensions. In such a world, the total number of workers with pensions would equal the sum of workers covered by defined benefit plans and those covered by defined contribution plans. But that is not the real world according to the real data.

Although the data, properly interpreted, show that the share of workers in DC plans is growing and the share covered by DB plans is falling, no one seems to realize the consequences of this difference. When firms provide new workers with DB plans (this happens less and less), the increased number of workers in those plans is a true increase in the number of workers in a pension plan. But newly added people in DC plans do not expand pension coverage because these workers are already in a DB plan.

> **Bottom Line**   *Expanding coverage in defined benefit plans increases the share of the workforce covered by pension plans. An increased number of workers in defined contribution plans does not.*

Here is the evidence. The share of workers in DB plans fell severely, by more than 11%, in the seven years between 1999 and 2005 in the goods-producing sector. But, in those same years, DB coverage rose most for workers in small firms, representing the largest increase in overall pension coverage—a boost of 8.8%.[7] Also, pension coverage in the service industry increased by almost 6% as new workers were provided with defined benefit pension plans.

During the seven years from 1999 to 2005, union workers experienced very large increases in overall pension coverage rates, particularly in the proportion of workers covered by DB pension plans. Both increases are noteworthy

Table 3.2

Pension Coverage Growth is Correlated with DB Coverage Growth

Percentage of all private sector workers' pension participation in all types of plans, ranked in descending order by growth of overall participation rates.

	Coverage Rates in All Pension Plans		Coverage Rates in DB Pension Plans	
	1999	*2005*	*1999*	*2005*
1	2	3	4	5
All workers	48%	50%	21%	21%
Small firms 0–99	34%	37%	8%	9%
Service industries	44%	47%	17%	18%
Non union	44%	46%	16%	15%
Union	79%	85%	70%	72%
Goods-producing	61%	64%	36%	32%
Full time	56%	60%	25%	25%
Larger firms over 100	64%	67%	37%	36%
Correlations				

Source: National Compensation Survey: Employee benefits in private industry, author's computations from data available on the website: ww.nbls.gov/ncs/ebs

because union workers in 1999 had the highest overall pension coverage rate, 79%, compared to pension coverage rate for all workers, 54%.

During the seven years between 1999 and 2005, union workers experienced a more than 1% increase in their defined contribution coverage rate. Since unions usually collectively bargain for defined contribution plans to complement already existing or newly bargained defined benefit plans, you can be fairly certain that the growth in defined benefit coverage boosted overall pension coverage for the group of unionized workers.

For all workers there is an 88% correlation between changes in the overall pension coverage rates and changes in the defined benefit coverage rates. In contrast, the correlation between changes in the overall defined contribution coverage is only 11%. (See table 3.2, columns 7, 8, 9, and bottom row.)

Similarly, data representing all workers in 2003 and in 2005 provides more evidence that increasing the number of people in DB pensions results in increasing the number of people with overall pension coverage.

Coverage Rates in DC Pension Plan		Changes from 1999–2005		
1999	2005	Changes in Over All Pension Coverage	Changes DB Coverage	Changes DC Coverage
6	7	8	9	10
36%	43%	4.2%	0.0%	19.4%
27%	32%	8.8%	12.5%	18.5%
34%	39%	6.8%	5.9%	14.7%
35%	41%	4.5%	−6.3%	17.1%
39%	43%	7.6%	2.9%	10.3%
44%	50%	4.9%	−11.1%	13.6%
42%	50%	7.1%	0.0%	19.0%
46%	53%	4.7%	−2.7%	15.2%
			88.3%	11.3%

Consider that groups with above-average DB coverage rates also have above-average overall pension coverage rates. There is no such correlation with the DC pension coverage rates. Unionized female workers, who earn above average wages, have twice the pension coverage rates as part-time workers, who have the lowest pension coverage rates at 47%. What explains the high rates of pension coverage among these higher-paid union females? Their DB coverage rate is 300 times higher than that for female part-time workers. Again, simple correlation between a group's pension coverage rate and its defined benefit coverage, and the same group's pension coverage and its defined contribution coverage, shows that DB coverage rates are 94% correlated with overall pension coverage rates, while DC coverage rates are only 55% correlated with overall pension coverage (see table 3.3).

Much of the decline in coverage and participation rates—remember, participation rate is the proportion of workers participating voluntarily in pension coverage offered to them—is the result of the lack of expansion in the number of DB pensions, while the explosion in DC coverage has not improved workers' access to pension plans. Firms that would otherwise have

Table 3.3
Workers with New Pensions Are Likely to Have DB Plans
*Selected groups' pension coverage rates by type of pension, ranked
by coverage growth rates: calculations from the 2003 CPS*

	Pension Coverage Rates (ranked lowest to highest)	DB	DC
Part-time	47%	11%	37%
Part-time: Above-average wages	54%	12%	50%
Full-time	53%	16%	40%
Male	56%	14%	38%
Never-married women	58%	18%	28%
Married women	58%	19%	42%
Female	59%	18%	43%
Married men	64%	16%	38%
Male: Above-average wages	71%	21%	61%
Full-time: Above-average wages	73%	23%	62%
Union Female	78%	43%	39%
Union Male	80%	36%	53%
Female: Above-average wages	81%	33%	63%
Union Male: Above-average wages	91%	58%	56%
Union Female: Above-average wages	100%	72%	48%
Correlations between DB and pension coverage		94%	
Correlations between DC and pension coverage			55%

pensions are using DC plans, and the firms without pensions are not likely to offer a pension plan—not even when there is a new kind of pension to offer.

> **Bottom Line**   *Private sector workers' access to pensions is stagnating; coverage rates have hovered around 50% of the work force for approximately the past twenty years.*

The Paradox of Overall Pension Stagnation

Pension coverage—meaning, the share of workers whose employers sponsor a plan—is stagnating. Powerful demographic and economic changes should point to such trends as aging workers, an expanding economy, profitable firms, and firms' interest in retaining skilled workers. Reasons why pension coverage should be expanding include the following:

First, a rich economy with an aging workforce should be filled with people not only able to save for a safe and sound financial future, but also with a growing desire to do so.

Second, security is a "normal" good—that's the kind of good you want more of when your income goes up. So, when income increases, the demand for a normal good increases. Average income and wealth have consistently climbed, as American workers are aging and moving into their income-security- and health-security-conscious years. The average American worker, just by virtue of her age, would be expected to demand more pension coverage.

Third, firms' ability to pay for pensions increased as profits reached record levels in the 1990s and early 2000s. Firms that enjoy rapid growth often face employee retention issues—that is, they tend to target each other's employees with the intent to hire the same employees. These firms can afford to pay for pensions. Therefore, we would expect firms in high-growth industries to develop compensation devices that raise the cost for a worker to leave his job.

Fourth, defined benefit pensions have been a key retention device. As boomers retire over the next twenty years, companies will find it increasingly difficult to hire and keep workers without raising wages. Companies not providing DB pensions may come to regret it.

If these four fundamental issues point to what should be a growth in pension coverage, in general, and to DB pension plans, in particular, then what explains their decline? The answers will greatly influence the policies we Americans want from our government.

There are four explanations, not necessarily independent of each other; each helps explain the puzzle that pension coverage has remained stuck at half of the workforce when a higher percentage would be expected.

One explanation has to do with "weakened worker power." This expression refers to the vast number of firms that now avoid long-term employer-worker relationships, because, presumably, those firms can obtain the same level of productivity without such relationships.

The second explanation is that the natural evolution of the economy is what caused the shift in pension plan design. This explanation emphasizes that the kinds of technologies that produce the things that people now want to buy—for instance, high-speed video graphic cards, boutique software packages, services from an independent account—are technologies that do not need loyal employees. Since defined benefit pensions cater to employees who have attachments to one or two employers and these employees do not represent the new kind of worker, then firms merely evolved their pension plan to adapt to a newer, more nimble workforce comprising workers who may prefer individual accounts.

The third explanation blames both tax regulations, which are hostile to defined benefit plans, as well as public policy decisions resulting in laws that discourage DB plans while encouraging DC plans. Inherent in this explanation is that the DC vendors—the investment management firms, and some employers, specifically, employers that wanted to adopt cheaper DC plans—obtained the legislation and regulations that serve their interests.

The fourth explanation for the decline in DB pensions proposes a "perfect storm" of economic events, in which high interest rates and low financial returns drown DB plans in uncertainty and too much cost for an employer to provide them.

How government should respond to the changing nature of pension provision depends in large part on what explanation—weakened worker power, changing types of jobs and worker preferences, a public policy environment hostile to DB plans, or a perfect storm of bad economic events—is accepted. If defined benefit pensions have outlived their purpose—that means their ability to aid employers to hire and train the best workforce and for employees to accumulate retirement assets—then very little government intervention is needed to restore DB plans or reform DC plans. If defined benefit pensions are outdated and thus fading, not unlike the dinosaur, then we can expect an orderly exit—with some localized disruptions.

However, the government should intervene, if the decline in defined benefit pensions is due to (a) workers having less influence in determining their pay and working conditions; (b) commercial interests dominating pension legislation and thus promoting 401(k) plans; or (c) employers shifting the risks of securing retirement income onto workers.

If bad economic events—the perfect storm—caused funding uncertainty for defined benefit plans, then all that is required to advance pension protection is temporary relief provided by the federal government (for example, as when the airlines got a special provision to spread out their pension funding). Pension reform ideas are constrained by assumptions about what best explains the specific pension problems the policymakers seek to correct.

Consider though, the situation in which an environment with weakening union bargaining power became hostile to defined benefit pensions. In a strange unfolding of events, US Airways pilots and Alabama public employees were pitted against each other without intending to be in a zero-sum game for their pensions and jobs. In 2003, the retirement fund for Alabama state and local employees demanded that US Airways pilots forfeit half of their pensions.

In 2002 the executive director of the Alabama state pension funds got a lot of attention by buying a significant share of US Airways stocks and bonds for the pension fund. The executive director's stated intention was to save US Airways, which was an important employer in Alabama. One year later, the Alabama pension fund, which was then one of the most important creditors to the troubled airline, joined forces with other creditors—banks and bond holders—to demand that US Airways give up the pilots' pensions in exchange for the airline's release from bankruptcy and higher returns to the creditors. The pilots' union argued that their pension was deferred wages, an important part of their promised pay, and that by giving up their deferred wages, the pilots would have to bear most of the costs of US Airways management's mistakes, as well as the costs for adverse economic events out of their control, such as the attacks on the World Trade Center Towers and greatly increasing fuel costs.

The pilots lost. Their pension plan was terminated. This situation may seem unusual and not likely to happen again—that a flashy and powerful pension administrator would be able to invest a substantial share of the fund in a substantial amount of shares of a troubled company. In this case the pension plan took a large gamble on a single outcome—pension funds do not usually do this! But pension funds are becoming more involved in shareholder rights. Although the pilots' union fought hard in bankruptcy court against the loss of their pilots' pensions, pension claims have low priority in bankruptcy law. The risk of the loss of the Alabama state workers' pension fund investment in US Airways could have been shifted to taxpayers, to shareholders, to executives, and even to Alabama workers—but, instead, the pilots bore all the cost of someone else's risk.

It is clear that workers' pensions are not secure, not even from other workers' pensions.

Another explanation for the decline in defined benefit pensions is the expansion of low-paying jobs with high turnover. During the 1980s and 1990s, the relationships between U.S. employers and their employees changed. Workers have lost market power as jobs become more unstable and insecure, especially for men. The U.S. economy's "secondary" sector—that is the sector that does not use production processes that rely on experience, loyalty, or the high skill of its employees—is expanding.[8] The expansion of this sector can explain, in part, the loss of workers' bargaining power to secure pensions. To get a sense of the basis for this explanation, consider that retail and service industries are the fastest-growing industries, pay the least, are the least unionized, have the highest share of part-time and temporary workers, the lowest rates of pension coverage, and the lowest share of total compensation that is paid in employee benefits. These jobs pay primarily cash wages.[9] Overall, the rise in secondary jobs in secondary industries is correlated with the drop in the share of total compensation that goes to pensions.[10]

If the decline of DB pensions is caused by the dip in worker bargaining power and the rise of low-paying and more temporary jobs, then the erosion of DB pensions could actually be a mistake and an accident of history.

The hostile regulatory environment is another reason for the decline in DB pension plans. During the past twenty years, Congress has crimped the growth of DB pension plans by adding more and more stringent regulations while encouraging DC plans with very few regulations.[11] The Financial Accounting Standards Board—the board that regulates the methods used by publicly traded firms to report their finances—pressed for firms to measure pension liabilities and assets in ways that make a fund likely to report that it does not have assets to cover its liabilities. Liabilities can be measured in terms of what would be owed to workers if the fund terminated immediately, or the liabilities can be measured as if they were funded over a long time period. The analogy to a home mortgage is apt. Many people with mortgages cannot afford to pay off their mortgage loan, but can afford a mortgage paid over a twenty- or thirty-year period. How affordability and liability are measured matters a great deal—it can determine whether people live in a house or not. The way to measure pension liabilities and the way to measure assets—on a termination basis and on an ongoing basis—make sense; but favoring one over the other distorts the ability of the fund to pay its liabilities.[12]

The Pension Benefit Guaranty Corporation (PBGC) is a federal agency mandated by the 1974 ERISA Employee Retirement Income Security Act law to promote and maintain the defined benefit pension system. The PBGC is a quasi-governmental agency that pays for its operations by charging premiums to companies that sponsor DB pension plans in exchange for the assurance that the agency will take over the payments to retirees of a bankrupt company's pension. The PBGC also has the ability to terminate a pension plan before it becomes indebted during a troubled time leading up to bankruptcy.

In the early 2000s, the PBGC, in a departure from its previous stance, aggressively terminated many defined DB plans, claiming they did so to save them. Observers believe that the change in policy represented a philosophical position of the new Republican administration, which favored DC 401(k)-type plans over DB plans. The story of the United Airline pilots' pension plan, coming next, illustrates the PBGC's aggressive stance against DB plans and its alternatives besides advocating termination.

The Pension Benefit Guaranty Corporation had other choices in the United Airlines case, as I will explain in more detail shortly but will divulge briefly now. They could have extended loans to weakened defined benefit pension plans in the airline industry that would have extended their lives. Moreover, the PBGC supported the Pension Protection Act of 2006—a set of pension regulations that passed Congress in August of 2006—that most experts conclude will hasten the decline of DB plans. In supporting this set of regulations, the PBGC seemed to be giving up on the DB system, even though the 1974 Employee Retirement Income Security Act assigned responsibility to the Pension Benefit Guaranty Corporation to promote it.

Whether firms offered, or workers participated in, pension coverage was also affected by another public policy—the deep income tax rate cuts of 2001 and 2003. Although unrelated to pensions (and the effect on pension coverage was not considered when Congress and the President passed the legislation cutting taxes in those years), the cuts will have the serious and unintended consequence of reducing the incentives for employers to sponsor a pension plan. Tax cuts discourage pension coverage in this way: A smaller marginal tax rate reduces the advantages of sheltering income in a retirement account that exempts from federal income tax the contributions into that account and the earnings on those contributions.[13] As marginal tax rates decrease, so does the share of workers' compensation going to their pension accounts.

These developments are not adverse if workers' preferences had changed anyway, away from DB plans and toward cash compensation (and perhaps health insurance). It is entirely possible that the major drive behind the switch from DB to DC plans is that workers want to manage their own retirement finances. But the lack of protection in bankruptcy court, the decline in worker bargaining power, the growth of unstable jobs, the change in the Pension Benefit Guaranty Corporation's stance toward defined benefit pension plans, and the weakening of the tax code to promote pensions affect workers' desire for defined benefit plans.

Workers' Demand for Defined Benefit Pension Plans

In 2005, public sector unions fought to protect their defined benefit plans from "muscular" attempts to diminish them. California Governor Arnold Schwarzenegger hosted a state referendum (the voters would decide, not the legislature) to convert the state's public employees' defined benefit pension to defined contribution pensions. He lost. Merely the rumor that the University of California was going to replace nurses' pensions with a 401(k)-type plan was enough to prompt the nurses' union to authorize a strike in the UC hospitals.[14] In almost all the cases of the healthy pension fund terminations mentioned at the beginning of this chapter, and in many of the distressed terminations (like that of the pilots' pension plans) at Verizon, Sears, and IBM, workers and their unions protested vigorously. In collective bargaining situations, workers have been giving up demands for pay increases as trade-offs for pensions since the 1940s (see chapter 9 about unions and workers' demands for pensions). Unions bargain for pensions and, as women entered the labor market, the pension coverage rates among women soared. This is all evidence that workers want pensions.

Workers end up liking annuities—a stream of income for life—although they may not be apt to articulate the basis for their preference. Statistical studies of retiree satisfaction show that, given a DB pension and a DC pension, both having the same value, the form of pension payout matters a great deal for retirees. For example, given two retirees who are in the same situation with respect to retirement timing, marital and health status, and such, the one with the guaranteed stream of income is happier than the one with a lump sum (a lump sum that would pay the same annuity as the defined benefit if it were converted to an annuity). Merely having a 401(k)-type defined contribution pension does not add to a retiree's satisfaction.[15] That the elderly would rather have an equivalent level of income coming from a defined benefit annuity, or from a combination of a DB and a DC plan, rather than solely from a defined contribution plan, suggests that retiree satisfaction depends not only on how large their income is, but also on how safe it is. This is also borne out by the finding from the survey that having a supplement to Medicare or Medicaid—even for retirees who are healthy—substantially increases their satisfaction.

Nonetheless, there is a pervasive feeling that what workers want, workers get. When I was testifying in Congress in the late 1990s about the decline in pensions, a Republican Congressional member from Missouri, James Talent (he became Senator, then lost his seat in 2006), asked me a question based on this idea. He wondered if the lower-than-average spending on pensions on the part of employers in industries that were growing (my testimony was about this fact) was explained by the workers in those industries wanting cash instead of pensions and other employee benefits, commonly referred to as fringe benefits.

Without referring to it and perhaps without realizing it, Talent was applying neoclassical wage theory to make sense of who gets pensions and why. The explanation that "workers get what they want" is comforting from the perspective of a public policymaker from a political party that advocates few business regulations. According to neoclassical wage theory—by far the dominant theory taught in high school and colleges—workers and employers find each other and make the best match they can. In a good match, an employer gets the most productivity for the pay and workers get the best pay, best employee benefits, and best working conditions for their talents. (This is plain, old, simple supply-demand equilibrium.)

The theory of "compensating wage differentials" in competitive labor markets predicts that workers' desire for pensions (and other benefits and working conditions) is directly related to how much wage they will give up for pensions. According to this theory, employers are neutral to the combination of pay and pensions, so they pay whatever combination of compensation is required to hire the skills they need for the least cost. This means that any so-called inequality of pension coverage that we may observe among workers is really coming from their different desires for the makeup of their compensation. That white collar workers and highly paid executives are improving their pension coverage while blue collar and rank-and-file workers' pensions are going in the opposite direction is viewed primarily—in this theory—as the result of the choices workers are making. Workers are in the driver's seat according to this perspective, while employers, the government, and institutions such as insurance companies and consultants are merely the passengers in the "pension-coverage car," going wherever they are taken by the driver— the "driver" is the metaphor for worker's preferences for pay and pensions.

It's not that simple. For one thing, U.S. government social policy has always paid attention to what form compensation takes. Government policy strongly encourages employers to provide social insurance–type employee benefits. Tax breaks for employee benefits are designed to influence workers' and firms' preferences for the composition of the compensation. These tax breaks lower the cost of health insurance and pension insurance to workers, especially those workers who pay a lot of income tax. These tax breaks—they are called tax expenditures—add up to a lot of tax revenue that would otherwise have been collected if the tax code had not exempted them from taxation. The 2006 tax expenditures for employer benefits were equal to over $110 billion, and are justified because they advance social obligations of economic systems—such as providing for health insurance and supplements to disability and Social Security pensions, among others.

And firms are not neutral about forms of compensation. Firms care what form compensation takes. After World War II, most large firms, whether unionized or not, provided pensions to attract and retain the best workers. The managers of these firms also wanted to shelter their considerable pay from the increasing income tax rates. The compensating wage theory—that's the theory that workers get what they want and want what they get—is not an accurate way to explain who gets pensions and why the pension coverage rates are falling.

Defined Benefit Pensions and the Mobile Workforce

Regardless of the source of pension demand, less theoretical and more practical folks argue that defined benefit pensions are a kind of dinosaur and are not appropriate for the workforce of tomorrow because workers are becoming more and more mobile. They say that companies competing in an increasingly dynamic and global economy cannot be expected to keep long-term promises and provide a pension that rewards workers for loyalty. But many groups of workers, such as women, are less mobile now than they had been previously, because they are now more attached to the formal labor market. Also, a mobile worker who was covered under a number of different defined benefit pension plans may find that the credits accumulated in these plans over her or his lifetime are actually more valuable than if she or he had been covered by a series of 401(k) accounts. That may seem counterintuitive, but it makes sense when considering the difficulty mobile workers have with 401(k) plans. Most workers, especially mobile workers who have 401(k) plans, use their account balances paid out to them when they quit, are laid off, or fired, as though those balances were severance payments—they spend them. And that means job-hopping is bad for pension savings accumulation, in general, although it can be good if the next job results in a pay increase, better working conditions, more training, and is, all in all, a better match.

So how do mobile workers gain from defined benefit pension plans—plans that are considered best fit for these workers—if they do not settle into a long-term job until after age forty or so? It is because, it turns out, DB plans offer a way for middle-aged workers to accumulate a reasonable retirement income even if they changed jobs a lot in their twenties and thirties, or dropped out of the labor force. This turns out to help women especially.

Before arguing what kind of pension serves mobile workers better, we need to identify who should be considered a mobile worker. Mobility trends differ according to the time period and the industry. Mobility for much of the workforce has stabilized. The proportion of employees with more than ten years of service increased from 1996 to 2004: for men from 30.5% to 30.6%; for women from 27.9 to 28.6%.[16] Throughout the same period, women have increased their job tenure; the proportion of women who have been employed by their current employer for more than ten years has increased from 24.9% in 1996 to 28.6% in 2004. Yet the job tenure for older men has experienced a steady and dramatic decline. The likelihood that a male aged between forty-five and fifty has been with his current employer for longer than ten years has fallen substantially: from 57.8% in 1983 to 48.1% in 2004. (Note that the trends are mixed; tenure for older women has increased from 33% to 36.2% from 1983 to 2004.) This is especially important and worrisome because this job instability is happening at an age in which pension savings accumulation is supposed to be at its highest.

We also need to realize that worker mobility is *not* increasing in industries where the most new jobs are appearing. The average tenure for all workers over age sixteen increased from 3.5 years to 4 years from January 2000 to January 2004.[17] Yet tenure growth is expected to be higher in the industries projected to produce the most jobs in the next two decades. Industries adding the most jobs are retail trade, employment services, computer design, state and local government, food services, and health care—where the growth in jobs will be in offices of health practitioners, ambulatory health care services, and hospitals. In all but one of these large job growth areas, worker mobility is decreasing and job tenure is increasing. Overall, the average growth in job tenure for most of the fastest-growing industries is 16.3% compared to the average of 14.3% for all industries (see table 3.4).

Bottom Line   *Worker mobility has not changed considerably and certainly has not increased for everyone.*

Here is a simple simulation to help make clear how a mobile worker could be better off in a world where there were only defined benefit pensions. For starters, let us take a mobile worker in a 401(k) world. When the worker is younger than thirty years of age, I assume he has a 401(k) and every time

Table 3.4

More People Will Stay on Their Jobs Longer

Changes in job tenure for industries with the largest job growth

Industries Expected to Grow the Fastest (2002 to 2012)	Average Years of Tenure with Current Employer		Increase in job tenure
	January 2000	*January 2004*	
Retail trade	2.5	2.8	12.0%
Employment services and computer design*	2.6	3.6*	38.5%
State and local government **	5.5	6.4	16.4%
Food services	1.4	1.6	14.3%
Offices of health practitioners, ambulatory services	3.2	3.3	3.1%
Construction	2.7	3	11.1%
Educational services	3.2	3.8	18.8%
Hospitals	5.1	4.7	−7.8%
Average for all industries			13.3%
Average for all industries without hospitals	3.5	4.0	14.3%

* The job tenure figures often include categories that do not correspond with the employment growth categories. The tenure figures are for professional and technical services, which is a larger category than "employment services and computer design."

** The job tenure figures only include state employment because the employment growth categories are reported in larger categories than for job tenure. (Average tenure in local employment decreased slightly from 6.7 to 6.4.)

Source: U.S. Census, Statistical Abstract for 2004–2005

he changes jobs he saves 25% of the account balance from his previous 401(k), "rolling it over" to the 401(k) at his new job. That is pretty much what the average person who has a 401(k) does when he or she changes jobs when younger than thirty years of age. I assume in the simulation that, after age thirty, he rolls all of his 401(k) balance into the 401(k) at the new job. The Pension Protection Act of 2006 aims to raise participation in 401(k) plans by making it easier for firms to automatically enroll their workers in the 401(k) plan. Let us assume the Act succeeded, encouraging twice as many workers to participate than had participated in the past. I will assume that 56% of eligible workers under age thirty participate in 401(k) plans (which is a generous estimate because most people that age do not have employers who sponsor a 401(k) plan); and 88.4% of workers between the ages of thirty and forty-five are assumed to participate in a 401(k). I double the average participation rate again and assume it drops down to 77.6% at ages fifty-five and older.[18] Assuming that workers and employers together contribute 9% to a 401(k),[19] and the account earns 3% per year (after adjusting for risk and fees), then, under these real life circumstances, this worker accumulates almost $68,000 (exactly $67,248, table 3.5) in his 401(k) account by the time he is sixty-five. This amount is not far-fetched, since the median account balance for a sixty- to sixty-four-year-old is $59,000.[20] That $59,000 can be converted into an annuity, which would yield a stream of income equal to about $6,000 per year for life.

Now, if the same worker lived in a world with only defined benefit plans and had exactly the same work history, his annuity retirement income would be much higher—$35,364 per year for life. This is how I reached that conclusion. I assumed the worker has the same work history, but was vested in DB plans that had a formula that credited 2% of the average of the final five years of salary for every year of service. This generous formula is fairly common among DB plans. In this simulation, workers are automatically participating in a DB plan and the amounts are guaranteed by the government agency, the Pension Benefit Guaranty Corporation. And, as you have just seen, a worker with the same work history is better off with a series of defined benefit pension plans compared to a series of 401(k) plans.

However, in an ideal 401(k) world, the mobile worker has a better pension payout at retirement than would be provided to a mobile worker who participated in a number of DB plans. Under ideal conditions, the worker accumulates a large amount of money in his 401(k)—with the same work history, at age sixty-five he accumulates $647,379, which can buy an annuity worth $51,790 each year for life (see line 9 column 11 in the ideal world simulation). This is higher than the $35,364 per year for life for the worker participating in a succession of defined benefit plans.

There is very little evidence and expectation that workers can act in any way in the manner assumed in the ideal 401(k) simulation. The worker would have to exhibit a great deal of discipline, never skipping a 401(k) contribution, never withdrawing any money from her 401(k) account, not even when she changes jobs. (See table 3.5 for an illustration of the example.)

Table 3.5

Under Real Life Conditions, DBs are Better than 401(k)s

This is a simulation of a worker's pension accrual. This simulation assumes that the worker and the employer contribute the average to their 401(k) and participate at the twice the average rates if they are covered by a DB or DC plan. The resulting pensions under both types of plans are compared with a career where the worker has the ideal rates of contribution, withdrawal and participation.

					Real Life 401(k) plan		
Job	Age	Salary	Years on the Job	Contribution Rate 9%	Withdrawal Rates	Participation Rates	Net at Age 65[a]
1	2	3	4	5	6	7	8
1	20	$35,000	2	0.09	75%	0.5	$2,647
2	22	$36,050	3	0.09	75%	0.5	$3,971
3	25	$37,132	1	0.09	75%	0.5	$1,211
4	26	$38,245	1	0.09	75%	0.5	$1,211
5	27	$39,393	3	0.09	75%	0.5	$3,634
6	30	$49,241	15	0.09	0%	0.8	$28,685
7	45	$50,718	10	0.09	0%	0.8	$14,656
8	55	$52,240	10	0.09	0%	0.8	$11,233
Retired	65	same	0	0.00	lump		$53,807

a. Each year for life (based on a $67,248 lump sum).

Why Workers Don't Like Defined Benefit Pension Plans

Workers would not like DB plans if they feared that their firm would de-fault on the defined benefit pension promise. As more bankruptcies cause terminations of DB plans and more healthy companies freeze—that is, pre-vent future accruals in—DB plans, this fear becomes reasonable. It can be-come evident to workers that a DB pension default in one firm "dominoes," as other firms in the same industry scramble to lower costs. This domino effect threatens the government agency that insures pensions—the Pension Benefit Guaranty Corporation—because it is funded only by insurance premiums and earnings from defined benefit plan providers. The threat is to the sol-vency of the PBGC as it takes on higher liabilities—the benefits owed to workers of bankrupt companies' pension plans—than there are assets in the defunct pensions. The threat of default on a defined benefit promise is cer-

This simulated worker has eight jobs, retires at age sixty-five with an ending salary of $52,240. Ideally, she would have $647,379 in her account and take it out in an annuity of $51,790. The ideal 401(k) is better than the average DB plan, which yields $35,364 for life. However, under real life conditions, the real-life 401(k) is worth $33,335 or $2,667 for life.

	Ideal Behavior in a 401(k) Plan			Average DB
Withdrawal	*Participation*	*Lump and Annuity*[b]	*Formula 2% for Each Service Year*[c]
9	10	11	12
			$21,177
0%	1	$32,718	0
0%	1	$11,233	0
0%	1	$11,570	0
0%	1	$35,752	0
0%	1	$223,452	0
0%	1	$153,437	$14,772
0%	1	$158,040	$10,144
0%	1	$51,790	$10,448
			$35,364[c]

b. Each year for life (based on a $647,379 lump sum).
c. Each year for life.

tainly credible to workers who may already be insecure in their jobs; they distrust how much their employer values them; and they suspect DB promises because employers appoint the trustees who control DB plans.

Wariness toward DB pension plans makes sense. The eagerness for DC pension plans may not. Human beings tend to underplay longevity risk—they predict a younger death date than do the actuaries—so they think that their 401(k) will not run out of money, and they do not value the assurance that the DB plan will always pay a benefit until the date of death. People also underplay the investment risk—most people think stock values rarely fall so their 401(k) plans are completely safe—which further makes DB pensions look less valuable than a 401(k) plan.

On the other hand, humans are overconfident about their ability to resist the temptation to spend money set aside for retirement and just as overconfident that they are able to invest well. Many firms rely on the irrationality of the DC pension's appeal to workers to erode the DB pensions of their workers and to promote 401(k) plans in their place. (How common human judgment mistakes cause workers to overvalue 401(k) plans, relative to defined benefit plans, is discussed in chapter 4.)

One of the fatal flaws in 401(k)-type plans and, increasingly, in defined benefit pensions, is the payout of the account balance in a lump sum instead of as an annuity to people at retirement age. Not long after retiring, most retirees realize they should have taken annuities, but that is too late because the lump sum is already diminished. At the point of making decisions immediately preceding retirement, they prefer lump sums and regret it as they grow older.

Allowing lump sum payouts in DB and DC plans has ruined the pension system.

Lump Sums and Defined Benefit Plans: A Cure That Creates the Disease

Pension reform should tackle head-on the problem of lump sum pension payouts and how they erode retirement income. Merely promoting DB pensions over DC pensions—which all pay lump sums, if the retiree wants—will not work. Half of defined benefit retirees now take their pension in a lump sum instead of an annuity; although annuities are better for retirees, they want lump sums.

These lump sums can be dangerous to a pension fund if everyone asks for them at the same time. Just as a bank can fail if all depositors ask for their account balances in cash on the same day, so can a pension fund fail in the same way. Like a depository bank, a pension fund does not have enough funds to cover all of its liabilities at every moment in time. A pension fund that did have assets to cover its liabilities, if everyone lost their jobs and had to be paid immediately what their promised pension was worth, would have more than enough assets for the corporation and employment to continue. An ongoing pension system expects retirees to be paid their pensions over a period of time, as the fund earns money over time, and the employer contributes year after year. A fully funded pension plan has enough projected assets to cover projected liabilities. The Federal Deposit Insurance Corporation (FDIC), established in the Great Depression in the 1930s, was created to avoid bank runs—which is what happens when panicked depositors rush the bank and demand their bank balances all at the same time. Since the FDIC insures bank balances, there is no need for depositors to demand their balances in cash in such a rush, and bank runs are prevented.

But lump sum pension payouts in certain circumstances can have the same effect as a bank run on a pension plan—and this was never anticipated by the regulation that allowed DB pension plans to give participants the option of a lump sum or annuity. Here is some math that helps to understand why the lump sum option was not a problem in the 1980s (when the regulation was passed), but became a death knell to DB pensions in the 1990s. When a worker with a DB plan retires, she is promised a stream of pension benefits over her lifetime (the amount of the pension is based on her years of service and her pay). That stream of income has a monetary value called a present value. The present value is calculated based on an estimate of the number of years a retiree will live and an estimate of the interest rate she could earn on a lump of cash invested to pay the same pension over the same length of time. The value of the lump sum depends crucially on the interest rate. Here is an example.

A $10,000 per year pension promised to a retiree who will live twenty years is worth only $105,940.14 if the annual interest rate is assumed to be 7%, and a whopping $148,774.75 if the annual interest rate is 3%. So, when the assumed interest rate is high, the lump sum is relatively low, and vice versa. Since 2000, interest rates have been freakishly low during the same time when workers have been suffering freakishly high fears that they will lose their jobs due to company restructuring. This is a toxic environment for DB plans. Workers who are eligible for pension benefits will more likely opt for a lump sum when interest rates are low, and the fear of pension default and job loss is higher than when the future of ongoing employment looks bright and interest rates are high. (The Pension Protection Act restricted lump sum pension payouts from pension plans that have a ratio of assets to projected liabilities under 70%, which is a step toward protecting these fragile pension funds from becoming more insolvent.)

Ironically, neither rank-and-file workers nor their unions initiated the IRS ruling that allowed lump sums to be paid from DB pensions. That came from—guess who? And guess why? Upper-level managers of a large corporation in the mid-1980s asked the IRS if they could pay themselves a lump sum out of the DB plan. The IRS ruled if they paid lump sums to themselves they had to extend the same provision to all workers. So, instead of the IRS ruling to prevent all lump sums, many companies extended the lump sum option to all workers, as the IRS expected. The lump sum became attractive as interest rates fell and the stock market boomed, as happened in the late 1990s. When

82

Box 3.1

The Story of Lump Sum Payouts

Polaroid sponsored a typical defined benefit pension plan. Until 1995, workers did not have the option of taking a lump sum payout instead of their promised annuity. The Pension Benefit Guaranty Corporation did not insure all of the pensions promised by the Polaroid pension plan. The PBGC only insures "core" benefits, which are pensions owed to someone retiring at the "normal retirement age," as defined in the pension plan, although it is commonly age sixty-five. Some companies, like Polaroid, also provided early retirement benefits that enhance the normal benefit, allowing workers to retire at ages younger than the normal retirement age and still obtain pension benefits as if they retired at the "normal retirement age." Enhanced pension benefits are not insured by the Pension Benefit Guaranty Corporation. The intention for not insuring these benefits is clear—the government insurance for pensions is designed to help pensioners in catastrophic circumstances, such as when their company goes bankrupt and there is not enough money in the pension fund to pay benefits. The PBGC considered that only firms having a well-funded pension plan and a bright financial future could afford to and would ever offer enhanced pension benefits. So there was little or no need for the PBGC to insure enhanced benefits. Further, lawmakers intended workers and their unions to monitor their firms' promises to pay enhanced benefits and insist that any uninsured promises be funded sufficiently. This intention is based on lawmakers' "faith" that unions and workers have some influence over the firm's pension funding and can independently assess the firm's finances and ongoing ability to pay benefits.

Polaroid did offer enhanced pension benefits that provided the option to retire early. Over 75% of men at the company retired before age sixty-five (yes, the women worked longer). In 1998, Polaroid changed the pension plan to permit lump sum payouts at retirement—an option more to the advantage of the company than to retiring workers. Lump sum payouts saved Polaroid money; in one swoop the company could pay out a lump to a retiring employee and in the same swoop wipe its pension debt to that employee off the corporate books. Under the newly instituted corporate accounting rules that went into effect at that time, annuity payments due a retiring employee would have to remain on the books, reducing the company's corporate earnings.

The trustees for the Polaroid pension plan were Polaroid executives (all single-employer defined benefit pension plans have this arrangement). As trustee-executive persona, they had conflicting interests—to serve their own self-interest, to serve the interests of the company, or to serve those they were charged to serve as "impartial" trustees of Polaroid's pension plan participants. Guess what they did? Okay, it wasn't hard to guess! It turned out that their duty as trustees to the pension plan participants was sacrificed. The panic around Polaroid's imminent bankruptcy (due in large part to the popular and rapidly increasing use of the digital camera), in combination with enhanced lump sum benefits, doomed the pension plan. More workers stampeded for the doors and retired than the actuaries had predicted and allowed for. These retirees—not

Box 3.1   *(continued)*

trusting Polaroid's promise to pay all pensions, realizing that the Pension Benefit Guaranty Corporation did not insure early retirement pensions, and seeing that interest rates were at historic lows (so that lump sum calculations were at historic highs)—wanted their pension accumulation paid up front in a lump sum. During the same time, the stock market was not cooperating—investment losses to the Polaroid's pension plan were over $136 million (compared to its $981 million obligation in pensions due to workers). In the first part of 2002, 675 Polaroid employees retired, taking $81 million in lump sum benefits—which came out to only about $120,000 for each retiree, or the equivalent of between $8,000 and $10,000 annual annuity for life.

What happened at Polaroid is a case of moral hazard, a classic problem in insurance markets, which refers to insured people changing their normal behavior just because they are insured. For example, bicycle owners may start to neglect locking up their bicycles after they purchase bicycle theft insurance—knowing that if the bike gets stolen the insurance will cover the loss. In much the same way, it seemed that, because the pension fund was insured, Polaroid management may not have been concerned that the lump sum payout provision could endanger the fund, because the core benefits for the workers would be insured by the PBGC. We don't know what the motivations actually were—no fly-on-the-wall reported the trustees' discussions—but it is a reasonable scenario to infer. By the time the PBGC took over the Polaroid pension plan, which was when the company filed for bankruptcy and began to pay the core benefits, the pension plan had assets of $657 million and liabilities of $981 million.[21] The PBGC was not the only entity that swallowed the pension deficit. Former Polaroid workers who had been retired and did not take their pension in a lump sum also paid the price; the enhanced pension benefits they were receiving as annuities were terminated because the Polaroid pension plan went bankrupt. Because the amount of benefits covered by the PBGC depends, in part, on how much a pension fund can still afford to pay—in distressed terminations it is usually not much—retirees who took early retirement lost benefits. The lack of full insurance means that retired workers could lose their enhanced pension benefits (their core benefits would remain intact), effectively forcing the retired workers to bear the brunt of an insolvency. Lawmakers did not intend that to happen; they intended that not insuring enhanced pension benefits would serve as an internal check, to the extent that there was on the pension board an active employee representative to discourage or prevent management from promising pension benefits they could not afford to pay. Indeed, Polaroid workers and their union advocated for more pension funding, but ultimately funding is the company's decision, and Polaroid refused. The refusal stuck the PBGC, the healthy defined benefit pension sponsors who pay the insurance premiums to the PBGC, and pensioners with the shortfall in Polaroid's pension funding.

Polaroid continues to survive as a company[22]; it is owned by individuals as a privately held company. The current employees have only a 401(k) pension plan; the PBGC pays the core pension benefits to Polaroid's retirees.

more than expected lump sums are paid, the pension fund is weakened. Just ask any worker at Polaroid. The Polaroid executives could only get their lump sum distributions if every worker at every level could also do the same. The optional lump sum was the pension policy at Polaroid, and it destroyed the workers' pensions. (See Box 3.1, "The Story of Lump Sum Payouts.")

Why Firms Like Defined Benefit Pensions

As mentioned at the beginning of the chapter, in the first week of 2006 the International Business Machines Corporation (IBM) and Alcoa followed the lead of the Sears Holding Corporation and more than sixty-seven other companies, which froze or closed their defined benefit plans to new hires in 2005. IBM and the other "defined benefit freezers" have instead opted for 401(k) pension plans. New economy companies like Microsoft and Wal-Mart never adopted DB plans, and old economy companies such as Sears, IBM, Coca-Cola, Verizon, Lockheed Martin, and GM are freezing and otherwise reducing future DB pensions. Yet DB plans may have some productive purpose. There is actually a slight expansion of defined benefit pensions in retail and financial services, and they are holding steady in industries enjoying high profits and employing younger workers, for example, pharmaceuticals. Defined benefit pension plans also dominate the public sector—nearly all federal, state, and local government employees are covered by DB pension plans. Four companies in finance and communications—SBC Communications Inc., United Microelectronics Company, U.K. Barclays, and TransCanada—adopted DB plans in 2004. Why? One interpretation is that these firms want to retain mature workers as the workforce ages, and DB plans engender worker ties to their company. Women workers[23] at age sixty-five covered by DB plans and men between the ages of forty-five and fifty-five with DB pension coverage are less likely to retire than those without coverage or those who are covered by DC pension plans.

What made defined benefit plans a good employment strategy for some companies or workers? To answer that question, we have to understand why firms sponsored DB pension plans in the first place.

For decades, economists have claimed that employers are motivated to sponsor DB pensions for practical reasons. Defined benefit plans provide incentives for workers to be loyal to a firm and acquire skills and judgment important to the firm. There is a straight line connection between DB plans and productivity. This straightforward explanation owes much to "neoclassical" labor economics, and the explanation makes some sense, but it is not the entire explanation. Neoclassical economics presumes that workers trade off wages for employee benefits and make those trade-offs according to their own preferences. This neoclassical model is what most policymakers understand. It tends to make intuitive sense because this free-market way of thinking presumes that what workers and firms agree to is the most efficient and fair outcome and should not be interfered with.

That's the theory. The practice, with respect to pensions, is that employers decide what kinds of pensions to offer or whether to offer them at all. The worker has very little say. The fact that much of the reality in labor relations is not readily explained by the neoclassical model is the main reason institutional economics is a prominent alternative theory in labor economics. This sidetrack explanation of the "ins and outs" of various economic models is necessary because it explains the wildly different views of why pensions exist. If we understand why pensions exist we might be able to see what can be done to save them.

Institutionalists are not as guided as are neoclassical economists to explain outcomes. They tend to examine patterns and relationships in order to interpret outcomes. Institutionalists—I consider myself one—tend to view outcomes as compromises that balance many competing needs, including maximizing profits, wanting to survive, keeping a workforce happy, and even meeting a moral obligation to operate ethically. Institutionalists emphasize human limitations to process information, limitations that make it unrealistic for people to make rational decisions. That perception implies that decisions can be better made, or only made, by a union and a firm, together, to provide employee benefits, such as defined benefit pensions and health insurance, both providing for workers' long-term needs. Perhaps this may justify what could be considered derisively as the "paternalistic" view of unions and firms.

Institutionalists emphasize that outcomes can be explained by customs and power relationships; more so by the latter, where "power relationship" means that one party needs the relationship more than the other. The problem with this balance-of-power view is that some workers are less able to walk away from an employer than others. These differences create "segmented" labor markets, that is, firms and workers are divided into groups that do not compete with each other because of racial and gender discrimination or because of socioeconomic class or luck. These noncompeting groups persist because workers and firms strive to create structures to insulate and protect themselves against competition and other threats. We can think of labor markets as divided into two main groups—primary and secondary labor markets.

> **Bottom Line**   *Pensions are provided in the primary market but not in the secondary market, as you will see in the detailed discussion and examples below.*

Institutionalists explain that the United States stands alone in not providing national health insurance, nor pensions that provide sufficient income to most retirees, and this is not something that came from maximizing self-interest. They explain that it came from cultural norms, power relationships, and historical happenstance.[24] The primary sector—comprising unionized firms, firms protected against global competition, like construction, transportation, and utilities, and occupations where the workers are educated and have some market power because they can move freely between firms and for other reasons—is characterized by employment relationships that promote long-term contracts between workers and employers.[25] Firms in the primary sector are much more likely than firms in the secondary sector to offer employee benefits, pay above-average wages, have the latest technology and equipment, and innovate and invest in research and development. Firms in the primary sector strive to create meaningful long-term relationships with their employees or with a group of employees, such as professional engineers, doctors, or teachers. In contrast, firms in the secondary sector are characterized by high turnover among workers and little concern for that turnover. Some of the employers are small and compete with each other for business from larger firms, such as auto parts manufacturers. Or employers in the secondary sector can be large but operate in competitive markets, like Wal-Mart. Since these firms use low-wage labor and adopt production techniques where workers can easily be trained and replaced, they tend not to offer many employee benefits, such as pensions.

Therefore, we can see that the distribution of pensions is explained by the structure of labor markets. If more employers were primary employers and not secondary employers, then more workers would have employee benefits. The evolution of the American coal-mining labor market is a key example of how secondary employers can be transformed into primary market employers. (See Box 3.2, "The Story of the Miners' Union Pensions: How Secondary Markets Are Transformed.")

Part of the legacy of worker-based employee benefits are pension plans—whether 401(k)-type plans or traditional defined benefit plans—designed to affect employee loyalty and reduce turnover. In 2004, University of

The Story of the Miners' Union Pensions:
How Secondary Markets Are Transformed

In the 1950s, the United Mine Workers of America (UMWA) was both plagued and blessed by mechanization. Mechanization required less inhumane work, which also meant less work for humans. In response to the plague and the blessing, the union developed a brilliant pension plan: Employers' pension contributions became based on the output of the machine, not the input of the human mine worker—the mining company's pension contribution base switched from input hours worked to tons of output mined. The machine that replaced the human mine worker would pay for his disenfranchisement, his depreciation. The industry became more concentrated—fewer and fewer companies provided more and more of the coal being sold. As the companies got bigger and bigger, the smaller companies could not afford the costly machines. Productivity in the mines soared, although so did the amount of coal dust and black lung disease. The increase in productivity both increased the firm's ability to pay workers more and increased the union's bargaining power to pressure the firm to pay more.

However, good jobs are jobs in the primary sector—they pay well and are safer than jobs in the secondary sector. The miner's job was not yet a "good job." The same mechanization that produced the conditions for higher pay and pension benefits brought an alarming increase in workers' injuries. Dangerous jobs and high pay were positively correlated. It might be tempting to conclude that the mine workers' high-paying jobs are high paying because the employer pays a premium to compensate the workers for the risk of greater injuries. Looking at it this way would imply an equilibrium—a stable outcome was achieved between the pay employers were willing to pay and the number of workers willing to work for that pay. The neoclassical model would stop here. The institutionalist recognizes that workers who have some bargaining power explore options to make firms provide the highest paying and safest jobs the firms can afford. Workers want primary jobs because primary employers provide higher pay, pensions, and safety. Workers also seek to persuade employers to adapt, help them adapt, and accommodate their needs.

In the 1960s, the share of miners who sustained injuries or were killed—where mechanization was clearly the cause—continued to increase. Danger in the coal mines led to upheaval in the miners' union, the United Mine Workers of America. The union members weren't agreed on the trade-off between the increased risk of injury or death for higher pay. The awareness of black lung and health and safety campaigns of the 1960s were among the young Ralph Nader's first areas of consumer activism. Nader helped articulate and promote the needs of the group of union members who criticized their union's leadership for failing to press employers to enforce health and safety standards as set by law and labor contract.

(continued)

Much turmoil has settled down over the years, and mining is now safer—though not as safe as it is in Europe—and unionized miners have pensions and middle-class wages.

This is an example of how an institution—that is, the union—and activism adapted and worked with management to create a primary market out of what was a decidedly secondary market.

Virginia economist Leora Friedberg, and Federal Reserve economist Michael Owyang, found that DB plans are associated with very high levels of loyalty among middle-aged workers. What they found was that middle-aged workers are much less likely to search for another job and leave if they are covered by a DB plan. In the same year, Federal Reserve Bank economists Stephanie Aaronson and Julia Coronado published a study that showed that firms that have a higher than average increase in worker mobility are correlated with firms that have DC plans. These correlations can lead to the interpretation that workers who are mobile want DC plans instead of DB plans. But that is an unwarranted conclusion because it is more likely that firms that choose to provide defined contribution plans are the same firms that do not value long-term employer/employee relationships.

In fact, Freidberg and Owyang note that large firms that provide DB plans outsource to smaller contractors for strategic purposes unrelated to compensation design. In doing this, the larger firms are responsible for some of the growth in DC plans of the smaller companies, which makes the larger firms also responsible for the foreshortened careers of the mobile workers going from small company to small company. Employees of a new, spun-off, smaller firm had likely once been long-term workers of larger firms covered by DB pension plans. Those workers employed by the new smaller firm likely have no DB pension. A statistician could wrongly infer from this that workers with short tenure prefer not to have DB plans.

A human-resource consulting firm warned employers not to accept the notion that employees generally prefer DC plans, particularly 401(k) plans, rather than DB plans. The consulting firm's research found that younger employees, when exposed to the pros and cons of each type of pension plan, preferred that the employer make investment decisions and bear the various risks, and so they chose a defined contribution/defined benefit hybrid over a

401(k) plan. When a large electronics employer offered its workers a choice between a traditional DB plan and a DC plan with an employer match, two-thirds of the workers chose to remain participants of the traditional DB plan, foregoing the DC alternative.[26]

The common explanation for why employers provide pensions in the first place is the tax breaks employers receive, resulting from employers' pension fund contributions and earnings on those contributions, both not subject to federal income tax. But this tax-incentive view of pensions gets the story backward. The tax advantages came after the pensions. Firms that employ workers in high tax brackets, in other words, employers in primary markets, have a lot of power, including political clout. These large firms used their political clout to pass tax legislation that favors the employee benefits they provide and get those benefits partly subsidized by taxpayers—the subsidy exists because tax revenue that would have been collected on pension contributions and earnings has to be made-up from somewhere else.

Primary Labor Markets: High Wages and Good Pensions

Inspired by the then Congressman Talent's argument—what I call the "workers-choose" explanation of pension decline—that workers in new jobs are choosing cash wages over pensions, I conducted a test. I used statistical analysis to explain changes in the proportion of workers' total compensation package that was made up of employee benefits, mostly pensions and health insurance, and how much in cash. I examined a ten-year-period for different industries and occupations.[27] I assumed that the share of total compensation spent on employee benefits was affected by how fast the industry and occupation were growing (Talent's unwitting neoclassical hypothesis), how fast health insurance costs were increasing, what proportion of total employees were women, and what proportion were part-time employees. The most significant factor explaining the portion of total employee compensation spent on employee benefits is the health insurance expense, but it is not the only significant factor.

Let's take Congressman Talent's conjecture that employers in tight labor markets have to use cash, instead of benefits, to lure employees who may prefer cash and individual retirement accounts. I found the opposite phenomenon, supporting an institutionalist view. When the demand for workers increases, the employers in these growing markets, such as in business services—for example, software design and custodian services—have to offer more employee benefits. The share of total compensation paid in the form of employee benefits increased the most in industries and occupations where the numbers of workers employed increased the most.

Furthermore, workers more likely to enroll in their employers' pension plan have the largest wage increases. Women's wages grew faster than men's wages from 1979 to 1999, which is the same period of time when women workers achieved their greatest increases in pension and health insurance coverage.[28] This means that pensions and health insurance are complements to, not substitutes for, cash wages. The institutionalist view—remember, that's the view that power relationships matter, and people can't always compete in the same labor markets—is further supported by the finding that whether a person is in a union or not greatly affects their chances of having employee benefits. Union workers have twice the pension coverage of nonunion workers.[29]

Support for the chilling view that the "haves" have more is in the research on occupational health and safety. Between 1970 and 1995 on-the-job danger—as measured by the number of occupational injuries—fell in the very industries where workers' compensation rose the most. This is the opposite of the trend in the 1960s, when the risk of injury rose in high-wage industries. In the 1960s, workers seemed to be paid for bad working conditions, which is consistent with the neoclassical view that workers (a) compete for jobs and sort themselves out by their preferences for security and safety; and (b) require pay that reflects the extra risk they have to take on to work for an employer that provides an unsafe workplace. Since the 1960s, labor markets have become more polarized. The better jobs, the primary sector jobs that pay well, have a high degree of employee benefit coverage, and are safe, are pulling ahead of secondary sector jobs that do not pay as well, have a high turnover, and poor work conditions.[30] The overall decline in pension security, first, is not shared across all workers, and second, is a consequence of the growing inequality between workers and the growth of secondary sector jobs.

Employers Who Do Not Sponsor Defined Benefit Plans Prefer 401(k) Plans—or Nothing

Although employer-provided pension plans help employers, especially in the primary sector, achieve higher levels of productivity, the management in large and profitable firms fought against their workers' pension demands. Pension plans were contested terrain in the 1950s as unions struck and bargained for retirement plans. But, as the fight was not too fierce, employers soon saw that defined benefit pensions could be valuable loyalty-enhancing personnel tools, and so they provided that coverage.

What explains the decline in DB pensions forty years later? Defined benefit pensions served their purpose, but their purpose was no longer needed—labor relations and managers no longer cared about employee loyalty. Wharton economist Peter Cappelli wrote in 2003 that employers do not care about worker loyalty because baby-boom workers are abundant and unions are in decline. Without a motivation to cement long-term ties between employer and employee, job-tenure-related employee benefits, like pensions, lose some of their purpose.[31] This is the view that DB pensions are dinosaurs—they cannot survive in a new kind of environment. I once agreed with this view. But I have come to appreciate, in the face of mounting evidence, that there are other factors explaining the decline in DB plans aside from shifting labor relations caused by a change in the kinds of things produced in the economy, like services rather than manufactured goods.

Permit me to use metaphors of dinosaurs and panda bears. Defined benefit plans seem more like panda bears than dinosaurs, in the respect that pandas are creatures that are going extinct because powerful forces are destroying their habitat. Modern day corporations managed their pensions badly, and in the face of a string of bad luck, bad law, and bad vision, they have permitted their defined benefit plans to collapse. As examples of all that "badness," it is clear that DB pension liabilities soared at the same time the stock market plummeted, which is predictable bad luck, dooming whatever DB pensions survived. However, it is the federal government's stunning promotion of defined contribution pensions, the 401(k)-type pension plans, that put pressure on the defined benefit model. Public policy enabled 401(k) plans to be cheap and inferior substitutes for DB plans. Employers were able to freely convert their traditional DB pensions into DC plans even though workers would lose pension benefits from the switch.

In the fall of 2004, when the DuPont Corporation switched from providing defined benefit to a 401(k) plan, declaring that its workers would like the modern design—a portable pension plan in which the employee has ultimate control rather than the old-fashioned defined benefit plans—*New York Times* columnist Floyd Norris wrote,

If those new employees are really enthusiastic about a program that DuPont estimates will save it—and take away from employees— around $46 million a year, after taxes, then the state of economic education in this country is worse than you may have thought.

The simplest explanation for why firms prefer 401(k) pension plans is the plain fact that they reduce pension costs. By providing 401(k) pension plans—and calling them pensions—firms can reduce their pension funding expenses considerably. Overall, employer expenditures for pensions fell by a whopping 22% between 1978 and 1998.[32]

My study of more than seven hundred firms that had sponsored pension plans since 1981, showed that (a) 401(k) plans lower the firm's costs; (b) the firm's pension contributions per worker dropped from $2,140 in 1981 to $1,404 in 1998; and (c) the defined contribution (mostly 401(k) plans) share of employer pension contributions increased from 23% in 1981 to 68% in 1998. Changes in the design of pension plans made it possible for employers to commit less cash to pensions.[33] (This is discussed further in chapter 4.)

> **Bottom Line**   *What that increase means is that a 10% increase in the employers' use of defined contribution plans is associated with somewhere between a 1.7% and a 3.5% reduction in employers' pension costs per worker. Therefore, taking into account how much DC plans, including 401(k) plans, have expanded, the average firm lowered its pension costs by more than 10% by adopting DC plans, or by expanding the DC plans that were already provided by firms.[34]*

Legacy Costs: Defined Benefit Plans Do Not Kill Companies

A company that has had a defined benefit plan for a number of decades will have a growing ratio of retirees to workers. That is the nature and intended purpose of employee pay systems that extend past retirement. The costs of providing pensions and health care to retirees are called legacy costs. It must be noted that legacy costs come paired with legacy benefits, which are benefits such as worker loyalty, labor peace, and enhanced productivity that comes with the firm's promise to pay pensions and retiree health benefits. Workers pay for these promises through reduced wages, and the employers are obligated to take those wage sacrifices and fund the promises in a reasonable way.

Many DB plans took on legacy costs by giving pension credit to workers who had not sacrificed any wages to fund their pensions—these workers were given credit for what is called "past service." Crediting past service in a pension plan makes good sense.

The motivating idea behind a pension plan is to care for older people, encouraging them to retire, and enabling them to retire in dignity. At the time a pension plan is formed, an older generation usually needs pensions in order to retire. Convincing young workers to accept what they consider to be a "tax"—whether it be Social Security payments or a deduction from pay for their share of an employer-provided pension—usually requires appealing to the younger workers to be concerned for the older workers who will need pensions soon even if they did not spend a work life contributing to a plan. There are many cases where past service costs are not paid for completely and where a company, or an industry, encounters rough economic conditions, motivating more and more workers to head for the exits, demanding their pension on the way out.

Pension promises are like home mortgages. Paying off a mortgage, which is a debt, over a period of time, is a reasonable way to live in a house before it is fully paid for. But if the payments become too high and unaffordable, the mortgage might go into default and the house will be lost. If the pension promise does not have enough funds when times are bad, the pensions might go into default, which is the risk the workers took by accepting a defined benefit plan. But just because some firms defaulted does not mean that paying off the promise over time is not a reasonable way to fund pensions, just as some home foreclosures do not mean that mortgage financing is not a safe way to fund housing.

The widely reported airline defaults of 2004, which are reminiscent of the 1980s steel industry crisis, have left many people with the impression that pension obligations cause bankruptcies. This view is a fallacy—the causation actually is in the opposite direction. Poorly funded pension plans do not destroy good companies. Badly managed companies destroy good pensions.

It just so happens that, under U.S. law, pensions and other labor costs are easier to avoid than other obligations, such as obligations to bond holders, to property owners, to vendors, and to taxes. Defined benefit plans are, in fact, associated with successful ventures, as in the defense industry, where pensions do not make front-page news.

In the United Kingdom, where a similar boom in the stock market and popularity for DC plans occurred during a financial boom, some key employers are implementing DB plans. In 2004, the investment banker, Barclays PLC (PLC stands for public limited company, in the United Kingdom or in Ireland, a type of limited company whose shares may be sold to the public) converted its DC plan into a DB plan. The Marylebone Cricket Club and the property administration for the British royalty, Grosvenor Estate, London, also replaced their DC plans with a DB plan. The U.K. regulatory environment has been warmer toward defined benefit plans than corresponding regulations in the United States, the U.K. warmth allowing more flexibility in the design of benefits due. For example, the U.K. government instituted DB pension insurance—a version of the Pension Benefit Guaranty Corporation—twenty-eight years after the PBGC was formed in the United States.

After 2001, despite the U.S. economy recovering, especially in industries where companies provided workers with defined benefit plans, DB pension plans faced an uncertain future. It may be surprising to realize that the proportion of large companies that sponsored at least one DB plan, remained constant from 2000 through to 2004. However, more companies froze or terminated at least one of their DB plans (companies commonly provide more than one pension plan to different groups of workers). The number of companies that backed away from at least one of their defined benefit plans rose from 7% of all defined benefit plan sponsors in 2003, to 11% in 2004.[35]

Smaller and less profitable firms providing DB plans are more likely to retrench their pension plans. Between 2001 and 2004, about half of the companies that terminated their DB plan dropped off the "Fortune 1000" list. Half of the companies that had frozen or terminated their DB plans had below investment-grade credit ratings—that means the experts in financial markets deemed these companies to have shaky finances and to be more likely to go bankrupt—which is twice the rate of the large firms with active DB plans.

> **Bottom Line** *Many of the companies whose pension plans are not 100% funded—alas, their assets do not equal their liabilities—would have gone bankrupt regardless of their pension costs. The institutions, like unions, and the rules, like the rules in bankruptcy and pension funding, are not strong enough to allow a firm to shrink its pension plan assets in relation to its liabilities before it defaults on other obligations, such as the phone bill or maintaining dividend payments to shareholders. Distressed companies diminish their defined benefit pension plans; healthy companies maintain them.*

What Should Government Policy Do?

An appropriate government policy toward pensions should look like a retirement policy designed on purpose and with a purpose. Pension regulation should be adaptable to production needs and patterns of work. As workers become more and more mobile, portable pension plans need to be encouraged. If workers do not need to be loyal to be skilled, and turnover costs are low, then pension plans promoting longevity with an employer may not matter for a productive and efficient economy. However, pension policy should not be reactive to high-profile events, it should not be short-sighted, and it should protect pension promises and secure workers' choice to retire.

Efficiency

Unfortunately, the federal government's permissiveness toward defined contribution plans has ignored the principle that a pension system should be efficient and practical. Defined contribution pension plans create losses that could be avoided. A dollar spent in the DB world earns more than it would earn in a DC world. Moreover, the administrative costs for DB plans are lower than for DC plans. In 2001, in the depths of the recession, and at the beginning of the crash in the stock market, the median DB plan returned −3.8% compared with −7.3% returns for the median 401(k) plan; defined benefit plan investments lost less than the investments in defined contributions plans. The year before, in 2000, DB plans outperformed DC plans by 4.3%. Only in the bull market years of 1998–99 did median returns from 401(k) plans exceed returns from defined benefit plans. Even worse, companies that only offered a 401(k) plan experienced lower 401(k) returns than the 401(k) plans in companies that offered both DB and DC plans. In fact, Alicia Munnell and her team of researchers at the Boston College Center for Retirement Research confirmed the obvious common sense prediction that professional money managers—those who manage DB pension plans—obtain safer and higher returns than the individual pension beneficiaries themselves who make investment decisions for their own 401(k) plan. The research team found that in the period from 1988 to 2004, defined benefit plans outperformed 401(k) plans by 1%.[36] There are two reasons for the differences in rate of returns between defined benefit plan and defined contribution plans:

- defined benefit plans are managed by professionals, while individuals direct their own 401(k) investments; and

- workers pay larger fees for the investment and administrative services of the 401(k) managers, compared to fees of the managers of defined benefit plans.

The pension administrator for the gigantic Texas Municipal Retirement System, Gary Anderson, and researcher Keith Brainard in 2004, underscored the DB plans' advantages, claiming that governments could make no better investment—alluding to getting the most for taxpayer dollars—than in the DB retirement funds.

Adaptability to Changing Employment Structures

Workers are thought to be more able to change geographical location than a firm is able to move its production or completely change its workforce. But, in many cases, firms are more mobile than workers. Any new form of pension plan should recognize that employees can have more loyalty to a job than a peripatetic employer does to a work site or employee. For example, in the late 1990s, a group of nurses in a New Jersey hospital finally obtained their long-standing demand to join the multi employer pension plan that the hospital's operating engineers belonged to. Why operating engineers? The hospital had changed ownership many times, and each time it did the nurses' current pension plan. The workers, the nurses, were not mobile. Their employer, the hospital, was. Joining the multi employer plan let the nurses accrue years of service credits in one defined benefit plan.[37]

Policy Options

Defined Benefit Plans Need Help: Taking Down the Barriers

In nearly every year since 1978, legislation designed to encourage people to save in individual retirement accounts has sailed through Congress. Only 401(k) plans can accept voluntary tax-deferred employee contributions, employer matches, and profit-based contributions. Moreover, Congress has expanded the limits on how much income can be sheltered from taxes in 401(k) plans.[38] The American Academy of Actuaries conclude that most of the decline in defined benefit plans is due to the favorable regulatory treatment of defined contribution plans over defined benefit plans.

Despite the hostile environment for defined benefit plan hybrids—that is, cash balance accounts—and the dearth of legislation to facilitate the growth of hybrids, it is remarkable that the number of U.S. companies threatening to freeze their DB plans is not higher.[39] There are several interesting ideas to make DC 401(k)-type plans more like DB plans. One idea is DB/DC hybrids, which are versions of cash balance plans. Another idea is the defined benefit (401)k.[40] And a third idea is traditional multiemployer portable defined benefit plans that exist in dynamic industries with mobile workforces. These three will be discussed in later chapters.

Real Problems in the Pension Benefit Guaranty Corporation Should Be Fixed

There is no question that the Pension Benefit Guaranty Corporation is facing a shortfall. In 2004 its budget plummeted into a $23 billion hole from a stock-swollen surplus of $10 billion in the year 2000 (although the agency has enough reserves to pay for all probable terminations for "a number of years").[41]

The key to understanding the PBGC's exposure to underfunding is that the Employee Retirement Income Security Act of 1974, for good reasons, intended to give firms that voluntarily provide defined benefit plans funding flexibility over business cycles. I, and most everyone else, view this as a very sensible feature for a voluntary program. The aim of funding flexibility is to enable firms to build up surplus funds during periods of high profits and revenue, and then allow them to draw on the surplus when the corporation is experiencing an economic slowdown. The Government Accountability Office, the agency that audits the federal government by investigating whether laws are being enforced, argued that this method did not work. The surplus is called a "credit balance," and surplus funds are valued using an expected rate of return, over a period of time. Many of these surplus credit balances were accumulated in the late 1990s and were, of course, valued at historically high rates of return that were fueled by the stock market boom.

Encouraging firms to build up excess assets above a minimum balance makes sense. Alas, the way they were valued turned out to be fatal. Every expert concurred with the assumption that double-digit rates of return would exist forever! It was music to the ears of employers. They were told, using these optimistic valuation methods, that the pension fund was flush and no contributions were needed. Many firms took pension "holidays" based on the advice of their expert pension professionals. The herd mentality of the consultants, actuaries, and investment experts is widely recognized as a contributing cause to the lack of sufficient funds in defined benefit pension funds when the expected hefty returns did not materialize. Credit balances were called upon when firms were in financial distress. Too late, that's when it became clear that their credit balances were worth much less than had been assumed.

In each year from 1995 to 2002 most of the one hundred largest defined benefit pension plans were fully funded. A significant 39% were less than 100% funded by 2002 (25% were less than 90% funded). Almost two-thirds of those pension plans had not made cash contributions in any previous three-year period and, instead, used credit balances to fulfill their legally required contributions. These pension plans were especially vulnerable to two pressures—many people were retiring at ages much younger than anticipated (because of the recession), and the rock-bottom interest rates (also caused by the recession). Both caused pension liabilities to soar. The low interest rates and the unexpected liabilities caused the asset-to-liabilities funding ratios to fall short. Many blamed the credit balances for causing the shortfalls. This is the "bad law" scenario: poorly written guidelines about credit balances caused pension shortfalls.

What I call the "bad luck" scenario gives an alternative interpretation of events. It's like the "perfect storm," the confluence of several severe storms merging from different directions. In simple words, the confluence of unanticipated misfortunes, or bad luck, is the reason defined benefit plans were in trouble. The scenario goes like this: A bear financial market and historically low interest rates caused pension funds to fail. Because interest rates are inversely correlated with liabilities, the sluggish financial market and low interest rates raised pension fund liabilities and lowered pension fund assets—not a happy combination. When interest rates and the value of stocks and bonds fell, many companies faced the prospect of either keeping their pension plans intact and meeting skyrocketing requirements for cash contributions to these plans—or terminating the pension plans. The former head of the PBGC, Steve Kandarian, was the first to refer to these circumstances as "the perfect storm," implying that this freak confluence of events—the recession, the crash in the stock market, and the record low interest rates—was causing the DB pension system to sink and drown.

The "bad behavior" interpretation of the causes of the PBGC's forecasted deficits can be melded with the "bad luck" and "bad law" interpretations of the causes for the deficits. According to the "bad behavior" interpretation, some corporations manipulated assumptions about future rates of return on their pension plan assets to reduce their pension contributions, and in some cases their motive in doing so was to use what they would have spent on pension contributions to fund rising health care insurance premiums. The allowable level of pension contributions that qualify for tax deductions depend on the level of pension surplus the firm is already sheltering from tax. Assets minus liabilities can be adjusted—within limits—by adopting different assumptions pertaining to the retirement age, death rates, interest rates, and earnings of the workers (workers' earnings are a factor in that "adjustment" equation because DB plans base the final benefit on the workers' salary). As noted previously, many firms took pension funding holidays, meaning they did not put any real cash in the pension fund. Especially troubling to policymakers, and therefore the focus of the 2006 Pension Protection Act, is that weak firms, mainly in the airline and steel industries, had also stopped contributing to their pension funds because their poor financial health was obscured by rosy assumptions about the future.[42]

The PBGC is not as defenseless as might be inferred from the events just described. For some of its history, they aggressively intervened to cajole corporations to fund their plans; in 1994, the PBGC encouraged General Motors to keep its funded status near 100% by contributing massive amounts of stock and cash. The PBGC's early warning system that monitors corporate transactions, mergers, and acquisitions, and, when necessary, intervenes to persuade a company to "fund up" its pension plan, won a Harvard School of Government Award.[43] Firms, in fact, do follow the law's intention to build pension fund surpluses in good financial times.

Furthermore, most firms actually behave as though they are committed to fulfilling the promises workers expect from their pension plans. My survey of more than six hundred firms over a nineteen-year period, 1981 through 1998, showed that when the assumed rate of return on assets was high—in good times—the firms contributed more to both their defined benefit and defined contribution plans, just as was intended by the 1974 pension law, the Employment Retirement Income Security Act. The airline and steel industries stopped contributing to their pension funds when both industries faced crises and when the funds in their DB plans were earning high rates of return. There are two, not mutually exclusive, explanations for these two industries cutting back on their pension fund contributions. One is that these industries decided to offload their liabilities not only onto the PBGC but also onto their workers—this is the bad behavior interpretation. The other interpretation is that when the rest of the economy was doing well, these industries were experiencing their own sector-specific recessions—this is the bad luck interpretation. Beyond these sectors, few firms withhold contributions to the PBGC during flush periods.

This evidence suggests that blaming firms for gaming and, in essence, cheating the system is an imprecise interpretation of events. It's imprecise because the vast majority of firms did not reduce funding during periods of high profits and earnings, only to find they needed more pension funding when profits and earnings were diminished—surely this would be a perverse outcome. The airline industry and steel industry are exceptions; they decreased DB plan funding even when the rest of the economy was doing well.

The blame is imprecise also because the bad luck and bad behavior interpretations ignore a crucial flaw in the Pension Benefit Guaranty Corporation. The flaw is that, unlike other insurance companies, the PBGC has no "reinsurance" mechanism for losses that it might suffer due to catastrophe. Most insurance companies have such insurance; the PBGC does not. The problem underlying the flaw in the PBGC's insurance mechanisms is that employer-based pensions—designed to supplement Social Security and personal savings to achieve retirement income commensurate with the standard of living a worker achieved in his working life—are voluntarily provided by employers. In addition, because the U.S. pension system is voluntary, healthy companies can switch from DB pension plans to 401(k) plans when they purchase a financially weak company, and avoid paying for the purchased firm's losses with higher insurance premiums. Therefore, the PBGC needs reinsurance for catastrophic events inherent in such purchases.

The dramatic fall in the Pension Benefit Guaranty Corporation's surplus during the early part of the twenty-first century was mostly caused by mass bankruptcies and defaults in the steel and airline industries that crippled firms in those industries. The PBGC was designed to cope with isolated cases of default, not sector-wide crises and restructurings. Since 2002, 70% of the PBGC's liabilities have been related to steel and airline defaults. Cyclical and secular events—recession and competition from nonunion carriers, respectively—dramatically affected five of the major firms in the same industry.

This is an extraordinary circumstance that was recognized by Congress when it created the Air Transportation Stabilization Board (ATSB) after the terrorist attacks in 2001. United Airlines (UAL) argued that an ATSB loan would, among other things, help maintain its pension plans. The ATSB rejected UAL's loan guarantee request in the summer of 2004 and set in motion the events leading UAL to default on its pensions in May 2005.[44]

At this juncture, the PBGC made a policy choice. If it were intent on preserving the defined benefit system, it could have jaw-boned the Air Transportation Stabilization Board, the credit market institutions, and other airline companies, to create and foster public opinion that pension obligations were inviolable and must be maintained.[45] Inhibiting this possible course of action was the PBGC's intention of pursuing a short-term and narrow goal, which was to minimize its own exposure to UAL's liability defaults. Further, a White House intent on modeling the PBGC after a private insurance company, by advancing a long-standing conservative agenda to privatize it, would have chosen for the PBGC to stem its exposure to the defined benefit liabilities and seek to terminate the UAL pensions as soon as possible.

Chapter 10, on pension policy, elaborates a plan to merge unfunded pension plans that are sponsored by one employer, referred to as single-employer pension plans, into a pension plans that cover many employers, called multi-employer pension plans. Multi employer plans have the best of DB and DC pension plan characteristics—workers collect a defined benefit and employers contributions are steady and level. Multi-employer pension plans are more portable among employers; these kinds of pension plans help employers and workers retain and advance skills in a particular occupation. There is precedent to move bankrupt, single-employer plans to a multiemployer system; the precedent goes back to when the railway retirement system was created in 1920.

Conclusion: When Bad Things Happen to Good Pensions

The pension landscape is not a cartoonish battlefield between a new world of 401(k) pension plans and an old world of defined benefit pension plans. Many firms have stopped sponsoring DB pension plans to reduce costs and many have shifted to DC pension plans despite workers having to take on higher risks and higher administrative costs. Nevertheless, the case for DB pensions has never been stronger. As the workforce ages, public policy regarding pensions needs to husband the precious dollars accumulating for retirement benefits and to make sure they are contributed consistently, invested well and efficiently, and provide income for the rest of a retiree's life.

Defined benefit pensions have several important social and economic benefits:

- DB plans are associated with higher levels of pension coverage (including coverage in DC plans) which result in more wealth accumulated for retirement purposes.

- DB plans are insured by the Pension Benefit Guaranty Corporation; they can be easily paid out in annuities; investment fees are lower; and they earn higher rates of return than DC plans.

- DB plans yield more retirement income with less risk; provide more return; and require fewer administrative costs.

The argument that policymakers and employers have been caught flat-footed by the soaring costs of defined benefit pensions—mainly because maturing pension systems are more expensive, as well as because they have been mismanaged—is not entirely correct. The changing nature of work relationships is the fundamental cause of the decline of pensions based on work done.

Employer-based defined benefit pensions were once regarded as an important aspect of the productive life in the nation, at least for two-thirds of full-time workers. However, 401(k) plans have become profitable for consulting firms, actuaries, pension lawyers, money managers, all pension vendors, and employers.

A dollar in a DC plan is less likely to be used as retirement income because of the many leakages of individual accounts.[46] And, if there is anything left in a worker's DC fund at retirement, it is most likely paid out in a lump sum to the retiree, not as an annuity, which makes 401(k) pensions less secure, which, in turn, lessens the well-being of older people.

Despite the advantages of the DB form of pension, the 2006 Pension Protection Act will likely result in the defined benefit pension becoming employment compensation's Cheshire cat—the beguiling creature in Lewis Carroll's *Alice in Wonderland* whose body faded until all that was left was its toothy, friendly grin. The DB plans that persist will be well funded, and will be secure for workers who will retire on these pensions and for retirees already drawing income from defined benefit pensions.

APPENDIX 3.1: The Pension Protection Act of 2006

Worse Than Enron

The United Airlines (UAL) May 2005 default on its pension contributions made headline news. U.S. House of Representatives member George Miller (D-California) sponsored the first-ever Internet-based Congressional "E-hearing," in which more than 2,000 people, mostly victims of the default, wrote what the lost pensions meant to them. One respondent was Ellen Saracini, widow of the UAL captain of hijacked Flight 175 flown into the south tower of the World Trade Center on September 11, 2001. She received a monetary award from the 9/11 victims' fund, which was established by the federal government to compensate victims of the terrorist attacks. The amount given her was reduced by the expected amount of her husband's UAL survivor's pension. Worse, two years later, the amount of that UAL survivor pension was reduced by two-thirds. She has no recourse, none, to ask for more from the compensation fund.

> "I can't help but to ask myself at what point are companies allowed
> to take away so much from the lives of dedicated employees and their
> families?," Ellen Saracini wrote. "At what point does our government
> step in and stop atrocities such as this before they are allowed to
> irrevocably change the lives of so many?"

United Airlines

Here are the facts about the United Airlines pension situation. On August 20, 2004, a federal bankruptcy judge gave UAL thirty days to devise a corporate restructuring plan, given that the Air Transportation Stabilization Board unexpectedly rejected UAL's bid for more loans earlier in the summer. The judge rebuffed union demands to appoint an outside trustee for the pension fund because, the unions claimed, UAL illegally halted payments to its pension funds in June 2004. Just two years before, in 2002, UAL had declared bankruptcy, and four years earlier, in 2000, it had halted pension payments because the airline's four pension plans had surplus assets—the funds' assets were greater than the liabilities—thanks to unusual increases in the equities values underlying the pensions' assets. In May 2005 the bankruptcy judge, UAL, and the Pension Benefit Guaranty Corporation together agreed to terminate all of UAL's defined benefit plans. That agreement (a) not only ignored more creative and less harsh proposals suggested by retirees and the International Association of Machinists—the union representing baggage handlers and mechanics at several airlines—to modify or develop new defined benefit plans; (b) it did worse in bypassing UAL and union negotiations. The press gave some attention to the pilots and the retirees who lost the most accrued pension rights.

> Hillegas said he's not looking for sympathy. He knows pilots make a lot of money. But he doesn't think it's right that United workers and retirees, who have made sacrifices, should have to give up the retirement benefits they were promised. "What kind of morale are you going to have for the people who are still there? What's it like to work there for 30 years and have the rug pulled out from under you?" (Griffin 2004)

When the Pension Benefit Guaranty Corporation took over the pension plans, UAL pilot Hillegas and many long-tenured, more highly paid airline employees lost up to three-fourths of their expected pension benefits—the PBGC insures basic or core pensions up to a maximum of just over $44,000 per year. Many of the pilots with thirty or more years of service received over $100,000 per year in a pension. All core accrued benefits are insured. However, benefits that were promised for participants retiring at younger than the fund's normal retirement age, usually sixty-five, were not insured, nor were pension benefits that served as severance payments due to layoffs—both were considered enhanced benefits.

Senator Ron Wyden (D-Oregon), during the Senate Finance Committee hearing on June 7, 2005, inferred that the UAL pension situation was the result of "bad" company behavior. He mused whether events revealed a double standard with regard to workers' pensions and executives' pensions. Wyden asked UAL chief Glenn Tilton why Tilton's $4.5 million trust was preserved when other employees lost their pensions. Tilton denied his trust was a pension, though it replaced a $4.5 million retirement plan he forfeited when he left his previous employer after thirty-six years of service. Tilton said that UAL promised him the payment when he accepted the job as chief. He did not acknowledge that UAL workers were also given promises by virtue of their pensions. This notion of a double standard between worker pensions and executive pensions became the Democrats' way of distinguishing themselves from Republicans, and was the basis for their proposals for a moratorium on pension terminations and their opposition to the Republicans' Pension Protection Act, which eventually was passed in August 2006.

The Pension Benefit Guaranty Corporation's decision in the UAL case is more difficult to explain than Tilton's reasoning. The PBGC bypassed union/company negotiations[47] that could have saved union workers' benefits at the expense of the other creditors—banks and bond holders. Future pension accruals and benefits promised before age sixty-five—so-called early retirement benefits—are not insured by the PBGC. The PBGC's decision to cut its own deal shifted the company's financial problems onto the oldest and most loyal workers, long-service employees who were promised the option to retire before age sixty-five. At the same time, three problems occurred: a sharp increase in oil prices, reduced revenue due to the recession and the terrorist attacks, and debt overhang from the massive expansions in the boom years of from 1998 to 2000.[48]

The UAL pension default helped the President's proposals along, in much the same way as the Studebaker Company's pension collapse in 1964 helped pass the 1974 pension law, the Employment Retirement Income Security Act, which secured defined benefit plans according to the standards followed by most corporate pension plans. Corporate sponsors of ERISA hoped to prevent competition from companies that promised pensions but did not fund them. Some activists felt that the UAL pension default represented the imminent decline of all airline and airport workers' pensions, and called for those workers to picket the airports.[49] But massive protests did not materialize. Nevertheless, Congress responded to generalized anxiety about pension security with the president's 2005 pension reform proposals. These proposals promoted 401(k) plans at the expense of DB pension plans, despite the fact that 401(k) plans suffered widespread suspicion when Enron defaulted on its 401(k) pensions in 2001.

When Enron workers lost most of their 401(k) pensions—because the 401(k) accounts were dominated by Enron stock, which pension participants could not sell—it seemed that 401(k) reform was unavoidable. Instead, the Enron situation spurred the Sarbanes-Oxley reforms that force companies to be more diligent about their auditing and accounting practices, and no 401(k) pension reform was passed. Congressional bias toward 401(k) pension plans is even more peculiar because, in stark contrast to the Enron 401(k) plans, the Enron DB plans were secure. Nevertheless, the Pension Protection Act of

2006 will hasten the erosion of existing DB plans and inhibit the formation of new ones, all the while encouraging the growth of 401(k) pension plans.[50]

This public policy bias in favor of DC pension plans is unfortunate because 401(k) plans do not function as "real" pensions in the sense that workers having 401(k) pensions can use them as "rainy day" funds or as savings accumulated for the purchase of consumer durables, such as cars, or as down payments to buy a home. Chapter 4 will show that there is little evidence that 401(k) plans will provide meaningful pensions for middle-class workers—the median 401(k) pension value at retirement age is $50,000, which yields about $300 per month. Though workers indirectly trade compensation for employer contributions to 401(k) or DB pensions, only for DB pensions plans do employers have to fund and insure the "compensation." Despite Enron's unethical and illegal default on its workers' 401(k) plans, it was the UAL-insured DB pension default that prompted legislation to encourage individual accounts.

One of the reasons the UAL default produced little pension reform to protect DB plans is because there are three deeply divided interpretations of what went wrong. Bad behavior on the part of corporate defined benefit sponsors is one interpretation. Another interpretation is the bad luck of low interest rates and low financial returns, occurring together, bloating liabilities and shrinking assets and imperiling DB plans. And a third interpretation is that a bad environment for DB pensions is caused either by firms' preferences for 401(k) plans, or by both workers' and firms' preferences for 401(k) plans. More important, no matter the interpretation of what happened, experts disagree about how secure governments or companies should make anyone's pension, and that disagreement causes ambivalence about needed reform.

The pension reforms of 2006[51] were aimed at improving funding for defined benefit plans based on the bad behavior interpretation. Despite their intentions to improve the pension system, pension sponsors testified in Congress that the requirements that assets must equal liabilities at all times and any deficit must be paid off in seven years, rather than the current requirement of thirty years, would hurt the DB system. Pension plan sponsors argued that these reforms would be similar to requiring much higher down payments and seven-year mortgages for home buyers. Surely, home buyers who could afford the higher down payments would be less at risk of default and debt exposure, but home ownership rates would tumble. Just as the requirements for better funding and shorter payoff periods would make the existing funds more secure, there would be far fewer DB pensions.

The campaign to save pensions may destroy them.

The Pension Benefit Guaranty Corporation contributes to bad behavior similarly to companies, mainly bad behavior in the form of moral hazard—when an insured person or entity engages in more risky behavior just because the insurance lowers the cost of the consequences. The PBGC's moral hazard is the main cause for pension underfunding because it adheres to the same principle as private insurance: insuring entities with the lowest risks. The PBGC minimizes its losses when it terminates insurance coverage as early as possible, raises insurance premiums, and seeks to limit the benefits it covers.

If it is the internal flaws of the pension system that cause pension underfunding and defaults, which is tantamount to bad company behavior, then the pension reform supported by the congressional Republicans makes sense. Their proposed legislation assumes that firms game the system—that is, firms manipulate their estimates of actuarial and investment returns, and otherwise engage in moral hazard—so that they engage in increased risky behavior because the insurance coverage pays for the negative results. This motive is plausible. There are no obvious trade-offs for firms taking on risky assets in their pension funds—the downside of the risk are losses that are insured by the government agency, the upside of the risk are gains that are entirely the firms' to keep.

On the other hand, if the pension decline is caused by employers, in general, deciding to withdraw from the kinds of labor relations that engender defined benefit pension plans, then their decline would be made worse by reforms that significantly raise DB costs. Serious threats to the DB pension system are not from corporate misdeeds, they are from a hostile environment created by external economic and political events and trends. Among these externalities are the dramatic acceleration of the transfer of U.S. manufacturing offshore; strong U.S. dollars boosting cheap imports; the decline in employment standards; the decline in unions; and new employers paying lower wages and providing no pensions. These factors together have pummeled the airline and steel sectors, which represent the bulk of the Pension Benefit Guaranty Corporation's deficits. Bethlehem Steel, Delta Airways, US Airways, and United Airlines, plus one large company in another sector, Polaroid, have offloaded $324 million in pension liabilities onto the PBGC during the years 2001 through 2005.

Defined benefit pensions are threatened by what the airline situation reveals: that there are markets where older companies with long-term labor contracts are now competing with new firms that have young employees. Those new firms use the industry's infrastructure—in the airline industry, the infrastructure comprises trust in airline travel, airports, research and development that spawned reservation systems, among many other things. Employers make promises to pay pensions in the future, so as to obtain labor productivity in the present. New companies, including Asian firms, are not burdened by high pension costs and retiree health care costs, both of which come from having an aging workforce, even though the new firms offer DB pension plans. The entrance of new firms in an industry puts pressure on older firms to minimize their legacy costs, which mainly consist of DB pension costs, as well as retiree health insurance promises, among other similar costs. Defined benefit pension plans are also threatened by less costly and newer 401(k) pension plans that emerged in the early 1980s, first as supplements to DB plans and then as substitutes. The existence of these alternatives meant very few young workers were coming into the DB pension system, so that thsose plans became top-heavy with older workers and retirees.

Still other components of the bad environment for defined benefit pensions are unintended consequences of past congressional decisions. Looking at these consequences suggests that Congress unwittingly assisted firms in reducing their DB pension funding with the 1987 revenue-saving tax and spending bill. This act was a desperate attempt to garner more revenue for the federal budget—as a consequence of Reagan tax cuts—by reducing the amount of money firms could shelter in their tax-favored pension funds.[52]

One interpretation of these three pension problems—the United Airlines' pension trouble, the Pension Benefit Guaranty Corporation financial shortfalls, and flaws in the current pension system—is that most companies, like UAL, are using the PBGC as a bankruptcy solution, and liberally using DB funding rules to avoid pension contributions. Another interpretation is that the UAL's default is emblematic of a wholesale employer move away from "good" pension plans to "bad" pension plans.[53]

The first interpretation of events leads to bankruptcy law reform. The other interpretation leads to legislation like the Pension Protection Act of 2006, which uses the principles of commercial insurance to restructure social insurance.

The Pension Protection Act: Destroying
the Defined Benefit System as the Way to Save It

The United Airline pension situation triggered the introduction of the Pension Protection Act in June 2005, which was a weakened form of President

Bush's pension proposals, introduced February 7, 2005, one week after he announced in the State of the Union address his aim to transform Social Security into private accounts (more on this in chapter 5). The PPA was passed by Congress and signed into law in August of 2006 and it aims to shore up pension funding. The PPA also aimed to limit the liability of the PBGC, but there are two ways to limit that liability.

One way is to expand the base of what is insured so more plan sponsors are paying premiums to the PBGC. A system refreshed in this way helps employers fund the pensions at lower costs and increases PBGC's revenue from premiums.

The other way to limit risk of potential insurance liabilities is to limit that which is insured. Insuring DB plans against default costs is less risky if fewer pension benefits are insured and more pension funds are frozen. That is the direction the PPA took. The PPA limits which, and to what extent, enhanced pensions can be paid by underfunded plans, for example, enhanced benefits such as "shut-down" benefits that are paid by pension funds to workers who lose their jobs because a plant or establishment ceases operation. An auto insurance analogy helps describe Congress's choice in reforming pension insurance. Auto insurers could limit their risk by promoting safer cars and safer driving, or by advocating less automobile use. The auto insurance industry of course wants to insure and encourages automobile use. Likewise, in establishing the PBGC back in 1974, the government sought to promote DB pensions.

In a reversal of federal government pension policy, the PPA seeks to limit the PBGC's exposure by shrinking DB plans and encouraging individuals essentially to self-insure against events that were once insured by government or employers.

The Pension Protection Act of 2006 makes defined benefit plans less attractive in a number of ways. One, it hikes premiums per pension participant from $19 to $30.[54] Second, the Act increases pension funding by requiring funds to use an interest rate derived from a complex yield curve calculated by the Treasury Department. Here is how the yield curve works: A DB plan's liability is calculated by summing up the value of the expected pensions for all the participants. The interest rate is a key factor in valuing a future payment of income—the lower the interest rate, the higher the liability; the higher the interest rate, the lower the liability. Before there was the Pension Protection Act, firms used the interest rates on long-term "graded" corporate bonds. Since these bond rates were for the long term and the bonds did not have to be high quality, the interest rates used to discount the liabilities were quite high, making the liabilities appear to be quite low.

Under the PPA, pension plans will need to use three different interest rates depending on the expected period over which the liabilities are paid—within five years; between five and twenty years; or more than twenty years—after the valuation date. The idea is to match the measurement of the liabilities to the date when the pensions are expected to be paid. Firms complain that these rules make administering a DB plan much more complex. Crucially, the new reform has a distributional effect by age of plan. Older mature plans will be forced to use lower interest rates to value their liabilities; the younger plans will be able to use higher interest rates. This may lower the cost for new DB plans and may encourage (at least this provision won't discourage) employers to construct new plans. Employers opposed the complexity of the provisions and the variability of the yield; however, firms with older populations have a particular concern about using a yield curve to value liabilities.

Third, the Act requires pensions to be 100% funded—the assets must equal the liabilities at all times (current law required a 90% ratio of assets to liabilities)—and limits the use of credit balances. Previous law also allowed firms to anticipate bad times by overfunding their pension plan—within limits—and creating "credit" balances that could be used to fund the pension, rather than cold hard cash, in bad times. Credit balances caused problems in 2001 and 2002 because their estimated value was based on unrealistically high rates of return. When those credit balances were called upon during the recession, their true value was much lower than their estimated value. The PPA would allow more overfunding (firms' pension contributions are exempt from federal tax, which surely means firms are encouraged to shelter profits in the pension fund, vexing the Treasury by depriving it of revenue) but constrain the use of credit balances for funds that are less than 80% funded.

Fourth, the PPA of 2006 privileges individual accounts, making them more attractive by easing up on the rules that prevented an investment firm that has a conflict of interest—the conflict is that the investment firm sells its products in the employee's DC plan—from counseling the employee about what to invest in. This provision of the PPA clearly represents a belief that biased advice is better than no financial advice at all because it focuses individuals on their 410(k) pension plan.

The provisions of the PPA are better understood in the context of the pension funding practices of the 1990s. Professional actuaries use asset-liability studies to determine pension funding and investment strategies. Assets and liabilities are projected by assuming death rates, separation (from job) rates, salary increases, rates of return on all types of investment vehicles, and all other factors effecting the future value of assets and liabilities. If actuaries assume stocks will earn high rates of return, they recommend that the portfolio become more heavily invested in stocks, which most financial managers recommended in the 1990s. Over 39% of DB private sector pension fund assets were invested in stocks in 1989; by 1999, over 64% of assets were invested in stocks, in what financial analysts called a love affair with the equities.[55] Many insist that pension funds should hold only bonds because stocks are too risky. Ironically, Bush's Social Security reforms called for individuals to hold stocks in the proposed Social Security personal accounts because government bonds are too risky![56] The share of stocks in pension funds fell after the stock market bubble burst to 59.3% of the value of the average portfolio, because the value of the stocks in the portfolio was less in 2002.[57]

When pension funds experienced actual returns twice as high as forecasted returns, expectations could have been revised upward to reflect the recent past, or revised downward to recognize that stock returns above a historical average will eventually revert to that historical average. The implications of this rule of thumb are devastating. If the average return on stocks is 7% and the average return for ten years has been 10%, then the stock market rate of return is predicted to be −3% for ten years. Most firms revised their expectations about the permanent average stock market return upward, with encouragement from their consultants in the late 1990s—this "irrational exuberance" is well documented in a book with the same title.[58] Ironically, five years later, a Wall Street rating agency ranked one-third of the largest firms in the United States "poor" or "below average" in the quality of reported earnings because they almost always understated their financial difficulties. Why did they understate? Strangely enough, over 64% of the firms understated their pension liabilities because they used unrealistic assumptions in calculating future pension liabilities and assets. Halliburton, Archer Daniels Midland, Best Buy, Bristol Myers Squib, Corning, Eastman Kodak, EDS, Gap, Janus Capital, Motorola, and the Walt Disney Company are among the poorly rated firms.[59] When firms revise their profit rates downward (because they had overstated the expected returns on their pension funds), pension funds are affected. They have to lower their rate of return assumptions on the stocks their pension funds hold, and those lowered return assumptions cause their profit expectations to decline. This has a domino effect, as other firms holding the stock of these companies must lower their own profit expectations downward.[60]

Although Harvard economist Benjamin Friedman in 1983 found that firms in financial trouble became more conservative, holding more bonds and less stock in their pension fund investments, the Government Accountability Office found that behavior reversed in the 1990s. For example, Bethlehem Steel, whose bankruptcy was the largest claim to the Pension Benefit Guaranty Corporation until UAL and, with other steel firms, contributed to 80% of the PBGC's past problems, had a whopping 73% of its assets in stocks in 2000. Bethlehem Steel might have been holding so much stock because it was desperately trying to obtain high returns. Most analysts believe that attempt had the invidious effect of raising the pension fund's projected asset-to-liability ratio, and reducing pension contributions, which conserved the desperate company's cash. Bizarrely, immediately before the PBGC took over Bethlehem's massive $4 billion pension debt, IRS funding rules prevented Bethlehem from making tax-exempt contributions to the pension fund in 2001.[61] Similarly, Polaroid's pension plan was terminated by the PBGC with a $321.8 million deficit, and the pension plan had a credit balance, so Polaroid could not contribute tax-sheltered assets to its pension in 2000. Government pension accounting regulations, aimed at discouraging companies from sheltering profits in tax-exempt pension funds, are targeted for blame for the perverse situation where a pension plan deemed to be overfunded in one year is massively bankrupted the next.[62]

The Effects of the Pension Protection Act of 2006

The Pension Protection Act of 2006 aims to correct the problem just alluded to. But it does so without recognizing a much more serious problem facing the pension system. The more serious problem is that more defined benefit pension systems are not being formed. The PPA advances the ideas that DB plans have become unsuitable and obsolete, and that pension reform should be following the principles of commercial insurance companies. The PPA aims to reduce risk by proposing to improve pension funding, which would decrease the risk it faces. Commercial insurers offload the risk they do not want to insure. For example, homeowner insurers offload a lot of homeowner risk of floods and earthquakes to the Federal Emergency

Management Administration (FEMA). Similarly, the PPA aims to eliminate insurance for DB plans by offloading to the insured individuals the risks of securing their own retirement income. By doing so, the PPA seems to serve the administration's larger vision of workers funding their own retirement from individual retirement accounts—such as the proposed Retirement Savings Account (RSA), which allows higher levels of individual contributions on a tax-favored basis—and the personal Social Security accounts. (RSAs and Social Security personal accounts advance the same principles, substituting for social- and employer-provided insurance vehicles used by individuals to self-insure, such as Health Savings Accounts, for example.)

The Pension Protection Act of 2006 may have been prompted by the Pension Benefit Guaranty Corporation's deficit, but it does not address the two most fundamental causes of the PBGC's financing troubles:

- The Pension Benefit Guaranty Corporation loses premium payers when companies replace their guaranteed DB pensions with DC plans. Thus, the government regulations that privilege DC plans over DB plans help accelerate the PBGC's losses by discouraging the formation of new plans that would bring in more premiums.

- Two industries have caused unusual Pension Benefit Guaranty Corporation outlays. In 2004 less than 5% of all defined benefit participants were in the airline and steel industries but those constituted over two-thirds of the claims to the PBGC. Underfunding DB plans is not as prevalent as commonly believed; a small number of companies underfund, therefore this is not the largest problem facing DB plans.

The Pension Protection Act of 2006 seeks to shore up pension rights by preventing firms from dumping their liabilities on the PBGC. But there are other ways to prevent dumping besides requiring more pension funding when a firm is in troubled financial times. Many have argued for amendments to bankruptcy laws to prevent companies and shareholders from avoiding pension liabilities. In addition, the PPA does not recognize that defined benefit pension terminations produce lemming-like behavior and a race to the bottom; firms deciding to opt out of the DB pension system give their competitors little choice but to opt out as well. The United Airlines termination of its pensions may provoke Delta and Northwest airlines to do the same. The PPA should have sought to slow down terminations and make them subject to negotiations between workers and firms.

Any pension reform should be evaluated according to: whether the reform encourages better and more stable funding; whether the reform is fair to workers, retirees, executives, shareholders, customers, and taxpayers; whether the reform encourages the formation of "real" pensions—where "real" implies a definite stream of lifetime income; and whether the reform helps firms adjust to business cycles and industrial trauma.

The Pension Protection Act of 2006 reforms focused on funding rules, not on the survival of the entire defined benefit pension system. Nor do the reforms come close to meeting the conditions suggested in the preceding paragraph. Instead, the approach of the PPA hastens firms out of the DB pension system; it makes no provision for slowing down firms' terminations of DB pensions, and it does not prevent the use of lump sum distributions from DB plans. Under current law, the DB pension plan—which is the contract to pay a stream of income for life—can be converted into a present value paid in a lump sum. Before the PPA, lump sums were calculated using the thirty-year U.S. Treasury bond rates (5% per year at mid-2005). The reason for using thirty-year T-bond rates was that workers would invest the lump sum in conservative assets. Severely underfunded DB plans, under the PPA, are constrained as to how much the benefits can be lumped. There are two major problems with lump sums: it is difficult to purchase an annuity with a lump sum; and many DB plans are not designed for lump sum distributions, meaning that they are funded assuming the fund's liabilities will be dispersed over a retiree's lifetime. In short, lump sums do not result in real pensions. What they do is bleed DB funds dry. (The defined benefit plans in many firms started in the 1990s to use lump sums instead of annuities, mainly because of pressure from the firms' executives who wanted their own pensions in a lump sum.)

Many pension fund sponsors consider that paying lump sums is a mistake, so they would like to stop doing it. But the first firm that stops will attract a lot of negative attention because lump sums are very popular among employees. This is a classic collective, action problem—most firms want to end lump sums, but no one firm has an interest in doing so without the others also revoking them. Congress could solve the collective-action problem by prohibiting lump sums payments from DC pension plans and DB pension plans. Accepting the prohibition against lump sums should be the price employers and employees pay for keeping the generous tax break.

Conclusions: The Pension Protection Act of 2006

The "pension reform" of 2006 continues congressional coddling of 401(k) plans, discourages defined benefit plans, and will further erode traditional DB pension plans. The PPA does not require firms to automatically enroll employees in their companies' 401(k) plans; rather, it simply makes it easier for those who want to enroll to do so.

Although research shows (as you will see in chapter 4) that automatic enrollment increases savings significantly, especially among low- and middle-income workers, no one knows how many companies will actually adopt that feature. Congress did not mandate automatic enrollment for defined contribution plans. It could have. The PPA also reverses a prohibition against investment companies offering financial advice to employees, even if the employers' 401(k) plan offers the investment companies' products. Lifting this ban was a key goal for the securities industry lobby, while labor groups opposed it strenuously. Congress missed a chance to help companies and employees—and both will need defined benefit plans in the future—when it passed the Pension Protection Act of 2006.

Chapter 4

Do-It-Yourself Pensions

It's ironic that employees seem to prefer the new species of retirement plan although it might not be as good for them.

—Michael Clowes,[1] conservative writer and editor of the influential pension industry publication, *Pensions and Investments*, regarding workers' irrational preferences for defined contribution savings plans

Pension coverage is stagnating while the share of employees with a defined contribution savings plan is growing. (Defined contribution plans include 401(k) plans [about 80% of participants in DC plans are in 401(k) plans]; profit sharing plans; money purchase plans; individual retirement accounts; and 403(b) plans, which are 401(k) plans for employees in the public sector.) That paradox is explained largely by DC plans replacing traditional DB plans. The disappointing lack of growth in pension coverage (discussed and documented in chapter 3) is not the only consequence of the shift from DB to DC pensions. Other consequences include

- inefficiency (the nation is not getting the most retirement income security out of each dollar saved for retirement),

- inadequate retirement savings, and

- inequality of income and risk-bearing between employers and workers, as well as between upper- and middle-class workers.

These three consequences—the three "i's"—stem partly from the nature of defined contribution and defined benefit plans and partly from how they are used.

Defined benefit plans are a form of insurance. Workers pool the risk of retiring without income from their main job. Those who move on to another employer without significant pension credits subsidize those who don't. In contrast, workers self-insure with DC plans. Workers decide how much to save, how to invest the savings, and how to withdraw funds. But "doing-it-yourself" is vulnerable to the tragic consequences of amateurishness; specifically, saving too little, investing poorly, paying fees that are too high, and spending too fast. These are mistakes that can last for the rest of a pensioners' life. Firms find sponsoring 401(k) plans more profitable than sponsoring DB plans. For firms, DC plans are less costly, less risky, and can be funded with their own stock, not with cold, hard cash.

Trends in 401(k) Plans

DATA TO DIGEST   *In 1999, 36% of workers were covered by a defined contribution plan. By 2005, 43% were covered an increase of more than 19%. During the same time period, overall pension coverage increased 2%, from 48% to 50% (according to employer-based surveys described in chapter 3; see table 3.2).*

Most defined contribution plans are now 401(k) plans. Several corporations asked the IRS in the mid-1970s if their highest-paid employees could avoid taxes on their cash bonuses by directing the bonuses into a deferred compensation account. The executive could avoid paying income taxes until the income was withdrawn, presumably at a lower tax rate because the executive would be retired. The earnings would accrue tax-free. The tax benefit to the executive would be significant because the top marginal tax rate was over 50% at the time. The IRS said yes, but warned that this option would have to be available to everyone. A section of the tax code—yes, Section 401 subsection (k)—allowing pretax contributions into an individual account was inserted by Congress in 1978. An entrepreneurial consultant, Theodore Benna, designed a generic plan to comply with the new tax code section and, once the IRS approved of the plan in 1980, he marketed it to employers as a way their workers could delay paying taxes by making contributions into an account maintained by the employer. Many employers adopted 401(k) plans to supplement their existing DB plans. Yet 401(k) plans have become the predominant pension form.

One consequence has been the stagnation of pension coverage in general; another has been a tilt in pension coverage toward higher-income workers, according to economists Alica Munnell's and Annika Sundén's book, *Coming Up Short* (2004). This book is an excellent and dependable resource

on 401(k) plans, as is Boston College's Center for Retirement Research updates.

> **DATA TO DIGEST**   *In 2004, 73% of prime-aged workers, those between
> forty and forty-nine, who earned annual incomes between $20,000 and
> $39,999 (just under the median), participated in a 401(k) plan when eligible; yet
> 96% of those earning $100,000 or more, who were eligible, participated in a
> 401(k).*
>
> *In terms of eligibility to participate in a 401(k), among those earning in the
> $20,000 to $39,999 range, only 56.9% were eligible to participate, while over
> 75% of those earning annual incomes of $60,000 and over were eligible.[2]*

Even if an employer does sponsor a 401(k) plan, and a worker wants to
participate, the plan likely excludes the lowest-income groups because they
do not have enough service or they are part-time workers—working less than
2,000 hours per year. Hispanics and African Americans populate this category. Therefore, among the most likely to be ineligible to participate in their
employers' pension plans[3] in 2004 were 28% of Hispanics and 25% of African
Americans, compared to 21% of whites who were ineligible.

Advantages and Disadvantages of Defined Contribution Pensions

The question is, Why did 401 (k) plans take off?

Without doubt, workers find 401(k) plans appealing, especially because
of their visibility—that is, workers can usually confirm their value on the internet or telephone 24 hours, 7 days a week; and perhaps as well because
401(k)-type plans are immune to employer business failure or workers failing
to remain at work with the employer. And workers can adjust the size of their
retirement income by saving more or less. Nevertheless, in practice, any
worker with a 401(k) faces two challenges: accumulating enough assets to
provide enough income during retirement, and choosing the appropriate
payout method to result in desired retirement income flow. Alas, the challenges are not distributed equally. Middle-class and below middle-class
workers are more likely than higher-income employees to pay higher 401(k)
plan administrative fees, make wrong investment choices, and also believe
they are not able to afford to participate.

Advantages of 401(k) Pension Plans

What a 401(k) plan is worth is easily known at any time—each employee has control over the amount of her and his own plan and how it is invested. These are attractive features as you shall see, especially in comparison with defined benefit plans. Also, 401(k) plans reduce two key risks found among traditional DB plans: employer risk—that the employer will stop providing the DB plan—and employment risk—that you will not be working for the same employer.

Employer risk is high in a DB plan because an employer's financial health greatly determines the pension's value over time. Employer risk was painfully well illustrated when bankrupt Bethlehem Steel and United Airlines, among other firms, defaulted on their DB pension plans. The defaults ended further accumulations into the DB pensions and slashed expected benefits for airline workers, steelworkers, and other groups of workers; the workers also lost many benefits not covered by Pension Benefit Guaranty Corporation (PBGC) insurance. In some cases, the losses are colossally unfair. Airline pilots are forced by law to retire at age sixty; then they retire, start collecting their pensions—but the PBGC does not insure pensions collected before age sixty-five! In effect, the law makes the retired pilots vulnerable to loss of their pensions! Many retired United pilots lost over half their pensions.

Employer risk creeps into 401(k) plans, too, however. Over 40% of 401(k) assets are invested in the employers' own stock, whereas DB assets (according to the 1974 Employee Retirement Income Security Act) are allowed to hold up to only 10% of the employer's stock. Moreover, the PBGC insures most, not all, DB plans, which reduces the employer default risk. For these reasons, 401(k) plans pensions could be more exposed to employer risk.

Traditional defined benefit plans are valuable to workers who stay with their employer and in their employer's benefit program for a long time—the longer the better. Nevertheless, the short-term worker feels short changed. If a worker stays fewer than five years, she or he usually earns no credits toward a pension. This is "employment risk," so-called because it alludes to the risk that a worker will leave employment with a firm before vesting or building up significant pension credits. There is no employment risk under 401(k)-type pension plans because all DC plans are fully portable. If workers do not spend the balance in their 401(k) plans before they retire—and the temptation to spend before retirement is usually present in one way or another, for one need or another—the funds accumulated remain in a worker's 401(k) balance, no matter what the vagaries, the whims, or the mistakes of their employer. Nevertheless, employers do pose some risk to DC participants. Employers could stop or shrink their 401(k) contribution matches—many employers reduced or stopped matches during the 2001 recession. (These issues will be considered and discussed in the next section.)

Workers who own DC pension plans, for the most part, own every penny and know where every penny is. A worker whose 401(k) plan is not loaded with his employer's stock is surely relieved that his nest egg is not dependent on his employer's financial future, especially when an employer is failing and that employer's DB plan goes down in flames. Owning and controlling the assets in a DC plan is certainly an advantage of 401(k) plans.

Disadvantages of 401(k) Pension Plans

The disadvantages of 401(k) plans stem from the three challenges that workers must face in their own planning for retirement: accumulating enough assets; investing in them safely for optimum growth and returns; and choosing the appropriate way to take assets out of the plan.

First, let us consider accumulating enough assets to provide expected retirement income. Only about a third of Americans say they have thought about retirement *and* have done something about it. Surveys of retirement preparedness routinely identify three groups of people, each group having about the same numbers of people.

A third of respondents can be referred to as "smug prepared" rational savers: they are confident they are saving enough and are on the right financial investment path for retirement. Only about half of these smug savers have any savings at the age of forty! Another third admit they know they should be saving more but do not—let us call them the "shamed rationales." And still another third say they do not worry about retirement and do not plan for it. These might be irrational or have other things warranting their attention on financial matters, like saving for a house or saving for other financial needs. Let's call them "present-minded."[4]

The pitfalls of the do-it-yourself pension lurk in the rule of thumb that almost every pension expert and on-line pension-advising website will say you must save between 7% and 15% of every paycheck[5] when you are in your thirties and forties so that you can have the same preretirement standard of living during your retirement. Americans have difficulty saving anything at any time, let alone saving that much of their pay regularly over the long term.

Retirement savings has to be *continuous* and it must start at the beginning of a person's working career. If workers in their twenties save, they are usually saving to buy a house or to pay for children's education.[6]

Accumulation Risks

Assuming a worker is a planner, or turns into one, she must be able to calculate her retirement needs, estimate wisely what she must do to get there, and periodically review how well she is doing. There are some so-called retirement calculators—programs that help people determine how much they have to save to reach certain retirement income targets—that account for how inflation will erode income as the person ages. Accounting for inflation, of course, raises the estimate of how much would be needed to maintain a certain standard of living. If you plan on receiving $80,000 per year starting when you are sixty-five and inflation fluctuates closely at around 4% per year, you will lose a quarter of your buying power before you are aged seventy-five, and half by the time you are eighty-five.

Assuming there is no inflation, to keep the math simple, let us look at what amount of money is needed at retirement, usually referred to as a lump sum, to provide a monthly flow of retirement income. A reasonable estimate of the relationship between a retirement lump sum and the retirement income flow it will produce is that approximately $230,000 is needed at retirement for every $1,000 of income per month you want guaranteed for life at age sixty-five. The value of a Social Security benefit promise is a bit over $240,000, and the average Social Security benefit is about $1,000 a month, so the rule of thumb just mentioned works fairly well. Someone wanting $4,000 per month (in 2008 dollars) for the rest of his life would need about $1 million at retirement. (This simple estimate would lead to severe mental depression for someone planning too late for retirement.)

In addition, there is temptation risk, inherent in human nature, to consider in do-it-yourself pension planning. Temptation risk exists in 401(k) pensions because they make it possible to yield to the temptation to spend the 401(k) assets before retirement.

Another risk, also inherent in human nature, is the tendency toward "myopia," the shortsightedness that leads to people "discounting"[7] future income at rates higher than the going interest rates. People with a high personal discount rate value a dollar today much more than they value a future dollar plus the going interest rate. These people may collect early Social Security benefits and in doing so sacrifice the automatic 8% Social Security benefit increase granted for every year collection is delayed after the normal retirement age. These people could not earn a risk-free 8% per year anywhere else on the planet. This is not the only example of myopia; there is a great deal of behavior suggesting financial myopia at all ages. Many people[8] (there are no good estimates of how many) are not future-oriented, either because of their personalities or because of pressing present-day problems, so it's likely they do not save.

Federal judge and economist Richard Posner describes the myopia alluded to in this way: Funding retirement is a conflict between current self and future self. The future self is old and rickety, a self for which a current younger self has little sympathy. From that, it follows that the current self is subject to the shortsightedness afflicting his vision of his future self.

Let's say you care about your old self and you start to plan for retirement by turning to Google. Entering the words "retirement planner" and ".org" retrieves the not-for-profit sites that contain a retirement savings calculator to simulate various savings scenarios. The website www.RetirementPlanner.org is the first returned nonsponsored site. Its instructions are simple. It prompts users to follow four easy steps:

1. Estimate how long you'll live.

2. Determine how much you spend now.

3. Subtract expenses you will not have after retirement and add additional costs you are likely to have after retirement.

4. Determine how much your investments will earn after inflation and after fees are deducted.

So, just how easy are these four steps to follow? Let's see how well you do.

Longevity, Investment, Financial, Inflation, Political, and Poverty Risks

Longevity Risk

Ask yourself: "How long will I live?" Obviously, you can't answer and be 100% sure of your answer. Here is the point. You face the longevity risk of underestimating how long you will live. (Leave it to an economist to identify living too long as risky!) This risk is not the general risk that in retirement your buying power will fall and your expenses will rise, so that eventually your expenses exceed your income. That's not what longevity risk is about. Longevity risk is the risk that, despite planning carefully for the increasing cost of living, you live past the age you planned for. Longevity risk is the risk that you outlive your retirement money. Annuities, as from defined benefit plans and Social Security, are designed precisely to eliminate longevity risk.

You may find it interesting to learn that people have different estimates about their longevity, and how widely the range of estimates varies across gender and ethnic categories. Based on past information and guesses about the future, actuaries routinely make estimates of the probability people will live to age seventy-five. When people are asked about their chances of living to age seventy-five they are usually not in agreement with the actuarial tables. For instance, based on a survey in 2004, African-American women said their probability of living until age seventy-five was 14% less than the actuaries' estimates. European-American women think they will live 6% fewer years and European men 3% fewer years than they actually do live to on average. People who think they will die sooner than actuaries' estimate will spend their retirement money too fast, resulting in having too little to live on until they die. Only African-American men overestimate their longevity, 9% more years than the actuarial tables predict. (More about this in chapter 6.) This is the only group comprising individuals that we expect would want to buy an annuity, or save more than needed, or work longer. The idea is that if you think you will live longer than the insurance company thinks you will, you will collect more than you paid to the insurance company (see table 4.1.).

One possible reason for underestimating longevity is a pessimism that is a form of cognitive dissonance. What that means is this: By avoiding thinking about what you know, that you won't have enough money for the rest of your life (that's the "cognition"), when you cannot do anything about it (that's the "dissonance"), you take a psychic shortcut to alleviate the frustration and anxiety. You change what you think you know (back to "cognition") and begin to believe you will have a shorter life (back to "dissonance"). Cognitive dissonance is a subconscious coping mechanism. For some people it is easier to change what they believe to be facts than to understand and believe the facts.

This form of cognitive dissonance makes a lump sum payout look more attractive. But when you take a lump sum payout, that's all you get! The lump sum payout disconnects you from other workers, from other retirees. Furthermore, be sure you understand that this kind of subsidy exists only in a subsidy pool, much the way it exists in an insurance pool. If you "self-annuitize"—that is,

Table 4.1

Most People are Pessimistic about Their Own Life Span

People's estimation of how much time they have to live, compared to what actuaries predict

	Men	Women
White	97%	94%
Nonwhite	109%	86%

Source: Author's calculations from the Health and Retirement Survey (University of Michigan, http://hrsonline.isr.umich.edu/. The white male n = 907, nonwhite male, n = 188, white women, n = 706, nonwhite women = 216.

take your lump sum payout, put it in the bank or similar investment, and then distribute to yourself the interest and principal in equal amounts over time—there is no subsidy because you have constructed for yourself a one-person annuity pool. In such a one-person pool, your periodic payments will be less than periodic payments from a large annuity pool. And another thing you will have to understand about being a "self-annuitizer" is that you will likely pick an age that is too young to have your interest and principal go to zero. In other words, your annuity will die before you die!

By not being in an annuity pool, a retiree loses out on the cross-subsidization of people who die sooner than average to people who live longer than average. It is a strange fact that people enter a health insurance pool, home insurance pool, and auto insurance pool, without fearing that the insurance will pay to some other person in the pool the cost of repairing accidental damage to her expensive car, or that others will get a $100,000 heart operation. But people fear they will not collect their annuity.

Another field of the social sciences would be needed to explore why people avoid annuities, although Munnell and Sundén guess what may be the reason—that people avoid annuities because they think they can do a better job investing their lump sums and they don't want the insurance company to profit from their death. Munnell and Sundén suggest that people are unaware or unconcerned that, with an annuity, their death doesn't profit the company but actually helps the other people who live longer than they lived.

> **Bottom Line**   *The fact that most people think they will die sooner than the professional actuaries think they will means most everyone feels that the insurance company profits at their expense. This attitude is not conducive to*

people clamoring to buy annuities. From what you have read thus far in this section, you should have a good idea why most people do not buy annuities and why Social Security is a forced annuity program.

Inflation Risk

The second step in your retirement planning is to determine the amount of money you currently spend, as the basis to figure out how much you will need when you retire. You would think this is the easiest step. Let's say it is easy because you have previously established a budget and you have been sticking to it successfully. Now use that budget to project what amount of money you want to have and what you will need to buy when you are retired. Estimating retirement expenses has its own special uncertainties. Health care costs of the elderly have gone up much faster than expected, driving up out-of-pocket medical expenditures and the Medicare premiums deducted from Social Security payments. Dartmouth economist Jonathan Skinner sums up what we need to do to get along with lower incomes in retirement: cook at home, such as making our own spaghetti sauce, with little or no eating out; downsize and sell our house; and live[9] as frugally as we did when we were paying the costs of our children's educations. Even these unappealing economies may not be enough. The combination of eroding retiree health benefits and the risk of catastrophic future out-of-pocket health spending suggests that even conventional retirement planning recommendations, such as having ten times your final salary in your retirement account, could be too low.[10]

Clearly, unexpected inflation is an enormous problem for retirement planning. People managing and planning for their retirement with DC plans face inflation risks, but so do participants in employer defined benefit plans, which are rarely inflation protected. (Remember, inflation-indexed Social Security benefits bear no inflation risk.)

> **Bottom Line** *Workers face longevity risk, and within that risk is inflation risk, especially that of increasing medical costs.*

Investment Risk

The allocation of assets in a retirement portfolio and the level of administrative fees and investment fees can crucially affect overall return and risk in a pension plan. When 401(k) plans were first offered, employers that sponsored these pension plans invested the assets for the workers in the plan, although they provided them with very little choice of investment vehicles. Then there came a trend toward providing workers the opportunity to select among many different kinds of investment vehicle accounts—sometimes up to fifty-six choices, according to one study. We all know to diversify, which workers did when faced with choices. Participants would distribute their contributions evenly across vehicles when there were fewer than five choices, but that tendency changed as the number of choices expanded.[11] Whether workers chose wisely and diversified to reduce risk and maximize return is an open question. Enough doubts led vendors, such as Vanguard, to offer life-cycle funds to employers as 401(k) assets. Life-cycle funds are funds that automatically reduce the equity allocation as the participant ages, according to the (100 minus your age) rule. For instance, a thirty-year-old choosing a life-cycle fund is advised to have most assets in stocks, say 70% (100–30) in stocks and 30% in bonds. By the time the person is aged fifty, it is advised to have less equity, say, 50% in stocks and 50% in bonds. A life-cycle fund changes allocations automatically as the investor ages. This scheme makes it much more likely that defined contribution participants won't lose a significant amount of their assets because of their own poor allocation decisions. However, not everyone takes or has available the life-cycle option.[12]

What may prevent people from making the right savings and investment choices is overconfidence, which is necessary when falling in love, having children, and taking other risks (like driving to work or entering law school). What may be a vital trait for the survival of the species could be fatal for retirement planning. Investors must not overstate their ability to make the right decisions and must take into account all the risks involved in reaching a target retirement income.[13]

Although the life-cycle investment option takes many of these decisions out of your hands, the vehicles invested in cannot eliminate the downside risk that returns will be below average when you turn sixty-five. In DB plans, the employer took on that risk and you received a guaranteed pension. It wasn't hard for the employer to take on that risk because if investments were down when you retired there was a good chance they would be above average when your younger coworker retired. The only way you could insure that risk is to invest in the kind of U.S. Treasury bonds that adjust for inflation; these are U.S. Treasury Inflation-Protected Bonds, referred to as TIPS, and the rate of these bonds has not peaked over 3% per year.

I repeat: The only way to ensure you will have a certain level of buying power on a certain birthday or at a certain retirement date, is to have lower-earning assets. And if you assume a 3% annual return instead of 7%, then you need almost 40% more in your 401(k) account to reach the same target income as with the higher rate, if it is attained during the same term as the 3% return.

Also to be considered are the fees that must be deducted from the expected earnings. Fees are a key part of determining the final rate of return on an investment portfolio—but the fees as articulated in 401(k) plans are almost indecipherable. Workers pay much larger administration and investment fees in 401(k) plans than in DB plans. These large fees reduce retirement income substantially: 401(k) fees alone can reduce the value of an account by 20% to 30% after a thirty-year career.[14] Unlike the laws governing mutual funds, mortgages, and other loans, there are few laws that guarantee uniform and easy-to-understand fee disclosures for employer-sponsored retirement accounts. Because plan sponsors are able to pass on fees to workers, they have little incentive to use their clout to negotiate lower fees with financial managers of the plans. Workers participating in such plans bear the risk of high 401(k) pricing, yet they have no say in the choice of pension plan vendors.

Can financial education help participants make better decisions? Can they, given realistic scenarios of both what makes them happy and the uncertainty in predicting events, make decisions about investing, saving, and consuming, so as not to get caught short before the end of their lives in retirement? Financial managers who sell investment vehicles to employees through the 401(k) plans, and employers, who are genuinely concerned that their workers make good choices, urged Congress to allow employers to offer professional investment advice. The Pension Protection Act of 2006 allowed, not independent advice, but a "let-the-buyer-beware" policy that freed representatives of financial manager firms to give investment advice to employees. Congress did not mandate that employers must disclose 401(k) management fees in an easy-to-understand form or limit the amount of employer stock in their 401(k) plans. The investment education provided by the vendors will likely encourage workers to invest in the firm's product but not save more or diversify their investments. It is depressing to educators that workers who attend investment advice seminars are *less* likely to change their contributions or their fund's allocations than workers who do not attend.[15] The assumption behind the reforms in the Pension Protection Act of 2006 implies that workers' ignorance alone causes the limitations of 401(k) plans as a pension system.

> **Box 4.1**
>
> **Investment Management Fees: The Politics and Profits**
>
> In spring 2007, the House Education and Labor Committee held hearings on the level of fees for 401(k) plans based on a 2006 Government Accountability Office report that concluded workers often cannot understand, or in some cases cannot find out, what fees they pay to have their 401(k) money managed. The conclusion is that workers are charged between 3% and 5%, while 1.5% is more appropriate. An excess charge of 1% can seriously erode retirement money. A person investing $10,000 a year over thirty years and earning 5% per year, for example, would have more than $790,000 for retirement; if those same $10,000 yearly contributions only earned 6% the sum would be $664,000.
>
> In 2007, 47 million workers have more than $2 trillion invested in 401(k) plans, which represents about $42,000 per worker. A worker contributing $750 per year for the last thirty years, earning 4% after fees, would have accumulated $42,074. If fees had been 1% point lower, say 4% rather than 5%, the average worker would have had $7,765 more in their retirement account and the money management industry would have earned $364 billion less.
>
> To encourage Americans to save more for retirement, Congress passed the Pension Protection Act in 2006 to allow employers to automatically enroll workers in 401(k) plans. The Pension Protection Act did not include full fee disclosure by investment firms in their annual reports filed with the government, nor in contracts with employers or in publications given to workers. This legislation was enthusiastically supported by the investment industry!

Inaccurately following the four steps toward retirement planning, given at the start of this chapter, and poorly estimating future inflation and returns, plus a dose of overconfidence in making investment decisions, will add up to a wrong determination about how much will be needed and how much there will be to provide those needs in retirement.

> **Bottom Line**   *Workers are unsuited and unable to earn the maximum return on their pension savings when individual accounts are the vehicle to do so because of high and hidden investment management fees, the lack of investment experience, and the difficulty of saving enough to eliminate the downside risk of not having enough to retire on.*

(The risk of not having enough money at retirement goes beyond not saving enough or investing well. Consider the poverty risk old women face. Much of the risk of a drastic decline in income and the probability of poverty is due to family and health changes, such as the death of a spouse.[16])

Summary of all the risks: There is some employer risk in a 401(k) plan; the employer establishes an account but contributes on an ad hoc basis and usually contributes only the firm's own stock. On the other hand, DC accounts are portable and avoid employment risk. With a DB plan, employers promise benefits based on service, so the DB participant bears (a) employment risk, and (b) the risk that the employer may not fund the plan enough due to bankruptcy or some similar business distress. However, the employer that provides DB pensions bears the investment risk and longevity risks (only if the worker takes out an annuity). Both DB plans and DC accounts face poverty risk and political risk in the sense that the benefits may not adequately supplement other assets so that the elderly person lives in poverty. If the government changes tax rules and protections, this can affect the value of the pension—this is called political risk. Each risk is summarized in table 4.2.

Table 4.2
DC Plans Have More Risk
Comparing Risks in DB and DC Plans

Risk	DB	401(k)/DC
Longevity	No, if payout is an annuity; yes, if payout is a lump sum	Yes
Financial market	Not much	Yes
Investment mistakes and high fees	No	Yes
Inflation	Yes	Yes
Employer-default risk	No, if all benefits insured; yes, if many benefits are not insured by PBGC and the fund is underfunded	Yes, if the 401(k) holds substantial employer stock
Employment risk	Yes	No
Temptation risk	No	Yes (borrowing from it or cashing it out instead of rolling it over)
Political risk	Yes	Yes
Poverty risk	Yes	Yes

> Bottom Line   *Changing workers' pension plans from defined benefit to defined contribution does not eliminate risks: it shifts some risks, reduces others, and produces some new risks.*

Causes of the Shift to 401(k) Plans

The growth in 401(k) plans could be explained by executives attempting to accommodate changes in the labor market. But there is more to it. Globalization, declining unionization, and a rise in a new kind of worker are all pressuring firms to lower costs and be more efficient, and altering ways of rewarding employees. There is some evidence that workers, as they contemplate retirement, appreciate the future value of the DB pensions and are less likely to leave an employer, which helps employers reduce turnover and training costs. Yet workers in general might prefer the portable, easy-to-understand DC form of pension, which could be behind the growth of do-it-yourself 401(k) pensions. Economists basically assume that firms choose the type of pension plan that yields the most profitability at the least cost.

The Supply Side: Why Firms Want 401(k) Plans

Firms want 401(k) plans for several reasons. One reason is that 401(k) plans can cut employer pension costs. There are three main ways firms reduce their pension costs by providing a 401(k) plan instead of a defined benefit plan while maintaining the ability to retain and attract the same level of worker effort and skill.

First, if workers' actually prefer a 401(k) plan to an equivalently expensive DB plan (equivalent in terms of costs to the employer) the employer could actually reduce costs a little bit and not displease a worker just by changing the form of the retirement plan. But workers' preferences are not set in stone. The equity market boom in the late 1990s made it easy for firms to convince workers of the value of 401(k) plans. For several years all a worker had to do was select stocks and congratulate herself for the double-digit returns. Defined benefit pension plans—whose value is expressed in multiples of years of service, percentages, and some distant concept known as final salary or career average salary—were not even half the fun.

Second, the employers gain with 401(k) plans simply because not all workers participate in their employer's 401(k) pension plan and therefore do not cash in on the employer match. Unlike in Social Security and DB plans, workers are not obligated to participate in a 401(k)-type plan if it is offered by the employer. In fact, 26% of those eligible to participate do not. Most employers[17]—91%—match an employee's 401(k) contribution, though many employers reduced their contributions during the 2001 recession, but they did not take the drastic step of stopping contributions.[18] Employees who do not participate are exhorted for leaving "money on the table." Pension experts and academics invariably write this off as a quirk of human nature, ignoring the obvious reality that when workers leave money on the table, they are leaving it on their employer's table. Employers know that if they automatically enroll workers into a 401(k) plan, participation leaps.[19] In 2003, *Plan Sponsor* magazine celebrated companies that achieved above-average participation rates in 401(k)-type plans. The effective techniques were easy to spot.[20] Employers achieving 99% to 100% participation used a surefire way of boosting participation—mandatory participation. These employers were primarily government agencies and not-for-profit firms. Yet one for-profit company, Sun Coke Company, did get 100% participation even though the company did not require employee contributions to its DC plan, which is a profit-sharing plan, not a 401(k). Although profit-sharing plans are called retirement plans because workers face penalties for withdrawing assets before age fifty-nine-and-a-half, employers serious about providing compensation do not offer only 401(k) plans.

Despite knowing ways to increase enrollment, only 14% of employers providing a 401(k) have adopted automatic enrollment—perhaps it works too well! What I mean to imply is that employers may not mind if workers opt out; firms save money when they do. Between 2002 and 2004, if all eligible workers had participated in their employers' 401(k) plans, employers would have had to contribute 26% more to their workforce plans than they did—that would have come to an annual total of $3.18 billion more contributions.[21] Simple? Yes.

My own studies back up much of the data (see Box 4.2: "Are 401(k) Plans Cheaper Than Defined Benefit Pension Plans?"). When a firm concentrates its pension dollars on 401(k) plans, the firm has lower pension expenses than a similar firm that spends more on DB plans.[22] Specifically, my research shows that when a firm increases the share of its pension spending on its DC plans by 10%, its pension spending per worker decreases by 3.5%. Between 1981 and 1996, the proportion of pension spending going to DC plans increased by 190%. This means that firms decreased their per-capita pension spending by 53%.[23]

Third, the non mandatory feature of 401(k) plans benefits the employer in another way. Precisely because 401(k) contributions are voluntary, employers can learn something about the workers who participate in the 401(k) and the ones who don't; say, the workers who plan ahead are more productive and are also savers. Social Security economist Kimberly Burham, drawing on the work of economist Richard Ippolito, argued that this connection between saving and productivity means that the employer's 401(k) match goes to the most productive workers.[24] This in turn means that the employer is paying a higher wage to the most productive worker, which makes sense economically. In these ways, 401(k) plans not only reduce pension costs but are also clearly efficient forms of compensation.

> **Bottom Line**   *Firms save money by providing 401(k) plans instead of defined benefit plans. No wonder pensions are eroding and no wonder firms have large incentives to persuade workers to favor DC plans over DB plans.*

Other Reasons Firms Like 401(k) Plans

Three other considerations make 401(k) and other defined contribution plans more attractive to an employer than defined benefit plans. A firm can contribute unlimited amounts of its stock instead of cash to the workers' 401(k) plans. And a firm can time its stock contributions when the stock is cheapest. A firm's administrative costs are lower for 401(k) plans than for defined benefit administrative costs. Third, a firm can stop contributing to its workers' 401(k) plans, but cannot discharge its financial responsibility to a defined benefit plan.

Employers can contribute their own stock to their employees' 401(k) plans because it usually costs less to do so than contributing cash. (Employers can also contribute stock to defined benefit plans within limitations and with approval from both the Pension Benefit Guaranty Corporation and the Treasury Department.)

Enron executives, who had more information on their firm's finances than was available to their workers, protected their own 401(k) balances by selling their stock before workers sold, or tried to sell, theirs. All of Enron's contributions to the 401(k) were in Enron stock—a neon read-out of the Enron's share price greeted employees in the company's lobby and elevators. Enron maintained a rather typical 401(k) plan for a company of its size. It offered

Are 401(k) Plans Cheaper Than Defined Benefit Pension Plans?

Economists who study why firms choose the kinds of pension plans they offer to employees sidestep directly examining firm behavior because extensive firm-level data are hard to come by. The quality and type of data available usually drive what questions are asked in economic research. What happens is that flawed research results from flawed data. It's not unlike this old joke: Late at night an agitated man realizes he has dropped his keys. He asks a passerby for help finding them. The passerby crosses the street to look on the ground under the light post. "No," the man says, "I lost the keys here on this sidewalk, not there." The passerby says, "But this is where the light is best to look for your lost keys." Most studies of the 401(k) phenomenon only describe the trends because that's where the lamppost light may be. There isn't much light from the lamppost to study firms' motivations for sponsoring 401(k) plans.

I analyzed a unique data set of firms that have sponsored pension plans since 1981. Using "time-series" analysis of over seven hundred firms over nineteen years enabled me to observe detailed changes in a firm's pension plans and workforce. This is the most comprehensive existing data on pension plans. I combined the data from the form firms use to report their pension finances to the Internal Revenue Service (IRS Form 5500) with data publicly traded firms report to the Securities and Exchange Commission on a data set called Compustat. The firms in my sample are larger than the average firm because small firms are less likely to sponsor pension plans. The firms in my sample are also different because they have survived for nineteen years.[25]

Analysis of the sample confirms what we know: Firms dramatically reduced their tendency to provide only DB plans, offering other types of plans, in the 1980s and 1990s. Focusing just on DB pension plans and DC pension plans, the share of firms that sponsored only DB plans dropped from 44% in 1981 to 11% in 1998, as firms added DC plans to the pensions offered workers.[26] In 1981, 42% of firms sponsored both types of plan. In 1998, however, the percentage of firms offering both types rose to 71%. At the same time, the share of firms that provided only DC plans changed little, increasing slightly from 14% to 17%. At first glance, this supports the claim that DC plans are complements of, and not substitutes for, DB plans. In other words, the predominant trend in this period was for these firms to offer both DB and DC plans by adding defined contribution plans. (Also note that, in this sample of large surviving firms, defined benefit plans are not dinosaurs—86% of these firms, surprisingly, had them in 1998.)

(continued)

(continued)

This data also confirm that there was a great upheaval in the kinds of pensions offered among the large firms in my study. Starting in 1981, more firms adopted 401(k) plans and, at the same time, DB plans became more regulated and more expensive to administer.[27] Not until now could we answer questions about what kinds of firms changed their pension policies and, just as important, which did not.

> **Bottom Line**   *Firms that had both defined benefit and defined contribution plans before 1981 maintained relatively high pension contributions throughout the 1980s and 1990s. But firms that adopted a defined contribution plan, and a 401(k) specifically, were able to lower their pension contributions.*

twenty investment options; its own stock was just one of those options. Yet its match of 50% of employee contributions—up to 6% of an employee's salary—was Enron stock, and only Enron stock, which employees were not allowed to sell until they turned fifty years of age. (This age restriction is common for "gifted" stock, although Enron employees were free to sell Enron stock they had purchased.) At the end of 2000, 62% of the value of employee 401(k) accounts was held in Enron stock. This was not unique. In 2002, Procter and Gamble's fund was 95% company stock; Abbott Laboratories fund was 90%; Pfizer's, 86%; and Coca-Cola's, 82%.

After the Enron collapse, the administration and some members (not enough members!) of the Senate proposed to: restrict the amount of company stock in a 401(k) plan to 20%; reduce the tax break that companies get for matching contributions with in-house stock; allow participants to sell company stock after three years; and permit companies to give financial advice to their 401(k) participants. Only the proposal to allow financial advice was passed in the Pension Protection Act. But no reforms limiting employer stock in 401(k) plans were ever passed (the Pension Protection Act allows workers to sell their stock after holding it for three years in their 401(k) plans). At companies where employee contributions are matched with employer stock, the average worker has 41% of her 401(k) account assets invested in the employer's stock. Remember: employer 401(k) matches are not required; the employer can function as an administrator of a deferred compensation scheme and even pass the administrative costs on to the employees. Thus, employers can act as administrators, set up a plan, and not contribute—but, because employees see their contributions netted from their paychecks, they tend to believe the employer is providing their retirement plan.

Administrative costs are a factor affecting the value of defined benefit pensions and defined contribution pensions. For employers, DB plans are more expensive to administer, while the administrative cost advantage of DC plans is growing over time. A 1998 U.S. Department of Labor report, showing that firms are shifting administrative costs of 401(k) plans directly to workers, tends to explain the attraction of these plans to employers, and therefore the basis for arguing that DC plans help firms offload pension expenses to employees.

An analysis of the administrative costs of over 17,400 pension plans in 1989 shows that the larger the plan in terms of participants and assets, the lower its administrative costs (because of economies of scale); and the higher the ratio of retirees to current participants in a plan (not yet retired), the higher its administrative costs (in this sense, it appears to be more expensive to cut a check than collect contributions). The data from that analysis in 1989 show that a shift from a DB plan to a 401(k) plan reduces administrative costs by 3%; and a shift from a DC plan to a DB plan increases administrative costs by 25%. In 1998, these differences were just as stark. From a firm's point of view, what is not to like about 401(k) plans?

Worker Demand for the 401(k) Plan

Perhaps workers now prefer defined contribution to defined benefit pensions because they expect to have shorter employment relationships with each employer. In addition, if workers are becoming more confident about managing their pension money, we expect more demand for DC pensions. However, there is little evidence for this reasonable demand-side explanation. People are holding their jobs for longer periods of time in the fastest-growing occupations, which are health care and finance. The job tenure for occupations in these fields is not shortening.

If workers doubt their employers' commitment to DB plans, then DC plans will be a better, but a second-best, choice. Workers' preferences for DC plans did not increase the popularity for and increase the number of defined contribution plans.

> **Bottom Line**   *Although, on balance, DB plans reduce the risks of secure retirement income relative to DC plants, there is what looks like a preference for DC plans. This preference is likely if workers exaggerate, and otherwise "overvalue," the risks associated with DB plans and undervalue the risks associated with DC plans. Workers may view their jobs as very insecure and not trust their employers. In addition, workers undervalue longevity risk and investment risk and may not appreciate inflation risk. Therefore, rationally speaking, if workers drive what kinds of pensions are offered and workers weigh risks in a certain way, the relevance of the calculated superiority of DB plans falls away.*

Good pension plans take on the best features of defined contribution and defined benefit plans. A species of pension plan offered in some unionized sectors—construction, coal mining, trucking, textiles, and food stores—is a cross between DC and DB plans. The plans are called multiemployer plans, and the amount of the pension accrued in a multiemployer pension plan is portable between the employers a worker is most likely to move between (employers that require the same skills). Each employer in the plan makes a defined payment for its share of the benefits accrued by a worker. The largest DC pension plan is Teachers Insurance Annuity Association and College Retirement Equities Fund, the plan for faculty at universities and related research institutions. It is considered an efficient and effective delivery system for pensions in the academic professions, and it is a multiemployer plan. (Other, and hybrid forms exist and these and others are discussed in chapter 10.)

Conclusion: Do-It-Yourself Pensions

It looks as if the 401(k) plan is here to stay. But that doesn't mean there are not problems with it; and we must first recognize those problems, and then begin to solve them. And it doesn't mean that taxpayers have to subsidize the 401(k) plans at the current level.

The largest problems with 401(k) plans are that employees, ordinary people with ordinary skills, manage the plans, and that employers and workers are not required to participate in the plan. In short, the problem is that they are self-directed and voluntary.

The people who successfully plan for their retirement with 401(k) plans have much higher incomes than most of the population. And most of the population has small 401(k) accounts or no other pension plan besides Social Security. Voluntarily accumulating enough money for retirement is difficult for all but the highest-income earners. There is no evidence that education in retirement planning among the lower-income earners will change that.

It is more than likely that retirement income in a lump sum will be spent rather than annuitized; an annuity is the only way to stretch wealth across a retirement lifetime. Particularly affected by inadequate retirement income are the elderly—most over the age of eighty are nonmarried women; one out of four elderly women is poor; as women get older, they get poorer.

Leakages in the system—fees, unlucky investments, cash-outs—diminish accumulations. Cash-outs are a key problem. Two-thirds of workers leaving jobs with 401(k) plans spend a significant portion of their accumulation (even though withdrawals before age fifty-nine-and-a-half are subject to an extra 10% tax in addition to regular income taxes). At any one time, 14% of participants have borrowed from their 401(k) plan, which—unless the borrowed amount is invested (most of the uses for borrowed 401(k) funds are for education, consumer durables, or home buying) and the investments earn more than the 401(k)—cause the 401(k) to lose value.

In their 2004 book, *Coming Up Short*, Boston College economists Munnell and Sundén present a comprehensive agenda for 401(k) plans to help restore some features of a defined benefit pension plan. These proposals would require that 401(k) plans automatically pay out an annuity that is indexed to inflation, and provide a benefit to a surviving spouse. The worker could always opt to take the benefit in a lump sum. In other words, they call for a joint and survivor inflation-indexed annuity as the default payout option. They want more education of the public about life expectancy and how important annuities are.

The Munell-Sundén critique of 401(k) plans is severe, but their proposals to fix them are weak. They do not suggest banning lump sum distributions at retirement, and there is little evidence that financial education changes the way people save or invest. These reforms are bolder than some but focus only on fixing the workers' shortcomings in dealing with their 401(k) plans and ignore how employers use 401(k)s to limit their contributions to the highest-paid employees and decrease their pension obligations and expense.

Employers have adopted 401(k) plans precisely because they are not pension plans; they are rather savings plans. Employers sponsor what they call a pension plan but are not required to contribute to it, and the financial accumulation, investment, and inflation risks are all borne by the employee.

Implementing the Munnell-Sundén proposals—making it more difficult for people to take their 401(k)-type plan in a lump sum and to borrow from the accumulations—would make a savings plan less attractive to workers and participation may start falling. Reforms of 401(k) plans won't mean much to most workers because a high proportion do not have any type of pension, not defined benefit plans nor defined contribution plans. Although reforms can reduce the inefficiency, inadequacy, and inequality in the voluntary 401(k) pension world, reducing flaws is a meager goal. Pension reform can aim higher—a program is laid out in chapter 10. But no pension reform will work if Social Security is not cared for.

Chapter 5

The Future of Social Security

Who should pay for the old? How should we pay for the old? Should the old work to help pay for themselves?

These questions are not new for governments, but they persist and are becoming increasingly part of public discussion. Just one indication of the growing concern is the media's interest. I used the newspaper search engine LexisNexis to count the number of times the phrase "old-age crisis" appeared in the headline or lead paragraph of major papers. In the five years between 1990 and 1995 it appeared 73 times, between 2000 and 2005, 170 times. Modern industrialized societies expect governments to address these questions, determine the answers, and decide how best to implement those answers.

This chapter unpacks the policy debate over what to do about Social Security's finances and benefits, and describes how Social Security works now and how it came to be the most secure and predictable source of retirement income for American workers. Much of this chapter covers the debate about Social Security's affordability—although antagonists agree on most of the numbers, they draw very different conclusions from them. The proposal to transform Social Security into a system of personal savings accounts—a person's Social Security taxes would go into an account owned exclusively by the individual—is described, followed by an explanation of why most experts believe personal savings accounts will make things worse for Social Security. The political history of the Social Security program helps predict what can be done and what will probably be done to reform it.

How Does Social Security Work?

Most all workers pay a tax—commonly recognized on payroll stubs as FICA, which stands for Federal Insurance Contributions Act of 1939. FICA authorized payroll deductions to fund Social Security, which is a system that provides retirement benefits, survivors' benefits, disability benefits, and health insurance to eligible people. The Social Security system is financed mainly by taxes on the salaries and wages of workers, to a lessen extent by taxes on the income from Social Security to retirees receiving higher than average incomes, and to an even lesser extent by interest received on the Social Security trust fund. The breadth of coverage and participation in the Social Security system in the United States is remarkable, considering that the pension systems in many other nations have lower participation rates and there is widespread evasion of government pension taxes.

A worker's Social Security benefit is based on calculations using the data in her Social Security records. The mechanics of the calculations show how the system favors lower-income workers while making sure that the more years someone works and the more income the employee earns, the higher will be that person's Social Security benefits. Social Security benefits are earned benefits; they are not charity nor government assistance.

The first step in the calculation establishes what is called the "average indexed monthly earnings," which has a friendly acronym—AIME. This step considers the thirty-five years in which earnings are the highest. For workers having fewer than thirty-five earnings years, all years are considered in the calculation and the nonworking years are entered as $0. Therefore, if you work fewer than thirty-five years you will have a lower AIME and a lower Social Security benefit.[1] I concentrate here on how the formula is applied to provide a progressive benefit and more benefits to higher-income individuals.

The basic Social Security benefit is calculated by first establishing a person's "average indexed monthly earnings," and then applying a formula on the AIME to get the basic benefit amount. The formula used to calculate the basic benefit (called the primary insurance amount) is progressive because

- the first few hundred dollars of monthly earnings is weighted 90%, which is

- nearly three times more than that of the second tier of earnings which is weighted 32%,

- and the third (and final) tier is weighted by 15%, slightly less that half the weighting of the second tier monthly of earnings.

Can you see a pattern in the weighting and why it is progressive?

The earnings amounts defining each of the tier levels are called "bend points"; the bend points change annually according to average wage increases across the economy. As an example, let's say that a person retires at the normal retirement age, which in 2007 was sixty-five years and ten months. The first bend point was $680 and the second was $3,689 (these specific dollar bend points change every year, as already indicated, and as will be shown in another example to follow). The amount of income between the first and second bend points is weighted by 32%, and everything after the second bend point is weighted by only 15%. If the person in our example has a $3,689 AIME, then the benefit is calculated by

- adding the first-tier replacement income, which is 90% of $612, or 0.90 × $612 = $550.80, to

- the second-tier replacement income, which is 32% of the second tier of income, or 0.32 × ($3,689 − $612) = 0.32 × $3070 = $984.64, which is added to

- the third-tier replacement income, or 15% of the third-tier income, or 0.15 × ($3,855 − $3,689) = 0.15 × $166 = $24.90;

- adding up the replacement income at each tier, $550.80 + $984.64 + $24. 90 = $1,560.34, which is the replacement income for $3,689.00 AIME.

- The replacement rate in this example is 42.3% = (1,560.34 ÷ 3,689) × 100.

The amount of retirement benefit paid depends on the age at which a person elects to receive benefits. Social Security reduces benefits taken before the normal (or full) retirement age and increases benefits taken after the normal retirement age.

To help make clear how a monthly benefit is calculated using an AIME, here is another example using the 2005 bend points instead of the 2007 bend points and showing how a high earner is treated.[2]

Say that a worker's average indexed monthly earnings is $8,500.

- The first component of her monthly benefit is based on 90% of the first $627 of her AIME, which comes to 0.90 × 627 = $564.30; the Social Security Administration thinks of that $564.30 monthly benefit as replacing the first $627 of her average indexed monthly earnings.

- The second component of her monthly benefit is based on 32% of the part of her AIME between $628 and $3,779, which comes to $0.32 \times (\$3,779 - \$628) = \$1,008.32$; in this step, that $1,008.32 monthly Social Security benefit replaces $3,151 of her average indexed monthly earnings from $628 up to $3,779.

- The third and final component of her monthly benefit is based on 15% of the part of her AIME between $3,880 and $7,500 (that's the cap), which comes to $0.15 \times (\$7,500 - \$3,880) = \$543.00$.

- By now you get the idea that that amount is the monthly Social Security benefit that replaces her average indexed monthly earnings from $3,880 up to the cap, $7,500.

- The part of her AIME exceeding the $7,500 cap gets zero consideration in calculating her monthly Social Security benefit according to the 2005 formula; in other words, the Social Security Administration provides $0 to replace any part of her average indexed monthly earnings exceeding $7,500.

So, this applicant with a Social Security earnings record of over forty years and an average indexed monthly earnings, AIME, of $8,000 would receive a monthly check from the Social Security Administration of $(\$564.30 + \$1,008.32 + \$543.00) = \$2,145,62$, which is higher than that of the average earner, but the replacement rate is lower at $25\% = (\$2,145/\$8,500 \times 100)$.

Note that the earnings used in the calculation are indexed according to the increase in wages. As long as wages increase faster than prices, Social Security benefits will have higher buying power for subsequent retirees. This means that each generation of retirees will have more income to consume than the immediately preceding generation, or cohort (as it is commonly called) of workers. If wage increases reflect ongoing productivity improvements, then a retiree's pension benefit reflects the productivity of his or her generation. After retirement, or the onset of the collection of benefits, the benefits are adjusted according to price changes, not the productivity of the current working generation. Every retiree has living standards reflecting the achievements of her or his generation. That the Social Security initial benefit is indexed to wages, and subsequent benefits are indexed to prices, both reflect a specific philosophical decision about the balance between retirees' standard of living and the standard of living of the workers who support them.

The second implication is political. In robust economies, each generation of workers increases its productivity and achieves a material standard of living that is higher than the standard of living of the preceding generation. If real wages lag behind productivity increases, or the economy enters a recession, the willingness of workers to support nonworkers may wane. Therefore, wage-earners and pensioners have aligned interests: to keep the economy growing so that real wages increase.

The Social Security system, structured as just described, is a pension system following the principle that replacement rates—the proportion of preretirement earnings that are replaced by the pension system—are fixed and the tax rates are variable. The replacement rates for higher-income workers are about 20% or less of their respective preretirement incomes; life-long, low-income workers—those with incomes near the lowest bend point—receive about a 90% replacement rate.

Even the massive reform in 1983 did not disrupt the idea of holding replacement rates constant (although the normal retirement age was raised). In 1982, in response to an immediate Social Security system financial shortfall, President Reagan formed a bipartisan commission, the so-called Greenspan Commission,[3] which recommended the usual fixes to increase Social Security revenue—a gradual payroll tax increase[4] and raising earnings caps subject to Social Security taxes. Congress took the plunge and decided the consequences of Social Security's insolvency must be shared; it cut benefits for future retirees by raising the normal retirement age to sixty-seven by 2020. The cuts are oddly shared, because the same workers who are paying the higher tax are also the future retirees with the benefit cuts. (Note that Congress did not raise above sixty-two years the age at which reduced benefits can be claimed.)

DATA TO DIGEST   *As a result, workers born after 1946 will not replace as much preretirement income as did the generation before 1946. Social Security benefits are scheduled to decrease by 0.05% for those retiring in 2018, and by 45% for new retirees in 2075.[5]*

Issues in Social Security Financing

TV ad in the year 2005.
Image: Close-up.

> Your grandmother (or someone just like her), with a hairnet, is a
> server in a fast-food restaurant.
> Zoom out to her hands.
> A voice-over intones, "Those hands brought you the working
> lunch, the working vacation, and now George Bush's plans for Social
> Security will bring you the working retirement."

A liberal Internet political action group, MoveOn.org, launched this political advertisement during the week of the 2005 State of the Union Address. When he got to reporting the status of the Social Security system, President Bush declared that it was "headed toward bankruptcy" and that personal savings accounts are "a better deal."[6]

If the MoveOn.org ad was at all effective in changing the political climate against the president, it was because many Americans—the experts, too—suspected that transforming Social Security into a system of personal savings accounts would not make it more solvent. One week after that State of the Union Address, Federal Reserve Chairman Alan Greenspan admitted to Congress that diverting Social Security revenue to personal savings accounts would more than double the system's seventy-five-year financial shortfall. He added that he supports massive government borrowing to finance a transition to personal savings accounts only if Social Security benefits are cut. The MoveOn.org TV ad suggested this motive and its consequences—lower Social Security benefits will force seniors to work in low-wage jobs. Social Security's projected insolvency, and the inference that benefits are excessive, fueled the Republican argument for transforming Social Security into "personal savings accounts" (more on this to follow).

Social Security advocates in the 1930s had an advantage that is not enjoyed by today's proponents. The Social Security program back then cost very little. FICA was only 1% of covered payroll and was shared equally, 0.5% by employers and 0.5% by employees. As more and more workers were included in the Social Security system, their participation resulted in increasing funds going into the program. The growing accumulation of funds made possible two things: (1) more and more retiring workers who became eligible but never contributed into the program began to collect benefits; and (2) retirees living longer than prior retirees received more benefits than those who preceded them. Congress, with technical advice from the Social Security actuaries, regularly increased every worker's and every employer's FICA contributions not only to pay for the expanded benefits they legislated—Congress expanded benefits in many ways, including giving benefits to dependents and survivors of covered workers, increasing the bend points, liberalizing the definition of retirement, expanding the earnings considered in the AIME, giving credits for military service—but also to help alleviate Social Security's persistent shortage of funds caused by people living longer and longer.

Every time Congress passes a tax increase, the increase is supposed to make the system solvent for seventy-five years. The Social Security system has been insolvent for a total of twenty-two years since 1935. Only after it becomes insolvent does Congress hike payroll taxes. The history of Social Security funding makes clear that deficits are routine and expected. Nevertheless, Congress must "manually" raise FICA taxes because the taxes are not indexed to benefits, nor to costs, nor to any measure of solvency. In 2006, the seventy-five-year shortfall was 2.02%, which means that if the FICA had been raised by 2.02% of payroll in 2007, there would have been no projected insolvency for the next seventy-five years.

The U.S. Social Security system was originally designed to be a national pay-as-you-go pension system. However, because of recurring insolvency or the persistent brink of insolvency, Social Security really is an "adjust-as-you-go" system. Seventy years after the inception of Social Security, President Bush put the system's solvency front and center in a 2005 Jacksonville speech when he launched his personal savings accounts campaign by predicting the system's financial collapse. He said, "If you're in your twenties and by the time you retire, if nothing is done about Social Security, the system will be busted. In other words, there won't be anything for you."

Constructing Solvency

In 2007, Social Security was considered insolvent, meaning that it will not be able to pay all of the projected benefits with its projected revenue in about forty years. In fact, it is projected to be able to afford only 75% of benefits after the year 2041. However, insolvency is not equivalent to a financial crisis.

Insolvency is a long-term imbalance between expected revenues and expected liabilities.

Bankruptcy is a financial crisis.

"Flat broke" is an immediate inability to pay.

To assess Social Security's solvency, we need to examine it from six perspectives:

- the uncertain assumptions backing the predications for solvency, as well as the pessimism of the Social Security actuaries, who chose conservative assumptions about the future growth of the economy;

- the political gains obtained by predicting the system will not be solvent for seventy-five years;

- the magnitude of the tax hike needed for seventy-five-year solvency;

- the absolute size of the shortfall within a seventy-five-year time frame;

- the absolute size of a shortfall relative to the size of gross domestic product (GDP) and of other key national deficits; and

- the dependence of the projected shortfall on the particular seventy-five-year time period one is looking at.

Contested Assumptions: Why Insolvency?

In 2007, the system is expected to be solvent for thirty years and face a shortfall afterward. These expectations are based on the Social Security Administration's "intermediate set of assumptions" about economic and demographic changes to come during the next seventy-five years. As mentioned earlier, under these assumptions, if nothing else changes, then by the year 2041 the system will pay about 75% of benefits to recipients instead of the 100% they had been receiving or had expected to receive.

The first point to reflect on is why the 1983 reforms were said to fix the system for seventy-five years (the predicted year for trust fund depletion then was 2058 compared to the 2005 estimate of 2017 or the 2007 estimate of 2018). In 1993, the Social Security Administration actuaries announced that their projections were wrong. This admission was not a surprise, but the fact that the 1983 actuaries had been too optimistic was. The actuaries usually predict bleaker outcomes than what actually occurs.

Actuaries choose assumptions to ensure that their solvency predictions err on the side of having too much money, rather than too little. They would rather have a false negative than a false positive. In other words, because they want to be right in a certain way, they aim to be wrong in a particular way. They want to be nearly 100% right that the fund will have enough to pay benefits for at least five to ten years, so they plan it so that they have too much money five to ten years in the future. To appreciate how they do that, first consider how Social Security actuaries' assumptions are similar to more immediately recognizable experiences, where tilting toward what may not look so positive can appear positive.

A serious example comes from medicine. No medical test can be accurate, so researchers design tests based on assumptions that likely errors will occur. Tests for cancer and HIV err on the side of false positives: predicting there is cancer or HIV when there is not rather than erring on the other side by indicating there is no cancer or HIV when there is. In other words, it is safer for a test to be wrong in indicating that a person has cancer or HIV, so that he will seek a retest, than for a test to be wrong when there really is cancer or HIV. Similarly, Social Security actuaries choose to err by falsely predicting a shortfall rather than being wrong by predicting no shortfall and thereby lulling Congress into thinking that the system is in surplus.

A professional actuary, David Langer, reveals this professional practice among actuaries—making the downside risk zero—with a simple exercise. He compares the Office of the Actuary of the Social Security Administration's predictions with the actual levels of economic growth and concludes that the Social Security Administration's rosy or low-cost scenarios line up best with actual events. In table 5.1, I reproduce Langer's startling findings. The discrepancy between assumption and reality is displayed in each box. A negative number means that the system turned out to be in better financial shape than the actuaries predicted. Out of twenty sets of Social Security Administration's prediction versus reality, the numbers are negative in eighteen of them! The three scenarios—low cost, intermediate cost, and high cost—refer to a set of assumptions that predict conditions for economic growth as it affects Social Security revenues. High wages and low inflation rates are good for the system and are assumed in the low-cost scenario. The high-cost assumptions are about conditions that bode poorly for the system, for example, inflation (and therefore indexed Social Security benefits) increasing at the same pace or more quickly than wages, and low economic growth (which inhibits employment and payroll size).

Look at row 1, column 1, which displays the difference between the Social Security Administration's assumption about economic growth under the rosy scenario and what turned out to be the actual growth. The Social Security Administration predicted that GDP growth would be 5% higher than it was between 1992 and 1994. Fine, rosy was quite rosy. Nevertheless, under the

Table 5.1
The Enduring Pessimism of the Social Security Actuary
Differences between Social Security's assumptions about GDP growth
and the actual GDP growth in percentage points

Years	Low Cost Scenario	Intermediate Cost Scenario	High Cost Scenario
1992–94	5	−20	−46
1995–97	−8	−18	−28
1998–2001	−1	−1	−3
1992–2002	0	−11	−24

Source: Langer 2004.

intermediate assumption—the one that policy recommendations are based on—in the second column and under the high-cost scenario in the last column, economic growth was 20% and 46% higher than the Social Security Administration predicted between 1992 and 1994.

Look at the last row, which reports the record of the Social Security Administration's predictive prowess for the years 1992 to 2002. The SSA was "dead-on right" only under the rosy scenario; the SSA predicted 11% and 24% less growth than there actually was under the intermediate and pessimistic scenarios. Langer concludes that the rosy set of assumptions (low-cost scenario) is really the appropriate intermediate case and the pessimistic scenario is off the charts and should be taken off the table. He calls for the actuaries to develop a new set of optimistic, low-cost assumptions, and use the rosy scenario as the intermediate scenario and the intermediate as the pessimistic scenario.[7]

With all that generally in mind, now consider that the Congressional Budget Office, which also makes Social Security projections (although not required by law to do so), assumes higher economic growth and predicts that 100% of benefits will be paid until 2052. Alas, what's a policymaker to do?! What projections should they use?

Not only does tweaking assumptions yield an enormous number of projections[8] (the more the tweaking, the greater the number of projections), but many argue that forecasts far off into the future are simply not meaningful, even though the assumptions when made seem to be reasonable. Any small change in the assumptions or a change in their relationship—for example, in fertility and women's labor force participation—can yield widely different forecasts in the solvency of Social Security. Federal Reserve economists will not forecast past two quarters—they limit their forecasts to six months into the future. The Social Security actuaries themselves warn that predictions past twenty-five years are likely not to be accurate. To get a sense of what it would be like to make predictions for the United States far into the future, imagine you were predicting seventy-five years into the future for President Ulysses S. Grant. You would have had to predict World Wars I and II and the world-wide depression.

Because relying on projections forty years hence, and not seventy-five years, is more defensible and reasonable, and under two of the three scenarios projected by the Social Security Administration the system is solvent for forty years, the policy option of doing nothing about Social Security is defensible and reasonable. Not only is it reasonable because whatever action were taken based on projections would likely miss its mark, it is also reasonable because such important adjustments rightly belong to the voters during those future years. In fact, Congress actually follows this sensible political action, by treating Social Security as adjust-as-you-go. When the projected insolvency gets close, much closer than forty years, Congress acts. Congress also knows it will have to act because longevity is always increasing and FICA is not indexed to longevity. Congress has raised taxes and expanded benefits twenty-one times since 1935. The twenty-second time an insolvency was predicted, in 1983, payroll taxes were raised and future benefits were cut (the normal retirement age was gradually increased to age sixty-seven for those retiring in 2027).

Political Gains from a Perceived Social Security Crisis

Another perspective on solvency that we need to consider is the political motivation for declaring the system insolvent. Radically reforming a system is easier politically if the public perceives that the program is not working, but wants it to work. Though every Social Security expert agrees that Social Security is not "flat broke," nor is that a reasonable forecast, President Bush may have accomplished one of his goals. Polls showed that support for his plan to divert FICA revenue into a personal account slid each week during his national tour promoting it. But the same polls[9] revealed that confidence in Social Security was also sliding, which makes it possible for future cuts in Social Security to be politically acceptable. Insolvency predictions are not politically neutral.

Why Did the Greenspan Commission Get It Wrong?

Here's what caused the actuaries to be wrong about their projections made in 1983. To understand it, you first need to consider that a large part of any projected seventy-five-year deficit in 2005 is only a seventy-four-year forecast in the next year, which is the year after the seventy-five-year forecast was made. The seventy-sixth year causes a forecasted deficit because of increased longevity— every year, people can be expected to live, and are living, longer. For example, 59% of the 1.91 percentage, or $(0.59 \times 1.91\%) = 1.12\%$ of the increase in payroll taxes in 1994 projected to be needed to restore the seventy-five-year financial balance, was due to increased longevity.

In addition to some technical changes, the rest of the disparity between the 1983 forecasts and actual events was caused by a rare bit of optimism from the Social Security Administration's actuaries. The payroll tax rate set in 1983 was based on the actuaries' predictions that the same distribution of wage increases would continue; they never considered that there would be a wider earnings gap, causing the earnings cap to cover less and less payroll. If the earnings gap had not increased in the 1980s and 1990s, about 50% of the deficit would not exist. Note that the 1983 fix's failure had nothing to do with the changing ratios of workers to retirees. That was the easiest forecast to make. Rather, the 1983 fix did not work because, starting in the 1990s, more conservative assumptions were used for wage growth, inflation, and disability claims.

A key change was the forecast for the growth in the earnings base subject to Social Security tax. The actuaries did not foresee the growing gap in earnings inequality, nor that wages would not keep up with productivity.

> **Bottom Line**   *This is worth reiterating: Social Security works, and is funded best, when wages grow faster than prices, and the wage growth for those in the bottom 90% is as high as or higher than wage growth at the top.*

UFOs and Social Security

A survey in 1994 by the Third Millennium, a libertarian advocacy group, revealed that more young people believed in UFOs, Unidentified Flying Objects, than believed that Social Security would be there for them when they retire. In a real way, the results of that survey began the recent campaign to weaken support for Social Security. Although books on basic personal finance, and many parents as well, advise young people to plan as though Social Security will not be there when they might expect it, the advice does not reflect a sober look at Social Security's political and financial future.

Conservatives' warnings to young workers that Social Security will not be solvent when they retire appeals to the worst suspicions about government. On April 5, 2005, President Bush posed for a photo beside a file cabinet that holds the $1.7 trillion in Treasury bonds that constitute the Social Security Trust Fund and commented that those securities "were not real assets." Later in a speech he said, "There is no trust fund, just IOUs."[10]

Northwestern political scientist Fay Lomax and University of Minnesota's Larry Jacobs argue that statements by "political elites," even statements that are not supported by evidence, change people's minds about issues, especially highly visible issues like Social Security. Lomax and Jacobs cite the favorite flawed statement of promoters of privatization—that more young people think they will see a UFO than think they will get Social Security. Reports issued after the 1994 UFO survey, including one to the President's Commission on Social Security in 2001, exposed that the Third Millennium group's survey was manipulated. The 1998 Employee Benefit Research Institute (EBRI) report to President Bush's own Commission of Social Security Reform documented the misuse and falseness of the statement. Lawrence Jacobs writes: "A 1997 survey by EBRI offered respondents the direct choice that Third Millennium falsely claimed to have posed." EBRI asked, Which do you have greater confidence in: receiving Social Security benefits after retirement or that alien life exists in outer space? Repudiating the claims of Third Millennium, EBRI found that Americans overwhelmingly sided with Social Security over UFOs by 71% to 26%. (Even among Generation Xers [aged thirty-three years or younger], the margin remained a stunning 63% to 33%.) Although these polls may be silly, they clearly indicate the imprecision in any comparison about younger people's confidence in alien life and Social Security and thus cast doubt on the accuracy of Third Millennium's report.[11]

Yet, from February to April of 2005, President Bush repeated the manipulated survey results more than thirteen times. There is nothing new about young people having less confidence in Social Security than older workers. In 1995, 83% of workers about to retire compared to 44% of workers in their twenties and mid-thirties believed they would receive Social Security benefits when they retired. Those proportions have not changed much since 1970.[12]

Crises Are Relative

If Social Security was in crisis in 2007, there are no adjectives alarmist enough to describe what its condition was back in 1982, when the forecast was that it would not be able to pay any benefits at all within two years! But Social Security was able to pay all benefits due, not only within the next two years, but also during all the years since then. A third way to judge the projected shortfall is by its absolute magnitude. Social Security proponents would maintain that a shortfall that can be remedied by a small move, by a tweak, is not a crisis. For example, taxing incomes 2% more would make projected Social Security revenue cover liabilities for the next seventy-five years. This tax increase would be unpopular but would have little economic effect on job creation or consumption behavior, among other economic activities.

> DATA TO DIGEST   *The 2007 report by the trustees of the Social Security fund predicted that the taxable payroll for FICA would be 1.95 percentage points below what would be needed to assure solvency for seventy-five years. That prediction meant that if the FICA tax rate of 12.4% (that was the rate then and still is now) was increased to 14.5% (yielding over 15% more funds), then it would be possible to forecast that the Social Security system would be solvent for the next seventy-five years. (Raising the FICA tax rate is not unreasonable since it has not changed in fourteen years. Moreover, during the fourteen-year period before it was last changed in 1990, FICA was increased six times, from 7% in 1977 to 12.4% in 1990.) Presidents Carter, Reagan, and Bush senior oversaw FICA tax rate increases. Since FICA has been raised twenty-two times in the sixty-seven years since Social Security was established, increasing the FICA tax on pay is a routine part of maintaining the system. It can be argued that raising the FICA tax now is politically difficult because there is a surplus of more than $1.5 trillion in the Social Security Trust Fund, and the trust fund is projected to grow in absolute value until 2017, when the size of the trust fund will be overtaken by the liabilities in Social Security.*

A fourth way to judge the shortfall of the Social Security system in the United States is to look at similar social programs in other nations. Compared to other nations, it looks as if we can easily afford social pensions. Here's why: Americans seem to tolerate a great deal of poverty among the elderly, and because we accept poverty among the elderly, our social programs are less expensive than in nations that do not allow their elderly to live in poverty. In the United States, 12% of the elderly were poor in the mid-1990s. At the same time, in Italy, Germany, France, and Canada, only about 3% to 5% of the elderly were poor. Also, because workers are young and reluctant to support social programs to keep the elderly out of poverty, the United States' projected Social Security expenditures measured as a share of GDP are low relative to the same kind of projected measures in other nations.

DATA TO DIGEST   *In 2050, the United States will spend 7% of its GDP on Social Security; only the United Kingdom predicts less at 4%. Italy is projected to spend 20% of its GDP on its public pensions, Canada 8.7%, and France and Germany are in the 14% to 18% range.[13]*

A fifth point of reflection in assessing the amount of unfunded liabilities in Social Security is to compare it to other debts. According to the Social Security Trustees' intermediate assumptions, the seventy-five-year Social Security debt is equivalent to 0.68% of GDP, yet the Congressional Budget Office predicts that the seventy-five-year Social Security liability constitutes only 0.35% of GDP. Meanwhile, the Medicare improvements for prescription drug benefits will cost 1.8% of GDP and the 2001 income tax cuts, made permanent in 2005, represent 1.95% of GDP.[14]

Infinity Is Forever

In 2003, the Social Security Trustees inserted into their computations a factor that had never before been part of their report on the system's financial future. That factor is an "infinite time horizon," which displaced what until then was the standard time horizon, seventy-five years. The infinite time horizon made the Social Security liability larger. The United States is only one of two nations (Canada is the other) that uses a seventy-five-year time horizon for its social insurance projections (the typical horizon in other countries is between thirty and fifty years). The United States is the only nation to make an official projection over infinity, and doing so raised the Social Security projected shortfall in 2003 from 1.92% of payroll, $3.5 trillion, and 0.68% of GDP, to a deficit of 3.80% of payroll, $10.5 trillion, and 2.3% of GDP.[15]

The Personal Savings Account Plan

That which was called a "rose" in the 1990s, by any other name today is still a rose. Moreover, that which was called "privatization"[16] in the 1990s, by any other name is privatization today.

The Cato Institute initially used the word "privatization" to describe the type of plan President Bush proposed, but does so no longer after focus group research showed that people negatively viewed the concept it conveyed. The president's plan to transform Social Security was thus called "personal savings accounts." Since that focus group, Republicans favor the phrase "personal savings accounts" and accuse Democrats of using the word "privatization" as a scare tactic.[17] And, of course, Democrats use it all the time, as do the media and the general public. Again, I judged the public discussion about Social Security by using LexisNexis searches, and found that "privatization" combined with "Social Security" turned up in over 1,000 articles between December 2004 and June 30, 2007. Only 179 articles in major newspapers contained "personal savings accounts" and "Social Security."

President Bush never presented a formal plan, so most analysts used one in the 2001 report of the President's Commission on Social Security. This proposal, called Model 2, allows workers to divert 4% of the total 6.2%, or nearly two-thirds, of the FICA tax on taxable earnings to establish a personal account. There will still be $(6.2\% - 4.0\%) = 2.2\%$ remaining of the worker's FICA tax that goes into his Social Security account. Once the 4% contribution is initially diverted to a personal account, the worker who participates in a personal account gives up rights to collect the ordinarily prescribed Social Security benefit payment, based on what that 4% would have entitled him to. Because the diversion is voluntary, the obvious question for a worker trying to make a decision is whether the 4% of pay in a personal savings account will end up being more valuable than the benefits provided by the 4% put into the traditional Social Security account. The determination of which is more valuable depends on (a) the accrued benefits using the risk-free rate of return on the diverted taxes under personal savings accounts, and (b) what the traditional benefit would have been under Social Security with no diverted taxes. How the system under personal savings accounts will calculate the prospective benefit accruing on the diverted taxes is crucial to determining whether the benefit is greater than, equal to, or less than, what the benefits would have been under traditional Social Security. Nevertheless, keep in mind that once an individual chooses to divert that part of the FICA tax to participate in a personal savings account plan, her Social Security benefits will be reduced by an amount presumed to be replaced by the personal savings account.

A rate of return (after fees and risk are accounted for) must be estimated to determine what the diverted taxes in a personal account would earn. President Bush's staff members admitted they were "costing the proposal out" assuming a 3% real, net return. Yet proponents and detractors both concluded that a 3% return was higher than could really be expected, given past performance on individual accounts. Most people would have a greater than 50% chance of doing worse with a personal account savings plan than if they kept the traditional benefit.[18] The higher the assumed rate of return on diverted taxes, the lower the likelihood that the personal savings accounts plan will be better. In other words, when the projections assume that the accounts will earn higher rates of return, the projected costs of the reform plan are lower; when the assumed rates are lower the reform is more expensive. The personal savings account plan does not provide independence from government, does not assure earning a higher rate of return, and does not escape from a flagging Social Security system. In short, it does not make a worker's retirement pension income any more secure.

Even if the assumed 3% return is considered too high and is changed to a lower return, there nevertheless remains a basic contradiction between how well the president says the economy will do when he finally predicts both the cost of personal savings accounts and the expense of the Social Security system. For the value of the personal savings accounts to be higher than traditional benefits, economic growth and productivity would have to be robust. If economic predictions yield a rosy scenario for equities and rates of return on the personal savings accounts, well then they also yield a rosy scenario for traditional Social Security. The rosy scenario is comparable to the low-cost set of assumptions for Social Security, which predicts no shortfall in Social Security.

By mid-2007, the personal savings account plan was headed nowhere, either in Congress or in the minds of the broader public. But it remains a key part of a Republican agenda.[19]

Progressive Price Indexation

A plan to transform Social Security into personal savings accounts would surely fail if the private plan did not allow people to voluntarily opt out of the traditional Social Security plan. In mid-2005, a "progressive price-indexation" plan was revived by the proponents of a smaller Social Security system through Robert Pozen, President of Boston-based Massachusetts Financial Services (MFS), a large mutual fund company, as an alternative to the rapidly increasing unpopularity of the personal savings account proposal. Before describing a progressive price-indexation plan, remember that one of three ways to eliminate the Social Security projected shortfall is to cut benefits (the others are to raise revenue by raising taxes or to raise the rate of

---

Box 5.2

Advance Funding Retirement: No Seed Corn

Saving to prepay for a future expense works for individuals, but is trickier for a whole society. A nation cannot set aside "real assets" to prepay a future liability. Individuals can buy claims to future income with bonds or other IOUs invested now with their savings, but it does not work that way for a government. The taxes paid now for retirement benefits later oblige the government to pay those benefits in the future. They are claims inherent in those taxes. The Social Security system buys U.S. Treasury bonds with Social Security taxes; it does not spend now to pay benefits according to the provisions of the Social Security program. When those benefits are due, the U.S. Treasury bonds held by the Social Security system will come due and the taxpayers will need to honor them. This is a way for the government to keep track of where future tax dollars are supposed to go. Just as anyone who buys corporate bonds today obliges that corporation to pay benefits in the future, the only way those bonds can be redeemed is if the corporation is alive and well in the future. Contributions to Social Security provide the funds for retirement in the same way as buying corporate bonds would: the security and quality of the future claim on the assets of an entity depend on the future financial health of that entity when obligated to pay. The Social Security system now invests in Treasury bonds, so the government spends the money as the voters indicate in elections—to pay for bombs, freeways, and other things voters want. In a privatized social retirement system, the tax revenue buys corporate bonds, and the private sector spends the money on things the private sector wants. Which is preferred is partly subjective, hinging on feelings about private spending and public spending, and partly objective, hinging on such concerns as transaction costs and risk and return. In neither the Social Security system nor the personal savings accounts system are "physical assets" saved—seed corn is not piled in a silo waiting to be planted in one's golden years. In both the Social Security Trust Fund and personal savings accounts, the assets are financial claims to future income.

return on the Social Security trust fund). One way to cut benefits is to do so gradually, and progressive indexing would do just that. Under progressive price indexing, 30% of workers with the lowest incomes are isolated from the remaining workers and would have their benefits calculated as they are now. The method is quite complicated—the Boston College Center for Retirement Research, written by Alicia Munnell and Maurico Soto, provides a very good (and short) 2005 report on how progressive price indexation works—but the result is that over time the weights for middle-class and higher earners would fall so that most everyone would receive the same benefit regardless of how much they paid into the system. By 2075, the benefit for the average earner would be lower than it would be under the current formula by almost 30%. (This would solve most of the Social Security financial shortfall.)

Social Security beneficiaries earning more than the currently established earnings cap, which was $97,500 in 2007, receive only a small percentage—about 10%—of their preretirement earnings from Social Security. Under progressive price indexation, Social Security would be transformed from an earnings-based insurance system—where benefits to retirees are based on their working lifetime earnings—to an income replacement program for the elderly poor, providing little or nothing for those who earned average and high incomes during their lifetimes. The average- and higher-earning workers would need to resort to personal savings accounts to retire.

If the same principle were applied to Medicare, Medicare benefits would be prorated according to income. For example, poor retirees would have their medical expenses fully paid; retirees who had higher incomes would pay higher deductibles and co-pays.

Motives for and Likely Effects of Personal Savings Accounts

There are eight possible reasons for the resistance to personal savings accounts:

1. suspicion of the motives of the proponents of a privately run Social Security system;

2. doubt whether people could actually manage their own personal savings account;

3. doubt whether low-income earners could realistically have inheritances

left over from their personal savings accounts after using it for
retirement;

4. concern that personal savings account benefits might not do as well
compared to the benefits of the Social Security system;

5. the effect of personal savings accounts on inequality between people
with different incomes and wealth;

6. the benefit to financial service companies at the expense of those
leaving Social Security;

7. the effect on employer pension plans; and

8. the high costs of transition from Social Security.

Motives. The MoveOn.org ad implying that the Republican Social Security reform aimed to increase work effort among the elderly, coupled with Federal Reserve Chief Alan Greenspan's admission that Social Security benefits needed to be cut, confused the public about the goals of personal savings accounts. Harvard economist Jeffrey Lieberman[20] argues that some motives for personal savings accounts were ideological, such as diminishing government's role in providing income security and redistributing income. The personal savings account plan eliminates the redistributive and insurance aspects of the Social Security system. However, in revised versions of the personal savings account plan, President Bush said he would add an explicit welfare component requiring individuals to buy an annuity which, combined with a basic Social Security benefit and a subsidy, would reach the official poverty line. Yet the capacity to prevent old-age poverty already exists in the current Social Security system; increasing Social Security's survivor's benefits and Supplementary Security Income (SSI) could be effective antipoverty devices.

Some of the most popular features of the personal savings account plan were not based on ideology. People who worried about the future of Social Security embraced personal savings accounts as a second-best option to a secure retirement income. Many economists and business groups considered the idea of diverting payroll taxes to buy corporate equities as a good thing because the diversion would increase the supply of loanable funds, resulting in lower costs of investing and expanding capital growth. At the very least, personal savings accounts would enliven the financial industry.

Detractors of personal accounts emphasize the high costs to transition from defined benefit plans; the high administrative costs of personal savings accounts; and that personal savings accounts would "crowd out" or entirely displace employer pension plans. The ideological arguments against personal savings accounts emphasize that they would reduce Social Security's redistribution of income from high-income to low-income earners through the progressive formula described earlier in this chapter. One of the strongest arguments against the personal savings account plan is that it directly creates a government program designed to inevitably expand the financial services industry at the expense of a well-run government agency. (As mentioned several pages back, Bob Pozen, CEO of a mutual fund company, promotes a "progressive price-indexation" plan, which would be especially profitable for the mutual funds industry because only workers in the middle class and above would have personal savings accounts, and only these accounts would be large enough to be profitable. The mutual fund industry does not want the personal savings accounts of low-income workers!)

Individuals controlling their own assets. That individuals will be expected to control their own assets poses for them potential gains and potential pitfalls. Economists in the growing field of what is called "behavioral economics"—a field that considers the way real people make decisions—are alarmist; they see a snake pit of enduring problems if individuals are expected to act like rational professional investors. (These issues are outlined back in chapter 4, where I covered problems with worker-directed 401(k) plans.) Nevertheless, there is ideological appeal to allowing the more important decisions affecting our lives to be made by the individual. University of Chicago economist Edward Lazear argues that personal savings accounts uphold "fundamental economic principles." He says, "We ought to honor consumer sovereignty and keep the market free of significant distortions."[21] Yet the Bush administration admitted that retirees would be required to buy annuities if their benefits did not exceed poverty line income from benefits, and that retirees' investment choices would be limited. President Bush promised that no one could take his or her Social Security account to Las Vegas. Personal savings account advocates restated the government's aim to guarantee income for the very poor—they are those who have incomes up to 30% of the average wage. (Most international poverty standards are higher—up to 45% of the nation's average wage.) Advocates had the difficult task of arguing that personal savings accounts gave personal control to workers, while realizing that too much control could result in fatal investment mistakes, and because of that, worker control had to be limited.

Personal savings accounts' promise of bequests. Many lower-income wage earners were attracted to the idea lurking within personal savings accounts, that a personal pension account could make it possible to have a personal estate. This possibility was contrasted against an individual's contributions (meaning FICA taxes) to Social Security, which do not provide an estate for the individual. Anyone within the Social Security system does have wealth, as such, within that system, but that wealth cannot be realized as an estate. However, the Social Security system does provide benefits to a deceased participant's eligible spouse, dependent children, dependent survivor's caregivers, and survivor's dependent elderly parents. The implication of a personal savings account system is that, if a retiree's personal savings account were large enough and not annuitized, the retiree could bestow bequests to her or his adult children. This element was directed at African Americans who, on average, have no wealth and are more likely to die before collecting benefits or shortly thereafter. Yet African-American workers disproportionately face other risks that Social Security insures: they are overrepresented among beneficiaries receiving disability benefits and survivor's benefits, and overall African Americans pay 9% of Social Security revenue and receive 9% of Social Security benefits.[22] Behind the disproportionate life expectancy of African Americans is a complex set of social justice issues that needs solutions, but the cause is not Social Security, nor can Social Security solve them.

How the personal savings account would affect benefits. Reducing traditional Social Security benefits for workers born after 1950 was an obvious part of the personal savings account plan. All Social Security benefits would be reduced, regardless of whether a worker chose to divert FICA taxes, because there would be less money in the system.[23] For this reason alone, most workers would be expected to choose to divert two-thirds of their payroll tax into a personal savings account, especially if it promised to pay a 3% real return. Yet proponents and detractors of personal savings accounts both concluded that a 3% return on the diverted taxes was too large to expect; most people would have a greater than 50% chance that the return would be less than 3%.[24] The personal savings account proposal was greatly weakened by that admission. For the value of Social Security benefits, which are based on financial markets and financial asset returns, to be higher than traditionally anticipated, economic growth and productivity would have to be robust. However, if predictions about the economy yield a rosy scenario for financial markets and financial asset returns, then they yield a rosy scenario for traditional Social Security revenues. The scenario is comparable to the low-cost set of assumptions for Social Security, which predicts no shortfall.[25]

The predictions that the personal savings account plan would result in cuts in overall Social Security benefits and that individuals would take on more financial risk clearly caused consternation among the public. By mid-2005, the personal savings account plan was headed nowhere.

Impact of personal savings accounts on inequality. When José Piñera, former Chilean Labor Secretary under General Pinochet, was asked by a CBS interviewer whether the highest paid Chilean workers get the best financial advice (implying they have an advantage under Chile's personal savings accounts retirement system), he said, "Higher-paid people generally get better goods and services in our life than a lower-paid worker. Life is unfair, as your President Kennedy mentions."[26] Higher-income workers can take more risk with their assets, have lower costs of administration because of the larger amounts in their personal savings account, and therefore would likely obtain higher rates of return than low-income workers. This is true in Chile and everywhere else. The structure of the personal savings account benefits the higher-income workers, while the traditional Social Security system redistributes funds in the form of benefits to the lowest-income workers. The distribution of retirement income determines the distribution of retirement time. Because the most likely scenario is that middle- and lower-income individuals will not garner higher benefits from individual accounts, but higher-income workers might receive more benefits, means that retirement time consumed may be redistributed to create and expand an already existing gap in retirement leisure.

Impact of personal savings accounts on the financial management industry. Most people who considered the personal savings account plan saw it as a straightforward assist to the financial management industry. Obviously, the personal savings account plans will be administered on a for-profit basis, producing fee revenues to financial management firms. Despite the potential of those new sources of revenue, the financial industry itself remains concerned about its current overcapacity (more financial managers, more financial management firms, than needed) and its projected declining growth. A personal savings account system of Social Security would create a permanent demand for financial services, which could help relieve these Wall Street concerns about the decline in volume of financial transactions. People growing older than their fifties and into their sixties—approaching their retirement years—will be in the phase of their lives when they will be selling their financial assets, which will reduce the liquidity of their funds and also reduce the demand for new products. The financial markets need financial liquidity to support the demand for financial services. (The increase in Wall Street's fee revenue has been estimated as high as $950 billion over the next seventy-five years.)[27] The Pozen plan of progressive indexing is even more helpful to the industry than President Bush's plan because, by carving out lower-income individuals, it eliminates them from the population of prospective retirees, effectively eliminating personal savings account plans that are too small for the financial industry to handle well and remain profitable.

The effect of personal savings accounts on employer pension plans. Employer pension plans would have to adjust to Social Security personal savings accounts. Employers sponsor pensions for sound economic reasons; one reason is to attract and retain valuable employees. Social Security personal savings accounts will obligate employers to collect and sort each employee's contributions into her and his personal savings account. This will create an additional administrative expense if the firm, like many small employers, does not already have an administrative system to do so. Under the traditional Social Security program, employers submit payroll contributions several times a year to one place, the Social Security Administration. More employers may reduce offerings of DC plans, such as 401(k)s, as Social Security personal savings accounts expand. Employee pension accumulations outside the Social Security system may be displaced, detracting from aggregate Social Security fund savings.[28] Personal savings accounts will likely increase the administration costs of small firms and firms that employ low-income workers. Not only will these additional costs fall particularly hard on some kinds of firms, they also represent a decrease in efficiency because they did not exist before.

Costs to transition from Social Security to personal savings accounts. Diverting taxes to create a personal savings account encounters the unavoidable math of a pay-as-you-go retirement system. Contributions (they are the FICA taxes) from current workers are what pay for the older generation's retirement, and also the current generation's retired and disabled beneficiaries and their dependents and survivors. Since 1983 some of the contributions have been going to the trust fund that will start redeeming the U.S. Treasury bonds held in the Social Security Trust Fund. (In 2007 it was estimated that the T-bond will begin to be redeemed in 2018, or thereabouts—the prediction of what year the bonds will begin to be redeemed fluctuates a little every time an annual Social Security Trustees Report is issued.) Diverting some of those contributions to a personal savings account leaves less available to pay current obligations. The Social Security annual report estimated in 2007 that $2 trillion would have to be transferred in 2018 into the Social Security system—either from general revenues or by borrowing. This $2 trillion amount is in addition to the $4 trillion needed to fund full benefits during each year of the next seventy-five years. Phasing out the pay-as-you-go Social Security system requires the current generation to pay double—they have to pay taxes to maintain current benefits, they have to pay the transition costs, and they have to pay taxes that contribute to their own personal savings accounts. If the transition costs are borrowed by the federal government, then the costs of transition will be even greater. They will be greater because of the interest we would pay to the lenders—now primarily Asian governments—and will have to be paid by generations too young to be working now and then by generations not yet born. Most scholars agree that the high transition costs will probably doom any transformation of a mature pay-as-you-go system—a system we know by the name of Social Security—to a system entailing personal savings accounts.

The famous aide to President Ronald Reagan, David Stockman, short-circuited the Reagan administration's plan for personal savings accounts by admitting that progressive price indexing, as previously described, could cut benefits to help pay the cost of the transition. The idea of privatizing the system by cutting benefits was political suicide, and the midterm congressional elections in 1982 were a bloodbath for Republicans. Peter J. Ferrara—viewed as the intellectual founder of the privatizing idea (the Cato Institute promoted versions of his Harvard College thesis analyzing the pay-as-you-go, defined benefit program, in the early 1980s)—proposed a personal savings account plan that would not engender cuts or transition costs, in effect, proposing all gain and no pain. He wrote[29] in the summer of 2003 that the Republicans' personal savings account plan proposal to pay for the transition by moving from wage indexation to price indexation "will not produce nearly the same benefits for workers and the nation, and offers the prospect at best of only a very costly and bloody enactment."[30] He repeated his warning to Republicans in February 2005 with this snide critique: "Only this White House staff would send the President out to sell personal savings accounts for Social Security with the message that private accounts don't really solve the problem. Is it any wonder then that the more George W. Bush talks about personal savings accounts, the lower they sink in the polls?"[31]

The politics are such that the only winning plan for reforming Social Security is a plan that raises benefits and cuts taxes. Ferrara had a plan that raised projected Social Security benefits without tax increases on households! He proposed cutting federal spending by 1% per year for ten years and dedicating the revenue gained from the federal spending cuts to Social Security. Moreover, he proposed a new corporate tax to be dedicated to Social Security and to help pay the transition costs. He justified this new corporate tax by asserting that personal savings accounts would increase economic growth and corporate profits.

The Libertarian think tank, the Institute for Policy Innovation, argues that there are no transition costs. They say that refinancing the current unfunded Social Security liability and placing it on the federal balance sheet (formalizing the debt) is not a new cost. According to Libertarians, these newly recognized, but preexisting, costs would merely become part of the unfunded federal debt obligation that will be paid off from sources other than workers' FICA contributions. Refinancing enables an eventual elimination of the liability. Their argument is that personal savings accounts may create near-term debt of approximately $2 trillion (in present-value terms), but when personal savings accounts replace traditional Social Security in providing retirement income, $12 trillion of debt (projected out to infinity) will be eliminated by general revenues. Ferrara's and the Institute for Policy Innovation's plans aim to surpass the president's plan by proposing that general revenues pay the transition costs and restore solvency without cutting benefits. General revenues are on the table!

Fixes that Maintain Social Security's Basic Structure

The usual fixes used to alleviate the Social Security solvency have worked over the past sixty years or more, if we acknowledge that full solvency is not a measure of the success of those fixes. The Social Security system was never fully funded; so, in a way, insolvency has been built into the system. Since the system decided in 1940 to pay benefits to older people who did not contribute, these legacy costs are a one-time cost, carried through time, and amount to about 30% of the current deficit in Social Security.[32] A measure of success of the Social Security system is whether it regularly achieves a balance between meeting social goals and the costs of meeting those goals.

The Social Security system should not distort efficiency—what economists mean by efficiency is that the program itself should not cause people to act differently than they otherwise would to game the system or avoid being penalized for it. For instance, the Social Security system should not make people save less than they would save, nor cause them to retire much sooner than they or their employers want them to, nor reduce productivity; at the same time, the Social Security system should be flexible enough to keep up with the changing economy.

Those who aim to keep the basic structure of Social Security as it is emphasize its flexibility. The Social Security system has a history of enhanced benefits as living standards improved, adapting to changing circumstances as defined by a technical advisory committee, although, in 1983, for the first time, benefits were cut and taxes were raised. The last time payroll taxes were increased was in 1990, which means nineteen years in 2008, the longest stretch between tax increases. This long stretch was not caused by Congressional sloth or timidity. According to the Social Security 1983 reforms, it was intended that tax revenue exceed benefit costs so a surplus could accumulate to pay partially for boomers' retirements. This makes economic common sense, yet it may doom the system. The Social Security Trust Fund tops the list of the American public suspicions about the Social Security program. Many people view the Trust Fund as a fiction at best, and at worst, as theft. The president knows this and promoted the suspicions. When he posed for that photo next to a file cabinet that contained the $1.7 trillion in U.S. Treasury securities held by the Social Security trust fund and made the comment that the bonds were not "real assets." Later he said: "There is no trust fund. Just IOUs that I saw firsthand." In 1936, Republican Candidate for President Alf Landon said Social Security is a "cruel hoax and the trust fund was nothing but IOUs." And so also have the Cato Institute and other think tanks often referred to the Trust Fund as nothing but government IOUs.[33]

Not surprisingly, proposals to reform Social Security that avoid privatization advocate more tax increases and benefit cuts than benefit improvements.[34] The reform plan by MIT's Peter Diamond and Brookings

Institution's Peter Orszag,[35] and versions of the reform plan by former Social Security Commissioner Robert Ball,[36] both separate out the legacy costs and dedicate a separate source of income to pay legacy costs. (In 2005, a proposed source of revenue to pay for legacy costs was taxes on "legacy wealth," that is, taxes from a reinstated estate tax, estimated to alleviate about 26% of the seventy-five-year shortfall in Social Security.) The specifics of Ball's plans[37] are often the most up-to-date because, although the Social Security Administration's actuaries are obligated to cost out all "serious" proposals—the Social Security Administration determines what is serious—they are especially responsive to Ball because he is a former Commissioner. In mid-2005, the Ball plan included mostly tax revenue increases, a way to boost the rate of return on the trust funds, and some benefit cuts, yielding more than one-fifth more revenue than needed to restore long-run solvency.

The details on the revenue side were:

- gradually raising the cap on earnings covered by Social Security to cover 90% of all income to be taxed and counted for benefits; and, beginning in 2010, dedicating to Social Security the revenue stream from a tax on estates above $3.5 million (or $7 million per couple);

- investing part of the trust funds in equities; and

- raising the payroll tax from 12.4% to 13.4% in 2023, which it was estimated would solve 108% of the solvency shortfall.

On the benefits side:

- trimming Social Security cost of living adjustments; and

- by 2010, covering all new state and local employees under Social Security, estimated to yield another 28.5% of the solvency shortfall.

Diamond and Orszag would make similar changes but they propose to cut benefits by indexing them to average increases in longevity. Let us look at each part of the Ball plan to reform the Social Security program.

Raising the earnings cap. The Social Security's earnings cap is the highest salary on which FICA is based. Raising it became an attractive, populist, easy-to-understand alternative to the Bush Administration's proposal. Even Robert Pozen and the Breaux-Gregg bill, both favoring personal savings accounts, endorsed raising the cap and imposing a tax on general revenues to pay for legacy costs. The appeal of the proposal to raise the earnings cap is that it is progressive and raises a lot of money.

> DATA TO DIGEST   *Raising the cap would affect only the top 6% of wage earners, the ones who received most of the 2001 and 2005 income tax cuts. And the current cap is a mistake. The rationale for the 90% of covered earnings target was the Greenspan Commission's establishment of a cap that taxed 90% of wages. However, because top earners enjoyed faster income growth than others, a growing share of earnings escaped the Social Security system over the years.[38] As mentioned earlier, the Social Security actuaries did not forecast that earnings growth for top earners would diverge so much after 1983—the surprise inequality caused Social Security revenues to be half as large as expected. Only 6% of workers covered under Social Security earn incomes above the Social Security base, which was $90,000 in 2005 (the base is indexed to wages annually), and they earn 15.1% of all earnings. The highest-earning households have so much money that if the cap were eliminated (as it has been for the Medicare tax since 1990), not just raised to cover 90% of earnings, the entire Social Security seventy-five-year deficit would be gone, according to a February 2005 memo from the Social Security Office of the Actuary.[39]*

Tax increases. For calculation purposes, each year the actuaries compute the tax hike needed to achieve seventy-five-year solvency. The hike is small—about 2 percentage points of payroll. Though a small tax hike might be acceptable, it would accumulate even more assets in the trust fund—and that would be a downside of the hike because politicians would have to explain the need for real taxes now to pay forecasted debts in the next forty years. (And the looming Medicare debt might rightly clamor for attention—and for some of that trust fund.) Political leaders would have to convince voters that the surpluses were "real" and nonviolable. A nonviolable promise is a commitment to redeem the Treasury bonds to pay Social Security benefits starting about 2018. If there is no government surplus to pay for the redemption, then tax revenue will finance it, just as it does for any other Treasury bond coming due. However, these bonds are special, unlike bonds held, say, by the Germans; when these Treasury bonds are paid off, the buying power will stay in the United States.

Perhaps we can get inspiration from former Republican Treasury Secretary Paul O'Neill. He opposed across-the-board federal income tax cuts and instead proposed that federal income tax cuts be triggered by a realized federal

Table 5.2
Reforms to Solve the Social Security Shortfall

Proposed Reforms	Percentage of Shortfall Solved[a]
Revenue Enhancers	
Make all earnings subject to the payroll tax and raise benefits accordingly	92.6%
Make 90% of earnings subject to the payroll tax (cap = $140,000) and raise benefits accordingly (protects top 1%)	39.7%
Increase Social Security's Trust Fund investments in equities (assume 3–5.5% real return)	34.9%
Cover newly hired state and local workers	11.1%
Diverting revenue from a reinstated estate tax to Social Security	29.0%
Raise payroll tax by 1% each for employer and employee in 2020–2049 and by 1% more each in 2050	104.0%
Benefit Increases	
Raise the minimum benefit to the poverty level for workers with 35 years, 60% for those with 20 years	−7.0%[b]
Benefit Cuts that Should Be Rejected	
Reduce COLA by 0.5%	41.8%
Speed up increase in retirement age to 68	
(speed up the increase to age 67 and then index the normal retirement age by 1 month every 2 years until the normal retirement age reaches 68)	27.5%
Economic Changes	
Restore equality of earnings growth across the income distribution through social policy such as raising the minimum wage and solving the national health insurance problem	25.0%[b]
Assumptions	
Assume the economy will grow as fast as it needs to yield real 3% net return in a diversified portfolio[c]	100.0+%

[a] Unless otherwise noted, statistics are from Ball 2004.
[b] Diamond and Orszag 2003.
[c] Baker 2005a.

surplus. (This proposal was fatal to his career!) In a similar fashion, a FICA payroll tax change could be triggered by changes in the seventy-five-year forecast for surpluses or deficits every five years or so. Not an unreasonable proposal, considering that employer pension funds change contribution rates every year based on much shorter (and more variable) time horizons of five to thirty years. Tax rates could be automatically changed every five to seven years to bring the system into balance. Some other fixes, characterized in table 5.2, include raising revenue by Social Security covering all newly hired state and local workers to phase out the separate public sector plans in selected states. (Of course, without compensating the state and local plans, this idea will go nowhere.)

> **Bottom Line** *I like the symmetry of diverting taxes on legacy wealth to pay for legacy benefits by diverting revenue from a revived estate tax to the Social Security system.*

Assessing what fix is most likely to be accepted and put into effect requires a review of the Social Security system's political history.

Political History of the Social Security Program

The Republican majority's bid to undo the New Deal program in 2005 was as bold as the New Deal program itself was in 1935. The case for a national Social Security program to secure elderly income was bold, but the case for it was fairly easily made because employer pensions were collapsing and unemployment was soaring. It was not simple to get the proposal through Congress, but Americans were receptive to a scheme that promised to transition older workers out of the workforce as employer pensions diminished.[40]

The Social Insurance Appeal

The appeal of Social Security was that it was based on the same principles as social insurance. Unlike welfare or charity, there is no means test—assessing an individual's financial need, which is an expensive administrative requirement. Under social insurance, an individual who experiences the requirements of a specified insured event—such as retirement; becoming a dependent of a retired, deceased, or disabled insured worker; becoming disabled—gets the benefits regardless of that individual's wealth or income.

Voluntary, private insurance systems suffer in two respects: the highest-risk people are most likely to select insurance (known technically as adverse selection); and people having the lowest risk will avoid or try to avoid paying the premiums (technically known as moral hazard). States needed the federal government to conduct the large-scale coordination required to prevent adverse selection and moral hazard. If any one state provided old-age support, individuals in other states may likely change their behavior in reaction to the existence of the insurance—that's moral hazard—and migrate to the state providing the insurance—that's adverse selection. The possibility of moral hazard has the perverse effect that the insurance entity, whether it is a state or an insurance company, actually increases the risks it sought to insure against. Mandatory insurance solves the problems of adverse selection and moral hazard. Only mandatory insurance broadens the risk base and therefore makes premiums affordable.

> **Bottom Line**   *Mandatory insurance is preferred to welfare programs because, in welfare programs, whether the beneficiaries are deserving of the aid is always debated and the income is usually inadequate. Insurance plans that do not mandate that everyone pay premiums but insure against what most everyone in a market economy faces—the risk of not having income because of unemployment, sickness, or being too old to work—would have to charge high premiums to pay for the losses. Insurance companies know that, in insurance systems where participation is not mandatory, only those people who know they are likely to need the insurance—the high-risk individuals—are likely to buy it. Therefore, the insurers charge premiums according to these expectations, and only the rich and very desperate buy the insurance. That the rich buy it serves little social purpose since the rich can self-insure.*

The Social Security Idea and the Cato Institute Aim to Dismantle It

The Social Security proposal presented by President Franklin Roosevelt was well crafted by national experts with evidence from state demonstration programs, especially the one from Wisconsin, from input obtained from international technicians, such as visiting European actuaries, and from the German and British experiences in social insurance.[41] Two movements—a grassroots movement in California to provide all people over age sixty-five with a flat benefit of $100, and the railroad retiree activists in the 1920s—were part of a widespread movement for a guaranteed income to the elderly; they provided a political imperative for Congress to adopt the Social Security system. Social Security's original design was less radical than plans that would guarantee monthly income to the elderly. Social Security was designed to be paid for by the workers in advance—benefits were not scheduled to be paid until 1942. It was also designed to not be self-financing until 1962, when one-third of Social Security's revenue was expected to come from general taxes. Social Security was a compromise by a president who was not a Republican but wanted an entitlement to income that was not contingent on work. Though the collapsing economy in the 1930s propelled the well-crafted proposal through Congress for the willing president's signature, Republicans opposed Social Security. In addition, the Republican Party has remained steadfastly opposed to social insurance in great measure because of core philosophical beliefs that government should not provide a social wage.

The political history of Social Security demonstrates the effectiveness of expertise and bold ideas; and so also did expertise and bold ideas inspire the formation of the Cato Institute in 1972. Initially, the Cato Institute had one item on its agenda—gathering expertise and creating an intellectual framework to shrink government by privatizing the largest, most popular government program. Their target was clearly Social Security. The Cato Institute has since expanded to encompass other issues competently, while never losing sight of its main goal. It was the first organization to establish the domain name "socialsecurity.org." In 1982, President Ronald Reagan, then enjoying the popularity that often comes from surviving assassination attempts, mused to reporters on an airport tarmac that he was exploring making Social Security voluntary. The always present and large transition costs, his budget advisors explained to reporters in an honest way, would be paid for by cutting benefits through price indexation of the benefit base. The advisors' honest explanation of priced indexation was lethal to Reagan's exploration of voluntary Social Security.

Within a few weeks of Reagan's exploration, the negative political response resulted in the bipartisan Greenspan Commission. That Commission led to the Social Security reforms in 1983, which fixed an immediate shortfall brought on by the rapid increase in prices and the devastating jobless numbers in the 1970s.[42] Republicans would lose political power every time social insurance principles in a program were reaffirmed. They lost when Medicare was passed in 1965, and they would lose elections to Democrats every time Congress raised Social Security benefits. Capitulating, Republican President

Richard Nixon approved of making the benefits automatically indexed to prices so that the Democrats would no longer get credit for increased benefits in Congressional races. The conservative agenda to reduce Social Security through partial privatization comes genuinely from the party's long-standing investment of political[43] and intellectual capital into the idea that government should be smaller.

The Debate over Social Security: Some Things Never Change

Issues debated in the 1930s and afterward are being debated again in the twenty-first Century. Seven issues, at least, are always present in the Social Security debate:

1. How much should the elderly work?

2. What should the federal government do when employer pension plans fail?

3. Will increased longevity cause insolvency?

4. Does Social Security squelch initiative to save for one's own retirement?

5. Can Social Security (and tax-favored retirement systems) mitigate rising income and wealth inequality?

6. Does a crisis require major reform? And,

7. Are advanced-funded programs or pay-as-you-go programs more affordable?

I consider these issues one at a time.

1. In the 1930s and again in the twenty-first century, work remains a major source of income for the elderly. More than 50% of men aged sixty-five years and older worked in the 1930s (when, generally, elderly women did not), compared to the fewer than 20% of the elderly (men and women) who work today. Nevertheless, earnings then, as now, make up an important source of income for elderly retirees. In 2004, work was the fastest-growing source of revenue for the elderly! Working in retirement is a growing reality revealed in a number of

ways, including the increase in the labor force participation of the elderly and the growing importance of earning as a source of income in retirement. Estimates show that losing half of a retired person's wealth could boost by 4% the likelihood that they would be or want to be working.[44]

2. A collapse in the private sector's ability to provide pension security and keep its promises accompanied the passage of Social Security. Whether a similar loss of faith in employer plans exists—and if it exists, whether it provides the intellectual and emotional momentum for bold or mild reform—remains to be seen. Certainly, high-profile, defined benefit retirement plans are defaulting, and in their place employers and workers have accepted defined contribution retirement plans, and have resigned themselves to a do-it-yourself retirement planning process.

Of course, this scenario is similar to the way it was before there was Social Security, back when workers were responsible for their own retirement income.[45]

3. That people live longer is an enduring prediction (except, recently for the first time, some researchers suggest that obesity will lower longevity)[46] and is used to support calls for increasing the normal retirement age—the official age at which full Social Security benefits are available. Longevity rates are often displayed by gender, but it is not the only, nor the main, determinant of mortality variance. Mortality varies widely by socioeconomic class, more so than it varies among people of different genders. Women's mortality probabilities are 83% of men's mortality probabilities, but the gap is larger by class. Women or men with the most education have mortality probabilities that are about 70% below the mortality probabilities of those with high school educations.[47] Older British men are expected to live 1.3 years, or 9%, longer than older Turkish women, but only 3.5 years, or 22%, fewer years than Japanese men (see table 5.3).[48]

4. Large populations of researchers and experts throughout long careers have concluded that Social Security has competing effects on individuals' motives to save.[49] Most concur that Social Security boosted retirement savings and demand for annuities for retirement, and also that increases in Social Security benefits did not suppress Americans' rate of saving. In fact, savings rates fell in 1983 after scheduled decreases in Social Security benefits took place.

5. An increase in the gap between the high-income group and low-income group, i.e., income inequality, spurs political agitation for income security programs. The concentration of wealth during the decade before Social Security was instituted fueled populist calls for income and wealth redistribution.[50]

Table 5.3

The Surprising Bad News about American Women's Slow Rise in Longevity

Longevity and longevity improvements for selected groups, 1991–2001

Group	*Years Expected to Live after Age 65 in 2001*	*Improvements in Expected Years of Life after 65 between 1991 and 2001 (%)*
Japanese Women	22.7	12.4%
U.S. Women	19.2	0.5%
U.K. Women	18.9	5.6%
Turkish Women	14.3	2.9%
Japanese Men	17.8	9.2%
U.S. Men	16.3	6.5%
U.K. Men	15.6	10.6%
Turkish Men	12.7	2.4%

Source: OECD 2003.

Recent sharp increases in income and wealth inequality may cause a similar demand for social insurance. Among all the sources of income to the elderly, only Social Security reduces the income and wealth differences, whereas financial assets create a gap or widen existing gaps.[51]

6. Democracies produce bold reforms only during immediate crises. During 1935, the jobless rate was 25% and the Communist and Socialist parties swelled with new members in the United States. Without these economic and political dislocations, the conservative agenda would have presented a case that Social Security was too expensive; hence, no revenue could be dedicated to it.

7. How best to fund the Social Security system, whether it should be pay-as-you-go or advance-funded, turns out to be less relevant than whether and at what level workers want to finance the consumption needs of children, the elderly, and other nonworkers. Workers' willingness in part depends on who enjoys the proceeds from productivity gains. If the productivity gains go to workers, then payroll taxes are a stable source of transfer to pay the costs of benefits to nonworkers. If the productivity gains go to profits, then a revenue base of interest, dividends, and capital gains is a stable source of income to nonworkers. From this perspective, the issue of how Social Security is financed depends on who is foreseen to be the beneficiary of economic growth—labor? or capital owners?

Bottom Line   *The financing mechanisms do not change the fact that working people or corporations or governments that promise to redeem and pay interest and dividends on corporate and government bonds and stocks will have to provide income to nonworkers; this is the reality in any pension system.*

What Is New in the Social Security Debate?

The Speaker of the U.S. House of Representative, Dennis Hastert, third in line to be U.S. President, stood outside the U.S. Capitol during President Bush's campaign to transform Social Security into personal savings accounts. Hastert was standing beside a 1935 brown Ford auto, which he expected to use to make obvious the point that, just as that Ford is out of date, so is the Social Security system. He said he would not ride in such an unsafe, old car. (Reportedly, the car collector who owned the Ford winced and told the reporter he was proud of his well-cared-for car.) Old-fashioned phones and other such props were also on display, conveying somewhat awkwardly that the Social Security system is old and needs new technology.[52] Democrats, going along with the metaphor, argued that Social Security, like all good machines, needs care and upkeep.

Despite the theatrics, all sides of the debate stipulate that much has changed since 1935. Here are four differences between the current Social Security debate and the debate in 1935.

1. *Social Security is a "countercyclical" tool*—an institution or program that increases demand by supplying income to consumers when the economy slumps. When the economy slumps more people retire, making the unemployment rates a little lower, but although retired, they continue to spend money because they have Social Security benefits. Without automatic payments from government programs and from private and government insurance, communities would suffer from the incidence of hurricanes, economic downturns, plant closings, and so would everyone identified as "too old to work." When older workers face layoffs and high unemployment rates, significant numbers of them are expected to retire and collect Social Security benefits and defined benefit pensions among those retirees who have such pensions. When jobs are scarce and earnings are down nationally, both the Social Security benefit payments and the payments from DB pensions— considered countercyclical sources of income—increase aggregate demand. Without these sources of income, workers would surely need to stay in the

labor force, as well as go into debt, all of which may further depress economic activity. Social Security, along with unemployment insurance and DB plans, serve as automatic stabilizers. These stabilizers would not be needed if the job market had plentiful jobs, enough for everyone who sought them, and there were no recessions, so that a laid-off older worker would merely look for and be able to find another job and maintain consumption.

> DATA TO DIGEST   *The share of total personal income coming from Social Security increased on average 6% per year during the past six decades. However, the increase was 8.7% per year during each year of a recession—when more people retired and started collecting. Social Security income is not only higher during recession years, it is concentrated in some places—in particular, Florida and shrinking farm belt towns in the Midwest.*[53] *Over 27% of the population in Florida, Iowa, and Oregon are over age sixty-five, and most of their income comes from Social Security. These places greatly enjoy the stabilizing effect of Social Security income.*

Again, unlike during the 1920s when populist demands for government protection helped spur federal program growth, earnings inequality now has weakened Social Security by depriving it of funds. If earnings growth had not been skewed toward the top 10% and above that, the top 1%,[54] then half of Social Security's seventy-five-year deficit, as projected in 2005, would have been eliminated. Instead of 90% of wages being taxed—which was the benchmark set in 1983 when the earnings cap on FICA taxable income was indexed to wage growth—only 83% is taxed, so that the highest earners have garnered a growing portion of national income.

2. *The increasing expense of the employer-based health insurance system* was unexpected. This expense relentlessly requires wages to be diverted to pay employer-based premiums, thus escaping the Social Security earnings tax base. When Social Security was initiated in 1935, the practice of paying workers in company store credits and company housing allowances in company towns was fast disappearing and becoming illegal. Now workers are increasingly being paid in noncash items, as with health insurance. A modern Social Security system could be built on payrolls that truly reflected what people were being paid and, taken together, would reflect the value of the nation's labor force. Yet employer and employee costs of health insurance are absorbing more and more labor compensation. The average annual decrease in the ratio of earnings to compensation was 0.3% from 1963 to 2003—this means that cash is becoming a smaller and smaller share of total compensation, which

includes the value of health insurance—and noncash compensation is not subject to FICA taxes. Rising health care costs account for much of the increase in the role of employee benefits in total compensation. Not only does employer-provided health insurance, as well as other employee benefits, cause "job lock" (reduces workers' mobility in ways similar to the effect of company housing), it weakens social insurance. Compensation in the form of health insurance escapes the tax base for Social Security and deprives the Social Security system of revenue. Under the Social Security trustees' intermediate assumptions, the ratio of wages to employee compensation is projected to decline from 80.6% in 2004 to 69.6% for 2079.

3. *Confidence in financial markets* has evolved alongside Social Security— a confidence that certainly did not exist for decades after the Depression. There is no greater contrast between then and now than Americans' faith and confidence in financial markets. This confidence, coupled with a broader base of ownership of stocks—over half of Americans own equities—helps explain results of surveys showing that, even after the financial market crashes in 1987 and 2001, a large portion of the public believed stock values always appreciate; the question was merely by how much. Low inflation rates and the preeminence of the U.S. dollar in world commerce still, also help make credible expert economists' arguments that markets are more trustworthy than a government. Referring to 2000 presidential candidate Al Gore's incessantly repeated promise to put Social Security accounts off budget and the surplus "in a lock box," one such commando, Edward Lazear, a former University of Chicago economist who is now at Stanford, simply asserts, "Investments made privately provide a stronger lock box than any offered by the government."[55]

4. *Affordability was not much of an issue in the early years.* At the start of the Social Security program, the ratio of workers to retirees was millions to one; about ten years later, it was sixteen to one and remained there for about a decade. For most of the life of the Social Security system, the dependency ratio—so-called because it reflects the number of workers paying FICA taxes that are needed to pay benefits to one retiree—has been three to one. Affordability and solvency grow to be larger issues, as they do in a mature defined benefit retirement plan that takes on "past service liability." That is the specific liability for services performed by workers before there was a system, and who became part of the system when it was created—but who contributed very little, if anything, to the system. Identifying how the economy has changed and the system that changed with it reflects back on the question

about whether Social Security is suitable for the current economy and answers it. Flexibility makes it suitable.

Conclusion: The Future of Social Security

Henry Paulsen of Goldman Sachs became Treasury Secretary in the summer of 2006. He announced that transforming Social Security to a system of personal savings accounts was a high priority. Ironically, by 2008, Paulsen's priority is to fix damage done by a highly private financial industry.

The decrease in benefits from Social Security is not emphasized in the Social Security debate. Nor has the implication for disability benefits been assessed.

Those who have longer than average lives, those who depend most on Social Security, and those prone to overestimate their abilities in investing and underestimate longevity, will lose from not having a guaranteed floor of income.

Writer Peter Ferrara, a fearless advocate of personal savings accounts and progenitor of the Cato Institute, argues that the fundamental philosophical goal behind the proposed Social Security reforms was to shift away from reliance on government, on public taxes, and on spending, and toward reliance on private investment.[56] Do these changes—the need for activist fiscal policy, employee benefit growth and inequality, and mature and expansive financial markets—make the case for retooling Social Security or changing it to personal savings accounts? Retooling is less drastic.

The diminishment of Social Security is part of the attack on retirement entitlement. With personal savings accounts, there will be no secure form of pension. Insecure pensions mean more work. The increase in work effort will likely come from individuals who most depend on Social Security as the way they will need to fund retirement. The meaning of retirement will be debased if it is a forced working retirement.

Part II

What Is Good about America's

Retirement Income Security System

Chapter 6

The Short History of Old Age

Leisure in America

American workers are spending more time in retirement today than they did thirty years ago. But that has started to change. The amount of retirement time is beginning to shrink.

This chapter reviews the evolution of retirement in the United States and how retirement is changing. Policymakers and pundits say Americans should work more. They argue that working more is a win-win solution to rising Medicare and Social Security costs and to the upward pressure on wages caused by so-called future labor shortages.

But working more is not a win-win solution. There are losers. The losers are the people who lose their pensions, the people who lose a viable choice about whether to work in old age or retire with a reasonable income. Though some elderly find work attractive as retirement income fails, they lose the ability to seek work on their terms. They lose to terms that are more favorable to employers.

Retirement Leisure by Generation

The elderly are working more now at the beginning of the twenty-first century than they worked in the 1980s. There was a time when Americans worked less and had more retirement time.

DATA TO DIGEST

- *A man born during the 1930s, reaching his sixty-fifth birthday in 2000, could expect 13.4 years of old-age leisure—those are retirement years I refer to as the time after work and before death.*

- *A sixty-five-year-old man born twenty-five years earlier, say in 1910, could expect only 10.8 years of retirement leisure.*
- *Men born in 1900 who reached age sixty-five—which was in 1965, the year Medicare was adopted—could expect 9.2 years of retirement leisure.*
- *Going back further, men of the inaugural Social Security generation—those born ten years after the Civil War—could expect fewer than 6.9 years of retirement leisure.*

Looking back through the generations, it's clear that retirement time was increasing. Before the 1980s, retirement time had been increasing because men were retiring earlier, at younger ages. After the 1980s, any increase in male retirement leisure resulted because men were living longer. Crucially, though, the increase in the "death age"—another way of saying, improvements in longevity—grew more slowly than did the increase in the age at which people retired. The result? Retirement time got squeezed.

You need to be aware that I have been speaking in terms of averages, and alluding to averages can mask significant information, for instance, average changes in work effort and longevity that hide important racial and socioeconomic differences. Though longevity improved for almost everyone during the last one hundred years, white male longevity improved the most.

DATA TO DIGEST   *Between 1979 and 1998, the longevity for sixty-five-year-old white males (born between 1914 and 1933) improved by 13%; for African-American males, it was 8%; for white females, longevity improved 4%; and for African-American females, only 2%.*[1]

Significant increases in male longevity came soon after 1965, when the Medicare program and President Lyndon Johnson's War on Poverty raised incomes for the elderly. It seems that more income and health care helped men live longer. Life expectancy rates for men turning sixty-five in 1965 compared to men who turned sixty-five in 1960 were not very different. But ten years later, men turning sixty-five in 1975 could expect to live an impressive ten more years than men ten and fifteen years older. However, since the mid-1980s male longevity improvements have slowed down. Male longevity improved an average 11% between 1970 and 1985, and 12% between 1985 and 2000. Female life expectancy at age sixty-five rose 9% after the Medicare program was implemented (1970–1985) but the gains have since flattened out to 4% between 1985 and 2000 (see table 6.1).

Table 6.1
Life Expectancy Improvements Are Slowing Down
Changes in life expectancy by sex, by five year increments

Year Turned Age 65	Male Life Expectancy Change from Previous Five-Year Cohort (%)	Female Life Expectancy Change from Previous Five-Year Cohort (%)	Male Life Expectancy at 65 (years)	Female Life Expectancy at 65 (years)
1950	—	—	12.8	15.0
1955	0.8%	3.3%	12.9	15.5
1960	−0.8%	1.9%	12.8	15.8
1965	0.0%	2.5%	12.8	16.2
1970	2.3%	4.9%	13.1	17.0
1975	5.3%	6.5%	13.8	18.1
1980	2.2%	1.1%	14.1	18.3
1985	2.8%	1.1%	14.5	18.5
1990	4.1%	2.2%	15.1	18.9
1995	3.3%	0.0%	15.6	18.9
2000	4.5%	1.6%	16.3	19.2

The Inaugural Social Security Generation

A person born in 1875, ten years after the Civil War ended, could collect Social Security benefits (having met the criteria) in 1940 at age sixty-five even though he or she had paid Social Security taxes for only three years. That was a good deal for anyone in this group—they certainly benefited from the massive political mobilization for government-provided and secured employer pensions.

The original blueprints for Social Security engineered an "advance funded" program—the benefits would be paid from a trust fund that had accumulated sufficient funds. The idea was that workers would contribute for many years before anyone would collect benefits. But social and political pressures to help the elderly, who suffered greatly from the Depression, grew too persuasive; as a result, the first benefit was paid just four years after the start of collecting premiums (the FICA taxes) for the Social Security Trust Fund.

Though conceived as a program that would assist older adult male "breadwinners" and their wives and survivors, the first Social Security recipient was a working woman—Ida Fuller (a New York legal secretary in an influential congressional member's district) had worked all her life and paid $21 in premiums. She lived one hundred years, died in 1975, and collected $21,000 in lifetime benefits. She was the first recipient but, clearly, because of her unusual longevity—women's life expectancy at age sixty-five was fifteen years, not thirty-five years—and the fact that she was a working woman, she was a typical recipient in only one way—women who worked retired in far greater proportions than men. Almost half of the working men Fuller's age stayed in the labor force, whereas 90% of former working women her age were retired.

> **Bottom Line**   *A male born ten years after the Civil War ended, who worked all his life, and survived to age sixty-five could expect six years and eleven months of retirement leisure. A similarly situated female could expect over thirteen years of old-age leisure.*

The Medicare Inaugural Generation

By the time workers are in their thirties they have already defined their work; they may have experienced some comforting wage growth, begun savings plans, and started to accumulate home equity. Urban families were not likely to have owned a home in the 1910s and 1920s, but they established families and financial futures by age thirty. For people born in the early 1900s, extreme levels of uncertainty marked this generation's financial futures. In their thirties at the beginning of the Great Depression, many not only suffered economic setbacks, but later, as parents of the "Greatest Generation" they also had to watch their sons go into battle in World War II.

Though the Great Depression and World Wars I and II pockmarked their early work lives, these men and women gained the most in retirement time. By the time they reached age sixty-five in 1965, 27.9% of the older men who had lived past sixty-five were still working or looking for work; this is a far smaller proportion than the rates of older men born five years earlier in 1895; these older men's labor force participation rates were over 33.1%.

Indeed, the parents of the Greatest Generation—the inaugural Medicare generation—were much more likely to retire at age sixty-five than their parents had been. They were also the first older people to have complete access to health insurance through Medicare and Social Security benefits. Social Security provided recipients with another generosity spurt—this time in increased benefits, not just expansions of coverage—under President Nixon. Benefits increased 23%, and inflation indexation in Social Security income was instituted; both occurred in just three years between 1969 and 1972.[2]

> **Bottom Line**   *The expected post–sixty-five retirement leisure for men born in 1900 was eight years and seven months, compared to that of men born in 1975, for whom it was almost seven years.*

The Greatest Generation

The so-called Greatest Generation of American men and women—those born between the years 1920 and 1935—helped "save" the world from communism and fascism. After they did that, they begat the baby boom that fueled the American economy after World War II. In 1940, almost half of households were living in their own homes, and both men and women had some of the highest education rates in the world. When they reached age sixty-five—in the years 1985 through 2000—Medicare paid for most of their medical bills, and most of the retirees who had pensions had defined benefit pensions, which last a lifetime. The small portion of elderly households who happened to own stocks benefited from buying stocks in the 1970s and 1980s and selling them during the largest American financial boom of the 1990s to finance their retirement. Compared to their fathers, the men of the Greatest Generation lived 2.5 years longer once they reached sixty-five. The women of this generation lived 2.7 years longer than their mothers did. This generation coupled their longer lives with more pensions and got enormous improvements in the length of time spent in retirement. (See figure 1.1 to review the fast pace of improvements in retirement time and its significant flattening out in the 1990s.)

Wal-Mart Greeters and the RV Generation

People born in the mid-1930s have become what I call the "Wal-Mart greeter/ RV Generation." This generation has two dimensions represented by these two stereotypes. Elderly men who were born in 1935 increased their labor force participation rates since 2000. Despite the increase, this generation has many expectations for old-age leisure. Although most men over age sixty-five do not work and are expected to live seventeen more years, we see older men, men without enough income, greeting customers in Wal-Mart.

What about women? All women, including older women, who have always worked fewer years than men, have relentlessly increased their participation in paid work since the 1950s. Yet, when business cycles are taken into account, older women, like older men, tended not to work when jobs were scarce. The 2001–3 recession was different, however. That was when a greater share of elderly men and women were in the labor force than during any previous recession (see chapter 8). The free time for America's elderly, as measured by the leisure participation rate (one minus the labor force participation rate), has fallen.

Policies for older Americans have, since the 1980s, reinforced working during older ages in a variety of ways. The United States is the only Organization for Economic Co-operation and Development (OECD) nation that bans forced retirement, pays full Social Security benefits to people who have not retired,[3] and has raised the normal retirement age to sixty-seven, a much higher age than its European counterparts.

Repositioning the Retirement Idea

Despite the intense pace at which Americans work, or because of it, policymakers persist in presenting longer work lives as a solution to the problems of rising Medicare and Social Security costs and to the predicted upward pressure on wages when the baby boomers retire and shrink the labor force. The human-resource industry reassures its clients that the feared coming labor shortage will partially take care of itself: 75% of older workers said they would continue working when they got older because "they didn't have sufficient financial resources to retire."[4]

Despite the potential gains of work—many older people find work financially and mentally rewarding—raising Social Security's normal age to seventy is fiercely contested and opposed by most working people. Yet support for cutting either Social Security or employer defined benefit pension benefits by raising the retirement age comes from both sides of the political spectrum. Those who advocate individual retirement accounts and "personal responsibility" view retirement as a choice, like choosing between apples and French fries, that should be financed by the individual. They feel that cutting benefits merely puts the responsibility for financing retirement back on the individual, where it belongs.

Repositioning retirement rests on a conviction that boomers are very different from the generations who came before. One difference is that future retirees' life expectancy is increasing. True. But because it's true does not mean boomers should, could, and want to, work longer. In most surveys, respondents in the boomer age group say they expect to work after age sixty-five. This is often used as evidence that boomers *want* to work longer. The question is whether boomers want to work longer because they like it or because they don't expect to have enough to retire on? Redesigning pension systems so that a worker has to continue to work longer to get full benefits is a policy prescription shared widely among policymakers and academics. But workers (and voters) tend to reject it.

Convictions for More Work: Winners and Losers

Deeply felt convictions usually have roots in material incentives. There are clear winners to a repositioning of retirement as an event to avoid. We know white-collar male workers' longevity has grown faster than the longevity of women workers or blue-collar workers. We also know that older workers who enjoy and control their work pace and tasks are more likely to want to continue to work. Educated professionals, who likely began working full time in their mid-twenties, have worked fewer years by age sixty-five than have non–college-educated workers, who generally started work in their late teens. Study of the linkages between these characteristics has barely begun—this book is a beginning—yet it is likely that workers with high socioeconomic stature lose the least when working longer is a norm.

When workers try to replace lost company pensions with more individual retirement account managers and personal finance counselors, many niche businesses—the money managers, consultants, and other private-sector vendors—win.

Employers also clearly benefit from new retirement norms, and that is why they are the biggest champions of a working retirement. The pressure faced by employers to raise wages is relieved when more people are in the labor force. An increase in the supply of labor invariably redistributes income toward profits and away from wages. In general, an expanding labor supply helps employers tame pressure to pay more, to improve working conditions, or to conserve labor by investing to boost labor productivity. An expanding labor supply also improves and expands the pool of applicants for jobs, making it cheaper to hire good workers. Working "retirees" help manufacture healthy profits.[5]

Praising and Promoting Work

That we should eschew leisure and promote work until about age sixty-seven or seventy is based on the idea that work is good for older people. In the 1970s and 1980s, retirement expectations shifted subtly. Psychologists uncovered linkages between ill health, depression, and early death among retired men. This research supports arguments for raising Social Security's normal retirement age—the age people are eligible to collect full benefits. The problem with the research is that the causation can clearly run the opposite way—that is, health problems could cause retirement, rather than retirement being the cause of health problems. Research with my colleague, Kevin Neuman, found that retirement improves the health of those enjoying retirement leisure, although workers in poor health are more likely to retire at earlier ages (this research is discussed in chapter 7).

A second question is whether personal tastes and cultural norms—the rules of thumb people use to determine when they should retire, based on when they expect other people to retire—are shifting to explain the work increase among the elderly. If changing tastes for work versus having free time are the cause for workers retiring later, then nothing is amiss, and government need not act. However, if the elderly are working more because they need to compensate for pension erosion, then rules of thumb about when to retire have merely been accommodated to cope with a negative economic reality. Cultural norms developing for later retirement could represent collective cognitive dissonance. That means the members of a society, when faced with a change that is not wanted—like not being able to retire—and also realizing that the change is inevitable, consider the change is acceptable. They consider it acceptable because it causes less psychological dissonance. A good example of collective cognitive dissonance is people working in a job they need while not complaining about the health hazards, preferring to think the job is safe. A growing acceptance of later retirement could represent a coping strategy and acquiescence in the decline in retirement income security.

Youth Culture and Promoting Work

Old is not so old anymore—that is one of the fetching arguments supporting the idea that more work among older people is good for them. A 2003 issue of the Association of American Retired Persons (AARP) magazine *Maturity* has a sultry Lauren Hutton on the cover with the caption, "Is Sixty the New Thirty?"[6] At the same time Naomi Wolff, known famously in the 2000 presidential campaign as a fashion advisor to Al Gore, warned in the first chapter of *Beauty Myth* of an insidious form of labor market discrimination—discrimination against the "unattractive." The chilling example was an older news anchor being fired because her appearance did not "match viewers' expectations." Viewers expect women to look how? We can only imagine. But it was clear that an older physical appearance was not acceptable. Wolff wanted women to take to the streets and mobilize politically against this specific kind of bias—grey hair and wrinkles. The $80 billion health and beauty industry successfully taps into the anxieties of aging Americans.

Concerns about achieving a satisfactory personal appearance are not unconnected to anxieties about pensions. Fear of age discrimination and failing pensions can help explain what vexes the World Health Organization and public health advocates. For example, pharmaceutical companies pursue cures for hair loss while research projects on diseases affecting the impoverished young go begging for funds.[7] A charitable view of the American obsession with youthful looks is that Americans, alone among the globe's wealthy citizens, have to work and look ready to work at older ages. We are a nation of individuals who have fewer pensions; therefore, we have to do what is needed to make ourselves as employable as possible at older and older ages. In this light, paying for botox is not a vain frivolity but a case where low-dose botulism can help a person get and keep a job.[8] The rise and maintenance of a youth culture connects to economic global agendas in profound ways; what appears to be social and cultural actually reinforces the interests of those who want us to work longer. The pain of diminished pensions is met with less resistance if the financial threat of having to work until age seventy is muted with flattery. Believing seventy is the new forty helps older people to psychologically repress the negative feelings that come with having to work longer than they wanted.

In 1983, Congress moved to change retirement norms. In addition to political safety, Congress cut benefits for retirees seventeen years in the future[9] by incrementally raising the normal retirement age starting in 2000.[10] Besides the primary goal of reducing future Social Security pension liabilities, Congress aimed to raise the age Americans use as "anchor" for what they consider to be the "normal" retirement age.

Can the Elderly Work More?

Believing that the health and vigor of the elderly workforce is greater than ever before makes raising the retirement age a favorite choice in retirement policy proposals. But no one really knows because there are no reliable long-term data as to if and how the physical and mental capacities of Americans to work have changed.

> **DATA TO DIGEST**   *Self-reported work limitations have been collected from a survey of workers since 1981 and show that*
> - *self-reported limitations on ability to work increase with age (which makes sense and makes the self-reporting believable);*
> - *90% of people aged fifty-five through sixty-one report they are able to work (meaning most Americans approach retirement able to work); and*
> - *surprisingly, the prevalence of work limitations (those that last a year or longer) since the 1980s is increasing, from an average of 9.37% during the economic expansion of 1983 through 1990, to over 10.81% in the economic boom of the 1990s.[11]*

In 2000, 11.3% of people aged fifty-five to sixty-four reported physical limitations that prevented them from working or seeking work two years in a row. In any one year, the share of older adults who report work limitation for just one year is almost double that. Though subjective assessments of health continue to increase, there is no indication that elderly workers are suited to or accommodated in the jobs that exist.[12]

Therefore, more older people seeking work may not be motivated by work's pleasures. Working longer could be a second-best solution to having lost pension income. Having the option to work is a genuine improvement over not having the option; but having to work does not expand choices. The elderly give up valuable time when their real income falls, inducing them to work. There is considerable evidence that the elderly enjoy free time, as we all do, but for a reason that is particular to older people.[13] Berkeley economist Clair Brown (1994) ranks living standards along a continuum, with a chronic state of want at one end and extreme comfort at the other. Being extremely comfortable requires more than material goods: comfort means mobility, the freedom to "change your mind," and the resources to blunt the consequences of a mistake. If every relevant aspect is the same, a retired person is better off than an older worker because the retiree has more time to change her or his mind. An older worker may need time off from work to recover from a mistake. The boost in time can help compensate for many losses in the aging process.

Affordability: Are Pensions a Form of Fiscal Child Abuse?

Economist Laurence Kolitkoff told hundreds of Notre Dame students in 2005 that the high taxes necessary to make Social Security solvent would be "fiscal child abuse." Therefore, he declared that Social Security benefits should be cut to enhance intergenerational justice. His argument is that, under the current Social Security system, workers pay for benefits they will never get. The young could benefit if the older people worked longer and retirement is made more "unaffordable" for current workers. This is clearly a claim that the "old eat the young" and positions the young as winners when pensions fail and the elderly work longer.

But having to work longer and give up retirement time is not the only policy reaction that is sustainable in the face of population aging. Many have made the opposite case. University of California-Berkeley's demographer Ronald Lee, in 2003, argued that many nations are in a classic demographic transition—fertility is low, infant mortality is low, and lifespans are longer.[14] The changing elder-to-worker ratio may startle national budgeting agencies, but it is an expected result of an aging society. Lee argues that, in the first phase of a demographic transition, when infant mortality decreases, nations and families find themselves with more children to support. The next phase is when those children start to work and the dependency ratio of youth to people of working age and the dependency ratio of elderly to people of working age, both fall—a happy phase that can last fifty to sixty years. That is followed by a phase where, not surprisingly, there are fewer workers to support the growing number of elderly. In this phase, it appears inevitable that pensions become more expensive as the number of workers for every retiree falls, but that is demography, it is not a clearcut prediction of what the economic consequences will be.

The economic effects of the demographic transition can be surprising, especially if the perceived wisdom is that an aging society becomes "too" costly. If the economy becomes richer and more productive because of, or co-incident with, an aging population, then pensions and end-of-work retirement leisure are affordable. What is affordable or not, of course, is a political issue, not an economic one.

> **Bottom Line**   *The change in worker-to-retiree ratios could cause great strides in labor-saving technologies, resulting in fantastically productive workers. In this case, fewer workers could support leisured elders if the elders invested in human and physical capital innovations through their pension funds, tax payments, and other savings and investment institutions. At the other extreme of possibility that emanates from an aging population transition, is the gruesome situation that few low-paid workers are taxed at very high levels to pay for the leisure of healthy older people.*

America's Unique Pension Debate

Political leaders will be forced to make decisions dealing with the expense of aging populations. Although obscuring future expenses with rosy economic projections and using other delaying tactics are tempting, policymakers will have to chose among three options—all politically unpleasant: (a) retrench, usually by raising the normal retirement age; or (b) refund, by raising taxes; or (c) restructure, by privatizing.[15] These are the three "r's" of political reality. For twenty years (barring the exception of the Medicare expansion), the U.S. system of retirement income security has retrenched, starting with the 1983 Social Security cuts, and continuing with employer pension erosion in the 1980s and 1990s when defined contribution pension plans (that is, 401(k)-type plans) usurped defined benefit pension plans.

Global economic agendas are expressed both by governments and by international organizations. The World Bank's report on pensions in 1994 became a manifesto for more individual responsibility in retirement planning, for changing social norms to reward and make legitimate longer work lives, to penalize "early" retirement, and for private individual pension accounts to replace national Social Security and company plans. In short, one clearly expressed global agenda is to retrench—to get the elderly to work more.

The aging population in the United States presents a problem that is mild compared to that of other nations. It's less a problem here because fertility rates and immigration rates are higher than in other developed nations. In 2050, the United States is projected to spend only 5.5% of our gross domestic product (GDP) on pensions and health care, compared to Italy, which is projected to spend 18.5%. A common way to display statistics about pensions is to list the projections of an aging population alongside projected expenses of paying for the elderly, alongside how much men aged over sixty-five work. Displaying the data this way suggests that the solution to the expense of paying incomes to the nonworking elderly is to have the elderly work. In other words reduce pension costs by reducing the number of pensioners!

The nations with the largest projected expenses associated with aging unfortunately also have the smallest labor force participation rates, barely above 1% for older men. Among German men, 4% over the age of sixty-five work, compared to 16% of American older men who work. The rate of Japanese older men who work is the highest among nations, but their projected expenses are still high relative to the projected expenses for elderly in the United States. The positive correlation between current labor force participation rates for men, and lower future expenses for the aged, suggests that older people working more can relieve the expense of an aging population. However, this is not a perfect correlation. See table 6.2, which is reproduced from a similar

Table 6.2
Americans Spend Less on Pensions and Older Americans Work More
Work effort, expense, replacement rates in five nations

	Average Labor Force Participation Rate of Workers Age 60 and Over	*Share of GDP Spent on Old Age Programs in 2000[b]*	*Average Replacement Rates from Old Age Programs in 2002[b]*
United States	18.7%	5.2%	51.0%
Japan	30.3%	6.4%	59.1%
Britain	15.5%	7.7%	47.6%
Germany	8.8%	10.8%	71.8%
France	4.2%	10.4%	68.8%

[a] International Labor Organization 2000.
[b] O.E.C.D. 2005, and Whitehouse and Whiteford 2006.

table constructed by the Organization for Economic Development, a voluntary organization of thirty of the world's richest industrial democracies dedicated to promoting economic growth and trade.

The information in table 6.2 implies another lesson: that more work among the elderly is not inevitable. Other nations with higher costs associated with an aging population choose to pay the costs for more elderly leisure. Looking at the data in this way makes the case for *lowering* retirement ages in America. Actually, the United States has a lot in common with poor nations. Old people in nations with half of our per capita GDP work just as much as they do in the United States.

> **DATA TO DIGEST**
>
> ▪ The U.S. GDP per capita was over $44,000, and the male labor force participation rate of people aged fifty-five to fifty-nine, was about 79% in 2001.
>
> ▪ Nations with a per capita GDP in the $2,000 range have a male labor force participation of 83.7%.
>
> ▪ In 2001 in the United States, the labor force participation rates of men between ages sixty-five and seventy ranged from 38.7% to 24.5%,[16] which is similar to rates in North Africa at 29.2%.
>
> ▪ In Asia, 42% of men over age sixty-five work; in Europe 14.9% work.[17]

Policy Implications of Repositioned Retirement Norms

There are many possible scenarios for responding to the aging population. The U.S. General Accountability Office (GAO), the nation's auditor, warns that European nations' zeal to encourage the elderly to work is causing "overwork"—a concept not recognized by the economics profession, though it is absolutely clear what it means. "Overwork" denotes people working because they have lost income. If push factors are dominant—meaning people are forced to work because they don't have sufficient financial resources—then the United States is experiencing a reversal of decades of improvements in workers' retirement opportunities and workers' living standards. If people are being pulled into a strong labor market with enough bargaining power, then work is enticing to the elderly, life for them has never been better, and the overall increase in work—for everyone—is a win for the economy and for all workers themselves.

> **Bottom Line**   *It matters a great deal whether older people are living longer, leading healthier lives, and happily seeking work, or are being forced to work because their incomes have fallen.*

Conclusions: Old-Age Leisure in America

Forming a new social contract on retirement depends on understanding what was the old social contract. The old social contract was that people could choose to retire or not, even if they were healthy and able to work past a certain age. This expectation developed in the post–World War ll period and came about because of economic growth negotiations among labor, capital, and the government.

However, the contract is changing as the erosion in pensions and Social Security and increases in health care costs mean the elderly can maintain their buying power only by working more.[18] That Americans must "consume" less leisure—in other words, Americans have less free time at retirement age—represents a reversal of fortunes for working-class and middle-class Americans. Policies aimed at delaying retirement create classes of winners and losers; the winners are tempted to overstate the benefits to society from a change that benefits them, and the losers are not speaking up. If the increase in work is occurring among groups with lower life expectancies, then they are losing the most retirement leisure, and the distribution of retirement leisure, as well as income, is getting worse.[19]

In the United States, the attack on retirement is pressing forward with both carrots and sticks. The carrots are analogous to enticements to work in response to increases in Social Security benefits in return for years of delayed eligibility, as well as the various ways public policy and popular culture—consumption and youth oriented—promote work and demean leisure. The sticks are analogous to punishments for not working, in terms of smaller and more insecure pensions. One "pro-work" policy change—raising the retirement age[20]—presents itself as a carrot, but it functions as stick by penalizing retirees through pension reduction.

The matter for public debate is whether the increase in retirement and the increase in longevity "overshoot" the amount of free time an older person in America "deserves" to have. The answer partly depends on an empirical question: How much time do workers have for themselves after they retire and before they die? Social scientists have depended on the average retirement age and its flip side, average labor force participation rates, to give rough indications of old-age leisure. These are approximations, and confuse averages with people's experiences. Chapter 7 explores the mistakes made when we use this method of calculation.

Chapter 7

The Distribution of Retirement Time:

Who Really Gets to Retire?

Yes, the average American is retiring earlier and living longer. However, these two facts do not mean that people are spending more time in retirement. Jumping to that conclusion means assuming that longevity is going up faster than the retirement age is decreasing for everyone. We do not know that. Besides, only some people are living longer and only some people are working more. Stunningly, no one has considered that the reason we are living longer is precisely that we are retiring at earlier ages. There is credible evidence that retirement improves health, and evidence that working more would reverse those improvements in longevity.

The amount and distribution of how much time people spend in retirement—I will call this retirement time—are tricky to measure. After measuring accurately enough the distribution of retirement time across the population of the elderly correctly, I was pleasantly surprised. It seems that Americans of all different races and income levels have about the same amount of retirement time. The reason retirement time is the same is because the retirement date is flexible—Americans can start collecting a pension as early as age fifty (in some cases), and mandatory retirement is illegal so workers can stay in the labor market if they want.

Another way to explain the equal distribution of retirement time is that people can retire at different *chronological* ages so that they can retire at the same *real* age. Chronological age is measured by how much time has elapsed after your birth; real age takes into account how much time you have left. An eighty-year-old with such a healthy profile that she is predicted to live ten more years is the same real age as a feeble seventy-year-old who only has ten years to live (you will see more about this distinction throughout this chapter). For now, consider this: as we get older, measuring our age is less relevant than measuring the time left before our death. Think about it. When we are young, chronological age is a pretty good predictor of how long we will live. All five-year-olds are predicted to live about the same number of years. Their chronological age and real age are about the same. However, the correspondence between chronological age and real age gets fuzzier as we get older. A seventy-year-old retired coal miner is a lot "older" than a seventy-year-old retired college literature professor. If the professor has the same number of years to live as an average sixty-five-year-old, then his real age is sixty-five. If the seventy-year-old retired coal miner has as much time to live as an average eighty-year-old, his real age is eighty.

This chapter measures retirement time—the time between the day we retire and the day we die—and also discusses how retirement time is distributed among people with different wealth levels, different races, and genders. In 1994, the World Bank argued that pension annuities were regressive, that they were unfair to the poor. The World Bank's reasoning was that, since high-income workers live longer, they collect more lifetime benefits than people who die sooner—leading to the conclusion that annuities favor the well-to-do. But I see it a different way. Professionals are also likely to work longer than blue-collar workers. Therefore, such a system can be more balanced than it would appear. In fact, pension systems that pay out annuities *and* let people retire earlier could end up being very progressive. If people who die earlier also retire at younger ages, they could conceivably have the same amount of retirement time as higher-income people who live longer.

The U.S. retirement system allows people to retire at different chronological ages, which helps equalize the amount of retirement time across socioeconomic classes—time spent in retirement is surprisingly equal across class and race.

The Value of Time and the Link between Paid Work and Health

Having the option to retire is very important to the quality of our lives. Retirement time matters a great deal to people. Retired people engage in more healthful self-care activities than people with full-time jobs—the opposite of what was the common wisdom that retirement made men (especially) sick and depressed because they gave up their identity and the meaning of their lives when they gave up their jobs.

Studies have refined assumptions about what makes work beneficial to some old people; it is not so much identity, but keeping mentally active and maintaining close relationships, which is almost always what healthy, satisfied old-age people do.[1] There is no evidence linking paid work with those features.

The thinking that work kept us young and healthy was mostly based on observations that, when people retired at younger than the usual ages, they were likely to be less healthy. But the causation is not clear. Less hardy folk often have to retire earlier. Researchers armed themselves with the idea that "work is life." Better data and statistical techniques untangle the causation.

It is likely that the explosion in early retirements is causing the increase in longevity. Instead of the two trends—earlier retirement and longer lives— being two unrelated events, they are likely related. More time in retirement may actually be the cause of longer lives! University of Wisconsin economist Kevin Neuman finds that retirement improves women's health and slows down the deterioration of men's health—meaning men who are not retired report that their health becomes worse and worse as time passes, compared to men who are retired. In other words, the rate of change of health decline is faster for working older men than for retired older men.[2] If retirement leads to healthier outcomes, then pension reform aimed at getting Americans to work longer might inadvertently cause Americans to die sooner, which would slow or reverse longevity gains.

Although most economists use income and wealth to measure well-being, time may be a significantly more important measure for older people. Why? Time becomes more valuable as it becomes more scarce. The "Levy Institute measure of economic well-being" index[3] reveals that adding time to household income reduces the measured disparity in total well-being between the average American household and the average elderly American household. In 2000, the elderly had 87% of what an average American household had in command of resources. A comprehensive measure of "command of resources" includes time away from paid work. The elderly have 55% of the cash income of an average American household. Adding "free" time significantly reduces "well-being" inequality in the entire population, which corresponds with the findings represented in this chapter.[4]

*Major Finding: The Distribution of Retirement
Time Is Strikingly Equal*

Retirement time from the age of retirement to the age the person turns
sixty-five (data limitations prevent us from computing all retirement time, the
point of retirement to death) is fairly equally distributed across the socio-income
spectrum. This means that if Social Security pension eligibility and employer-
provided pension eligibility ages were raised, that would risk taking leisure time
away from the people at the bottom of the income and wealth distribution.
Among all people who are between the ages of fifty-one and sixty-five and who
are retired, the richest—those in the top quintile of the wealth distribution—do
not have more than 20% of total pre–sixty-five retirement time.

DATA TO DIGEST

- *Older men in the top quintile of asset distribution—those with assets worth
  over $271,000, had 5.57 years of retirement time per man and 22% of the
  total amount of retirement time (see figure 7.1).*

Figure 7.1
The American Retirement System Distributes Retirement Time Fairly Equally across
Race and Sex: The Share of Retirement Time before Age 65 by Income and Sex.

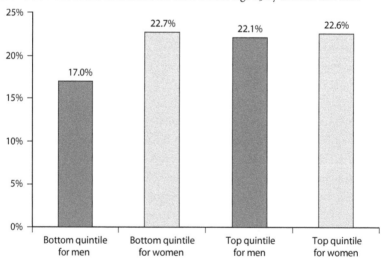

Source: The data to calculate the years of expected years of retirement time is from the Health and Retirement
Study sponsored by the University of Michigan. The calculation is made based on a sample of workers who retired or died before age 65. I observed the actual amount of retirement time in years and months until a person
reached 65 or died. I then calculated what the share of total retirement time each income group by sex had.

■ *Men in the bottom quintile—those with an average debt of $6,000—obtained 18% of retirement time.*

■ *There is still a disparity, but, compared to 20% of the men having 85% of all the wealth and the poorest 20% having debt, the distribution of retirement time before age sixty-five is almost equal.*

■ *For women the distribution of pre–age-sixty-five retirement time is equal. The top and bottom fifths of women get the same share of retirement time—22.6% for the top and 22.7% for the bottom.*

Real Age and Chronological Age

Real age varies widely for people who are born on the same day in the same year.[5] A retirement system that allows retirement ages to vary over chronological ages is the only way to ensure that people have access to retirement time at approximately the same real age. For example, a disabled fifty-five-year-old with a chronic disease expected to live only ten more years is the same real age as an average seventy-seven-year-old expected to live until eighty-seven. The "old" fifty-five-year-old should be allowed to retire younger. In a retirement system allowing retirement only at sixty-five years—the chronological age—the chronically ill fifty-five-year-old gets no retirement time.

Though raising the retirement age and reducing benefits in workplace pensions might make "younger" older people work more, it may deprive older people of retirement time. Cutting benefits by raising the normal retirement age wrongly assumes that the effect is neutral because every group in society has obtained the same rates of increase in longevity.

The case for raising society's normal retirement age to solve economic growth, labor shortages, and fiscal imbalances[6] is not supported. There is no evidence that "too much" retirement is being consumed in America.

Who Has the Most Retirement Time?

Yet a number of trends suggest that people are consuming more retirement time. On average, people are living longer; on average, older men are working less; and on average, older women's labor force participation rates are increasing more slowly. Further, the proportion of Social Security recipients collecting early retirement benefits, which was two-thirds in 2001, has increased over the last thirty years.[7]

The belief that average retirement time has increased resides in those who propose to increase the normal retirement age. But we all know that averages do not tell the whole story. There are many reasons to expect—besides the differences in health and attitudes about work and leisure—that there would be systematic differences in both longevity and retirement behavior; for instance, rich people would have better jobs and better health care, making work more attractive. Some groups die sooner and some retire earlier than others. If these groups overlap, then retirement time might be equally distributed; if they are negatively correlated, then retirement time is unequally distributed. The evidence is clear as you will see in the data that follow.

Who Lives Longer?, and Is the Longevity Gap Widening?

You saw in chapter 6 that white men are enjoying the most improvements in longevity.

DATA TO DIGEST   *In 2000, at age fifty-five the life expectancy for all men was twenty-three years and ten months, a 26% improvement from 1950.*

- *Likewise, female life expectancy at age fifty-five increased 23% from 1950 to twenty-seven years and five months.*
- *However, these average improvements hide significant differences by race. For the same time period, at fifty-five years of age white male life expectancy improved by 26% (from nineteen years and one month in 1950), while the corresponding life expectancy for African-American men rose by only 19% (from a much lower 1950 level of seventeen years and four months).*
- *African-American women experienced greater growth than white women, at 27% compared to 22%, although they still expect to live over two years and six months less than white women—twenty-four years and eleven months compared to twenty-seven years and six months.[8]*

The few percentage point differences in the growth rates may not seem significant. However, small differences in growth rates add up. In 1950, the longevity gap between white men and African-American men at fifty-five years of age, was 7%. In 2000, the white male longevity advantage grew wider, to 9%. If the same differentials persist, then approximately forty years from now, in 2050, the white male advantage at age fifty-five will have almost doubled—to 12% longer than black men of the same age. As Hunter College social psychologist Virginia Valian says in another context, small differences in rates of growth may look like mole hills but, "Mountains are mole hills one piled on top of the other."

Race and sex are not the only divisions that explain mortality differences. Blue-collar workers have lower life expectancies than do white-collar workers. This fact, along with the findings that, unfortunately, blue-collar men and men in lower-skilled white-collar jobs have slightly less retirement time than white-collar professionals and those who do not work in "goods-producing" industries, suggests that inequality in retirement time exists now by social class. Furthermore, medical and public health researchers find that people in jobs that are subordinate in a hierarchy have higher mortality rates than workers who have control over the way their work performance is judged, and some say over how secure their jobs are.[9] This suggests that longevity gaps between socioeconomic groups could widen over time if jobs become more insecure due to outsourcing and offshoring, among other human-resource strategies.

If employees in subordinate, and otherwise lower-status, jobs cannot retire earlier than those who have more control over their work life, they will have less retirement time before they die. If workers at the bottom of a work hierarchy cannot retire earlier, then the inequality in work life will carry over and magnify in old age, when those at the top have more retirement time before they die. The possibility that this is happening is troubling, so I set out to investige the matter.

Who Retires Earlier?

The study economist Kevin Neuman conducted, and that I was closely involved with, sought to discover if the same people who retire earlier are those who are likely to die sooner than the average person. There is some evidence that retirement timing is not always a person's decision made alone. Only one-third of retired people retired at an age they expected to. Most retired earlier than they had planned, and most of those who retired earlier than they had planned did so for health reasons.

DATA TO DIGEST   *A 2006 McKinsey Company survey of 3,000 retirees found that*

- *Only 36% retired when they expected to.*
- *57% retired earlier than they had planned.*

■ *Of those who retired, 70% were forced to retire because of health problems or job loss, 47% because of ill health, and 44% because of job-related issues; the remaining 9% retired to care for a family member.*

Of the three groups who retire earlier than average—through poor health, job-related reason, or preference—two groups are unfortunate and probably die sooner than average; the third group, who prefers leisure, is fortunate and more likely lives longer.

Poor Health. This group retires because they are in poor health[10] but do not qualify, or do not apply for, Social Security disability insurance. Their poor health may limit their ability to work but may not be severe enough to qualify them for disability insurance income. Or they are disabled but have not met the insurance eligibility requirements—women are the majority of the early retirees who could have qualified for disability benefits if they had had a long enough work history.[11] Of early retirees (those who collect reduced Social Security benefits, aged sixty-two to sixty-four), 20% report substantial health problems. This means the Social Security retirement program acts like a quasi-disability program. Because disability administrative law judges can use an applicant's work history and the conditions in the applicant's labor market in qualifying an applicant for disability insurance, the disability program also acts like a quasi-retirement program. (Collecting Social Security disability insurance is a better option than collecting Social Security early retirement benefits because Social Security disability insurance beneficiaries obtain full Medicare coverage before age sixty-five.)

In the 1970s, researchers were concerned that men who retired early commonly responded to surveys with "poor health" as the reason they retired in order to avoid being stigmatized as lazy. Verification of their poor health status with objective assessments by a number of means—including reports from a person's doctor, the person's body mass index (the body mass index is a number calculated from a person's weight and height, and provides a reliable indicator of body fatness for most people; it is used to screen for weight categories that may lead to health problems), whether the person had diabetes, or abnormally high blood pressure—confirm that a person's own assessment of his or her health is usually accurate.

Because it is not far to leap to the conclusion that people in poor health also die sooner, and there is plenty of other evidence that shows people in poor health have lower average income and wealth levels, we can understand why, at the beginning of the twenty-first century in America, the distribution of retirement time is distributed as equally as it is. People who are not well and expect to die early retire earlier.

> **Bottom Line**   *Poor health and high mortality are not randomly distributed, as if the only cause of early death were longevity genes randomly distributed across a population. Early mortality is not all "nature." "Nurture" plays a large part. People in "bad" jobs are more likely to die earlier than people in "good" jobs. Fortunately, some people in "bad" jobs tend to have pension plans, in conjunction with Social Security and retiree health benefits, that facilitate early retirement.*

Job-related reasons for early retirement. The second group of workers who left the labor market before age sixty-five retired because they were laid off: they lost or left jobs because either their plant or company closed or moved, or there was insufficient work for them to do, or their position or shift was abolished. Workers laid off must have bargaining power to get early retirement pension benefits. Alas, for too many workers, what would have been a severance payment is called a "pension." What is really a layoff or unemployment is called "retirement." In the manufacturing and mining industries, collectively bargained labor contracts commonly allow collection of retirement benefits after thirty years of service, no matter that the retiree is younger than the usual retirement age. Workers having put in that time in these industries exhibit earlier retirement ages, but they probably did not retire early because collectively bargained labor agreements promote it. Industries with insecure jobs, such as manufacturing, may orient their personnel policies toward early retirement. Retirement is not entirely under a worker's control. It should be known that retirement is often a joint decision between employers and workers, not just the workers' decision.

Early pension eligibility ages often indicate slack labor demand. Industries characterized by massive layoffs—airlines, communication, manufacturing—since the 1970s have used early retirement packages and other attractive benefits to encourage exits from their firm.[12] It may look as if workers and their unions favor and bargain hard for generous early retirement provisions that sometimes appear in defined benefit plans, when in fact these benefits are second-best alternatives to a secure job.

Pensions that encourage early retirement are more likely to appear in unstable industries, which suggests that workers who retire early may not be obtaining windfalls in terms of years of retirement. A closer look at the details and incentives for early retirement in company pension plans reveals that they usually occur in places where the job characteristics are linked to bad health and foreshortened lives. These jobs are such that they require performance under stress and extremely hot environments, repetitive manual processes, physical strength, coordination, and flexibility.[13] Therefore, the common interpretation that generous early retirement benefits induce early retirement is certainly wrong. The causality goes in the reverse direction. Job characteristics that induce early retirement also induce employers and employees to configure compensation in order to provide early retirement benefits, presumably because these jobs lead to physical deterioration, disability, and early death. In 2003, Princeton economists Angus Deaton and Anne Case found that people in jobs with these characteristics experienced early sickness, disability, and mortality. Therefore, early retirees may be consuming the same, or even less, retirement time than individuals who retire later.

Firms use retirement policies to handle fluctuating demand for their products and industry transitions. Older auto workers tend to retire well before age sixty-five, not only because their pension plans contain early retirement incentives, but also because auto firms use overtime, rather than hiring, in periods of increased production. Because older workers are less likely to tolerate 50- to 60-hour work weeks, they retire instead at a real age that may be far older than their chronological years.[14]

> **Bottom Line**   *Having a bad and an unstable job is the second reason workers may retire at earlier ages. And the opportunity to retire early helps explain why retirement time consumed before age sixty-five is so surprisingly equally distributed.*

Preference for Leisure. The third group of those who retire before age sixty-five is fortunate—they retire early because they want to. The people in this group retire for two reasons: because they have the pensions to retire, and because in our society it is not shameful to retire even if you don't have a disability or work limitations. But policymakers worry that the mere availability of early retirement benefits could create new social norms for early retirement, especially through inducements in that direction—inducements based on the notion that workers cannot stand the idea of not collecting benefits they are entitled to. This means people may be retiring at younger ages than previously because the pension is available to them.

Some researchers argue that early retirement is caused by generous early retirement pension benefits because many people have personal "high discount" rates. That is, some people discount the future at a high rate, meaning they live for the moment, and cannot tolerate the possibility of losing out on benefits later to which they are currently entitled, no matter that the benefits may be worth more later than currently.[15]

This explanation of why people retire early supports the policy suggestion that the early retirement age in Social Security be raised from sixty-two to sixty-five.[16] But this proposal is based on the assumption policymakers would have to make that workers weigh the costs and benefits of working one more year, with the objective of maximizing the value of their lifetime benefits, and retire when the costs outweigh the benefits, then boosting pensions for working longer would get people to work longer.[17]

> **Bottom Line**   If workers do not control their retirement age, and have to retire early for reasons other than a finely tuned cost-benefit analysis, then raising benefits for people who work longer and cutting benefits for people who can't work longer could merely raise benefits for people who are wealthier, healthier, and lucky to be in good, stable careers.

Who Actually Obtains Retirement Time?

Even if American workers can choose their own retirement age—aware that retirement ages vary in employer pensions, that Social Security allows collection of early reduced benefits, and that age-discrimination laws protect older workers from discrimination—workers cannot choose their own death age. Therefore, workers do not control how much retirement time they can obtain. If workers can partially compensate for what they think may be an early death by retiring sooner, then they may have as much retirement time as those with longer lives who retire later. This could mean that our retirement system distributes retirement time more evenly than it distributes income and wealth. To find out, I investigated further using the University of Michigan's Health and Retirement Survey (HRS), which is the most complete survey of older people's wealth, health, pensions, and retirement behavior.[18] I examined the data for more than one thousand men and nine hundred women who have worked more than fifteen years,[19] to uncover differences in the retirement time before age sixty-five. I looked at retirement time before ages sixty-five because these people were not old enough to have reached normal death ages. (As this group grows older and more people in the group die—the oldest in the group was born in 1935—the distribution of time between retirement and death will likely grow wider and likely become more unequal based on lifetime income, because lower-income individuals die at earlier chronological ages.) I defined "early re-tirement time" for each person in my study as the amount of time each had in 2002 between her or his retirement age and when she or he reached age sixty-five.

DATA TO DIGEST

- Men have slightly less early retirement time than women, five years plus a little over one month, compared to five years and about three months.
- Men and women retired at about the same age on average, age 59.3 years for men and 59.5 for women.
- Men and women have different financial and health profiles at retirement.
- Men have both more DC type pensions and more DB pensions than have women: 26.8% of men compared to 21.4% of women held a DC pension, and 55.8% of men compared to 39.6% of women held a DB pension.[20]
- Men and women report they have similar health, even though men die earlier—11.1% of men died before the age of sixty-five, compared to only 4.3% of women. (Either men systematically report better health than they truly experience, or men's deaths are less predictable.)

High and Low Retirement Time for Women

I divided the sample of individuals I just described into two groups, those with above-average retirement time and those with below average (see table 7.1.). High-retirement-time women—those women with more than the average 5.4 years of pre–sixty-five retirement time—are less likely to have pensions (it seems curious that pensions are correlated with more retirement time for men!), are more likely to be married, have more wealth, and are slightly more likely to be nonwhite. Nonwhite older women have more retire-ment time before age sixty-five!

The starkest difference between the high–retirement-time group and the low–retirement-time group of women is that the high–retirement-time group seems to have lower "real" ages. They have the life expectancy of people older

Table 7.1
Characteristics of Older Men and Women Who Retired before Age 65

Characteristic	Men	Women
Early retirement leisure (years)	5.23 years	5.37 years
Percent dead by age 65	11%	3.5%
Prediction of life expectancy compared to actual life expectancy [a]	0.99	0.87
	(about right)	(pessimistic about living long)
DB pension (percent covered)	55.8%	39.6%
DC pension	26.8%	21.4%
Financial wealth	$65,747	$53,496
Nonwhite	17.1%	23.3%
Married	86%	65.7%
Good health	75%	76.7%
	$n=1,094$	$n=921$

[a] The age-adjusted life expectancy includes fewer observations due to missing values ($n=1,019$ for men and $n=900$ for women).

then themselves, their health is worse, and they are more pessimistic about how long they will live compared to what most people their age predict. Be mindful that women who retire before age sixty-five are pessimistic about their longevity compared to women who are still working or who hardly ever worked for pay. Women who retire earlier think they will not live as long as the actuary predicts women their same chronological age will live. They think they will live only 87.2% as long as the actuary predicts they will. This is strong evidence that women are retiring according to their real age, and may be compensating for what they expect to be their shorter lifespans.

High and Low Retirement Time for Men

The interpretation that people compensate for a pessimistic view of their longevity by retiring early holds up when we explain differences between men with a lot of retirement time and men who have below-average retirement time. About two-thirds of men with more than average retirement time report being in good health compared with the 82.7% of men with less than

Table 7.2

Distribution of Retirement Leisure by Selected Characteristics

Average characteristics of "high-leisure" and "low-leisure" older men and women

	Men		Women	
Characteristic	*Above-Average Leisure*	*Below-Average Leisure*	*Above-Average Leisure*	*Below-Average Leisure*
Early retirement leisure (years)	9.35	2.76	8.85	2.9
Percent dead by age 65	7.56%	13%	2.9%	5%
Prediction of life expectancy compared to actual life expectancy[a]	.56 (pessimistic about living long)	1.1 (optimistic about living long)	.87 (pessimistic about living long)	.84 (pessimistic about living long)
DB pension (%)	64.6%	50.5%	33.9%	43.5%
DC pension (%)	16.1%	33.2%	27.2%	13.2%
Financial wealth ($)	85,094	54,228	64,467	45,929
Nonwhite (%)	17.3%	16.9%	22%	24.4%
Married (%)	82%	89%	69%	63%
Good health (%)	63%	83%	72%	80%
	n=684	n=411	n=373	n=548

[a] The age-adjusted life expectancy includes fewer observations due to missing values (n=1,019 for men and n=900 for women).

average time in retirement who report they are in good health. It also seems that men compensate for an expected early death because high–retirement-time men are pessimistic about their mortality. They think they will have much shorter lives—only 56% as long as the actuary predicts (see table 7.2.). It makes sense that men in worse health and pessimistic about their life expectancy would retire earlier.

The Difference between Survivors and Nonsurvivors

I refer to retired men who died before age sixty-five as nonsurvivors— they didn't survive until age sixty-five. And I refer to men who lived beyond age sixty-five as survivors. Nonsurvivors worked fewer years and retired at earlier ages than those who survived beyond age sixty-five. On average, the men who died before age sixty-five, the nonsurvivors, retired at age fifty-seven; men who survived beyond age sixty-five, the survivors, retired at age sixty. Early retirement time was almost the same—men who died before age sixty-five enjoyed five years and four months of early retirement time, compared to the five years and six months for the men who survived beyond age sixty-five. There were 121 men in my study who died before age sixty-five; these nonsurvivors differed from the survivors in several respects. The non-survivors had less coverage in defined contribution pension plans; they had less wealth[21] ($43,853 compared to $686,730 owned by the survivors); they were, as you would expect, less healthy; they were less likely to be married; and they had worked fewer years than men who did not die before age sixty-five. The nonsurvivors worked thirty-three years compared to thirty-nine years for the survivors. Interestingly, the survivors were not more likely to be nonwhite, nor did they come from any particular occupation or industry.

It seems that men who died early actually acted to compensate by retiring early. The nonsurvivors reported in a survey before they died that they felt they had a lower probability of reaching age seventy-five,[22] which further suggests that they considered their early mortality risk when deciding to retire. Similar conclusions are drawn from women's experiences.

Forty-one women, out of 921 in my study, died before age sixty-five. They retired almost three years earlier than the survivors and were more pessimistic than the survivor women about their lifespan. Consequently, among the women in my study, the survivors and the nonsurvivors obtained almost an identical early retirement time—5.43 years for the survivors compared to 5.48 years for the nonsurvivors.

Unlike the men in my study, the race of the women mattered in terms of who survived until age sixty-five; shockingly, 52% of women who died before age sixty-five were nonwhite and only 23% were nonwhite. Nonwhite women reported having worse health, but both whites and nonwhites reported they were limited in what health professionals refer to as activities of daily living, which are a measure of self-sufficiency.[23] Women who died prior to age sixty-five, the nonsurvivors, worked twenty-seven years, compared to thirty-two years of work by survivor women. Compared to the survivors, the forty-one women who died before age sixty-five had the same pension coverage but less wealth, approximately $9,000 compared to more than $55,000 for those who lived past age sixty-five. (Much of the wealth difference is undoubtedly that nonsurvivors were much more likely to be single.)

Is Retiring Earlier Really the Ticket to Retirement-Time Equity?

It looks as if people who die before living to age sixty-five—those cheated out of a long life—are not cheated out of retirement. Also, it looks as if race does not determine differences in retirement time, but wealth does. I use statistical methods that help me compare individuals who are alike in all relevant ways, except for a few key factors, to isolate the effect one factor has in explaining the differences in retirement time among individuals. Such a technique is called "regression" analysis and it examines the relationship between a characteristic or an outcome (that can be quantified) and another phenomenon or characteristic (that can be quantified) that may cause the outcome. For instance, we want to know what determines the amount of time between retirement and death. We can isolate one characteristic, for instance race, to see whether persons of different races, but who are the same in every other respect, have different amounts of retirement time.

Regression techniques were used to untangle whether the differences between retirement ages and longevity systematically influenced differences in retirement time for each different group. For example, African Americans retire earlier and die sooner than whites, but that could be because of how much money they have, or what kinds of jobs they hold on average, and not their race.[24]

Because social factors in retirement affect women differently than men, I considered how each of these factors affects women separately from men.

> **Bottom Line**   *The results of the regression analysis confirm that people act to compensate themselves for the differences in their longevity by altering their retirement age. However, men who died before age sixty-five did not fully act to compensate for their loss of retirement time by retiring early. Dying before the age of sixty-five reduces male retirement time by about one year and five months, which is 27% less retirement time compared to the average male. The more physical limitations a person reports in being unable to perform the activities necessary for daily living, the more retirement time that person will have, after considering the other factors that can affect retirement time: wealth,*

race, the kind of pension plan they had, and what kinds of jobs and industries they worked in.

In addition, because we know that people in good health work longer, it is not surprising that, after we consider when people die, good health reduces retirement time by over two years. A consideration of all factors that affect mortality reveals that men who die early have less retirement time because they do not fully act to compensate for their early death by retiring early. In stark contrast, women who are victims of early death have higher average amounts of early retirement time. Women appear to be able to predict their early deaths better than men and are able to act on that information by leaving the labor market. Interestingly, although participating in a DB pension plan helped men obtain one year more of early retirement time, women in a DB pension obtained ten months less retirement time. The differences between the effects of DB plans on men and on women could be a reflection of the dual nature of the plans. These plans are aimed to induce loyalty to the firm—up to a certain point in a worker's tenure at the firm; later they go into reverse, tending to induce retirement. Women, in this generation, have likely entered the workforce at older ages; so they are still within the point in their careers where loyalty is being rewarded, not at or beyond the point when eligible for early retirement incentives. For these women, the value of working compared to not working may be higher than it is for men.[25]

For men, having wealth increases early retirement time as expected, but the effect of wealth in the form of savings is small. For example, increasing an Individual Retirement Account value by $100,000, leads to an increase in early retirement time of less than four months for men. For women, the value of an Individual Retirement Account, on having low socioeconomic status, seems to have no effect on retirement time consumed by women.

Last, the study showed that whether or not a man is married does not seem to affect early retirement time—but the average married man says he considers his wife's retirement decision to be part of his decision to retire. This result suggests that the joint household retirement decision causes a married man, on average, to delay retirement until his wife is ready to retire. Women do not list a spouse's retirement plans as an important factor in their decision to retire (see table 7.3.).

These findings are represent good news about our retirement system. Race does not have an independent effect on retirement time and there are very slight, if any, differences by occupation. Wealth also does not have a large

Table 7.3
Factors Influencing Retirement Leisure*

Factors that might affect how much retirement time you had before age 65	When the factor changes, retirement leisure:	
	Men	Women
Dying before age 65	Decreases by 1.4 years	No independent effect
An increase in needing assistance with activities of daily life (ADLs)	Increases by 1.01 years	Increases by 1.25 years
Perception that one is in good, not poor, health	Decreases by 2.1 years	Decreases by 1.48 years
Having a DB pension	Increases by 1.15 years	Decreases by 0.82 years
Having a DC pension	Decreases by 1.36 years	Decreases by 1.69 years
An increase of $100,000 in IRA value	Increases by .000031 years (hardly at all)	No independent effect
Having a $100,000 increase in financial wealth	Increases by .000015 years (hardly at all)	Increases by 0.00000019
An increase by one in total years worked since started working	Decreases by 0.06 years	No independent effect
Answered that spouse's retirement is important in your decision	Decreases by −0.97 years	No independent effect
Being married	No independent effect	Decreases by 0.90 years
Constant	8.499 years	5.15 years

All these factors had no effect on retirement leisure: whether a person is white or non-white, white or blue collar, college educated or not, in the Armed Forces, in goods producing industries, being a home owner or not.

$$N = 1,449$$

$$Adj.\ R^2 = 0.1278$$

*Controlled for birth year, the younger the person the shorter the period of retirement leisure period, beginning at 1932.

effect. Men who die early consume less early retirement time. That these victims of early death were not able to retire could be due to institutional constraints, their inability to predict their deaths, or mortality expectations not mattering in their retirement decision.[26]

Equalizing Retirement Time with Disability Insurance

Advocates for raising the retirement age worry that doing so would cause workers who are borderline disabled to lose income. Raising the retirement age while at the same time liberalizing disability and unemployment eligibility requirements can help retirees who cannot work and lay these worries to rest. The eligibility rules for Social Security disability insurance are already liberalized in order to account for the job insecurity that almost all unhealthy workers face. It is possible that many older people are unable to work but cannot meet disability insurance requirements, even if the requirements are liberalized. These folks would be unintended victims of benefit cuts that come about by raising the normal retirement age.[27] Some of the distribution of retirement time is due to random factors and leaves little room for a clear policy recommendation on this issue. Many people die while working despite their health, and not all those who die prematurely are in poor health.

Conclusion: Who Really Gets to Retire?

This chapter makes the case that the U.S. system of retirement income security programs distributes retirement time fairly evenly across the population. Because the system is flexible, workers can adjust retirement ages to compensate for difference in "real" ages at the same chronological age. These findings support the claims that

- older workers with wealth have more retirement time than poorer workers, although the difference is not large; the reason it is not large is because poorer workers can retire earlier if they choose to;

- people with poor health and people who have limitations in daily life activities have more retirement time; and

- people who suffer an early death obtain less retirement time; raising the retirement age would make this disparity worse.

From the findings in this chapter, we can say that it is not just the privileged, as defined by wealth and longevity, who receive retirement time. Nevertheless, this does not mean that people in poor health and people who have insecure jobs welcome the retirement time. But there is no reason to presume they enjoy the choice to work or retire any less than others do.

Policies should aim to allocate retirement time equally across socioeconomic classes. A system that mandates that workers save for their retirement—I propose such a system, Guaranteed Retirement Accounts—is described in chapter 10 and can help all workers accumulate assets for old age retirement. For such a system to be compelling, the goal—making sure that people have the resources to decide to retire or not—has to make sense. Is retirement a good goal? Retirement makes living standards more equally distributed among people in different socioeconomic classes in the United States. Chapter 8 explores whether or not the labor market is attractive to older workers, and whether it is good for the economy that people make decisions about retirement based on the amount of assets in their defined contribution accounts.

Chapter 8

Working: The New Retirement's
Effect on the Economy

An online marketing company serving "today's dynamic population of leading edge Baby Boomers and over 40 set" concluded, "Most 40+ still plan to work in some capacity after retirement. This is especially true for skilled workers with higher education . . . they continue to work for personal fulfillment." Yet according to that marketing company's survey, being fulfilled at work is not widespread; only 35% of forty- to fifty-four-year-olds and 44% of workers over age sixty-five find their jobs rewarding.[1] Similarly, 55% of older employees say they are postponing retirement because they find their jobs interesting. In contrast, 75% report "not having sufficient financial resources" as a reason to continue working, and 60% say they need to work for medical benefits, according to the Conference Board's 2006 survey—the board is a research organization sponsored by large American corporations.

The elderly are increasing their work effort more than at any other time since World War II. Older people are postponing retirement or returning to work after retiring for many personal reasons, including the two that are this chapter's focus—to make up for lost income and to do what they can in response to diminished expectations for income security. That the elderly enter the job market when unemployment rates are rising and wages are stagnating suggests that they are pushed rather than pulled into the labor market. Despite what the increase in work effort means to an individual, the increase in labor force participation of workers over age fifty-five is likely destabilizing the economy because of the details about the timing of their increased work effort. As DC pensions make up more retiree income, people's pensions are more exposed to the ups and downs of the financial markets. The problem is that when the market is down, work effort is up, and when the market is up—and employers are scrambling for workers—workers are retiring with their fattened 401(k) accounts.

Box 8.1

**Age Is in the Eye of the Beholder, the Researcher, the Lawyer,
and the Retailer**

The Current Population Survey reports statistics about people in specific age groups. The relevant age groups for the discussion of older workers and retired people are "fifty-five through sixty-four years old" and "age sixty-five and over." I referred to the first group as "older" and the other group as "elderly." I made up those designations. (Everyone else does the same sort of thing. And that is okay so long as the designations are identified and used consistently.)

But age is a fluid concept (as anyone who has gotten old knows from personal experience). A psychiatric study investigated whether memory training had any lasting effect on memory for "older" adults; in that study older adults were defined as aged sixty and over. (The good news is that memory training improved memory for over five years.[2]) In the United States, you can sue for age discrimination if you have been denied employment, promotions, or equal pay, and are over age forty.[3] In France, you can be forced to retire at age sixty. In America, you can get senior citizen discounts to watch soccer, tennis, rodeo, and other sporting events, but the age requirements for these discounts vary depending on the event. Usually the discounts are available to those aged sixty and over, but some discounts begin at age fifty or fifty-five. Amtrak seems to choose Social Security's age of eligibility for early retirement benefits—age sixty-two. AARP memberships are available for anyone at age fifty. (And if you are seventeen or over you don't need your parent or guardian to see an R-rated movie in a theater!)

A note about age before we continue. One line of reasoning in this book is that defining who is old and who is elderly is not a matter of biology. Age is sociological, economic, and political. In this chapter, I use the terms "old" and "elderly" to correspond to the organization of the government data I am using. For a full discussion of the definitions of "old" see box 8.1: "Age Is in the Eye of the Beholder, the Researcher, the Lawyer, and the Retailer."

There are plenty of admirable examples of older workers being pulled into the labor market. For instance, Home Depot, Inc., and AARP made headline news by announcing in February 2004 their national training program for workers over age fifty-five. However, the Home Depot program is sensitive to push factors; it targets the middle-class elderly, who, the *Wall Street Journal* report noted, "may have trouble making ends meet because of an increase in medical bills and a decline in their 401(k) pensions."[4] This chapter measures the increase in work effort, assesses if pull or push factors are the dominant personal reasons why older people are working more, and explores the macroeconomic effect—the effect on the entire economy—of the increased work effort.

Older Americans Are Working More

As previously mentioned, American men obtained large amounts of retirement time during almost three decades after 1950. Men over age sixty-five participated 60% less in the labor force or, expressed in less conventional terms, had a 60% gain in leisure participation during the twenty-five years from 1950 through 1985. (The leisure participation rate for any group is 100% minus the labor force participation rate of that group.) Remarkably, almost three out of four men, or nearly 75%, over the age of 60 were either working or looking for work in 1950, compared to 16% in 1985 and 17.9% in 2003. Even more surprising, one out of two men, or 50%, over age seventy were in the labor force in 1950; the labor force participation rate fell by an enormous 70%, to less than one out of seven, or 14%, in 1985, and one out of six, or nearly 17%, in 2002, the year when two older men, Mr. Olbert and Mr. Magill, were working, as you will see next.

Florida newspaper reporter Jeff Kunerth described George Olbert, a seventy-four-year-old delivery man, who worked two jobs, six days a week, from 5:50 a.m. to 6:00 p.m.; he was a rank-and-file member of the 17.5% of men over seventy who worked in 2002. He admits that bad investment luck and a lifetime of self-employment left him with nothing for retirement. He and his cherished wife of fifty-three years live on his monthly $710 Social Security check, in a bedroom that was converted from the living room in their adult daughter's home. Olbert did not love his jobs; he worked for money he needed to live on.

In the same part of the country, Tom Magill, a high-energy seventy-year old, taught economics at Palm Beach Community College after a successful career as an electrical engineer. While I was visiting the college in 2002, I asked him why he taught what much younger university professors would consider a grueling five days a week schedule. Magill said, "Mary, my wonderful wife of forty-one years, said she married me for better or worse, but not for lunch. She wanted me out of the house."[5] Tom Magill joked about being pushed into the labor market but he was clearly pulled by his desire and his success as a teacher. Magill's story demonstrates that the increase in the labor force participation of older people is partly a result of enduring vitality and older people finding expression in a productive setting. There is a difference though: Olbert was working for money; Magill was working for love.

American women, in contrast, steadily increased their labor force participation in the post–World War II period. Despite the differences in work effort between men and women, an important similarity remains: older women's labor force participation rates rose more slowly than younger women's. Moreover, elderly women decreased their labor force participation by the mid-1970s. Contrary to what many analysts believe today, that the elderly started working a lot more in the mid-1980s, the significant leap did not occur until the mid-1990s. (Timing matters in the detective work of trying to deduce whether older people are working more now.)

The timing of the boost in the elderly's labor force participation can be pinpointed only by comparing the situation at the same point in the business cycle: that is, work effort at the peak of one expansion should be compared with work effort at the peak of another. People are sensitive to the availability of jobs when deciding to seek work or leave the workforce. Therefore, labor force participation ebbs and flows depending on the strength of employer demand for workers. Adults respond to recessions and expansions by deciding among the possibilities available, such as working more hours; looking for work; withdrawing into retirement; accepting disability benefits rather than working as a disabled employee; taking on the role of full-time homemaker; or enrolling in school for training in some kind of new work. A common choice for younger people in a recession is to look for work to make up for lost income in the family. This is especially the case when a spouse loses a job or suddenly is limited to a specific reduced number of work hours. For older workers, tough economic times may trigger a decision to retire—of course, only if there is a sufficient source of pension income.

In an economic expansion, bright job prospects may induce older people to hop back into the labor market if not currently working, or to continue working because employers have made the job more attractive. On the other hand, an economic expansion may make retirement nicely affordable. Observing how labor force participation rates change over the business cycle for different age groups and genders, tells us how America's older workers respond to different phases of the business cycle, if those responses differ by age, and how those responses have changed over time.

DATA TO DIGEST   *Older men, aged fifty-five through sixty-four, and elderly men, aged sixty-five and over, generally withdrew into retirement during good times; labor force participation rates fell by an average of 2.7% for older men, and −8% for elderly men, sixty-five and older, in the last ten business expansions since 1948.*

Yet, in the most recent completed expansion—the long one from March 1991 to March 2001—the withdrawal rate from the labor market for the group aged fifty-five through sixty-four was less than 1%; while for the sixty-five and older, the elderly men's labor force participation went up by a noteworthy 14.7%.

These rates of labor force participation of workers over age fifty-five are sharp reversals of trends, and they occurred well before Home Depot and AARP reached out to older workers.

Women's labor force behavior in the last expansion also departed from trends because both older women, aged fifty-five to sixty-four years, and elderly women, aged sixty-five years and older, have recently increased their labor force participation many times over what the average rate of increases in the post–World War II expansion had been.

DATA TO DIGEST   *On average, older women, aged fifty-five to sixty-four, increased their participation rates by 6.8%; but, in the last expansion, the increase was 17.4%. Women in the elderly group, aged sixty-five and older, increased their labor force participation rate by an average of 2.4% in all post–World War II expansions except the most recent one, in which the increase was a much larger 9.2%.*

Changes in the labor force participation patterns for both men and women in contraction periods are less pronounced, but they trend in the same direction—toward more work. On average, in the last ten contractions, men aged fifty-five to sixty-four, did not change their labor force participation, yet they did in the most recent recession, March 2001 to November 2002.

DATA TO DIGEST   *Older men, aged fifty-five to sixty-four, increased their participation by a significant amount, by 2.8%, in the most recent contraction.*

Elderly men, aged sixty-five and older, also acted differently in the most recent contraction, but not by working more. Older women also broke from the trend. In the recent recession, the labor force participation of women aged

Table 8.1

Older Men Once Left Bad Labor Markets

Changes in older people's labor force participation (LFP)
during contractions and expansions

	Labor force participation in the trough subtracted from the labor force participation in the next peak (%)			
	Men 55–64	*Women 55–64*	*Men over 65*	*Women over 65*
Expansion that ended March 2001	−0.9%	17.4%	14.7%	9.2%
Average since 1949	−2.7%	6.8%	−8.0%	2.4%

Note: The first expansion occurred from October 1949 to July 1953, and the last completed expansion occurred from March 1991 to March 2001 (the current expansion started in November 2002). The first contraction occurred from November 1948 to October 1949, and the last contraction to date is from March 2001 to November 2001.

fifty-five through sixty-four increased by 7%, whereas the average increase in all the contractions was only 3%.

DATA TO DIGEST   *Men over age sixty-five withdrew faster in the last recession, by −3.9 percentage points compared to the average withdrawal of −2.3 percentage points in the past nine contractions. I attribute the higher rate of labor force exit to this group being particularly well covered by defined benefit plans. Elderly women, aged sixty-five and older, unlike elderly men, also increased their labor force participation in the most recent contraction by 5.3 percentage points—a stark reversal of elderly women's tendency to leave the labor market when times are tough. In previous recessions, elderly women left the labor market at an average rate of −0.04 percentage points.*

(See table 8.1 for a summary of the labor force participation rate changes over phases of the business cycle since 1948, and how recent responses to contractions and expansions break from previous trends.)

Bottom Line   *Labor force participation trends speak clearly and with one voice: men and women between ages fifty-five and sixty-four years entered into a new era of work starting in the 1990s, not before.*

	Labor force participation in the peak subtracted from the labor force participation in the next contraction (%)			
	Men 55–64	*Women 55–64*	*Men over 65*	*Women over 65*
Contraction ended November 2001	2.8%	7.0%	−3.9%	5.3%
Average since 1948	0.2%	2.0%	−2.3%	−1.5%

The Quality of Jobs Available to Workers Over Age Fifty-five—More Push Than Pull Gets Them to Work

There is no evidence that the labor market is especially friendly to older workers. As a response to the popular movement against age discrimination (although the labor movement was conspicuously absent from the national debate), Congress banned employers from forcing people to retire because they reached a certain age. Congress outlawed mandatory retirement in 1986, three years after it raised the age at which one was eligible for full Social Security benefits. During the eight-year campaign against age discrimination— the protected age starts at forty—an earnest national effort to help older people to work began. The AARP, then the Association for Retired Persons, and the Department of Labor each established training programs for older workers. Yet, fifteen years later, economist David Neumark's exhaustive study of age discrimination in 2003 shows that the number of age discrimination suits has increased since 1980. The increase in workers over age forty suing employers for bad treatment could be explained either by more workers over forty being treated badly or by an increased willingness to sue or, more likely, by both.

If older workers are being enticed to stay in or enter the labor force, we would expect they are so enticed when wages are increasing and the risk of being unemployed is falling. Instead, the evidence suggests that older workers are facing employers who clearly have the upper hand. Many older workers are faced with stagnating wages, rising unemployment, and being offered low-status jobs in the 1990s and early 2000s. AARP analyst Sara Rix follows the jobs that workers over age fifty-five take, and publishes a report annually. In 2002, the year the upturn began, her report showed a rapid increase in the older people's labor force participation and comparatively bad working conditions compared to the experience of people ten years younger. If the older people were laid off, they had half as much chance as younger people of being reemployed, which suggests why the charges filed with the Equal Opportunities Commission began to increase starting in 1999, after falling from 1994 through 1999. The average duration of unemployment started to rise in 2002. The average search for job seekers over age fifty-five was sixteen weeks, up from 12.7 weeks in 2001.

Furthermore, one of the significant changes in the labor force since 1983 is increasing job insecurity for men over age fifty-five.

DATA TO DIGEST   *Older men's median years of job tenure—the number of years a person has been employed by their current employer—has fallen by almost 50% from 15.3 years to just 10.2 years for men aged fifty-five through sixty-four. The decline in job security has been much smaller for older women; the average job tenure for women over age fifty-five was 9.8 years in 1983, dropping only to 9.6 years in 2002.*

Besides looking at labor force participation rates and job tenure, we can also look at unemployment rates at the same points of the business cycle for help in identifying long-term trends. So I compared unemployment rates for groups of white workers over time. (The number of African Americans and Hispanics in the over-age-fifty-five workforce has been too small to make meaningful conclusions about changes since the 1940s.) The unemployment rates for older workers, those over age fifty-five are consistently much smaller than for younger folks, but unemployment rates have risen much faster for women over age sixty-five; between November 2002 and November 2004 elderly women's unemployment rates rose by 7.7%.

Note that the first expansion occurred from October 1949 to July 1953, and the last completed expansion occurred from March 1991 to March 2001 (the current expansion started in November 2002). The first contraction occurred from November 1948 to October 1949, and the last contraction to date is from March 2001 to November 2002. In the most recent completed recession elderly (over age sixty-five) women's unemployment rates rose by a large 33%, although in the recent completed expansion elderly women were the group most in demand (especially as home health aides and retail clerks), and their employment rates paced job growth.

Although the rate of unemployment for older men, age fifty-five to sixty-four, did rise in the most recent recession (March 2001–November 2002), it rose the least compared to other groups (see table 8.1). Also, there were no significant differences in patterns in wage growth by age to justify a conclusion that, despite the increased risk in unemployment, fast wage growth lured people over age fifty-five into the labor force.

In addition to wages and unemployment, another good indicator of labor market quality is job type at retirement age. Interestingly, women over the age of sixty-five are distributed among the occupations in ways that look very much like the distribution of much younger women, aged twenty to twenty-four. Using a simple statistical measure of the relationship between the distribution of old and young women across occupations, I found they are almost identical. The correspondence[6] between these two groups is 98%. This means that women over the age of sixty-five may be competing against young women in sales and clerical occupations. However, this is not the case for men. Men over age sixty-five are distributed along the same occupations as the group of men nearest in age, those aged fifty-five through sixty-four. The correlation distribution in each occupational title between the two age groups is 85%.

Bottom Line

- *Older men's job experiences are different from older women's job experiences.*
- *There is no clear evidence that older people who are looking for work, or who are working, are better off than younger workers.*

Government Accountability Office economist Sharon Hermes demonstrates that most people who leave retirement and hop back into the labor pool take jobs that are lower in pay than their career jobs. This suggests that financial need is pushing elders into the labor pool rather than enticing opportunities pulling them in. Her evidence suggests that insecure pension income propels some older workers to seek jobs.

How 401(k)s Destabilize the Economy

The timing and distribution of the return to work could have far-reaching and unintended consequences. The remainder of this chapter describes the effect of retirement timing on the economy. The consequences are rooted in the reasons why older people are working more—which is mainly because defined benefit pension plans and Social Security's replacement rates have declined, while 401(k) plans have become more popular, but not more valuable, forms of retirement accounts. Shaky financial markets in the early 2000s caused older workers to work more as they became less confident about the security of their retirement income. As financial, market-based, individual retirement accounts replace DB plans, the large U.S. economy, and specifically some smaller community economies, will have lost an important automatic stabilizer. When older workers cannot leave the workforce because they need jobs and cannot afford retirement during bad economic times, unemployment will get worse.

You can get a good sense of the adverse economic effects of retirement income based on financial assets by considering the following: Compare two similarly situated people. Person A has a secure pension, say a DB promise from an employer plan and Social Security, and retires when the economy slows. Person B's retirement income is based on financial wealth in a DC plan. When the economy dips, B works longer because her pension is linked to economic performance. The amount of money in B's DC account need not be large nor need there be vast changes in the S&P 500 index for her to realize that her retirement money is based on what happens in the market, that it is not a guaranteed annuity, and that it has a big impact on how she feels about leaving her job.

If pension income is linked to financial performance, and older people hang onto their jobs and those not working begin to look for work when the economy begins to slow, then unemployment gets worse and the labor market weakens for everyone. AARP reported in 2002 that younger workers were feeling stuck in their careers because senior employees were hanging onto their jobs.

Generation X and Generation Y are in a double bind. (Exact demographic boundaries of the generations are not well defined, but Generation X generally includes anyone born from 1962 to 1980 and Generation Y those born from 1981 to 1995.) They can't move up because retirement-age superiors aren't leaving their jobs, and the abysmal job market means there is less opportunity to job hop. Sharon Hermes and I found that the stock market crash of 2000 caused older workers to seek work or stay in jobs longer. We used two data sets: one that includes a large number of Americans in a single year from the Census Bureau (the Current Population Survey), and one that follows people over a period of time (ten years), a longitudinal panel of older individuals, by the University of Michigan Health and Retirement Survey (HRS). According to our results it is likely that the 40% decline in the stock market between January 2000 and October 2002 caused the labor force participation of older workers, those between age fifty-five and sixty-four, to increase by about 2.64% for men and 5.36% for women. (We accounted for the other factors influencing work and retirement decisions.[7]) The remarkably close correspondence between the increase in overall labor participation rates and the fall in stock market values can be seen immediately when changes in the rates for older workers are put on the same graph as changes in the value of the S&P 500 over the same years (see figures 8.1 and 8.2). When men's and women's labor participation rates are separated out, it is clear that older women aged fifty-five through sixty-four are driving the close correlation.[8]

A disappointed older worker described to a newspaper reporter the effects of the stock market crash in 2001 and his 401(k) collapsing. "I thought I would at least be able to take a break and think about what to do with the second half of my life." Mr. Pringle, aged sixty-three, went on, "but I didn't have a lot of options when the market went south." The reporter added, "To many Americans, the sustained slide in the stock market—particularly last week's nose dive—has been something to fret about, a darkening cloud. But to many people at or near retirement age, it has been a colossal jolt."[9] The correlation between what was happening to retirement and what was happening in the stock market is also expressed in a 2004 Met Life Inc. survey, which found that 48% of U.S. workers believed they would have to take on part-time or full-time work to maintain their financial stability in retirement.

If more people had defined benefit plans, some of these feelings of insecurity would be tempered and the economy would be more stable. Instead of older people having to work more when the economy slows, they could gradually phase out of working, as older people tended to do in past recessions. Social Security, of course, does not depend on stock and bond prices to pay out a steady and secure income.

Defined benefit pension plans and Social Security help prop up particular communities[10] as major industrial sectors shrink, in particular, manufacturing, mining, and transportation. Steel companies, automotive parts and assembly,

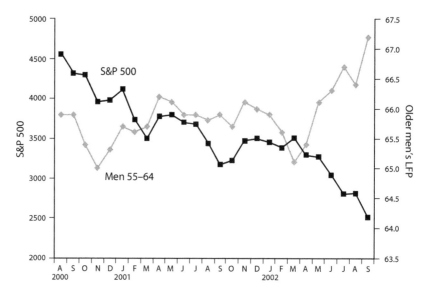

Figure 8.1
Older Men's Labor Force Participation Rose When the Stock Market Fell

airlines, and telecommunications used voluntary retirements that were induced by early retirement "incentives" in DB plans,[11] and also used layoffs to reduce payroll. Of course, voluntary "retirements" are a better outcome for the economy and for workers than layoffs, although, because voluntary retirements can be a way for a worker to avoid being laid off, it is necessary to accurately describe what retirement is. A retirement that substitutes for a layoff differs significantly from a voluntary retirement decision that is not made under duress. Further proof that DB plans can help stabilize the economy can be found in industries that provide DB pension plans, the same industries that have massive layoffs.[12] Every company with massive layoffs in 2001, except Dell and Amazon, had a DB pension plan (see table 8.2).

Unfortunately, these stabilizing effects, which are economy-wide, may be lost, because the industries with the fewest pensions are the fastest growing. Service and retail industries have been the fastest-growing industries in the last two decades. Employment jumped 23% from 1989 to 2001 in retail, where the percent of total compensation going to pensions is the smallest—only 1.4% in 2001 compared to the all-industry average of 3.5%. Service employment jumped 30%, while the share of pay going to pensions was only 2.5% in 2001.[13] The scarcity of pensions in these industries relative to other industries implies that, when downturns occur, layoffs are the dominant method of

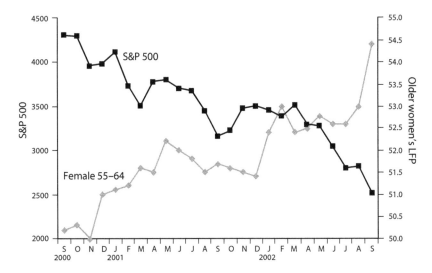

Figure 8.2
Older Women's Labor Force Participation Rose When the Stock Market Fell

downsizing, which makes more people look for jobs and exacerbates unemployment for older workers.

Furthermore, health insurance premiums have been increasing at a double-digit pace—projections for 2008 forecast a 10% increase in premium costs. In addition, since 1995 there has been a steep decline in health insurance provided by firms to their retirees.[14] The only way retirees can get health insurance (including Medicare supplements) is to work for an employer who provides it, and hope that the employer will continue to provide it. Paying for an individual health insurance plan is prohibitively expensive for most retirees. So older workers who have the opportunity make up for the loss and uncertainty of retiree health insurance by working.[15] Pension erosion[16]—employer expenditures for pensions have dropped by a whopping 22% between 1978 and 1998—has a similar effect—it induces the elderly to work more.

Bottom Line

- *Older workers eligible for Social Security and defined benefit pensions are more likely to leave the labor force and retire rather than be laid off and looking for work.*
- *When older workers have guaranteed retirement income they step back from the labor market in a recession, unemployment is arguably lower than it would otherwise be, and consumer spending does not fall quite as far.*

Table 8.2

Many Laid-Off People Have DC Plans That Can Lose Value in Recessions

Layoffs in the 2001 recession: companies and their pension plans

Company	Layoffs Executed or Planned (February 2001)	Percent of Pension Costs Spent on DC Plans (Based on 1998 Pension Data)
Daimler Chrysler	26,000	49
Lucent Technologies	16,000	1
Motorola	9,370	56
Goodyear	5,300	13
JC Penney	5,300	21
Dell Computer	1,700	100
Amazon	1,300	100

Source: This table is computed from information from Internal Revenue Form 5500, showing pensions characteristics of each firm; percent spent on DC plans calculated by the author.

- *Older workers, especially women, are entering or staying in the labor force more than they would otherwise because pensions have lost value and security.*
- *When compared to similar individuals with DB pensions, men and women aged sixty-three to sixty-four with only DC pensions experienced a significant reduction—between 20 and 24 percentage points—in their probability of retirement when the stock market fell.*
- *When older women and men move from a career job it is usually to a job that has lower status.*
- *Not only does an increased dependence on the labor market in a recession make older workers more vulnerable; it weakens the economy.*

Pension Surprises and Work

That the erosion of guaranteed pensions leads to an unstable economy is profound and chilling. It pays to explore further the link between pension instability and increased job-seeking during weak economies, and to review what other researchers think about that link. Imagine trying to get on with your life as an Enron worker in 2001. They learned, practically overnight, that not only had they lost their jobs but also that their 401(k)s filled with high-flying Enron stock were suddenly worthless. These educated and driven workers tended to buy houses in the same neighborhoods. In the "Enron neighborhoods," demand for houses lagged behind house supply so their home values plunged. In addition, corporate scandals, such as Enron's (and there were others, alas!), contributed to a national recession, making it difficult to find jobs anywhere. Some Enron workers would have been able to retire if they had had a DB plan, thus preserving some buying power for their household and communities. At the Congressional panel where I was testifying in 2002, Thomas O. Padgett, a thirty-year veteran of a chemical division Enron bought, said that he planned to retire and run a farm for handicapped children so that their caregivers could take short vacations. Instead, he underwent carpal tunnel surgery so he could keep working for another ten years in a lab.[17]

Other evidence suggests that workers postponed or planned to postpone retirement because of the unanticipated fall in retirement wealth in the early 2000s. In January 2002, the Gallup Organization reported that nearly 20% of people who owned stocks were considering postponing retirement by four years on average; the figure was higher, 26%, for workers aged fifty and older. Four months later, Gallup found that 45% of nonretired Americans over age fifty did not expect to have enough money to live on comfortably when retired and, on average, predicted they would retire at age sixty-three—back in 1995, the average estimated age of retirement was sixty.[18]

The reverse is actually true. People stop working if they receive a big increase in portfolio wealth or win the lottery. A 2002 study by venerable retirement researchers Alan Gustman and Thomas Steinmeier suggested that the stock market boom of the 1990s increased retirement rates by 3 percentage points. Congress's decision to boost Social Security benefits by a surprisingly significant amount in the late 1960s led to more retirements between 1969 and 1973.[19] Federal Reserve economists Julia Coronado and Maria Perozek in 2001 showed that one-third of people in their sample retired earlier than expected when the stock market boomed; among those who retired the earliest were those who had much larger gains in their stock portfolio values. The average increase in the value of stocks was $93,000 for early retirees, compared to an average gain of $58,000 for the entire sample. The greater the share of equities in the portfolio, the earlier the retirement date. Further evidence about labor force responses to changes in wealth is gleaned from studies on the effect of unearned income (such as lottery winnings) on labor earnings. Others found that people are apt to work less when they "come into the money," meaning when there is a sudden large increase in income from nonworking sources. A survey of lottery players in Massachusetts in the mid-1980s revealed that every 10% increase in income from not working decreased the proportion of people working by 11%; there were even larger effects for increased income from nonworking people aged fifty-five through sixty-five. Additionally, the survey found that low-income workers, in general, actually do not stop working when they win the lottery, but they do stop saving for retirement and increase their consumption.[20] This should give us pause when we try to predict the effect a stock market boom will have on retirement savings—it may actually cause us to diminish savings!—or what a tax cut or other windfall will do to people's choices about working, saving, and consuming.[21]

Economists Courtney Coile and Phillip Levine in 2004 refuted the claim that the stock market has any effect on retirement because, sadly, barely half of workers have pension accounts, and the average value of those accounts is a puny $15,000. For them, a fall in stock values would not affect a major decision like retirement. I don't think Coile and Levine are correct; even though only half of workers aged fifty-five to sixty-four have retirement accounts, the average value is a significant $71,040 (the median value[22] is $33,000). Though $71,000 is a lot of money, common sense would suggest that even if a large fall in stock values cut this in half, the money itself would not be enough to influence such an important decision as retirement. But the fear that other sources of income would fall or some other economic disaster occur certainly would be enough. Coile and Levine were measuring the wrong thing. I agree with Gustman and Steinmeier who argued in 2001 that small changes in wealth can cause big changes in people's perceptions of security.

That fear is a powerful factor in retirement decisions makes sense. Workers receive pension benefit statements once a year, while they are bombarded daily in the media with reports on the stock market. Because impressions about the value of financial wealth are influenced by imperfect knowledge and sensational information—the point made by Robert Shiller—it is not unreasonable to conclude that workers make their best estimate of retirement affordability based on easily available and widely accepted, though imperfect, information about the value of their retirement wealth. The S&P 500 became one measure for the value and perceived durability of retirement wealth. In addition, that recently divorced women work, on average 1.5 years longer than they expected, supports the prediction that people will work more when they lose income.[23]

Bottom Line *To cope with fluctuations in the industries in which defined benefit plans are offered, most DB plans induce people to retire almost two years earlier than they would otherwise. The increasing share of DC plans since 1983 is estimated to have raised the median retirement age by two to four months, and we find that it could increase the age of retirement by two to five months more as people rely increasingly on DCs for retirement income.*

Conclusions and Policy Implications: The New Retirement

It was possible to imagine that older people working more than they had in the post–World War II period has a positive contribution to social well-being. After all, civilized societies should allow anyone who wants to work to do so. Age discrimination against any workers is reprehensible, inefficient, and mostly illegal in the United States. More older Americans are working but there is little evidence that the U.S. labor market has become friendly to older workers and has made work more attractive.

It seems older people are postponing retirement and working primarily because their sense of pension security has diminished, along with losses in their 401(k)-type pension plans. If there had been more DB plans in place, it is likely more people would have retired when the economy could not employ everyone who wanted a job. Therefore, the change in the type of pension plan can affect the entire economy. Defined benefit plans, along with Social Security, help stabilize the economy by encouraging people to retire when jobs are more scarce. In contrast, DC plans do the opposite; they have a destabilizing effect on families as well as on the economy. The destabilizing effect will grow over time because younger workers, aged twenty-five through thirty-nine, are more than twice as likely as older workers to have only DC plans.[24]

The destabilizing effect will not affect all communities equally because industries where demand for their products is highly sensitive to conditions in financial markets, such as industries that use 401(k)-type plans and have substantial amounts of employer stock in those accounts, will also be more vulnerable. When the demand for their products falls and they need fewer workers, employers providing DC pension plans will be encouraging their older employees to stay put.

Women have to face peculiar risks at older ages. In the past, married women have been the most likely to be able to exit the labor force at older ages and have worked primarily for love of they work they do. As work becomes a more stable source of income than marriage, women may face increasing pressure to work in old age.

The United States is the only OECD nation (Organization for Economic Cooperation and Development) that bans forced retirement and expects the elderly to work for pay. Changes in the employer pension system may force workers to spend their longer lives in the workforce, which reverses decades of improvements in workers' retirement opportunities. A guaranteed stream of retirement income would help ensure that the elderly work for the right reasons.

The labor movement is the only organized political action group that has consistently sought the working person's access to jobs, retirement, and pensions. The next chapter explores unions' successes, failures, and the stakes in employer pensions.

Part III

The Rescue Plan for Retirement

Chapter 9

The American Labor Movement:

Advocating Retirement and Obtaining Pensions

Pensions did not spring forth from the brains of employers as Athena sprung forth from Zeus's head (but that was only because Prometheus took a rock and split open Zeus's head to relieve him of his headache!). Employers did not start out providing pensions to their rank-and-file employees until unions in a Promethean move—civilizing humankind by taking privileges once reserved by the gods—demanded that all working persons were entitled to a pension shortly after World War I. Pensions were, up to that point, a benefit reserved for management.

The American labor movement promotes employment-based pension plans and continues to advocate for improvements in Social Security. One challenge for organized labor is to create the conditions for firms to manage their responsibilities for pensions in an orderly way as their defined benefit plans and retiree health care plans mature and become more expensive.

Pensions are not merely a source of money for pills, poker, and cable TV every month. A second challenge for the labor movement is to manage the dual life of a pension fund. Pension funds are a source of pension income, and a source of financial power for the entities that control them. The American labor movement, starting in the 1920s, recognized the financial impact pension funds would have on the economy and demanded a role in managing pension investments. Labor union goals for managing money can be viewed from both offensive and defensive perspectives: offensive in the sense that unions use their position as representing the worker-investor to advance constructive actions to further their union goals; defensive, because unions aim to influence pension investments in order to defend their interests. At the very least, organized labor wants to ensure that its victories at the collective bargaining table and in government policy are not undone by its own pension fund investments, for example, by having their own pension funds buying equity shares or bonds in aggressively antiunion firms. The labor movement also aims to direct their members' pension fund monies to economic development that expands employment in areas where unions are already present or likely to expand. Organized labor wants the money in their members' pension funds to reward unionized employers and advance labor standards. In meeting the two challenges—helping employers manage pension costs and leveraging pension funds to promote union goals; and improvements in wages, hours, working condition, job security, and such—the successes have been mixed. But the labor movement's success in getting pensions to people who would not ordinarily have them is remarkable.

This chapter argues that, despite the American labor movement's weakness, its experience with pensions serves as a model for international pension reform. More unions in other nations are negotiating occupational pensions,[1] and have copied American pension fund and investment activism.

Unions Opt for Employee Benefits

What organized labor wants from pension systems has not changed much in the modern industrialized era. But labor unions have dramatically changed the composition of compensation between cash wages and employer-provided employee benefits—pensions, health insurance, sick leave, vacations, holidays, funeral leave, flexible hours, among similar other benefits. In addition, unions tend to favor defined benefit plans and, when one is created, a union usually initiates it for a job that never had a pension attached to it before.

Much has been made of the positive connection between collective bargaining and workers' preferences for employee benefits. What causes that connection is usually understood as the union reflecting the demands of the workers and providing that information to the employer. In this view, unions are efficient, low-cost, information providers—nothing more.

Nevertheless, I think the cause of unions' influence in the provision of employee benefits is in the reverse direction. Decisions move from unions to workers and from unions to employers, which makes more sense since a workplace union has profound effects on employers' and workers' opportunities, constraints, communication, and sense of identity.[2] The process of collective bargaining changes worker preferences for all aspects of compensation: cash wages; insurance; pensions; and pay for time not worked, such as vacation, holidays, sick and funeral leave.

I claim that unions do not simply poll their members and then communicate to employers that workers want a particular combination of pay and employee benefits. I claim that because the process of collective bargaining is a deliberate and formal way workers come together to discuss their financial futures, what their time is worth, and their aspirations for promotion and fair evaluation, it influences what workers regard as important. The collective bargaining process can move workers' preferences toward other aspects for compensation besides money—such as the long-term benefits embodied in insurance, pensions, and paid time off.

That union members are, in general, twice as likely to be covered by pensions as nonunion workers is one way to support this claim. Union members have higher levels of pension coverage across a range of earnings. In fact, the only way a low-income worker generally has a pension is if he or she is in a union.

DATA TO DIGEST

- *Unionization boosts pension coverage by approximately 20% for workers earning below the average hourly wage and by 11% for workers earning above average annual earnings.[3]*
- *The rate of increase in employer spending on worker pensions reveals significant differences by union status. The rate of growth for pension spending is 42% for nonunion workers, compared to 95% for union workers between the years 1988 and 2003.[4]*

Workers with the lowest rates of pension coverage are low-wage earners (income between 45% of the average wage and the average wage) working for firms with fewer than one hundred employees. The pension union premium for these at-risk workers is 100%. Being in a union doubles the likelihood that low-income people working in small firms have pension coverage.[5]

Where did this strong union effect come from? In the three decades after World War II, the United States employer-based benefit system grew to cover two-thirds of the working population for health insurance and one-half of the working population for pensions.[6] The American labor movement was always weaker than its European counterpart, and labor unions were not powerful enough to push forward national health insurance, a more comprehensive Social Security system, mandated vacations, and sick leave. Large employers, including some that were paternalistic and others that wanted to thwart efforts to organize nonunion employees into unions, created the American "welfare state" in the 1920s.

The labor movement molded its goals and constructed its strategies around what employers (including local and state governments and school districts) offered their employees. It is clear enough that employers may have agreed to provide employee benefits and to accede to union demands for business reasons—to attract and retain scarce workers. But, at the same time, those employers that provided pensions profoundly changed social expectations and beliefs about what good employers do—good employers provide pensions and health insurance.

Bottom Line

- *The American labor movement shaped employer pension design and retirement policy, as well as retirement expectations. Union contracts throughout the years have strengthened defined benefit plans, and in the last two decades unions have negotiated 401(k) supplements to those DB plans.*
- *The unions' effect is strongest for workers most at risk of not having a pension.*
- *The decline in unions (the portion of the labor force represented by unions fell[7] from 35% to less than 8% from 1953 to 2006) means a decline in pension coverage, and a decline in coverage in DB plans in particular.*

  Nevertheless, pensions are threatened, and whether workers have a right to them has been contested. Who owns these pensions depends on what form of payment they represent, as you will see next.

Are Pensions Deferred Wages, or Payments for Depreciation?

Unions had to make the case for working people's entitlement to pensions. They used competing metaphors and each metaphor had different and powerful implications. Sometimes pensions were described as representing "deferred wages" and sometimes as an employer's payment for the "depreciation" of workers' bodies and minds after long periods of work. Economist (and Jesuit priest) Paul Harbrecht in 1959 described the differences in the pension approaches of the progressive industrial workers, represented by the Congress of Industrial Organizations (CIO) and the more established craft unions in the American Federation of Labor (AFL). The CIO tended to describe pensions as a "payment for depreciation," whereas the AFL viewed pensions as "deferred wages." The payment for depreciation model implies that the employer owes a payment to workers. The idea underlying pensions as deferred wages is that employers are rather neutral and pensions merely help workers save for the future, because pension plans help facilitate an intertemporal—meaning between periods of time—transfer of consumption. On the other hand, the idea that pensions are deferred wages implies that workers pay for pensions by accepting a reduced wage.

Firms did not recognize pensions as deferred wages or depreciation payments—to them, pensions were gifts to be used as tools. From the 1900s to the 1920s, the largest American corporations adopted welfare capitalism programs, including pensions, and created personnel management departments that were linked to wide-ranging efforts to rationalize the work pay, recruitment, and promotion processes. The employers' goals in providing pensions were to delicately balance the conflicting actions of making some employees loyal while encouraging others to leave. More than three hundred pension plans, covering 15% of the workforce, had been established by 1919. By 1924, just four firms—two railroads plus AT&T and US Steel—covered one-third of all pension plan participants.[8] Of course, most workers would die, or leave the firms they worked for, before the age of compulsory retirement—age sixty at many firms—and rank-and-file workers were less likely to ever receive a benefit than were management employees.

At the beginning, the labor movement arranged the payment of pensions as charity, not an employer gift, deferred wage, or depreciation payment. In the 1880s, labor unions began as "mutual aid" societies whose major function was collecting funds from members to provide self-help aid, such as funeral benefits, which were not provided by employers. The contributions to mutual aid "trust funds" linked directly to payroll were an extension of this concept of self-help.

The Brotherhood of Electrical Workers and Electrical Contractors (Local 3) of New York was probably the first union to establish what is called a multiemployer pension plan, in 1929.[9] Multiemployer pension plans cover workers who have more than one employer, are in the same or similar occupations (may require similar training and skills), and are hired by employers in the same industry, such as workers in mining, needle trades, meatpacking, trucking, and the craft trades in construction.[10]

In other words, unions designed multiemployer pension plans (they are regulated by labor and trust law) in order to ensure that workers employed in industries where workers commonly move from employer to employer have pension coverage (health insurance plans are usually attached to the multiemployer trust). That unions control the multiemployer trust fund—financed by employer contributions, presumably diverted from wages—makes sense and is acceptable. Americans have the right to control their property. This pension model spurred the formation of multiemployer pension plans for other workers in the industries such as those just mentioned. The largest multiemployer pension plans include the Western Conference of Teamsters, the Central States Teamsters Plan, and the pension funds for plumbers, operating engineers, and mine workers. As these unions were directing their own pension plans, employers were developing their single-employer plans.

In the 1920s, the few single-company plans that had existed for thirty or so years became more mature and more expensive. Consequently, both union multiemployer and single-employer pension plans disappeared during the 1930s depression. Thirteen international union pension funds collapsed; only four survived after World War II. Public-sector workers, such as New York City employees, fared better—Massachusetts state employees, Civil War pensioners and dependents, and teachers' pensions in some states were public-sector pensions that stood in contrast to what private-sector workers lacked.

As industrial workers became organized in new firms in the post–World War II period, unions would demand in collective bargaining negotiations the same benefits management already had. Industrial unions aimed to make pension bargaining legitimate, claiming that pensions were payments for the depreciation that employers had extracted from workers.

The United Mine Workers of America (UMWA) was not the first union to negotiate pensions, but it significantly helped define the union role in establishing workplace pensions after the Great Depression.[11] The UMWA story describes the special ways unions strive to obtain job security from the collective bargaining process, and not just higher wages and more consumption. Declining coal demand and automation of dangerous debilitating coal mining jobs caused substantial miner displacement after the war. In 1945, the UMWA demanded a fully employer-paid, $100 per month pension for old and retiring miners, and the union characterized its demand as "payment for past service." Instead of arguing that pensions were a type of deferred wage (payment for services rendered) that had to be accumulated before paying out, the UMWA (and many other industrial CIO unions afterward) argued that pensions were depreciation payments owed to labor and thus were analogous to employer expenses for "wear and tear" (depreciation) on capital.

Although the term "legacy cost" was not used then, it was argued that pensions were owed because they represented payments for "legacy benefits" given. Legacy costs refer to the future cost of pension and retiree health benefits (and any other promise to pay in the future) that are not backed by financial assets in a dedicated trust.

Legacy benefits are a much less familiar concept, but they represent the toil and effort put out by the depreciated worker for the benefit of the employer and consumer. The more toil and effort, the higher the productivity, and presumably the higher the pay, and therefore the higher should be the pensions. Pensions, then, are complements—they accompany and exist because of higher wages. Pensions are not, in the depreciation view, deferred pay, that is, promises made in lieu of wages; in other words, pensions are not substitutes for pay.[12] Pensions, instead, are owed by employers and customers to workers. The depreciation argument firmly establishes the obligation of employers and consumers to pay the pension of the older and retired employers. The deferred wage argument also, like the depreciation metaphor, concludes that workers are owed all the promised pensions, but it turns out to be a much weaker argument.

During World War II, wage and price control policies had to solve two problems. Defense and related firms, desperate for workers, were making enormous, and socially unsavory, profits from the war; these firms were bidding up wages and putting pressure on wages and prices. President Roosevelt created the War Labor Board in 1942 in order to develop a "comprehensive national economic policy" to control prices, wages, and profits, and to stave off inflation that would be the inevitable result of businesses bidding up wages to attract scarce labor. Wages and prices were meant to be controlled, but the price controls were vague. The board controlled prices to ensure that profits were not "unreasonable or exorbitant" in the judgment of the board members. An Excess Profits Tax—the first was enacted in 1917—was used to raise government revenue on profits deemed to be earned primarily because the nation was waging war. Excess profits are defined generally as profits in excess of prewar earnings. Congress passed four excess profit statutes between 1940 and 1943. (In 1945 Congress repealed the tax, but imposed it again during the Korean War.) In a boost to pensions, the board deemed that money spent on employee benefits (such as pensions, heath insurance, vacation benefits) was not profit or wages and salaries. The board reasoned that since this form of payment did not cause labor costs to rise immediately, nor put money in people's pockets (consumer demand would not spike), company profits diverted to pension funds were exempt from the excess profits tax and wage controls. Companies wanted to pay pensions; but companies did not want to enter into contracts about how to pay for them. In the late 1940s and 1950s, Supreme Court decisions sided with unions against employers and made pensions a subject employers had to bargain over. The court deemed that pensions be included in the National Labor Relations Act as mandatory subjects of bargaining—wages, hours, and working conditions.[13]

If pensions are deferred wages, then employers and employees having joint control of a pension fund makes sense. Since the pensions are employees' money, they should have a say in how their money is invested. Because employers guarantee the full benefit, they should have a say in how the pension fund is managed and invested. Unions can negotiate a benefit but they do not have a claim to a fully funded benefit promise. In other words, if you divert your pay into a savings account, you are entitled to control your savings account but you are not entitled to a guaranteed specific amount of return. On the other hand, if pensions represent payments for depreciation, then consumers and employers owe replenishment, they owe secure income, and they owe retirement to the workers who provided the goods and services produced and consumed. In that way, the unfunded past liabilities, the so-called legacy costs, have a flip side. Legacy costs are accompanied by legacy benefits, which are the value of the work that employers and consumers enjoyed, which took a toll on the human beings who worked.

> **Bottom Line**   *Organized labor's demands for pensions were accompanied by a new entitlement claim.*
> - *Organized labor demanded that old but healthy workers should be able to retire, just as the wealthy were able to retire.*
> - *Unions demanded retirement as a state that was worthwhile for its own sake, not because old workers would happen to be more at risk of infirmity or superannuation. In other words, the claim that workers were entitled to leisure in old age because they were "too old to work and too young to die,"[14] evolved to become a claim for socially legitimate retirement.*

■ *The U.S. labor movement's evolution, from self-help to advocacy for retirement and a government pension system, is similar to the history of organized labor's retirement income agenda internationally. This is because "welfare capitalism" expressed itself more fully in the United States than anywhere else.* [15]

What Unions Do: Explaining the Union Pension Advantage

There are at least five economic reasons to explain why union members have more pensions than nonunion workers:

Efficiency wage and gift exchange. Unions raise wages and bargain for pensions that increase in value the longer a worker stays with her or his firm. Union workers not wanting to lose their jobs work harder to keep them. This extra productivity pays for the pensions.

Voice and facilitation effect. Unions can tell employers that workers want to trade off cash for pensions. Organized unions of workers can do this in a way that individual workers cannot. In addition, unions can make it less costly for employers to provide the benefit. Unions can reduce those costs in either or both of two ways: by spreading the administrative costs over a large number of workers; or by providing the employer with information about what workers want, information that would otherwise be expensive for the employer to collect.

Preferences for saving. Unions could be educating their members about the need for financial security.

Solidarity. Union members have a sense of community and affinity for their work group; this likely engenders their tolerance of, as well as their desire for, the redistribution of risk and income security implicit in group insurance, such as defined benefit pension plans.

Power effects. Unions provide workers with economic bargaining power to force employers to give up profits to provide pensions.

Most of these explanations help make clear that both unions and DB pensions increase a worker's likelihood of staying longer with a particular employer. The effect a pension plan has on employee loyalty partially explains why unions create an environment for DB pensions and why these pension plans create an environment for unions. This is clear in efficiency wage and gift exchange theory, which constitute one set of related explanations for employers providing pensions.

Efficiency wage theory views any type of pay that increases with more years of service (considered tenure-weighted pay), such as DB pensions plans, as "discipline devices." (Health insurance serves in much the same way, because older people find health insurance more valuable as they grow older, while putting in more and more years with an employer.) For example, DB pensions raise the cost of a worker losing his or her job. Middle-aged and valuable employees who are covered by pensions, according to the efficiency wage theory, work hard and shirk less because they fear losing their pension, which is likely rapidly accumulating value.[16]

The gift exchange theory refers to exchanges between employers and workers or managers, exchanges that are considered "gifts." They are gifts in the sense that they represent a valuable transfer of some type of pay that does not require a particular response, even though the effects of gifts are positive, such as tighter ties, trust, and loyalty. In the same regard, pensions represent gifts in the sense that they acknowledge loyalty on the part of the employer to their older workers, stabilizing relations between workers and employer, and in other ways improving the workplace.[17] However, what has happened is that "pensions as gifts" has faded in importance as a metaphor, replaced more and more by pensions as a deferred wage and depreciated payment. As the profitability of long-term contracts diminishes, employers adopt DC plans, which lower their costs and sever workers' relationship with the employer and with other workers.

In a widely read 1984 book, *What Do Unions Do?*, Harvard economists Richard Freeman and James Medoff argued that unions provide an example of the superiority of "voice" over "exit" as devices in market transactions. Unionized workers who want workplace improvements have a voice because of collective bargaining. Without the ability to complain and bargain for workplace improvements at the end of the contract period, workers might resign to find better jobs. Thus, unions reduce turnover, and this reduction in turnover increases productivity by creating long-term workplace relationships between workers and firms and among workers themselves. Long-term workplace relationships boost productivity by improving employers' chances of reaping the benefits from the cost of training, a benefit in the sense that the trained worker will likely not leave the firm. Similarly, a worker may accept lower pay at times, such as during training, knowing that eventually achieving seniority will yield a pension.

> **Bottom Line**   *The efficiency wage and voice effect predict that unionized workplaces have relatively low turnover, which encourages employer training and "tenure-weighted" employee benefits,[18] like pensions.[19]*

An extension of voice theory is economist John Budd's facilitation theory. The "facilitation" effect happens when unions inform their members about the value and availability of employee benefits, information that affects their members' preferences for different kinds of benefits. Unions help management provide this information to workers because it gives management the opportunity to please their employees, providing employee benefits in a way that is less costly; it is less costly to the company because the company can get lower rates for larger groups, for benefits such as pensions, health insurance, among others.[20]

According to a Peter Hart poll in 2006, 33% of all workers say that wages are one of the two most important aspects they want to see improved about their job, whereas only 30% of union workers said the same. However, when asked about retirement benefits and health care benefits, union workers were more likely to rank them as the more important aspects of their jobs needing improvement. Among union workers, 32% ranked health care as one of the top two job concerns, whereas only 25% of all workers said the same. For retirement benefits, the share was 27% for union members and 23% for all workers.[21]

I agree with a version of the facilitation effect, but I think it is too narrow, too flat. This facilitation interpretation does not capture the profound effect collective bargaining has on people's sense of the future—the entitlement to security and caring for one another.

Lower Discount Rates

Remember, union leaders are or were workers themselves. During their meetings in preparation for collective bargaining, they promote open discussion concerning, and solutions to, anxieties about difficult questions, like the financial implications of getting old. This is simply another way unions affect employee benefits—through the preparation for collective bargaining. These preparations bring workers together for analytical confrontations with difficult questions, rather than emotional and shortsighted confrontations and psychological denials of unpleasant realities. If left alone, human beings tend to discount the future, and overlook and downplay risks, such as poor health, disability, and living in old age without enough income. The main result is that union members become educated about time horizons, which enables them to place relative value on future consumption.[22]

Solidarity and Fairness

Unions also operate on the principle of solidarity—shared interests, responsibilities, and fellowship. This solidarity can explain why unions prefer defined benefit plans to individualized defined contribution plans. Economist Robert Shiller argues that DC pension plans have replaced DB plans because unions have lost influence in setting pay and benefits. According to Shiller, "a key factor appears to be an erosion of solidarity and loyalty among workers and an attitude that has come to be replaced by an individual business ethic."[23] Shiller argues that, without solidarity, which includes a desire to share risks, demands for social insurance (in the form of DB pensions) are replaced by demands for cash or individual accounts.

A social and political justification for the government legalizing and enforcing laws that allow workers to organize and obligate employers to engage in good faith collective bargaining[24] is to "level the playing field." Unions balance the power between workers and employers, which, the thinking is, generates markets that are more efficient. The idea is that unions counter the inherently stronger position of capital in setting wages, hours, and other conditions of employment.[25] Under this view, unions are able to extract pensions from employers through bargaining power.

Bottom Line

- Unions and unionized employers provide different "compositions of compensation" because collective bargaining extends the time horizons of workers and strengthens the notion of solidarity, which is consistent with support for an insurance-type employee benefit.
- Pensions serve as personnel tools that help employers achieve their goals.

How unions and employers established pension agreements and how they can disintegrate is discussed in the next section. The final section of this chapter highlights the fact that, since pension legacy costs are more likely to exist in unionized settings, the labor movement has only partially anticipated them.

Unions and Legacy Costs in Defined Benefit Plans

In 2002, an analyst at Morgan Stanley set off a customer relations disaster by criticizing unions, and in response union clients launched a massive letter-writing campaign from union trustees and other financial associates connected to unions, threatening to terminate millions of dollars of business. The analyst had written a report accusing unions of raising pension liabilities and lowering profits. The analyst warned investors to avoid putting their money in unionized companies. In a sense, he was right! Defined benefit funds are funded less well in union companies than in nonunion companies.[26] The proportion of pension benefits that are unfunded is higher in union firms. Some shareholder or customer in the future will have to pay for this legacy of unfunded benefits, which, from previous discussions here, you realize are legacy costs.

The most recent outstanding example of expensive union legacy costs is in the airline industry. If we add all the unfunded pension liabilities in the nation, the heavily unionized airline industry has 10% of those liabilities. Of course, airlines have a lion's share of the assets as well, although not as large as 10% of all pension assets.

Nevertheless, the connection between unions and legacy costs is not always complete. Southwest Airlines, which is unionized, is one of the financially healthy airlines that is reducing its fares, threatening the "high legacy cost" airlines. Although Southwest is a unionized airline, it provides its employees with only a DC pension plan. Southwest is one example that supports the view that the combination of unions and DB plans, and not unionization per se, is associated with high and unstable expenses. The relevant characteristic of financially troubled airlines is that they are older than the financially secure airlines, which do not have a spoke and hub system, so these airlines can pick the most profitable routes.

The railroad retirement fund, established in the 1930s, grew out of workers' demands for their mature DB pensions in the "legacy railroads" to be fully funded.[27] In the early 1900s, the pensions at the legacy railroads were amassing huge unfunded liabilities because the workforces were aging and the recession had severely reduced demand for their services. Moreover, young, lower-cost railroads were pushing down the prices for transporting passengers and goods. The railroad retirees and unions sought a federal solution, which became an industry tax on both the legacy railroads and the young nonunion railroads. The solution the federal government came up with was the Railroad Retirement System. The federal government's justification for this industry-wide solution was that the young railroads had the advantage of what the legacy railroads had already produced—a national dependence on railway transportation—and for that reason should fairly share the costs of those benefits.[28]

In a similar move seventy years later, the United Auto Workers (UAW) was involved in designing the defined benefit pension insurance agency, the Pension Benefit Guaranty Corporation. The PBGC was included in the comprehensive legislation—the Employee Retirement Income Security Act[29] (ERISA)—regulating most aspects of DB pension plans. The labor movement, at the time of this writing, is developing a defense of the PBGC and a rationale for it to be reinsured. Reinsurance is common in other insurance systems. Insurers buy insurance for themselves (Lloyd's of London is a well-known example of a reinsurer) to cover catastrophic events for which the normal insurance company is not prepared for financially. For example, house insurers can cover your house burning down but cannot cover a whole city—that takes a government agency. In the case of catastrophes the government steps in, effectively reinsuring home insurance companies. The PBGC is designed as pension insurance in case a company collapses; it is not designed to cover an entire set of DB companies collapsing at the same time in the same industry. The PBGC needs a system to insure pensions in the case of an industry collapse.

The U.S. labor movement adapted to employers' use of pensions as a tool to generate higher productivity among workers. However, the unions demanded that pension plans for workers be similar to pension plans provided for management. How unions gained pensions and how management used pensions to promote profitability can be found in the history of organized labor, particularly in the economic rationales supporting the demand for pensions. American trade unions advocated for employer-based pension systems primarily because if there were no employers for those workers, there were no trade unions for the workers. Therefore, what employers wanted helped shape organized labor's pension policies. Both employers and unions expected pensions to be used to motivate and retain workers and, importantly, to help laid-off workers transition to retirement rather than to unemploy-ment. Unions across the globe have endorsed or are just now accepting employer-expanded occupational pensions as second sources of retirement income.

Partially funded pension plans (fully funded pensions, if terminated, have assets equal to liabilities) are associated with trade unions mainly because unions and management benefited from the new pensions' ("new," meaning created fifty or so years ago) coverage of older workers who did not make con-tributions but who needed pensions immediately.[30] Unfunded liabilities—the difference between assets and termination liabilities—are called legacy costs because many of them come from crediting the past service of employees to-ward the final computation of their benefits. The labor movement usually set-tles for pension promises known to be unfunded. This is not a concern if the employer survives and maintains a balanced ratio of young and old workers. However, market dynamics are such that low-cost firms with younger employ-ees challenge the survival of older firms. The sources of the superiority of Toy-ota over GM are varied, and probably exaggerated, but no one questions that GM, Ford, and Chrysler suffer the disadvantage that they have an older work force, and unfunded retiree health benefits they can not renege on—yet!

How Things Fall Apart

What workers want and what employers want can be in stark contrast. Yet the labor relations history of the United States reveals that, under certain circumstances, securing workers' pensions served the interests of both busi-ness firms and workers. Pensions helped create complex and stable forms of cooperation between firms and workers; one example is that employers, as-sured of lower turnover, provided workers with costly training.

Pension reform in the early part of the twenty-first-century is not aimed at recreating those circumstances—where employer interests and worker in-terests about pension fit perfectly and harmoniously, although they should. Sociologist Erik Olin Wright[31] notes that compromises between employers and workers that could result in progress for both are not often made because of antagonistic relationships between them. They have different political ide-ologies and neither one of the parties wants to make the first move. Employ-ers have a history of resisting workers' demands because one employer, acting alone, is forced to define what employer interests are very narrowly. Secure pensions have certainly been compatible with high profits and productivity, especially when unions and government coordinated with competing employers to provide pensions. However, another route to higher profits, from the point of view of the employer, is to decrease the minimum wage at which people will work by decreasing pensions, which leads to higher profit rates simply because the decreased pensions effectively lowered wages. (The lowest wage for which they will work is technically referred to as their "reservation wage.")

Organized Labor And Social Security

Organized labor had a supporting role, not the main role, in the formation of the Social Security system. However, organized labor linked collective bargaining demands to the changes in the new Social Security program. Pensions were viewed as supplements to Social Security. The first pension plans ever negotiated by unions made it possible for an employee with both an employer pension and a Social Security pension to reach an established goal for retirement income, a target benefit. These integrated pension plans cost employers virtually nothing for lower-paid employees because for them the Social Security benefit exceeded the employer's promised pension benefit.

The United Auto Workers: Their Pension and Social Security Tactic

The United Auto Workers negotiated integrated pensions, which promise a certain level of pension income made up of Social Security and employer pensions. The more the government paid, the less the automaker would have to pay. The UAW reasoned that would encourage powerful automobile firms to lobby for higher Social Security benefits. Indeed, when Congress increased Social Security pension benefits in the 1950s, some pension benefits fell, while pension income stayed the same. The members revolted against their union leaders and against this clever plan. Social Security increases, workers reasoned, were supposed to improve retiree income, not improve corporate profits. Integrated pension plans within collectively bargained pensions began to disappear in subsequent contracts.

By negotiating for integrated pension plans, unions earnestly used whatever power it had to expand government programs, a goal about which they had been ambivalent. In the United States, organized labor did not initiate but rather joined with other social reformers to advocate for a universal, mandatory government program, which became Social Security in 1935. One of the reasons that organized labor was not a key player in passing Social Security was because unions were devoted to improving their scattered successes at persuading employers to extend managerial employer-based pensions to rank-and-file workers.

Fastforward from the pre–World War II period to 2008, when international pension reform is aimed at reducing government Social Security–type pension benefits in favor of employer-based pensions. Americans' eyes turned toward European pensions back in 1935; now in 2008 Europe is eyeing the employer-based pension plans in the United States and wondering how to diminish state pension obligations. But the shift in pension design from the traditional defined benefit to the defined contribution form that occurred in the United States[32] has generally not occurred in Europe (not yet), except in the United Kingdom and in Sweden. U.S. unions are foremost among opponents to transforming pensions into individual financial accounts.[33] International unions have similar principles for pension design: government pensions provide basic income in a mandatory pension system covering all employees, with supplements by employer-based plans.[34]

Labor's Capital

Unions, though weak and growing weaker, have taken the lead in claiming that workers' pension funds should be invested to meet workers' needs. Of the more than $6 trillion total in pension assets, about 50% of that amount is derived from collective bargaining and influenced by unions. Moreover, 50% of workers covered by defined benefit plans are under a union contract. Excluding the monies in individual retirement accounts, like 401(k) plans, by 2008 there will be over $2.7 trillion in single-employer pension funds and more than $2 trillion in state and local pension funds. About $250 billion in multiemployer pension funds is managed jointly by union leaders and firms' management representatives.[35] Management expert Peter Drucker declared in 1976 that America was "socialist" because workers, through their pension plans, owned the means of production. Nevertheless, ownership is not control, and unions have developed strategies to cope with that disconnect.

Ironically, the U.S. trade unions' strength as pension activists stems from their weakness. Unions have become less able to improve wages, hours, and working conditions through collective bargaining, and the U.S. labor movement has always been weaker than most other labor movements in the developed world. In the last twenty years, union strength has diminished fastest in the United States. The irony is amplified by the fact that the American labor movement is responsible for a large part of the U.S. pension fund wealth, which is larger, relative to annual gross domestic product than the GDP in most other nations. But elderly poverty rates in the United States are also larger than in most nations.[36] The unions' pension funds are large and growing while the unions are withering and diminishing. In contrast, European national unions are strong in terms of bargaining and political power, yet many are just beginning to exert influence over their pension funds' investment practices.

In the last thirty years, the enormous size of pension assets, accompanied by the weakness of traditional union tactics and the explosion in concern about corporate governance and the rights of the "Citizen Investor"[37] shareholder, provides American unions with opportunities to challenge corporate behavior in ways other than collective bargaining. Labor, as beneficial owners of pension funds, own pension assets (in both interpretations of pensions—the "deferred compensation" and "depreciation payment"). Of course, ownership does not confer control,[38] so unions in the United States, and increasingly unions in other countries, want control of workers' pension funds. Note that unions won their Supreme Court case that employers have to bargain over pension benefits but may not manage single-employer pension funds. In multiemployer plans, unions and management share control of the pension funds.[39] A well-known but misunderstood case of unions and management jointly managing pension funds is the Teamsters Union. The history of the Teamster Union's engagement in pension investments helps illustrate how, in the United States, aiming to secure pensions and to manage the funds backing those pensions has always been part of the impact organized labor has had on pensions.

In the 1940s, the International Brotherhood of Teamsters (IBT) was one of the innovators to use pension funds strategically to strengthen their members' bargaining power. The sophisticated and robust pension systems the IBT crafted were remarkable, given that at the time trucking companies and warehouses were small, fledgling, and undercapitalized, and their workers were among the most underprivileged in society. Often, IBT President James Riddle Hoffa and trustees awarded the business of administering the growing IBT pension funds to banks in the community. Doing this did not involve any shady investments; the union aimed to divide local businesses and thus weaken their unity, in turn weakening community resistance to the union's organizing efforts or its demands. Another reason why unions have control of just under $1 billion dollars of pension assets in the United States in the twenty-first-century is that employers did not fight unions to gain control of pension investments. A partial reason for this acquiescence is that the early pension plans operated essentially on a pay-as-you-go basis. That is, employer contributions in the pension plan were made on a per worker basis and most of the money was paid out to retirees. The employer's ability to pay benefits depended in part on the size of the workforce relative to the size of the population of retirees. As long as the former was large and the later small, this system worked fine.

But this favorable balance between the numbers of workers and retirees was threatened in the mining industry when the mines began to be automated. The union needed to change the basis of the pension contributions. The United Mine Workers of America's president, John L. Lewis, argued that, since employers garnered the benefits and workers paid the costs of automation, workers should be compensated with pension contributions based on tonnage mined per hour rather than on work hours. This caused contributions to explode, swelling the pension fund. Since the union already dominated the UMWA pension fund administration (though the fund had equal numbers of employer trustees and union trustees), the union ended up dominating pension investment policies.

The unions for workers in the large rubber, steel, and auto industries were aware of the importance of having a say in pension funding and investments. Pension funds were, and still are, a fast growing and important source of funds for corporate bonds and equities. Lane Kirkland, former president of the AFL-CIO, as a young researcher in the newly formed AFL-CIO in 1955, issued a ten-point pension-bargaining agenda for unions. The tenth point was to bargain for joint control of investments. Although the unions wanted joint control of investments, they did not have the influence to win control. Instead, they used their bargaining strength and something that turned out to be more valuable—"past-service" credits, which are credits for pensions based on service before the pension plan was implemented.

Since the 1970s, the labor movement's tactics in bargaining for pensions have grown in many directions as they lost traditional sources of power. For example, unions are prominent members of the Council of Institutional Investors, which was formed in the late 1970s by state pension funds, with California taking the lead. Public pension funds had become too big to "exit." That means if the pension fund sold stock to protest a firm's management—the old-fashioned way to complain—the stock price would fall precipitously. What can an investor do who doesn't merely *participate* in a market for a corporate equity, but *makes* the market because the investor is so large that the volume of the purchase or sale affects the price? The solution for pension funds who wanted a voice in how corporations are managed was "corporate engagement."[40] Unions wanting a voice work through the Council of Institutional Investors.

Unions still use the Hoffa tactic, which the unions once called corporate campaigns. The corporate campaign tactic goes to work when activists use pension funds to make the union an important client of banks and money managers. The unions want to influence financial institutions in order to pressure their corporate clients to make specific, pro-worker, decisions.

The organizing battle between J. P. Stevens and the Amalgamated Clothing and Textile Workers union is a well-known modern example of a union flexing its pension power in a corporate campaign. The movie *Norma Rae* was based on the real-life efforts of an organizer in a J. P. Stevens plant who ushered in a union victory in North Carolina. Left out of the movie is the chief reason the company agreed to negotiate a contract—a union victory in New York. Several companies whose officers, including the chairman of the Avon Corp, sat on the J. P. Stevens corporate board were threatened with union boycotts. In the once happy world of interlocking directorates, the J. P. Stevens chairman was asked to resign from Manufacturers Hanover Corporation's board of directors, because the unions threatened to withdraw pension funds from the bank unless he did. The union isolated J. P. Stevens and succeeded in gaining a foothold in the southern textile mills—until 75, 000 textile jobs in the South disappeared to off-shoring and imports between 1997 and 2002.[41]

Two other labor capital tactics include unions, as shareholders, threatening to launch shareholder resolutions against a corporation, which often relaxes their antiunion positions; and union pension funds investing in construction projects and owning buildings to ensure that the construction and the service work in the building is unionized, or the employer declared they will be neutral if a union attempts to organize.

The AFL-CIO's Department of Corporate Affairs was formed when John Sweeney became president (in a rare contested AFL-CIO presidential election) in 1995. The department's aims are to extend the AFL-CIO's activities to become a recognized analyst of corporate behavior.[42] AFL-CIO General Counsel Damon Silvers argues that legal, prudent investment conforms more closely to a workers' view of investing compared to "Wall Street's conventional wisdom."[43] The conventional principles of efficient market theory reward short-term-oriented behavior with exaggerated managerial compensation. Silvers argues that long-term growth and productivity are not pursued under the current system, and thus union engagement in corporate decisions helps all investors. (Bill Patterson, at a parallel unit of the rival labor federation, "Change to Win," conducts similar campaigns.)

Unions have filed more shareholder resolutions than any other group since 2000. In the 2000 proxy season, unions submitted 28% of all shareholder resolutions; they submitted 18% in 2003—far more than any other institutional investor. In addition, the union impact has grown. Out of 1,150 shareholder proposals filed in 2006, 345 were labor proposals (about 30%).

The effective influence of union shareholder activism was made obvious when unions were among the first to challenge the American company Stanley Works when it moved its headquarters to Bermuda to avoid paying taxes. This move became the symbol of corporate greed stressed by Democratic politicians in 2002.[44]

In 2007, Services Employees International Union President Andy Stern caught the attention of the *Wall Street Journal* both for sponsoring the website "BehindtheBuyouts.org," a site designed to expose and discuss private equity firms and actions, and for negotiating with the funds behind the scenes as they buy companies with Services Employees International Union members.[45]

> **Bottom Line**   *How does the labor movement resolve its paradox—as a challenger to capital and as capital owner? This is how I see it: Labor has one role as an agent that redistributes profits from owners to workers—what self-respecting union would do otherwise? Organized labor also represents workers who own shares in companies and when it engages companies, as a shareholder, its legal role is that of an agent maximizing profits for owners.*

The paradox above is more easily reconciled than it would first appear. The AFL-CIO Proxy Guidelines state clearly that the trustee "must not subordinate the interests of the pension participant to any other interest," such as to a striking union.[46] Union trustees are warned that they may vote for shareholder proxies only if the aim is to serve the interests of owners. For instance, a union trustee may wish to urge companies to maximize long-term value and implement corporate policies that maximize employment security and the wage levels of pension plan participants. Other issues include corporate policies that promote local economic development and stability; corporate policies that affect growth and stability of the overall economy; corporate responsibility to employees and local communities; and, safety and health considerations at the workplace.

Since proxies must be couched in terms that serve the interests of shareholders, labor's demands are couched in terms of goals to maximize shareholder value.[47]

Conclusion: Unions and Pensions

The U.S. labor movement had, and still has, an important role in bringing retirement to the working classes, because it links bargaining for employer-provided pensions to legislative goals for establishing and improving the Social Security system.

Social Security benefits in the United States are among the world's lowest (compared to average wages), which makes the employer a crucial source of pensions (and health insurance, since the United States stands apart from other nations in not providing national health insurance) and thus a focus for union efforts and bargaining power.

The dependence on social insurance at the workplace also has led to legacy costs.

One aspect of organized labor's role in the development of the U.S. pension system was unexpected—by changing the composition of compensation, the U.S. labor movement promotes savings, and because of their role as saver and investor, unions have become ardent representatives of capital owners in the United States.

The labor movement is, as Tom Geoghagan tells us, "flat on its back" and cannot organize many workers for the purposes of collective bargaining and the creation of pension funds. Where the labor movement goes, so goes the traditional way of expanding and improving retirement income security. However, pension funds and pension power are big and growing bigger; pension benefits are small and growing smaller. A new form of workplace pension is needed that does not interfere with the arrangements that companies and workers, unionized or not, have made work for them.

Chapter 10

Rescue Plan for American Workers' Retirement:

Averting the End of Retirement

Retirement with dignity and security after a lifetime of hard work is a cherished feature of a civilized society. To whatever extent and for whom it may have been possible, the ability to retire with adequate income is lessening in the United States. It is lessening because of a badly functioning system of retirement income security. That disquiet was expressed in the first chapter of this book and is the concern woven throughout all the following chapters as well.

The overall system of retirement is faltering not because Social Security, as the pillar of retirement income for Americans, replaces only 40% of preretirement income for the average wage earner when retired. Social Security is not designed to provide all the income a retiree needs. The system is faltering because pensions and savings are failing. Americans are expected to obtain the rest of what they need through employer pensions and their own savings. But that expectation is not going to be realized because the employer pension system is broken and savings rates are falling or nearly nil.

Much of the reason the employer pension system is broken is that defined contribution plans have replaced employer pension plans, and these new forms of retirement accounts—most of these are either 401(k) accounts or similar—will not fill the gaps created by the loss of employer pensions. (Defined contribution plans have different names depending on who is qualified to contribute, among other particular rules. The common types are Individual Retirement Accounts, SIMPLEs, SEPs, 401(k), 403(b), 457 plans, and Keoghs.[1])

Defined contribution plans are not good substitutes for employer pensions for several reasons: DC plans charge high administrative costs; workers make serious investment mistakes; and workers withdraw income from their accounts before they retire (reasonably, many of the withdrawals occur when workers have hardships or are changing jobs). Also, people who need DC accounts the most—the middle- and low-income earners—do not have them[2]; DC pension accounts are best suited to serve the needs of high-income earners. High-income earners have higher tax rates under a progressive tax system so they have bigger incentives to shift savings from financial accounts that do not defer taxes, to tax-favored DC retirement accounts. (These accounts are called retirement accounts only because if the account holder withdraws income before age fifty-nine-and-a-half there is a penalty. When income is withdrawn after age fifty-nine-and-a-half, the income from that withdrawal is taxed as ordinary income, with no penalty. The tax advantage comes about because the earnings and contributions were accumulated tax free and the account holder's tax rate is probably lower when the income is withdrawn.)

Because 401(k) plans were originally designed only to supplement traditional pensions and are now substituting for them, overall pension coverage has stayed flat rather than expanding, leaving half of all workers with no workplace retirement plan—the way it has been, unchanged for thirty years. Overall pension coverage has stagnated and the share of income from pensions will fall while the tax breaks for retirement accounts continue to increase.

DATA TO DIGEST

- *Workplace pensions are supposed to supplement Social Security but the share of income received by the median sixty-seven-year-old from traditional DB pension plans will drop from 21% in 2003 to only 9% in 2023.*
- *Defined contribution plans' share of retirement income—for the retiree at the median income level—is expected to rise from 4% to only 9% from 2003 to 2023.*
- *Tax expenditures for retirement accounts will have grown 11% from 2005 to 2009 although there is no expectation of an increase in the share of the workforce covered by pensions.[3]*

The nation's experience with voluntary, individual, tax-subsidized retirement accounts administered by commercial money managers, has failed. The consequences are stark. The baby boomers' parents may be the last generation to have enjoyed a more comfortable retirement than their mothers and fathers. Without major reform, only the privileged few will retire voluntarily. Without bold action, the American system of retirement income security could easily devolve into an inadequate, inefficient, and unnecessarily expensive failure like the American medical insurance system. If nothing is done, income replaced in retirement will be lower for retirees in the next half century than it has been for previous generations. This would be the first time since the Great Depression that the standard of living of the American elderly falls relative to the nonretired household standard of living, a relative decline that will force older people to work longer and accept less retirement time.

To help save the U.S. system of pensions, I propose ways to change it. Acting now can preserve the historical successes of the American mixed system (government, household, and employer-based) of retirement income programs. These successes made it possible for working-class laborers and middle-class white-collar workers to enjoy what once only the rich enjoyed—retirement leisure. Acting now means we can derail declining living standards and increasing poverty rates among the elderly.

A smart and fair retirement reform plan should be efficient—our pension dollar is precious, we should care for every cent. Reform should expand the productive capacity of the economy. In addition, a retirement, or old-age, income security system should not create unnecessary risks for the worker, the employer, or the government. And, last, a system of retirement income security should make it easy for anyone, especially low- and middle-income workers, to save for retirement.

A new system, called Guaranteed Retirement Accounts (GRAs), meets the requirements for an improved and more secure old-age income system. Guaranteed Retirement Accounts are less costly than the current system of tax breaks for defined contribution plans and will cover every worker, not just half the workforce. In addition, every worker, every year, under the GRAs will benefit from the tax system. Currently, in 2008, despite the tax incentives, in any one year only a fraction of workers actually contribute to a retirement account. For instance, in 2006 only 30% of workers voluntarily contributed to a DC retirement account. In that same year, less than 50% of employees earning enough to be in the top 20% of the earnings distribution contributed to any kind of retirement savings plans.

Guaranteed Retirement Accounts, combined with traditional DB plans and a strong Social Security system, will fix these gaps and secure retirement income for almost every worker.

Guaranteed Retirement Accounts

The pension rescue plan is a practical, affordable, and an effective solution to endangered American retirements and meets all the goals of a national retirement income security system. Guaranteed Retirement Accounts added to Social Security[4] (see chapter 5) would together comprise a comprehensive, straightforward way to insure adequate retirement income for everyone but the wealthiest. The wealthiest will have to supplement their GRAs and Social Security benefits to maintain their lifestyles acquired when they were younger.

Guaranteed Retirement Accounts will

- increase retirement savings, unlike the hodgepodge of tax subsidies that aim to raise retirement saving but instead induce savers to shift funds to tax-favored accounts from taxable accounts;

- benefit low- and middle-income families, not just the wealthy, and by supplementing Social Security will replace approximately 70% of preretirement earnings for the average worker;

- be professionally and efficiently managed in government funds—these accounts will not be charged high management fees;

- only allow withdrawals in old age;

- require mandatory participation, except for employees already enrolled in "qualified"[5] DB pension plans;

- provide a guaranteed rate of return, and will be self-sustaining; any financial risks will be borne by the government, not by the worker; the system will be advance-funded so the government will not accrue unfunded liabilities;

- have counterparts in other hybrid systems like TIAA-CREF—the pension program for academics and researchers in the United States—and pension systems known as "non-financial defined contribution accounts" operational in some European countries.

Bottom Line *Guaranteed Retirement Accounts will be a more efficient, more effective, and more fair way to patch holes in the current retirement system than other proposals, such as proposals for automatic 401(k) plan enrollment and adding new burdens for DB pensions while expanding tax breaks for DC plans.[6]*

How Will Guaranteed Retirement Accounts Work?

Participation. Participation in the program will be mandatory except for workers participating in DB plans where the pension contribution is at least 5% of earnings.

Contributions. Contributions will equal 5% of earnings, deducted along with payroll taxes and credited to individual, personal accounts that for now will be administered by the Social Security Administration. The cost of the 5% contribution can be split equally between employer and employee, but workers are required to make their share of the contributions every pay period (just as workers need to pay their Social Security taxes out of every paycheck). Mandatory contributions will be deducted only on earnings up to the Social Security earnings cap of $98,000 (the cap in 2007), but all workers have the option of making additional contributions with post–tax dollars. The option of additional contributions after taxes is a key feature and will sure to be welcomed by upper middle-class employees or anyone else who wants to replace more than 70% of their preretirement income.

Refundable Tax Credit. Because the 5% contribution can be a burden, a $600 refundable tax credit will be given to all workers regardless of income. This tax credit will replace the tax breaks for 401(k) type plans and will be indexed to wage inflation. The tax credit will take the place of tax breaks for 401(k)s and similar individual accounts and will be indexed to wage inflation. (The tax credit could be kept for 401(k) plans but it would cost the Treasury more.)

Fund Management. It is vital that the accounts be managed by professionals, efficiently, and in a manner so that workers may have the advantage of economies of scale. Public sector employees who have DC plans invested in the same funds the larger DB accounts are invested in, and federal employees in DC plans have professionals managing their accounts for the low fees that large institutions are charged. The GRAs can be managed by the Social Security Administration, who will collect the contributions, and invested by the

Thrift Savings Plan (Thrift Savings Accounts supplement a larger DB system for federal workers), which is a board that manages the DC accounts for federal employees. Workers may track the dollar value of their accumulations, just as workers who have the Thrift Savings Plan and other 401(k)-type DC accounts can often do now.

Investment Earnings. Workers will have their contributions invested in financial markets and will earn a rate of return guaranteed by the government. This means workers will not have to bear the full brunt of financial market risk. The accounts' guaranteed rate of return will be set at 3% per year adjusted for inflation, which reflects the actual history of economic growth in this country and its potential growth. However, if the economy does better, the board of trustees, selected by Congress and the president, can raise the guaranteed rate of return, although the trustees will be expected to keep a cushion, a rainy day fund, to ride out periods of low investment returns.

Retirement Age. Participants may start to receive income from their GRAs accounts at the same time they are eligible to collect Social Security.[7] Or, they may choose to delay receiving an annuity from their GRAs in order to let it accumulate larger balances.

Benefits. Account balances will be converted to inflation-indexed annuities upon retirement or later, to ensure that workers do not outlive the funds in their GRAs. However, any individual will be able to opt for a partial lump sum equal to 10% of her or his account balance, or to opt for survivor benefits in exchange for a lower monthly check.

A full-time worker who works forty-four years and retires at age sixty-seven can expect a benefit equal to roughly 30% of preretirement income, adjusted for inflation, assuming a 3% annual real rate of return (see table 10.1). Since Social Security provides the average worker with an inflation-adjusted benefit equal to roughly 40% of preretirement income, the total retirement income replacement rate for the average worker will be approximately 70%. Workers may opt to extend benefits to a surviving spouse, although the annuity will be reduced accordingly.

Guaranteed Retirement Accounts combined with Social Security will provide to workers, who have worked most of their adult lives, a guaranteed adequate retirement income irrespective of income level. Many people will

Table 10.1
Guaranteed Retirement Accounts (GRA) Meet Target Replacement Rates
(*Scenarios for three workers*)

Life-Long Earnings	High Earner	Average Earner	Low Earner
Earnings 2006	$61,914	$38,696	$17,413
Replacement rate provided by Social Security at the normal retirement age	34.4%	41.5%	56.0%
70% of pre-retirement earnings	$43,340	$16,400	$5,854
Lump sum that would achieve a 70% replacement rate with Social Security*	$327,920	$164,074	$36,269
Actual GRA accumulation at a 5% contribution rate*	$275,667	$172,291	$77,531
Annuity from the above GRA*	$18,500	$11,579	$5,200
Actual replacement rate with GRA and Social Security	64%	71%	86%

*Assumes 3% real rate of return.

want to supplement this retirement income with income from savings to pay for medical expenses, travel, and to provide inheritances to their children. The federal government and local schools should provide financial literacy to help people meet these saving goals.

GRA Efficiency, Fairness, and Shared Risk

Pension systems are key components of the social wage and they represent a substantial taxpayer commitment—two basic reasons why a pension system should be efficient, fair, and based on mutual responsibility and shared risk.

The GRAs I propose, as mandatory Social Security supplements, are *efficient* because savings in the accounts are managed by not-for-profit and publicly accountable agencies.

They are *fair* because if a person chooses a higher level savings, she will have a higher level of assets. (If the middle-class retiree wants, say, more income than 70% of her preretirement income, then she can use income from her personal savings or from work during retirement.)

The GRAs are based on *mutual responsibility and shared risk* because general revenues, which come from interest, capital gains, profits, and earned income, pay for the $600 refundable tax credit—to compensate for human depreciation at the workplace. If economic growth is low then the rate of return earned on these accounts will reflect that slow growth. Retiree income will be guaranteed but also reflect the living standards experienced by everyone else. The accounts are advanced-funded so people are responsible for funding their own retirements.

Guaranteed Retirement Accounts coupled with a solvent Social Security should comprise a retirement income system that is secure in the long-term future. Together they must achieve five specific objectives to rescue the current retirement income system:

1. A retirement income security system must help people be able to save for retirement so that living standards don't drop substantially after retirement. This means that access to retirement savings—savings that are subsidized by taxpayers to pay for all sorts of other needs including health care, job changes, buying a home, education, and other expenses unrelated to retirement or disability—should not be allowed. In addition, a retirement system should not exacerbate income and wealth inequality.

2. A retirement income security system must not penalize older people for working.

3. Risks should be shared across the economy. An individual must not bear all the risks of losing his or her job and losing all pension benefits; nor the risk of living longer than anticipated; nor the risk of financial market fluctuations; nor the risk that inflation will diminish the buying power of the investments income. Individuals must not bear these risks because they cannot control these risks. Employers and the government can bear these risks more effectively and at a lower cost.

4. Benefits must be predictable and portable, and employer costs must be stable so that the retirement income system doesn't burden the economy and instead, makes it grow. A retirement system must not help large businesses while ignoring small businesses. Pension reform must not crowd out defined

benefit arrangements. Defined benefit pensions will work better when the tax system changes. One goal of tax changes is that employers with DB plans are not punished

5. A retirement system must be cost effective, transparent, and accountable. It must take advantage of economies of scale and not waste money on marketing, on retail fees, nor on other unnecessary costs.

Achieving the Objectives of Guaranteed Retirement Accounts

Now, let's consider how the GRA plan meets each of these objectives.

1. The Guaranteed Retirement Accounts help people secure their own retirement income by requiring them to save enough. When people save enough they can choose to retire without experiencing a sharp drop in living standards.

Together, GRAs and Social Security will replace approximately 70% of preretirement income for the average worker. That is the income replacement rate generally considered the minimum necessary to avoid a significant drop in living standards upon retirement. Due to the progressive structure of Social Security benefits, the replacement rate is somewhat higher for low-income workers and lower for high-income workers.

The GRAs also help everyone, regardless of income, to save enough to retire because their refundable tax credits are progressive. The $600 tax credit, that everyone receives, will cover the entire 5% contribution for a full-time, full-year, minimum-wage worker, and will greatly reduce the effective contribution rate for other low-paid workers. These tax credits will be paid for by eliminating tax breaks for 401(k) plans and similar accounts which disproportionately benefit high-income households without increasing the national savings rates. (The 20% of taxpayers at the top of the income distribution received 70% of all the tax breaks for retirement accounts in 2006![8]).

Guaranteed Retirement Accounts effectively increase retirement savings, which the current system fails miserably in doing. All policies designed to promote savings are challenged by the crushingly inescapable fact that low-income households have little money to spare yet high-income households can shift existing savings from taxed accounts to tax-favored accounts. This would be true even if the savings incentives for rich and poor families were equal, but is exacerbated by these incentives, which generally take the form of tax deductions, providing a much larger "carrot" to wealthy families than to middle-class families—and no such carrots whatsoever for families too poor to owe taxes.

By converting these tax breaks into $600 refundable tax credits, GRAs will instantly boost the retirement savings of low- and middle-class-income households with no extra costs from the Treasury. The tax credits and mandatory contributions on earnings up to $98,000 are unlikely to have much impact one way or another on the savings of high-income households, except that these households will steadily contribute, which may make them better off at retirement. This high-income group, however, will lose tax breaks. (A modification that could be substituted, if a clean break from future 401(k) contributions could not be tolerated politically, is to allow a $5,000 contribution to a 401(k) type plan with a $400 rebate. This proposal will not cause any more expenditures on employer-based pensions than we have now and it would raise pension income considerably.) The effect on the distribution of after tax income is discussed below.

The Guaranteed Retirement Accounts are advance-funded; people pay for their own retirement! Unlike Social Security, which is partly a pay-as-you-go system, GRAs will be entirely advance-funded. Advance funding means that there will be no significant transition costs, although workers who begin participating late in their careers will receive reduced benefits commensurate with their lower contributions. However, as the system matures, workers will receive benefits roughly proportional to their lifetime earnings. Besides avoiding transition costs, the other big advantage to advance funding will be that it minimizes the problem of generational booms and busts because savings will automatically grow or contract as more or fewer workers approach retirement. In contrast, a pay-as-you-go system must grapple with the baby-boomer retirement problem—fewer workers will be supporting a larger number of retirees.

2. Guaranteed Retirement Accounts allow people to retire at an age they choose because they connect work with benefits and help older people choose to work. The longer you contribute to your GRA, the more you get. Each hour of paid work will count toward a higher benefit. GRAs will complement Social Security, which already provides a basic retirement benefit to workers with gaps in their work histories due to unemployment spells or care-giving responsibilities. GRAs will reward every worker who has both the good luck and the tenacity to work continuously over a longer period. Since individuals

will control how much they save (and work) in addition to the mandate, retirement income will be linked to each individual's responsibility, effort, and
preference. Guaranteed Retirement Accounts will be based on total lifetime
earnings, rather than average lifetime earnings, to recognize the longer work
histories of blue-collar workers who begin working at a younger age. There
will be, however, a minimum age of eligibility to collect the annuity, which
will be the Social Security early retirement age.

*3. Guaranteed Retirement Accounts promise secure lifetime benefits without
adding the risk that an individual will not have access to the best investment advice.* The third goal of a national retirement system is met because GRAs will
allocate risks to the entities that can best minimize them. They will reduce the
unnecessary risks individuals now bear because they have to manage their
own retirement accounts. The lowest income and least educated workers, under the current system, are punished because they have the least resources to
manage sophisticated financial accounts. Each person's GRA will be credited
with a rate of return tied to economic growth and inflation, a rate that will be
guaranteed by the federal government. Real economic growth (adjusted for
inflation) has averaged over 3% per year in the post–World War II period.
The guarantee means that workers can be assured of a positive steady return
on their retirement savings.

In contrast, 401(k) participants with funds invested in the stock market
face a significant chance of earning negative real returns on their investments
for periods as long as a decade or more, as happened during the fourteen-
year bear market that spanned the 1970s. If actual investment returns are
higher, the trustees will decide how to allocate the surplus, either to a rainy
day fund or to workers in the form of a higher return, or allocate the surplus
between the fund and the higher return. In effect, the government will serve
an insurance role, maintaining steady retirement benefits for workers retiring
during bull or during bear markets. The only significant risk the government
will be left with is financial risk, although this will be negligible because long-
term financial returns should at least keep pace with long-term economic
growth. The government is even better suited than pension funds are to guarantee a real rate of return because tax revenues tend to keep pace with inflation even in periods like the 1970s when investment returns were eroded by
inflation.

Besides providing a secure return on investment, GRAs will be automatically converted to inflation-adjusted annuities upon retirement to ensure that workers do not outlive their savings nor see them eroded through inflation.

4. Guaranteed Retirement Accounts make costs and benefits predictable for employers and workers. Every worker's contributions are always 5% of pay and are subsidized by a $600 refundable tax credit (indexed to wage inflation). And if the employer pays or shares payment of the employee's contribution the employee still obtains the refundable tax credit. Please note that many may want to structure the GRAs' financing structure so that it is like the current structure of Medicare and Social Security financing where the employee and employer split the cost. In that case, the employee and employer should then also split the refundable tax credit. Since I am one among the many economists who view the market as fairly competitive so that workers eventually would pay for the employer tax in the form of lower wages, the issue of who contributes is immaterial. Since it is administratively easier to have the employee pay, and acceptable because the contribution is a contribution to the employee's account (the employer could supplement), I propose the employee pay and the employee receive the refundable tax credit. Note that traditional defined benefit pensions still receive the full tax expenditure.

5. Guaranteed Retirement Accounts do not slight small business as the current system does now. Guaranteed Retirement Accounts will help overcome the small business pension gap: for a number of decades only one in five small businesses have sponsored a pension or savings plan. Small businesses have complained that the costs, monetarily and administratively, to start up a plan are too high and that their revenue is so uncertain they do not want to make the commitment of providing a pension plan. Since small businesses already pay Social Security taxes and the GRAs will piggyback on the Social Security Administration, they would face no monetary or psychological barriers. A firm will send the contributions to the GRAs when it sends in the employees' Social Security contributions.

6. Guaranteed Retirement Accounts do not crowd out defined benefit pension arrangements. Public policy has been mostly responsible for the failures of the employer pension system because it has scolded and restricted DB plans and has coddled and indulged 401(k) plans. It's sort of like the older child being taken for granted and bearing the brunt of the disciplinary scrutiny while the younger child is spoiled. Guaranteed Retirement Accounts will reverse the bias against DB employer plans.

Employers and workers will be able to substitute a DB plan that costs as much or more than the 5% mandatory contribution into a GRA. The case for DB plans and how to improve them is in the appendix to this chapter. The Guaranteed Retirement Account is modeled to a large extent on the Teachers Insurance Annuity and College Retirement Equities Fund (TIAA-CREF), the pension fund for university professors, which is one of the largest pension funds in the United States. The TIAA portion guarantees a 3% return on the employees' and employers' contributions, but the TIAA-CREF trustees have paid more than the 3% guarantee every year since 1948.[9] Although the TIAA-CREF is technically a DC plan, it is more like a DB plan hybrid and contributions to TIAA-CREF could be substituted for the GRA.

7. *Guaranteed Retirement Accounts incorporate the best features of defined benefit and defined contribution plans.* Like DB pension plans, GRAs will be efficiently managed and benefits will be guaranteed for life.[10] Investments will be diversified and professionally managed, and accumulations will be accessible only to fund retirement or disability. Like DC plans, GRAs will be portable and contributions predictable. The accounts will be easy to understand and their value transparent; they will also be immune from company default due to bankruptcy, malfeasance, or corruption. However, GRAs will correct three of the worst features of DB plans: variable and unknown rates of return; leakages into high fees and preretirement spending; and lump-sum benefits that do not provide a guaranteed income for life.

8. *Guaranteed Retirement Accounts meet the last objective of national pension systems because they are efficiently and inexpensively administered.* Mandatory automatic payroll deductions will ensure efficient and consistent payments in the system's accounts. The Social Security Administration has a proven track record of efficient management—its administrative fees are less than 1%—and it already maintains portable accounts for all workers.

One of the outstanding features of the American Social Security system compared to the social security systems in other developed nations is that the compliance rates are almost 95%, which is much higher than estimated compliance rates that are under 50% for Italy and other nations with high payroll taxes. The high compliance rates in paying taxes are an underappreciated but exceptionally valuable national asset and are taken advantage of in setting up this system of mandatory savings. Funds for GRAs will be pooled and professionally managed, taking advantage of economies of scale and dispensing with the high fees associated with 401(k) plans and other individual accounts.

Workers who contribute to the employer pension plans are paying retail fund management fees, which benefit the money management firms—the financial sector sits alongside the pharmaceutical and oil companies as the most profitable U.S. business sectors. In a retirement pension system dependent on commercial individual accounts, money management fees grow rather than fall over time because competition takes the form of firms struggling to gain market share and to increase profits through advertising and complicated expensive financial vehicles. The money management industry is not a free market. It is a market dominated by a few large firms—it is an oligopoly with oligopolistic pricing power. State Street Bank, Barclays, and a few other such firms have come to dominate the market as institutional investors want products that are more sophisticated and more global. In 2004, the top three financial management firms controlled 17% of the market; by 2006 they controlled 20%.[11] Another reason the fees are high is because employers do not pay fees—workers do. Vendors sell 401(k) services to employers, and one of the selling points is that the workers will pay the fees. It is not difficult to imagine the difference if employers were required to pay 401(k) fees—they would probably clamor for not-for-profit money management firms, as will be provided by the GRAs. As I mentioned above, in the United States, not-for-profit money management firms do exist—they are federal and state retirement systems, multiemployer pension trusts, and (up until recently) TIAA-CREF.[12]

The federal government will manage the GRAs through the Social Security Administration and the Thrift Savings Plans. I can imagine a version of the GRAs' plan that will allow workers to have their state and local pension plans manage their accounts. The point is that there are plenty of ways workers can have access to professional, not-for-profit, low-cost, money management services. When workers have such access, all the money accumulated for retirement will "go further" because fees will be lower. There is no reason policymakers should not make this so.

The Guaranteed Retirement Accounts plan will be revenue-enhancing for the U.S. Treasury. They will help balance the federal budget. Current tax subsidies for individual accounts will be replaced by a flat rebate of $600 (indexed to inflation). This will save the government money (as explained in the next section), which will help to reduce the federal deficit.

Furthermore, the system is self-stabilizing for the federal government. The federal government guarantees the rate of return on the GRAs and taxpayers provide the $600 tax credit. This program's costs do not sharply increase when the ratio of workers to beneficiaries shrink because the GRAs system will be advance-funded. Thus, it will minimize the problem of generational booms and busts.

The Guaranteed Retirement Account system is similar to the guranteed DC account systems in Sweden, Lativa, Italy, and proposed in Germany, that have replaced their defined benefit Social Security programs.[13] These systems are different from the proposed GRAs, however, because workers in these systems are not accumulating actual financial assets in their accounts—they are accumulating "notional" assets. The assets are notional because the workers receive promises for the government to pay an annuity based on the amount of credits accumulated in their accounts. The feature shared by the notional DC accounts systems and the GRA system is the automatic mechanism that allows the benefits to vary depending on the balance between liabilities and assets. If the generation (or cohort) retiring is much larger than that of the younger workers and/or the economy is in a recession, the trustees can vary the rate of return earned on the accounts. Retirees and workers both share in the upside or downside to a growing economy. The mechanism is part of the structure of the system. Congress will not have to approve of every change; benefits will be adjusted according the overall conditions of the economy because the trustees—they will be appointed by the president, with the approval of Congress, with terms similar to those of the Federal Reserve Board—can adjust the rate of return earned on the accounts.

Failure of the Current Tax Policy

Tax policies exempting contributions into, and investment earnings of, a variety of retirement savings accounts, at best are poorly targeted so they fail to meet their goals of increasing retirement savings for most people. At worst, they direct tax revenue to those needing the least help and forgo helping those who do need help.

> **DATA TO DIGEST**   *Economists at the Urban-Brookings Tax Policy Center found the following (I have compiled their findings in table 10.2):*
> - *70% of the tax subsidies go to those in the top 20% of the income distribution;*
> - *half of the subsidies go to the top 10%;*
> - *the top 3% receive almost 20% of the tax subsidies.*

Discerning who gets what from the way DC plans are treated, requires two steps best illustrated by an example. The Tax Policy Center divided all

Table 10.2
Who Receives the Benefit from the Tax Deduction Now?
Tax benefits of defined contribution (DC) plans and IRAs by cash income level, 2004*

Cash income level (thousands, $2003)	Average amount saved in taxes from the tax treatment of DC plans	In 2004, the percentage of heads of house-holds who actually contributed to a DC plan*	Share of the tax units	Share of the tax expenditures for DCs and IRAs
Less than $75K	$159	12%	87.8%	45.1%
$75–100K	$1009	36%	7.9%	15.1%
$100–200K	$1,985	43%	9.3%	34.9%
$200–500K	$3,495	47%	2.3%	15.2%
$500–1000K	$4,165	47%	0.4%	3.1%
More than $1,000K	$4,428	47%	0.2%	1.7%
Weighted Average	$528	29%		

*I choose the rate for the married filing jointly, which was generally higher than for singles or heads of households.
Source: Author's computations from Burham, Gale, Orszag, Hall 2004.

the tax units—there are three kinds of tax units: married couples filing jointly, single individuals, and what is called "heads of household"—by their cash income. Then the Urban-Brookings Tax Policy Center computed the taxes the folks in those categories would have had to pay if they did not contribute to accounts qualified for tax favoritism. Those tax units with cash income between $75,000 and $100,000 receive on average $1,009 of tax subsidy under the current tax system that allows people to contribute up to $20,000 a year tax-free in an individual retirement account. However, not everyone in that income range receives a subsidy. Those who do not contribute to accounts qualified for tax favoritism receive nothing. For instance, only 36% in the $75,000 to $100,000 income group contributed to tax-favored pension accounts in 2004. Since taxpayers with zero incomes are included in the average, the taxpayers who do contribute receive a much higher subsidy, $1,009.

In contrast, everyone will contribute to a GRA (unless they are in a hybrid or traditional defined benefit–type plan[14]) regardless of income. The $600 refundable tax credit will be the same for all tax filers regardless of income and will be received by all workers contributing to their pension funds. Currently, the bulk of the tax breaks go to the small minority of taxpayers at the top of the income distribution. For instance, in 2004 every household—not just the 29% (see row 7 and column 3, table 10.2) of the households who contributed to a DC plan—will set aside its own contribution and the government's contribution to its retirement account every year. Specifically, the 87.8% of taxpayers who received nothing in 2004 from the tax subsidy under the current system because they did not contribute anything to a pension fund or earned too little to pay taxes, will gain retirement income under the new GRA plan.

> **DATA TO DIGEST**   *The same Urban-Brookings Tax Policy Center calculated the impact of eliminating the tax favoritism for contributions made into individual retirement accounts and replacing them with a flat $600 refundable tax credit for the years 2008–2012. According to those calculations, the GRA system will save the federal government money compared to the system of tax expenditures for the elaborate system of individual retirement accounts.*
>
> ■ *Besides saving the U.S. Treasury money, the GRA plan will raise the after-tax income of the 87.8% of tax filers with $75,000 or less annual income by amounts ranging from 5.6% to 0.5% of income (lower-income taxpayers will*

get a larger increase in annual income from the flat-rate refundable tax credit (table 10.3).

- *The 8.9% of households with incomes between $75,000 and $100,000 would pay $142 more in taxes per year, which is on average less than 0.5% of income.*
- *The 11.6% of households with incomes between $100,000 and $200,000 would pay $1,486 more in taxes per year (table 10.3, rows 7, column 4).*

As mentioned above, if keeping some 401(k) tax breaks is politically expedient, a $5,000 contribution to a 401(k)-type plan (and individual retirement accounts) with a $400 rebate could be substituted and increase tax expenditures by $24 billion over a ten year period, 2008 to 2017. The Urban Institute Tax Policy Center calculated the impact of two forms of the GRAs. As we saw above, the first version eliminates all the tax favoritism for contributions made into individual retirement accounts and replaces them with a $600 refundable tax credit. The second version partially replaces the tax expenditures for contributions made into retirement accounts (up to $20,000 in some cases) with a flat $400 refundable tax credit and caps the allowable contributions to a qualified DC plan to $5,000 per year.

The Progressivity of the $600 Rebate Plan

The first version of the plan, the $600 rebate, helps balance the federal budget and raises the after-tax incomes of the vast majority of taxpayers. The 87.8% of tax filers with $75,000 and less of annual income, would experience not only an increase of annual after-tax income between 5.6% and 0.5% (lower-income taxpayers will get a larger increase), but they will also accumulate money into a retirement account (table 10.3, rows 1–6, column 5).

The taxpayers with the highest incomes will lose some of their current tax breaks. The 8.9% of tax units with incomes between $75,000 and $100,000 would pay $142 more in taxes per year, which, is on average, less than 0.5% of income. The 11.6% of tax units with incomes between $100,000 and $200,000 per year would pay $1,486 more in annual taxes (table 10.3, row 8, columns 3 and 4).

Table 10.3
The Distribution of Federal Tax Changes by Cash Income Group for Two Plans: $600
Rebate[1], and for the $400 Rebate, and $5,000 Allowable[2]

Cash Income Class (Thousands of 2006 Dollars)[3]	Tax Units Number (Thousands of 2006 Dollars)[4]	Share of All Tax Units (%)
1	2	3
Less than $10,000	$18,164	12.0*%
$10–20,000	$25,275	16.8%
$20–30,000	$20,401	13.5%
$30–40,000	$15,452	10.2%
$40–50,000	$12,430	8.2%
$50–75,000	$21,580	14.3%
$75–100,000	$13,470	8.9%
$100–200,000	$17,502	11.6%
$200–500,000	$4,784	3.2%
$500–1,000,000	$793	0.5%
More than $1,000,000	$421	0.3%
All and average	$150,867	100.0%

Source: Urban-Brookings Tax Policy Center Microsimulation Model (version 1006-2).
Notes: Number of AMT Taxpayers (millions). Baseline: 26.4 Proposal: 28.4
1. $600 refund: Calendar year. Baseline is current law. Under the proposal, all traditional IRA, Roth IRA, and defined contribution pension contributions added to taxable income. All taxpayers with wage income receive $600 refundable tax credit, except for wage-earning "married filing jointly" taxpaying units, which receive $1,200 refundable tax credit. The refundable tax credit is indexed to inflation. The revenue and distributional effects of the increased payroll tax rate are not included in the model, since the increased tax rate represents contributions to a TSP account that remain the property of the worker.
2. $400 refund and $5,000 allowable credit. Calendar year. Baseline is current law. Under the proposal, taxpayers can receive up to $5,000 in tax-free contributions to an employer-sponsored retirement account (employee and employer contributions combined). Taxpayers with positive wages receive a $400 refundable rebate,

GRA and a $400 Tax Credit and Defined Contribution Plan Tax Break of $5,000

If we offer a $400 tax credit and maintain tax breaks for DC plans, and individual retirement accounts, but cap them at $5,000, the plan is still progressive. The majority, 87.8%, of tax filers with $75,000 and less of annual income,

Average Federal Tax Change due to the $600 refundable tax credit[5]	Percent Change in After-Tax Income[6]	Average Federal Tax Change Due to the $400 Refundable Tax Credit and $5,000 Allowable[1]	Percent Change in After-Tax Income Due to the $400 Refundable Tax Credit and $5,000 Allowable[2]
4	5	6	7
$-309	5.6%	$-204	3.7%
$-363	2.4%	$-249	1.7%
$-415	1.8%	$-335	1.4%
$-408	1.3%	$-390	1.3%
$-355	0.9%	$-392	1.0%
$-233	0.5%	$-375	0.7%
$142	-0.2%	$-242	0.3%
$1,486	-1.4%	$529	-0.5%
$4,173	-1.9%	$2,383	-1.1%
$5,097	-1.0%	$2,734	-0.5%
$6,785	-0.3%	$3,584	-0.2%
$103	-0.2%	$-99	0.2%

with $800 going to married couples. The extra catchup contribution allowance for IRAs has been eliminated, so that taxpayers can contribute a maximum of $5,000 to an IRA annually. Working taxpayers, who automatically have a portion of payroll deposited in a retirement saving account, are subject to the IRA restrictions for taxpayers with employer-sponsored pensions.

3. Tax units with negative cash income are excluded from the lowest income class but are included in the totals. For a description of cash income, see http://www.taxpolicycenter.org/TaxModel/income.cfm.

4. Includes both filing and non-filing units but excludes those that are dependents of other tax units.

5. After-tax income is cash income less: individual income tax net of refundable credits; corporate income tax; payroll taxes (Social Security and Medicare); and estate tax.

6. Average federal tax (includes individual and corporate income tax, payroll taxes for Social Security and Medicare, and the estate tax) as a percentage of average cash income.

will have more after-tax income even after being required to pay 5% of their pay into an individual retirement account. After-tax income for the 12% of earners with the lowest incomes, less than $10,000 per year, increases by $204, which is a 3.7% increase (table 10.3, row 1, columns 6 and 7). For the 16.8% of taxpayers, with incomes between $10,000 and 20,000, after-tax income jumps even higher to $249 or 1.7% under the plan (table 10.3, row 2, columns 6 and 7).

The taxpayers with incomes between $40,000 and $50,000 per year get the largest increases in income, $392, or 1% of after-tax income (table 10.3, row 5, columns 6 and 7).

The after-tax incomes of the highest earners—the 8.9% of tax units with incomes between $75,000 and $100,000—would fall by $242, which is less than 0.3% of their average income (row 7, columns 6 and 7).

The 11.6% of tax units with incomes between $100,000 and $200,000 would pay $529 more in taxes per year. The 3.2% of tax units with incomes between $200,000 and $500,000 would pay a lot more in dollar amounts—$2,383 more in taxes per year; the extra tax represents 1.1% of their after-tax income. The very few affluent taxpayers, 0.5% of tax units with incomes between $500,000 and $1,000,000 would pay $2,734 more in taxes per year, but they should hardly notice because that extra tax represents less than 1% of their income, 0.5%. The very rich, the 421,000 households, 0.3% of taxpayers, with incomes over $1,000,000 would pay $3,584 more in taxes per year; perhaps, too, hardly noticeable because that extra tax is less than one-fifth of one percent of their income, 0.2% (row 11, columns 5 and 6).

Under either version, exchanging small tax increases for fewer than 15% of taxpayers gets pension coverage and increased savings for all Americans.

Are Guaranteed Retirement Accounts Politically Feasible?

The Guaranteed Retirement Accounts plan calls for wealthy people to pay more taxes! Could such a proposal "have legs"?

If GRAs were implemented—in exchange for a 5% mandatory contribution (up to the mandatory maximum Social Security contribution)—all workers, regardless of income, would receive a $600 rebate. Yet, because the current system favors the highest earners, more than 4 million households would pay over $4,000 more in taxes in 2008.

> **DATA TO DIGEST** *Under Guaranteed Retirement Accounts with a $600 rebate*
>
> - *more than 4 million households, or 3.2% of households, with incomes between $200,000 and $500,000 would pay on average $4,173 more in taxes per year;*
> - *the 0.5% of households with incomes between $500,000 and $1,000,000 would pay $5,097 more in taxes per year;*

■ *the highest-earning 421,298 households (0.3% of households) with incomes above $1,000,000 would pay $6,785 more in taxes, which is worth between 0.3% and 1% of their incomes.*

It would seem, of course, that these over 4 million high-income earners will provide formidable opposition to proposals to change from the current pension system to a GRA pension system. Perhaps not! Here are two considerations why not.

First, on average, the tax breaks these households may lose represents less than 2% of their total annual income. Nonetheless, the rich, like anyone else, don't like to pay more taxes. And the rich not only vote, they can afford the costs of swaying votes, which of course influences tax policy.

Second, and I was struck by this reality, only 47% of people in the highest-income groups (see table 10.2, rows 4, 5, and 6, column 2) contributed to a defined contribution plan in 2004! That means those who did not contribute to a retirement account did not receive a tax subsidy. Even these high-earning folks received nothing from the federal government. Under the GRA, each year everyone will increase their retirement savings and everyone will receive a tax subsidy.

Furthermore, the impact of GRAs on the federal treasury is remarkable. In 2008, if the GRAs had been in force, the government would have spent $5.4 billion less in tax subsidies for retirement accounts than it will under the current system. This means that if the $600 rebate for GRAs replaces the current tax subsidies to DC plans, the total savings for the U.S. Treasury during the five years 2008 to 2017 will be $343 billion. In other words, in exchange for eliminating tax subsidies—which distribute 50% of the total value of the tax subsidies to the 10% of households earning an average of over $3 million per year—we will get retirement accounts started for the majority of Americans who otherwise will have nothing. Under the GRA plan, in those ten years 2008 to 2017, the households in the top 10% will get $34.3 billion, and the bottom 50% will get over $170 billion instead of the $0 they now get from the federal government to help them save for retirement.[15]

Making workers save for retirement is popular. A 2006 survey conducted by the HSBC Bank found that, of all the ways to reform pension systems, workers in twenty-one nations, including the United States, preferred their government impose a "compulsory savings" plan rather than reduce pension benefits or raise taxes or make people retire at older ages, as the way to cope with the costs of an aging society.[16]

> Bottom Line   *It would not be difficult for a politician to defend the Guaranteed Retirement Account plan because all workers, even the highest-income earners, need a plan to force them to save for retirement. In addition, the GRA plan saves the Treasury money while it raises the savings rates of American households.*

The recent HSBC survey and, more important, the popular support for Social Security for over seventy years both suggest that people would rather be forced to save for retirement than have benefits reduced. Alas, a common way to cut benefits is increasing the age for collecting full Social Security benefits. However, pundits like Robert Samuelson, *Newsweek* magazine's economist, believe workers should think otherwise, that they should want to work more. Here is a quote from a column he wrote in 2005:

> Americans have to work longer, the economy will create needed part-time and part-year jobs. The real obstacle is the politics and psychology of the retirement revolution: the expectation that people in their early sixties are entitled to stop working. Undoubtedly many Americans prefer having someone else support their leisure.[17]

Samuelson demeans retirement and implies with his statement ". . . many Americans prefer having someone else support their leisure," that workers are not owed their promised pensions. Samuelson defends his harsh assessment because he says that changing demography destines harsh means and difficult choices. I claim that is it too harsh and too difficult to cut benefits any further since older Americans live on very small levels of income right now. This is probably why the HSBC poll found that Americans, as well as Europeans, argue for a mix of tax increases and benefit cuts to handle soaring pension costs.[18]

Although demography does not dictate political decisions, there is no escaping the math.[19] If the number of the elderly increases—and assuming nothing else changes—the costs of supporting the elderly increase. Increasing costs does not mean a retirement system is unaffordable.

Whether an economy can support nonworkers depends more on productivity growth and the size and strength of the tax base rather than on the ratio of workers to beneficiaries. Whether a society chooses to support nonworking older people depends on economic power, mostly on the power in the labor market. Pension policy is ultimately labor policy. Economists

Steven Nyce and Sylvester Schieber argue that older people should work more because a future smaller U.S. workforce will slow GDP growth (assuming everyone else is working) and lower consumption, which is something we all do not want to happen.[20]

Whether future labor markets are tight or slack depends almost entirely on the economy's future productivity. Furthermore, not all people who want to work can work. Instead of coming from the ranks of the elderly, the future labor supply should come from the working adults who want work and might need training, education, transportation, and protection from age discrimination in employment, pay, training, and promotion. Further, keeping wages low by boosting the labor supply can perversely affect productivity because labor that is paid lower wages will diminish employers' incentives to invest in capital. If labor shortages were caused by aging societies, then why in Europe, where the average age is much higher than in the United States, is unemployment high?

Wharton Business School economist Peter Cappelli notes (2003) that employers have a deep interest in the elderly working: "From the perspective of an individual employer, it is a real problem for them if they cannot find workers with the skills they feel they need at the wage they can afford to pay, even if that wage is below the market level, but it is not clear that is an issue that government policy should try to solve."

Because employers want to keep wages low is not why policymakers should cut pensions to force the elderly to work more. Employers could attract the older worker by raising wages and improving working conditions. See box 10.1, "A Persistent Policy Recommendation: Raising the Retirement Age," for a review of different perspectives on raising the retirement age or not.

Other Plans Fall Short of Fixing the Problem

The idea to supplement Social Security on a broad basis is not new. Republican Senator Jeff Jeffords and President Bill Clinton had promoted versions of proposals aimed at expanding simple, subsidized, individual retirement accounts.

Not long before he died in 1998, the late Northwestern economist, Richard Eisner, proposed individual account supplements to be administered by the Social Security Administration. Boston University finance professor, Zvi Bodie, argues that government inflation-linked bonds are the perfect retirement

A Persistent Policy Recommendation: Raising the Retirement Age

Even though most workers choose to retire before the "normal retirement age,[21] the age at which an eligible person can collect full Social Security benefits, advocates for postponing retirement are spread across the political spectrum—from Barbara Butrica, Kevin Smith, and Eugene Steuerle of the Urban Institute[22] to David John of the Heritage Foundation.[23] One of the most influential proponents for raising Social Security's, Earliest Eligibility Age, EEA, and lowering the benefits of those who retire before the Normal Retirement Age, NRA, is Alicia Munnell of Boston College's Center for Retirement Research. Munnell strongly believes that the government establishes retirement age norms by establishing the age of sixty-two as the earliest age eligibility to collect reduced Social Security benefits, and sixty-seven for eligibility to collect full benefits (in 2020). These ages, established by the government, tend to serve as signals about how people should act in a society. People who are shortsighted, myopic, and who live for the moment (for the professional economist reader that means people with a high time discount) would benefit from being encouraged to retire later when their pension income would be higher because they worked longer. Also, she suggests that having the government set retirement age norms at "young" ages encourages firms to practice age discrimination because firms are less likely to hire and train older workers, fearing they will retire.

I agree with Munnell that social norms are powerful influences on behavior. However, we cannot discount the reality that people want to work less as they grow older. That many workers stop work, or collect Social Security benefits early—incurring a permanent reduction in their benefits—may merely indicate their preferences for time over money. An Urban Institute study estimates that many workers would increase their retirement incomes by 25% if they delayed retirement from age sixty-two to sixty-seven.[24] Many workers may not be aware of that but almost all know they would get higher benefits if they work longer, which the Social Security Administration informs all claimants.

The most important argument against raising the retirement age to collect full benefits is that there is no convincing evidence that most older people can work longer just because they live longer. We do not know if longevity is in-

investment vehicle (in fact they were expressly created to do that) and everyone's retirement account full of them should supplement Social Security.[25]

Economists Christian Weller, Dean Baker, Alicia Munnell, Daniel Halperin, and the pension economists at the World Bank, have all made similar proposals. President Carter's 1988 Commission on Pension Policy proposed a similar plan, although Carter's proposed plan was mandatory.[26]

creasing because we are extending the lives of frail adults or because we are healthier at older ages. Also, we do not know how well-matched older people are to handle today's jobs. Since 1981, the share of older workers reporting limitations in their ability to work has been between 15% and 18%. While the share of jobs demanding physical effort is declining, especially for men, the share requiring good eyesight or computer skills is increasing.[27]

Many workers, such as those laid off or with health problems, do not choose to retire. It's a decision made for them. A recent McKinsey & Company survey[28] found that 40% of retirees said they were forced to retire earlier than they had planned and most of them reported it was because of their own poor health or a family member's poor health or because they lost their jobs. Age discrimination in promotion or pay or in assigning job duties also causes retirement earlier than planned. For example, an internal memo from Wal-Mart's Human Resource Department leaked to the a Wal-Mart reform advocacy group, encouraged managers to give all workers a physical task, such as requiring cashiers to gather carts from the parking lot, so as to discourage old and less physically able workers. The reasoning was that increased costs of training replacements were cheaper than paying higher wages because of seniority.[29]

Many older workers do not stay in their career jobs. Instead of "sixty" being the new "forty" (years of age), sixty has become the new "sixteen," as older people reenter the job market as retail clerks or in other similar, low-paid occupations once filled by teenagers. Overall, elderly workers over age sixty-five have jobs with less status than workers aged fifty-five through sixty-four.[30]

Advocates for raising the retirement age are aware of the physical limitations older blue-collar workers have, the changing nature of jobs, and the existence of chronic age discrimination. Like us, they want workers to get the jobs they desire at all ages. However, it is less likely that older workers will obtain jobs on their own terms if their retirement income is less secure.

Guaranteed Retirement Accounts will encourage healthy, employable, and satisfied workers to postpone their retirement if they want to, because participants in GRA pensions earn retirement benefits for every hour they work. However, they will also make it easier for the majority of workers who need or want to retire before age sixty-seven to do so by augmenting retirement incomes and by allowing workers to make contributions greater than 5% of their pay during their working lives.

The Guaranteed Retirement Account plan will go one step beyond many of these proposals in that it seeks to eliminate the ineffective and regressive tax expenditures for 401(k)-style plans and to use the assets in each individual's GRA to increase the retirement incomes of all workers. Not included in these other former proposals, and already discussed in this chapter, include: The GRA plan will cover all workers, not just those in low- and moderate-income families, and it will include mandatory contributions by employer or shared by both employer and employee, not just a government subsidy. While far-reaching, the GRA plan will be affordable because it will not worsen the federal deficit nor will it require a tax increase.

The Guaranteed Retirement Accounts plan will be more equitable and effective than proposals to close gaps in 401(k) plans through automatic enrollment and other measures.

Another key proposal comes out of the Hamilton Project written by Brookings Institution economist William Gale, MIT economist Jonathan Gruber, and Director for the Congressional Research Service, Peter Orszag.[31] (The Hamilton Project is a think tank formed in the spring of 2006 to elaborate policies in anticipation of a Democratic Congress; its financing comes from wealthy Democrats, among them Robert Rubin, Treasury Secretary, under Bill Clinton.) They propose that employers automatically enroll their employees in 401(k) type individual retirement account and put their contributions in a "life-cycle" fund. (A life-cycle fund allocates assets toward a greater concentration of bonds and away from stocks as the employee ages.) To lessen the ability of workers to spend the money when they change jobs, their proposal requires that the employer automatically move the workers' funds to another retirement account. If the employee retires, the employer is required to convert the account to annuities—workers can opt out of any of these default choices. Workers would receive a 30% match from the federal government.

This Hamilton Project plan, if adopted in its entirety, would increase retirement savings and make the tax subsidies more equitable because workers who do not pay taxes now because they earn little, would receive a government match to help defray their contribution. However, the Hamilton Project plan retains many of the previously discussed flaws of our current employer-pension system such as: workers continue to bear the financial risk and to pay high fees to commercial money managers; participation is not mandatory; employers are not required to extend coverage to all their employees nor contribute to their workers' individual DC accounts; and workers can continue to opt out of the annuity feature, take the lump sum instead, and spend it before they die.

At a conference for investors, I was on a panel with the director for the teacher's pension funds in West Virginia who explained why teachers wanted to return to the defined benefit plan from a defined contribution plan. The teachers realized they wouldn't have enough money to retire on. One reason they wouldn't have enough was the "red truck syndrome." Teachers retire take their lump sum, buy a new red truck, symbolic of some durable good, and then are remorseful afterward because they do not have enough left over to fund their retirement.

Tax Credits Targeting Lower-Income Workers

Alicia Munnell and Daniel Halperin declared they have given up on employers ever providing meaningful pensions for low-paid workers. They call for the government to directly subsidize the retirement of these workers and their spouses by depositing $300 tax credits into an individual retirement account, which was their version of a GRA. They call their proposed pension accounts, Universal Savings Accounts.[32] The tax credits would be phased out for middle- and high-income workers who could, instead, take advantage of government matching grants. These matching grants would be reduced in value at higher levels of income or they would have higher-income individuals using existing tax deductions for 401(k)-style accounts.

You can see that the issue of making the tax system more progressive is a constant theme in reform proposals, but there is a problem with their thoughtful plan. Munnell and Halperin would not require employers to offer workplace retirement plans, though they propose a patchwork of changes to the existing pension system intended to expand coverage and make retirement income more secure. This patchwork includes allowing employers' pension plans to exclude low-income workers because they would be eligible for the tax credits based on their low income. The idea behind excluding low-income workers is that they would be receiving tax credits; excluding low-income workers would make it easier for employers to provide retirement benefits to workers who are not receiving tax credits. Thus, the onus in the Universal Savings Accounts would be on the government to fund the retirement of low-income workers.

Munnell and Halperin propose paying for the tax credits by taxing pension fund earnings. Existing tax expenditures for commercial accounts will remain untouched, despite the problems with 401(k) plans—high fees, early withdrawals, spotty contributions, and top-heavy benefits—that the authors, among others, have documented. This certainly would make DB plans less attractive. Perhaps Munnell and Halperin wanted their proposal to seem reasonable, since for a time reducing cherished tax breaks for high income people was a nonstarter. The tax breaks may be cherished, but they are also broken. Also, the $300 monthly contribution is not enough; $600 a month earning a real annual return of 3% guarantees the worker bringing home income replacing 70% of his or her earnings at retirement at age sixty-five.

Conclusion: The Final Bottom Line

To determine what is needed for effective pension reform, it is crucial is to assess the evidence and just as crucial to stop pretending that the tax incentives for defined contribution plans do anything meaningful. (Note: tax incentives for many hybrid and defined benefit plans do work—DB plans pay annuities, provide no opt-outs for employees, professionally manage the funds with lower fees—and they are not divided into individual accounts that are more costly to manage.) This harsh assessment does not demean any earnest motivations for these large tax breaks—they just do not encourage workers to save for retirement.

The failure of tax policy to encourage retirement savings can be summarized starkly: The cost of tax breaks for retirement accounts grow, while retirement savings fall, and pension insecurity soars. Tax incentives for retirement accounts fail most Americans. Based on what we know did not work, we now have a better chance to ask and answer: What will work?

The answer, in short, is that GRAs and Social Security promote all the goals of a system of secure retirement income. For a pension system to be well managed, the collection of pension contributions and the investment of pension funds and distribution of pension income to retirees for the rest of their lives must be done, in the simplest terms, without wasting taxpayer money or wasting any of the money in pension accounts. Retirees should have enough to live on, the contributions and benefits should be fair—they should be linked to people's work effort—and the system should help the economy.

Adequacy with Guaranteed Retirement Accounts and Social Security will be met because no retired worker will have incomes below the poverty line. GRAs ensure that people accumulate enough for retirement.

Fairness under GRA will be achieved because workers in like circumstances will be treated the same and pension income will be linked to personal savings choices, work effort, and earnings.

Efficiency will be met because the GRAs pension system, administered by a not-for-profit professional money manager, will pay wholesale, not higher retail administrative costs. The GRAs eliminate the bias towards 401(k) plans and the tax subsidy for a system that does not work—this situation is the very definition of inefficiency.

Economic growth and stability will be enhanced to the extent that the GRAs will pay annuities not lump sums. Pension income—which is almost 10% of consumer spending—will not destabilize consumer spending because retirement income will not be affected by short-term changes in the values of financial assets. Also, pension investments, to the extent that they are directed toward productive domestic investment, will help finance economic development. In addition, because GRAs will encourage occupational and industry-wide defined benefit plans, the special human resource needs of employers and employees can be met.

Something must be done to prevent tragic shortfalls in retirement income predicted for: lower-income workers who will be facing Social Security cutbacks, consequently leading to higher poverty rates; and middle-class workers (third and fourth quintile) who do not have any DB plans or have only 401(k)-type plans. Though younger, lower-income, and mobile workers, and workers in volatile and retreating industries, such as steel and auto making, may also be disappointed by the shortcomings of DB plans, the GRAs will fill in the time workers are not covered by their DB plans.

At the extreme on the right, there is argument for Social Security to be essentially replaced by a tax-subsidized system of commercial 401(k)-type accounts. On the extreme left, there is argument for expanding Social Security by taxing all income from capital gains, interest, and work, and eliminating all workplace pensions.

The extremes do not talk to each other, and because there is no meaningful discourse, attempts at meaningful pension reform have faded. If the extremes communicated, perhaps they will see that a retirement pension income reform is exactly in the center—Guaranteed Retirement Accounts coupled with Social Security will preserve workplace pensions while encouraging voluntary pension arrangements between employers and employees. The GRA–Social Security coupling will make workers save for their own retirement. It will expand pension coverage to all workers. It will promote efficient money management of the investments in their retirement accounts. And it will help balance the federal budget.

American workers are facing a dramatic shift in what they can expect in

old age. Alas, it's a downward shift. The "right" to retire, as conferred by secure pensions, enabled American workers to have a powerfully reflective and
meaningful period at the end of their lives.[33] Pension security is an important
determinant of what reality is possible and likely, and crucially, how the quality of life in old age is distributed.

APPENDIX 10.1

Guaranteed Retirement Accounts: Questions and Answers

---

*Will Guaranteed Retirement Accounts provide enough retirement income
for all workers?* No. The GRA system is designed to provide a basic retirement
income for workers with a history of steady jobs. Workers, such as low-wage
workers or workers who took time off for care-giving or who experienced unemployment spells, will be able to supplement the funds in their retirement income account through additional contributions or through personal savings
or government transfers or job earnings. Workers who have the means and
simply want to enjoy a more comfortable retirement can likewise make supplemental contributions to their GRA funds or increase other forms of saving.

Is annuitization unfair to retirees who die younger? Annuitization serves
an important insurance function, preventing retirees from outliving their retirement benefits. However, benefits are tied to longevity which, in turn, is
tied to earnings. This may seem unfair to low-income workers and groups
characterized as having shorter lifespans. But when contributions, benefits,
and taxes are considered together, the GRA system is very progressive (as is
Social Security), since most low-income workers, even if they die younger,
will receive more in benefits than they contributed either directly or through
taxes.

*Can participants bequeath the savings in their Guaranteed Retirement Ac-
counts?* Much of the appeal of 401(k)s lies in the fact that workers can track
their accumulations and own the assets outright. When they die, they can bequeath the funds remaining in their 401(k) to their heirs. Although accumulations in GRAs cannot be bequeathed as lump sums, participants can opt for
a reduced annuity in exchange for survivor benefits. A retiree can declare that
after he or she dies, a designated beneficiary will receive a stream of income

for life or until a specified age. Many variations are possible and merely require technical decisions.

Lump sum bequests are incompatible with mandatory annuitization. If participants can bequeath untapped retirement funds, a participant who dies the day before her expected retirement would leave a substantial bequest, whereas a participant who died the day following the start of retirement would have nothing to leave to heirs.

Will the plan appeal to workers? A system of individual accounts with a guaranteed but modest rate of return might not have had much political appeal in the pre-Enron bull market of the 1990s. But as the hype around 401(k) plans has faded in the wake of corporate scandals and poor performance, most Americans are likely to welcome a well-designed, efficient, fair, and transparent pension plan that provides a guaranteed retirement income to supplement Social Security, especially if mandatory contributions for lower-income workers are heavily subsidized. Studies show that workers want pensions, are willing to pay for them, and appreciate a modest, steady, and secure annuity. Retirees report higher levels of well-being if their income is guaranteed and would, if offered the choice, prefer a DB plan over a DC plan with equal or slightly higher value.[34] Further, an HSBC bank survey found that, of all the ways to reform pension systems, U.S. workers preferred that their government impose a "compulsory savings" plan rather than reduce benefits, raise taxes, or be required to work longer.[35]

Why not simply expand Social Security? Social Security is the cornerstone of our retirement system, and will continue to be the most important source of retirement income for the majority of retired Americans. Moreover, estimates by the Social Security trustees predict that the trust fund will be solvent until the year 2040 and the Congressional Budget Office predicts that it will be solvent until the year 2052—even if Congress does nothing between now and 2052.

Both predictions are based on pessimistic assumptions, including economic growth projections below current and historical levels. Nevertheless, for political and practical reasons, we cannot ignore the possibility that a shortfall will eventually emerge, and it will need to dealt with—preferably by removing the cap on earnings subject to the Social Security tax. Meanwhile, the forecast for Medicare is genuinely bleak in the absence of major health care reform.

In contrast to the Medicare problem, GRAs will be fully prefunded and annuities will be adjusted to take into account increasing life spans. This means the GRA pension system will never need to be bailed out because of a decrease in the worker-to-retiree ratio. And, unlike Social Security benefits, GRA benefits will increase for each hour worked, which gives workers more flexibility in choosing when to retire.

Admittedly, GRAs are not as progressive as Social Security, which provides disability and spousal benefits as well as a higher replacement ratio for low-income workers. However, they will be a realistic, affordable supplement to Social Security, to provide an adequate and secure retirement for most workers.

Which defined benefit plans or hybrids qualify as exempt from the Guaranteed Retirement Accounts? Recognizing the valuable productivity enhancing features of occupational and industry pension plans, qualified DB plans will be allowed to substitute for a contribution into a worker's GRA. A qualified DB plan is one in which the plan sponsor contributes 5% of payroll per year; sponsors who make sporadic and uneven contributions would not qualify.

The arguments in favor of well-funded DB plans being able to opt out are compelling. For the majority of participants, DB pension plans work well, especially in public and private sector multiemployer arrangements. Employers can tailor the rules, such as on vesting and benefit dispersal, to meet the needs of particular workforces. Multiemployer plans, like those in the public sector or in trucking, mining, services, and building trades, are especially flexible in allowing workers to accumulate pension credits across jobs, giving workers an added incentive to invest in non–employer-specific job training.

There could be a concern that employers would use the GRAs to substitute for the single-employer DB plans, but they are no substitute for DB plans. The requirement for a continuous 5% of payroll contributions is more stringent than the funding rules in the recent Pension Protection Act. Also, DB plans will have tax advantages over GRAs, since an employer can exempt all the contributions to the DB fund that backs an annual benefit up to $180,000—a much larger figure than will remain tax exempt.

How much money would be handled and who would manage the investment? The accounts would be managed by a unit of the Thrift Savings Plans with its own trustees. The trustees will be independently appointed, half by the president (subject to Senate confirmation) and half by the House and Congress. They shall have terms structured in a similar fashion to the Federal Reserve Board of Governors, and will choose the commercial money managers. If the GRA had been in force, 100% of Americans would have retirement accounts—not 60%—and there would have been $100 billion more money in the system—oddly, the amount of tax expenditures for 401(k) and Keogh plans. This will represent new monies into the private capital markets.

Why don't 401(k) plans qualify as exempt from the Guaranteed Retirement Account and will now have to be taxed? The 401(k) plans may be convenient ways for employees to save and to direct their savings in investments of their choice (the employer's choice). But they are a waste of taxpayer money because the tax advantages overwhelmingly accrue to high-income households and to the financial services industry, with little or no impact on retirement savings. Some proposed 401(k) reforms, such as automatic enrollment, a cap on fees, mandatory annuitization, and converting tax exemptions to tax credits, would greatly improve them but would still leave the individual worker exposed to substantial financial risk.

The 401(k) plans will not be abolished, but additional contributions to them will no longer be tax-exempt. We expect that many 401(k) plans will survive because high-income employees appreciate the automatic savings feature and the possibility of an employer match. Accumulations in 401(k) plans and other retirement plans that exist before GRAs go into effect will be treated under the former tax rules earnings.

How do caregivers fare? Guaranteed Retirement Accounts will serve as a saving function and social insurance function but not as a welfare function. However, other pension income programs, such as Supplementary Social Insurance (SSI), funded through general tax revenues—from corporate, income, and other federal tax revenue sources—can provide assistance to eliminate old-age poverty, including subsidizing care-giving credits for unpaid caregivers. For example, economist Heidi Hartmann has proposed reviving an earlier Social Security reform proposal that gives the child's primary caregiver two years of Social Security credit for each of child. The credit will be calculated as if the care-giver earned 45% of the average wage in full-time work if the care-giver's earnings in those years are lower than that, which is often the case because parents reduce their paid work to care for the child.

Notes

Introduction

1. Lofgren, Nyce, and Scheiber 2003.

2. U.S. companies increased their share of GDP between 2001 and 2006 at an unprecedented rate, the fastest gain in labor income since World War II. The profit share of GDP rose from 7% in mid-2001 to 12.2% at the beginning of 2006. During the same period, labor's share of GDP fell from 58.6% in 2001 to 56.2% in the first quarter of 2006. *Financial Times* journalists interpreted the trends: "The negotiating position of U.S. workers may have been weakened by globalisation, giving companies the upper hand" and "Companies are aggressively shifting the burden of benefits on to the labour force and off their balance sheets" (Guerrera and Swann 2006). In the later part of 2006 the labor share of GDP recovered moderately; however, much of the recovery was because stock options for highly paid executives were included in the labor share, not because large numbers of employees received a larger share of GDP growth. Economists do not expect low unemployment rates—at around 4.2%—to cause "wage-push" inflation, because labor's bargaining power has shriveled in comparison to earlier times when labor markets tightened.

Chapter 1
Hope for Retirement's Future

1. Dora Costa (1998) provides an excellent review of American men's retirement behavior since the Civil War; she mostly uses data from surveys of individuals.

2. Russell 1935, 17.

3. The methodology for this calculation is as follows: leisure time after age sixty-five equals life expectancy after age sixty-five (in years) multiplied by one minus the labor force participation rate after sixty-five. For example, the estimated number of years of leisure for someone age sixty-five, expected to live for another twenty years, and with a 50% chance of participating in the labor force, is ten years.

4. Employer pension plans—mostly DB plans—allow early retirement and are more likely linked to health-deteriorating working conditions. In addition, the Social Security disability program, as well as employers' disability programs, also serve as a

source of income for those transitioning to retirement at younger ages and for those who are likely to die sooner.

5. The tempting self-help book advises us how to look and feel younger and live longer (Roizen and Stephenson 1999).

6. Employers pay lower investment and management fees per participant in 401(k) plans compared to DBs primarily because workers pay most of the 401(k) fees, which are commonly 3% of assets. In addition, employer-based 401(k) plans produce conflicts of interest between fund managers' and employers' interests. In contrast to DB plans, which are restricted by the Employee Retirement Income Security Act (ERISA) from holding more than 10% of sponsor stock, 401(k) assets can be entirely sponsor stock. This ability embeds conflicts for the persons who must both manage the pension in the sole interest of the participants and manage the company to advance the interests of shareholders and owners. There is no conflict of interest involved in managing Social Security.

7. Yet, even if the nation as a whole can afford the promised Social Security benefits, some employers have large pension burdens. Affordability is a chief concern for some of the employers—especially in legacy firms—who provide DB plans and retiree health care. For instance, the American Big Three auto companies are practically mini–welfare states, and some employers owe more pension and retiree health liabilities than the company is worth. In other words, the company is worth more dead than alive. However, employers' costs can be overstated because workers pay for most of the health care, pensions, and retiree health costs with lower wages.

8. Orszag and Diamond 2003, 65.

9. Neuman 2003.

10. Cappelli 2003.

11. Chernozhukov and Hansen 2004; Engen and Gale 2000; Munnell and Sundén 2004.

12. Bell, Carasso, and Steuerle 2005.

13. The Office of Management and Budget publishes the U.S. Budget and includes an analysis of the tax expenditures in an appendix to the budget that is called "Analytical Perspectives."

14. Current law provides multiple types of tax-preferred employer-based savings accounts (different rules apply to different employers) to encourage saving for retirement. The Bush administration proposes to consolidate these plans (401(k), SIMPLE 401(k), 403(b), 457 plans, SIMPLE IRAs, and SEPs) into a single type of plan—Employee Retirement Savings Accounts (ERSAs)—that would be available to all employers. Under one of the safe harbor options, a plan would satisfy the nondiscrimination rules with respect to employee deferrals and employee contributions if it provided a 50% match on elective contributions of up to 6% of compensation. The proposal substantially reduces complexity. Contributions to these accounts would be

on an after-tax basis but would grow tax-free. Individuals would be able to save up to $5,000 in a RSA per year and withdraw funds at age fifty-eight.

15. The idea is that with enough tax incentives workers will be encouraged to save more for retirement than they otherwise would. However, this effect is not well grounded in theory: Economists argue that people might actually respond to tax breaks by saving *less*, since the tax savings allow a target level of savings to be reached sooner. Under some versions of the 2006 White House proposal for Retirement Savings Accounts (the first proposals surfaced in 2001, among them the proposal that an individual could shelter $400,000 from taxes within a twenty-year period), the Tax Policy Center, sponsored by the Brookings and Urban Institutes, calculated that 13% of households with incomes over $100,000 would have received 94% of the tax expenditures, had Retirement Savings Accounts existed in 2005. Most of the tax breaks would have gone to households with incomes over $200,000. See Burman, Gale, and Orszag (2004). The analysis finds that the cost of the proposal after twenty-five years would be 0.3% of GDP.

16. The vision for individual accounts uncouples pensions from employers and takes the employer off the hook for having to comply with the antidiscrimination rules, which require low-income workers to be able to participate in the employee benefits given to the higher-paid employees. Expanding tax breaks for individual accounts would spur many employers, especially small ones, to eliminate all their employee pension plans. Under current law, in 2004, the maximum amount owners and executives of a firm could contribute to a tax-advantaged retirement account annually was $8,000. If they establish pension plans for themselves and their workers, and pay into their workers' pensions, they can save much more. That is an incentive for employers to sponsor plans. Under tax-subsidized individual accounts, however, owners and executives would be able to put $20,000 into a tax-favored savings plan without having to offer a pension plan for their employees.

Chapter 2
The Collapse of Retirement Income

1. Fernandez and Brandon (2006), working for the Securities Industry Association, showed that most Americans beyond the lowest quintile will not have enough to replace 70% of their preretirement income. In 2006, economists—not connected to the securities industry—estimated that fewer than half of older workers (average age fifty-five in 1992) have less than they need in retirement, based on their financial and housing wealth in 1992 and their current consumption levels. They assumed that the elderly would access 61% of their equity in their home when they retired and that they had no medical expenses while they were working. The target wealth levels were quite low—approximately $63,000 (in 1992) for the average earner and $2,500 for the lowest 10% of earners (Scholz, Seshadri, and Khitatrakun 2004).

2. The data for 1993 is in Employee Benefits Research Institute (2004a). Also see Employee Benefit Research Institute (2004b) report.

3. The data for 2006 is in Employee Benefits Research Institute on-line edition of their annual retirement confidence survey. See Employee Benefits Research Institute 2006.

4. Medicare Part B premiums are automatically deducted for most Social Security beneficiaries. Part B premiums have increased 60% between 2002 and 2007 while the Social Security COLA has increased only 14%. The COLAs are calculated to reflect the inflation rate experienced by the average consumer, and not for older people who buy different goods and services such as medicine and health care that typically have price increases higher than the average. Medicare Part B premiums cover outpatient care such as doctors' services, durable medical equipment, home health visits, and preventive care. The federal government pays roughly 75% of the total cost of Part B out of general revenues, and charges a premium to cover the remaining 25% (Centers for Medicare and Medicaid Services 2006). Individuals with incomes above $80,000 and couples with incomes above $160,000—about 25% of the population over age sixty-five (U.S. Bureau of Census Department 2006)—pay a larger portion of the premium, projected at over $162 for individuals with income over $200,000. For about half of Medicare beneficiaries, the premium's increases consume their entire Social Security cost-of-living adjustment. Medicare Part B premiums are based on the deficit between what the program was expected to cost and the actual costs.

5. EBRI 2003.

6. Rotenberg 2006.

7. Butrica, Iams, and Smith 2003, 45, table 6.

8. The elderly have record levels of mortgage and credit card debt (Draut, Tamara, and Heather McGhee 2004), and near retirees (aged fifty to sixty-two) represent 20% of households but hold 25% of the debt. In addition, 14.3% of elderly families compared to 10% of all families were considered heavily indebted in 2001—devoting at least 40% of their incomes to debt payments. Since debt is difficult to reduce without increasing income, the fear is that debt will force future consumption decreases (Soto 2005).

9. For two-thirds of the elderly, Social Security provides the majority of their income. For one-third of the elderly, it provides nearly all of their income. In 2002 Social Security provided 50% or more of the income of 66% of elderly people (those age sixty-five or older). Social Security provided 90% or more of the income of 34% of elderly people. For 22% of seniors, Social Security is the sole source of retirement income (Social Security Administration 2004a). Only 10% got most of their money from personal assets (personal assets include savings, the sale of a business, and defined contribution pensions).

10. EBRI 2003.

11. McDonnell 2005, 11, figure 3.

12. Butrica, Iams, and Smith 2003, 41, table 2.

13. Laurence Kotlikoff (Darlin 2007) and economists Scholtz, Seshadri, and Khitatrakun (2004) based estimates of retirement needs on consumption patterns

while people are working to project how much wealth people need before retiring. Their calculations are detailed and sophisticated and fundamentally assume that people have a fairly average tolerance for the risk of running out of money, a 4% chance of needing assisted living and nursing home care, will sell their home at retirement to downsize, and will keep consumption at 70% of preretirement levels. Smith, Love, and McNair (2007) also conclude that people will have enough income in retirement to maintain adequate consumption above the poverty level if wealth and poverty are measured correctly.

14. My calculations for the future come from Butrica, Iams, and Smith (2003, 42, table 3, and 60, table 5).

15. Weller and Wolff 2005, 17, table 4.

16. Weller and Wolff 2005, 17, table 4.

17. These data come from Weller and Wolff (2005, 17, table 4). The growth rates for older workers with average incomes is much different; pension wealth (mainly DC plans) grew the fastest.

18. The 1983 Social Security reforms increased the retirement age gradually from 65 to 67, starting in 2000 and ending in 2022 (Munnell *2003*).

19. Weller and Wolff 2005, 17, table 4.

20. The Congressional Research Service (see Purcell 2003 and *2005* for examples) provides an annual summary of participation and sponsorship statistics gleaned from the Census Bureau survey of the population called the Current Population Survey (CPS), which has the benefit of tens of thousands of observations. The drawback is the lack of detailed information about the worth of someone's pension or what type it is. Its report is titled "Pension Sponsorship and Participation." Full reports are available online.

21. Hinz and Turner 1998, 25.

22. See Even and MacPherson 2004; Geddes and Heywood 2003; Solberg and Laughlin 1995; Creedy 1994; Korczyk 1993.

23. In 1998, men aged twenty-five to thirty-four comprised 26% of the male workforce, down from 30% in 1983.

24. United States Department of Labor, Bureau of Labor Statistics, 2004.

25. See Ghilarducci 1992; Dorsey, Cornell, and MacPherson 1998.

26. Zion and Carcache 2002.

27. I obtained this data from an organization called "Cover the Uninsured." Their fact sheet was at this URL on July 5, 2007, http://covertheuninsured.org/factsheets/display.php?FactSheetID=113. Another article, using a different sample, found that between 1997 and 2003 the percentage of firms offering retiree health insurance fell from 32% to 25% (Buchmueller, Johnson, and Lo Sasso 2006). See also the Kaiser Family Foundation's website at http://www.kff.org for frequent studies on this issue.

28. Kaiser Family Foundation 2005.

29. Fisher 2006.

30. Requiring more research is the idea that human nature and optimism about mortality, pension rules, Social Security benefit structures, and family relations cause "young" older couples to take on debt, travel, and buy consumption goods over and above the "life-cycle" consumption of the longest-living spouse.

31. Rix, Rosenmann, and Schultz 1998.

32. The assumed interest rate is 4% and the rate of increase in the minimum wage is 1%.

33. This Government Accountability Office (formerly the Government Accountability Office) (2002) report on European policies toward older workers found that political leaders were concerned that people older than a "certain" age (what age workers were entitled to retire differed by society) wanted to work rather than having retirement leisure because their old-age income was meager.

34. Child labor is not considered voluntary or legitimate.

35. The ratio of average income of the elderly households in the top fifth of the income distribution to the income of those at the bottom currently is almost double at 1.93; for near-retirees the ratio will have gone up one-and-a-half times to 3.35 (Butrica, Iams, and Smith 2003, 42, table 3).

36. Grad 2002.

37. Butrica, Iams, and Smith 2003, 45, table 6.

38. In 2000 there were 6,123,059 women over age eighty, compared to 3,061,895 men; U.S. Bureau of the Census 2000.

39. Rose and Hartmann 2004.

40. Burtless and Smeding 2007.

41. See Bajtelsmit and Bernasek (1999) and http://www.census.gov/hhes/www/income/income03/statemhi.html.

42. Burtica, Iams, and Smith 2003, 45, table 6.

43. Rix, Rosenmann, and Schultz 1998.

44. Bajtelsmit and Bernasek (1999) reproduce the Employee Benefits Research Institute's compilation of CPS data to show a mixed pattern of pension coverage rates between men and women.

45. Butrica, Iams, and Smith 2003, 60, table 5.

46. The data for the sources of income to the elderly are from Grad (2002) and McDonnell (2005).

47. Miller and Gerstein 1983.

48. U.S. Department of Labor, Bureau of Labor Statistics 2005.

49. U.S. Department of Labor, Bureau of Labor Statistics 2005.

50. In 1993, Janet Currie investigated whether the sex pension coverage gap can be explained by sex differences in productivity or if fringe-benefit discrimination is yet another manifestation of pay discrimination by sex (Currie 1993, 3).

51. Currie controls for being offered a fringe benefit and actually accepting coverage, which improves on previous research that had underestimated women's health insurance coverage because they declined coverage, presumably because they were covered by their husband's benefits. However, Currie found that women were 8% less likely to be offered a pension, due mostly to differences in job tenure (perhaps a woman's choice). Currie looked at men and women with ten years of job tenure with an employer and found that women were 5% less likely to be covered by a pension plan. Women workers still get fewer pensions than similarly situated men, even though they have all the signs of being committed workers. Currie finds that nearly all differences in coverage would disappear if men and women earned the same, concluding that pensions and wages are complementary rather than substitutes and that women do not make trade-offs (Currie 1993).

52. Jacoby 1997, 97.

53. Jacoby 1997, 68.

54. Jacoby 1997, 98.

55. Blau and Ferber 1998; Rubery 1978.

56. Folbre (1994) argues that the pay-as-you-go system exploits women's labor, since the older male's benefit is based on the current and future productivity of children. Since children's ability to work is linked to the amount and quality of undervalued female labor, patriarchy is enhanced as men exploit women. See further elaboration and critique on the feminist argument in Ghilarducci (1999).

57. Each worker earns a Social Security pension based on her or his own earnings record. If a spouse's Social Security benefit earned on her/his own work history is higher than the dependent benefit (50% of the spouse's benefit), then the spouse receives her/his own. (The United States has had gender-neutral dependent benefits since 1975; the European integration treaty required gender neutrality by 1999.) Even though most married women in 1994 will be eligible for retired worker benefits, their spouse's benefit will be higher. This means only 29% of women have a worker benefit higher than her spouse's benefit and, thus, receive credit for their work (Holden 1996). Even when the early baby-boom cohort starts to retire in 2009, most women will receive wives' benefits because their own benefit is smaller than their husbands. See a similar argument in Bergmann (1986).

58. Levine, Mitchell, and Phillips 2000.

59. See Munnell and Sundén (2004, 57, table 3.2). The 1993 figures come from Basset, Fleming, and Rodrigues (1998).

60. The rules limiting the tax break for high-income employees are the Internal Revenue Services' so-called nondiscrimination rules. For an excellent short summary of the mechanics and possible economic effects of the nondiscrimination rules, see Carrington, McCue, and Pierce (2002).

61. Hinz and Turner 1998; Carrington, McCue, and Pierce 2002.

62. Reagan and Turner 2000.

63. American Academy of Actuaries 2004 b.

64. Only 33.8% of low-income men have pension coverage, yet of those few in unions, 70.67% have pensions. Similarly, 75% of middle-class men (earning between the average wage and 160% of the average wage) and 78.7% of middle-class women are offered a pension at work. If unionized, the pension coverage rates rise to 86.9% and 89.8%, respectively. The union premium for pension coverage in all firms is generally half of the premium in small firms (Ghilarducci and Lee 2005).

65. Young workers saving for retirement are constrained by events out of their control and by their own young minds. Retirement policy is predicated on the understanding that young and perfectly rational people do not (and should not) anticipate their older bodies' fragility and their older minds' desire for rest and reflection. Adam Smith admitted that young people are not aware of risk and do not demand compensation: "the contempt of risk and the presumptuous hope of success are in no period of life more active than at the age at which young people choose their professions. For this soldiers are poorly paid and sailors not much better" (Smith 1976 (original 1776) Book 1: chapter 10, part 1, paragraph 32).

66. Weller and Wolff 2005; Gale and Pence 2006; Munnell, Webb, and Delorme 2006.

67. Weller and Wolff 2005.

68. Thompson 2005.

69. The new Pension Protection Act of 2006 aims to lower the barriers to automatic enrollment, but does not eliminate the powerful financial incentive to leave things just as they are.

70. Author's calculations, based on Butrica, Iams, and Smith 2003.

71. Peter Hall, referenced in Béland and Hacker (2004), discusses the fact that, compared to workers in other developed nations (those nations in the Organization for Economic Cooperation and Development), U.S. workers receive much of their social insurance—pensions and health care—through employer plans and programs, whereas residents of other developed nations are covered by national health insurance and more generous Social Security benefits. This peculiarity is called by historians "American exceptionalism."

Chapter 3
When Bad Things Happen to Good Pensions—Promises Get Broken

1. This quote is on the first page of a website for Verizon workers http://www.verizonretirementwatch.com (accessed January 13, 2006).

2. Munnell, Golub-Sass, Soto, and Vitagliana 2006.

3. Elderly households in the middle of the income distribution (third and fourth quintiles) receive 14.5% and 24.9% of their total retirement income, respectively, from employer pensions.

4. The poorest households rely on Social Security and public assistance almost exclusively—94% for the first quintile and 86% for the second—and have very little income from employer-based pension sources. The middle-class elderly obtain only 3.6%–9.8% of their pension income from personal wealth.

5. The Department of Labor's survey of private employers reports slightly increasing rates of pension coverage and participation—no decrease. The 2005 National Compensation Survey (NCS) shows that 60% of workers in the private sector have access to (i.e., are offered) a retirement plan of some sort and that 50% of workers in the private sector participate in a retirement plan. (The comparable figures from the workers' survey [of those within the same age range], the CPS, are 57% and 46%.) The higher figures in the NCS may be caused by businesses probably having a better idea of who is covered than workers do. Also, many CPS respondents are not the actual worker but his or her spouse or other relative, and they may not know about the employee's pension plans.

6. Ghilarducci and Sun 2006.

7. Overall pension participation rates rose 4.2% and defined contribution coverage went up 19.4%.

8. Neumark 2000; Osterman 2000.

9. See Dickens and Lang (1985) and Ghilarducci and Lee (2005) for an extensive discussion of segmentation by industry and occupation.

10. Medoff and Calabrese (2001) and others have shown that industry shift does explain some of the decline in employee benefits.

11. Rappaport and Dragut 2004.

12. The total unfunded liability of the one hundred largest corporate plans fell 41% in 2003 to $88.7 billion from $151 billion in 2002, because firm contributions rose 72% and earnings rose 297%. Also, although long-term interest rates were famously stubbornly low (which raises liabilities) in 2004–5 (when interest rates increase the present value of the liabilities will fall) further closing the funding gaps, although it is doubtful this will save the PBGC from the severe financial consequences of the termination of the plans that are deemed highly likely to default.

13. Reagan and Turner 2000.

14. Raab 2005.

15. Note that this study also found that being forced to retire and being unhealthy dominated the determinants of satisfaction; being forced to retire decreased the level of satisfaction by 30% and being in poor health by almost 20%. Bender and Jivan 2005; Panis (2003) also covers the same material.

16. Wiatrowski 2005.

17. U.S. Bureau of Labor Statistics 2004, 2005.

18. Munnell and Sundén (2004, 56) provide the national averages.

19. Munnell and Sunden 2004, 58.

20. Munnell and Sunden 2004, 69.

21. Walsh 2003, 8.

22. Unfortunately, there is not much cheer in what happened after the company declared bankruptcy in October 2001. In August 2005 most of the employees in research and development were laid off as the company abandoned its "once-promising" printing division after changing owners twice. The employees lost lifetime health and life insurance and the value of Polaroid stock they had been forced to buy and hold for a decade. In ways similar to other company's transitions, many executives were able to claim their deferred compensation.

23. Women start work about ten years later than men; they, like men, are encouraged to work to accrue substantial years of service in a DB plan, though they are encouraged to do so when they are ten years older.

24. There is excellent scholarship on the "American exceptionalism" to universal social insurance programs; see Béland and Hacker (2004) for a good review.

25. Ghilarducci and Lee (2005) found that workers' pay and benefits depended somewhat on differences in individual productivity and job characteristics and also on whether a worker was in the primary sector rather than a secondary location. The dual labor market model predicts total compensation better.

26. Rappaport 2004.

27. Neuman and Ghilarducci 2004.

28. The average wage for women in the top third of the wage distribution in 1999, compared to the wage of comparable women in 1973, increased by 33%; their employers' costs for employee benefits increased by 78%. Women workers at the bottom of the wage distribution received smaller increases in average wages and a smaller increase in employer expenses. The data are comparable for men. (Ellwood 2000, 36–39, tables 1A.4–5.)

29. Budd 2005; Neuman 2004.

30. Hamermesh 1999, 1985.

31. Osterman 2000.

32. Medoff and Calabrese 2001, 134.

33. Twenty years ago 43% of women workers were covered by a pension plan; in 1996 just 39% were. The fall is worse for men. More than half of male workers had pensions in 1979; now only 48% do. This decline is affecting all workers at all income levels (Ellwood 2000).

34. Ghilarducci and Sun 2006.

35. One-third of employers with traditional DB plans said in 2006 that they were likely not to allow new employees to participate in their DB plans. Meanwhile, according to a 2005 survey by Hewitt Associates, 16% of employers providing DB plans said they were likely to freeze benefit accruals for all or a portion of current participants (Watson Wyatt 2004).

36. Munnell, Libby, and Prinzivalli 2006.

37. Ghilarducci 2003.

38. McCaw (2004) talks about the effect of a reduction in capital gains tax on reducing the tax incentives for high-income workers to participate in defined benefit plans.

39. Weller 2005.

40. The Academy of Actuaries' DB(k) proposal allows workers to supplement their defined benefit plan with their own contributions. This is an attractive feature for employees in the 401(k) context, for it helps an employee make personalized decisions about deferring current consumption to the future and gives individuals an important sense of control and connection to their retirement plan.

41. The independent monitoring organization Center for Federal Financial Institutions (COFFI) projects a program deficit of $16.2 billion in 2013. According to COFFI's founder, former Treasury staffer Douglas Elliot, the PBGC might require a program bailout of $56 to $100 billion by 2020 if DB pensions continue to decline and investment returns and interest rates are low. This number and the independent organization itself have been widely cited.

42. The American Academy of Actuaries (2004b) report argues that the range of assumptions depends on whether the sponsor is a not-for-profit or publicly traded company. The bottom line is that the publicly traded firms are more aggressive in their assumptions, which makes their pension funds look as if they have more potential earnings and fewer assets. In 2001, the smallest discount rate for not-for-profit firms was 5.5% and the highest was 6%; in contrast, the publicly traded firms had a much higher range, from 7.25% to 8%. A percentage point difference in the discount rate used to assess pension liabilities can reduce reported liabilities by half. Credit Suisse First Boston (Zion and Carcache 2002) analyzed each of the 360 firms with defined benefit plans in the S&P 500 and found the discount rates were the rates that changed the most, and the firms with the most conservative assumptions for discount rates had the most conservative assumptions for asset earnings. AFLAC and National Semiconductors assumed a 4.75% discount rate when the median rate was 7.3%.

43. On October 26, 1995, the John F. Kennedy School of Government and Ford Foundation awarded the Innovations in Government Award to PBGC for the Early Warning Program.

44. The loan board's unexpected rejection of United Airline's bid for more cash, the steep spike in its fuel bill (because cash-flow shortfalls prevented it from entering oil futures markets), and its persistent "bad" labor relations caused the sudden reversal in UAL's pension funding behavior. United owes the pensions $4.1 billion over the next four years, including $568 million in payments that the company said it would skip in 2004. United Airlines recanted, in the August 20, 2004 bankruptcy hearings, its own July public statements, explaining that when it lost its loan guarantee bid in June lenders would not allow the company to extend its stay in Chapter 11 if it made additional pension payments. That kind of agreement would be illegal under bankruptcy and pension law.

45. Legislation enacted in April of 2004 temporarily amends certain DB pension funding rules until the end of 2005. The change with the broadest effect (applicable to all but the smallest single-employer DB plans) changed the discount rate used to calculate pension liabilities under the deficit reduction contribution rules to a rate based on high- and medium-grade corporate bonds from thirty-year Treasury bonds. The legislation also included narrow revisions to the law that affect some underfunded plans sponsored by airline and steel companies and only a small number of multiemployer pension plans. As a result of all of these changes, smaller funding contributions will be required until 2006 for some plans than had been the case prior law.

46. 401(k) leakages occur because workers can borrow against their 401(k) and defined contribution pension plans; workers can withdraw funds before retirement; workers pay high fees for administration; and individuals make the investment decisions, the rates of return are lower than what they would be if professionals invested their fund.

47. Held under Section 1113 of the Bankruptcy Code.

48. What is happening in airlines happened in railroads in the early 1900s. The first private DB pension plans were established by railroads in 1865—they were the airlines of their day. In 1919 the maturing DB railroad pension plans were threatening to default for two familiar reasons: workers were beginning to retire in large numbers, and small start-up companies that paid low wages and provided no benefits invaded the legacy railroads' routes by slashing haul rates. The nation could have chosen to allow what the PBGC and UAL agreed to: let pensions default and have the workers pay for the industrial restructuring. But the American decision makers viewed that solution as unfair, and the government mandated a multiemployer pension plan, the Railroad Retirement Fund, that all railroads pay into. The rationale was that the low-cost start-up companies were taking advantage of the infrastructure the mature, legacy railroads and their workers created, and they needed to pay for the legacy benefits they were enjoying. To this day, railroad workers have a strong DB plan portable anywhere in the industry, regardless of the death and birth of individual railroad companies.

49. "The obliteration of the retirement for 134,000 United Airlines workers is a signal to corporate America that union-negotiated pensions are on the chopping block and can be raided, tapped or eliminated for financial gain. Back in the 1980s, when bankrupt LTV Corp. tried to cut retiree benefits, thousands of people took to the streets . . . everyone's pension is now in eminent danger" (Tasini 2005).

50. Enron did not terminate its DB plans. In 2002 Enron's pension plan was underfunded by more than $125 million. The plan has about 20,000 participants and about $220 million in assets.

51. On June 9, 2005, House Education and Workforce Committee Chairman John Boehner (R-Ohio) announced the introduction of the Pension Protection Act (PPA) (H.R. 2830), which included proposals for funding reform for single-employer and multi-employer pension plans, disclosure requirements, and provisions for par-

ticipants for access to professional investment advice (112 DLR A-8,6/13/05). The bill focused on solvency of the PBGC and funding rule changes aimed at increasing funding in DB plans.

52. Contributions that exceed 150% of current liability are not tax deductible. This limit was phased to 170% in 2005. Firms complained that the limits prevented them from funding plans more completely. Manipulation of actuarial assumptions also allowed many funds, including those that would terminate later (Polaroid, Bethlehem Steel) to take pension contribution holidays.

53. Defined benefit pension plans are compared to defined contribution plans and are often called "real" pensions because workers do not have access to the accumulations before retirement; they often—but not as often as they did formerly—provide a modest income for the life of a retiree; they have survivor options; and employers take the risks of bad investment choices and periodic downturns, as well as the gains of lucky and skilled investments. Defined benefit plans are also insured by the PBGC. However, DB plans are not without risk, as the airline industry case shows. Economists also attribute long-term productive contracts to DB plans. Comparisons are explored later in this chapter.

54. The bill's premium cost hike made sense. Doug Elliot at the Center for Federal Financial Institutions (COFFI) argued that if premiums had kept up with inflation there would be no shortfall in the PBGC. That would mean that Congress would have had to hike premiums when the PBGC was running a surplus and 401(k)'s were gaining in popularity. But to hike them when an industry collapses is also perverse. The firms with healthy plans begin to expect even more hikes and more cross-subsidization when catastrophe hits. The discouraging cycle occurs because the PBGC suffers from the serious flaw of having no real plan reinsurance other than by stiffing the healthy sponsors and taxpayers as a last resort. For example, a user-fee revenue stream could reinsure the PBGC for the airline industry problems. Future defined benefit sponsors need the confidence Congress could provide by reinsuring the PBGC for a catastrophe, such as an industry collapse, that the agency was never structured to deal with—for example, Studebaker failed but the U.S. auto industry was doing well.

55. Kruger 1999.

56. See a short review of the "all bonds" debate in Whitehouse 2002; and "Who to Believe?" *CFO Europe,* May 2004 (available on-line at http://www.cfoeurope.com/displaystory.cfm/2661813/l_print).

57. Government Accountability Office 2003b.

58. Shiller 2000; see also Shiller 2005.

59. Foster and Cordasco 2004.

60. Munnell and Soto 2005.

61. Because of the confluence of events that has been described as a perfect storm hitting all pension funds, which for Bethlehem Steel included three unfortunate events—a huge recession and layoffs, low interest rates, and low returns—its plan

assets fell 25% in 2001 and its funding ratio was 45% when it terminated in December 2002. To be sure, one of the more bizarre developments in the pension funding world was that corporate sponsors are required by law to use a long-term interest rate to value their long-term pension liabilities. This makes sense: the liabilities in a pension system span many human lifetimes. The government required corporate sponsors to use the thirty-year Treasury bond rate, which the government abolished on October 31, 2001. Their main complaint was not that the company stopped issuing thirty-year bonds but that the rate was very low.

62. Government Accountability Office 2003b, 2005.

Chapter 4
Do-It-Yourself Pensions

1. Clowes 2004, 1.

2. Munnell and Sundén 2004, 57.

3. Ghilarducci and Sun 2006.

4. Vanguard 2005.

5. The range of savings rates reflects a range of interest rate, wage growth, and Social Security assumptions.

6. My colleague, who does not wish to highlight his greyhound-betting past, while reading a draft of this book in summer 2005, said, "the only way I have a pension is that TIAA-CREF made me start saving at age twenty-seven—I put all of it in the stock market. I would have put it all on the dogs, imagine how rich I would be now!"

7. If you want to calculate out what a promise to obtain $100 one year from now is worth to you, you use this equation: the current value of the promise minus the future value of the promise, divided by (1+ your personal discount rate). So, if your personal discount rate is 5% per year you will give up $95.28 today to get $100 in one year. What this means is: Given a 5% discount rate you are indifferent—utterly indifferent—about the difference between having $95.28 now or $100 one year from now. Many a rational person uses the interest rate as their "discount" rate. But everyone has her or his own interest rate, and his or her own discount rate; it is a very personal thing that is related to how each person views the future.

8. See Gustman and Steinmeier (2001) on the implicit discount rate in pension funds; see also Thaler's article reprinted in 1991 and previously published in 1981.

9. Skinner 2007.

10. Skinner 2007.

11. Huberman and Jiang 2006.

12. Manning & Napier's Associates, Inc. 2004.

13. Shiller 2000, chap. 5, gives a good summary, among many others, of how these aspects of human behavior affect investment behavior.

14. See the Department of Labor's website for a warning on fee detection; see also Munnell and Sundén 2004, 78, and Turner 2005.

15. See Steve Venti's (2005) excellent overview of 401(k) investment behavior.

16. Rappoport and Dragut 2004. Anna Rappoport, at the Mercer Human Resource Consulting Group, has written many reports assessing the retirement risk people face and the individual's ability to handle risk. Many of the gems are located on the Mercer Human Resource Consulting website.

17. Munnell and Sundén 2004, 58.

18. Munnell and Sundén 2004, 32.

19. For workers earning more than $80,000 per year, participation rates increased from 76.3% to 85.9%. See Munnell and Sundén 2004, 64.

20. The magazine sampled 3,500 defined contribution sponsors and identified the thirty-five plans with the highest participation rates (Plan Sponsor, "Easy Does It" 2004).

21. I used information from Munnell and Sunden (2004) on participation rates, average contribution levels by earnings, and the distribution of employees by earnings to make the three billion dollar estimate. The average savings per worker is $156. Choi, Laibson, and Madrian (2005) calculated for their sample of over 800 employees in one firm that the employer saved over $250 per older worker who did not participate in the 401(k), even when they were eligible.

22. Teasing out the reasons that some firms lowered their overall pension spending per participant with multiple regression analysis reveals that the more the firm spends its pension dollars on DC plans, the lower the pension expense. On average, DB plan sponsors took advantage of favorable returns in the financial markets in the 1990s to stop or lower employer contributions to their DB plan. If these firms had maintained contributions to their DC plans, then the defined contribution's share would rise and the pension costs would fall. But this would have nothing to do with a firm's decision to emphasize DC plans; it has to do with the increase in the rate of return in the DB pension plan. Fortunately, a detailed data set does not have to make inferences using averages. When the rate of return in the DB pension plan and other items that affect DB expenses, such as their generosity, are controlled for, we still find that the higher the DC share the lower were overall pension contributions. This implies that the decision to emphasize 401(k)s lowers a firm's costs.

Evidence does not support the "perfect storm" explanation for DB funding deficits—that equity returns have positive and significant effects on pension contributions. Employers did not slack off in DB funding because of the boom market. Firms in poor financial shape reduce DB pension contributions. Even controlling for financial conditions, the share of DC pension costs has a significant and negative effect on pension contributions. Also, increasing the share of 401(k) contributions by 10% decreases overall pension contributions per participant by 2.7% (3.5% for public firms) (Ghilarducci and Sun 2006).

23. Ghilarducci and Sun 2006.

24. Ippolito (1997) and Burham (2003) argue that 401(k) plans serve a sorting function by attracting and retaining workers who are savers.

25. Other surviving firms that continually sponsored pensions since 1981 may have been missed if they changed Employer Identification Numbers (EINs), but there are no systematic reasons for EIN changes so I do not expect any bias in using EINs to identify firms.

26. 401(k) plans were distinguished from other DC plans starting in 1988: between 1988 and 1998, the share of DC assets that were in 401(k) plans ranged from 63% to 88%.

27. See Hustead 1998. Indeed, the cost of 401(k) administration relative to DBs is quite low and falling fast.

Chapter 5
The Future of Social Security

1. I recommend playing around with the official Social Security calculator— input your own work history, or a sample one, to get a feel for how the system works. It is found on-line at http://www.ssa.gov/planners/calculators.htm.

2. Here is an example of how an AIME is calculated from someone's earnings records. Please note, if you do the math, that this person worked for forty years at quite a high salary. The average drops the five lowest earnings years.

Year	Worked in These Years	Earnings before Indexing
1	1967	$14,049.75
2	1968	$15,031.50
3	1969	$15,917.00
4	1970	$16,725.50
5	1971	$17,583.50
6	1972	$19,327.00
7	1973	$20,556.25
8	1974	$21,802.00
9	1975	$23,454.75
10	1976	$25,099.25
11	1977	$26,631.00
12	1978	$28,776.00
13	1979	$31,325.25
14	1980	$34,182.50
15	1981	$37,661.25
16	1982	$39,776.00

Year	Worked in These Years	Earnings before Indexing
17	1983	$41,758.75
18	1984	$44,258.50
19	1985	$46,191.75
20	1986	$47,610.75
21	1987	$50,699.00
22	1988	$53,251.00
23	1989	$55,415.25
24	1990	$58,033.25
25	1991	$60,258.00
26	1992	$63,428.75
27	1993	$64,039.25
28	1994	$65,824.00
29	1995	$68,532.75
30	1996	$71,956.50
31	1997	$76,232.75
32	1998	$80,305.50
33	1999	$84,865.00
34	2000	$89,650.00
35	2001	$91,883.00
36	2002	$92,897.75
37	2003	$95,262.75
38	2004	$99,792.00
39	2005	$103,548.50
40	2006	$108,542.50
The average of the highest 35 years:		$102,021
AIME is the above, divided by 12:		$8,502

3. Merton C. Bernstein (1988), Emeritus Professor of Law at Washington University, was the executive director of the commission. The book written with his wife, Joan Bernstein, is an excellent and accessible reprisal of the technical considerations the commission faced, and is a reference guide to the commission's outcome.

4. The payroll tax (FICA) is regressive because taxable earnings are defined by earnings below a cap, and the income earners above the cap pay a smaller percentage of their income in taxes. Yet the earned income tax credit is in part intended to mitigate the regressivity of the FICA tax by giving a tax credit to low-income workers.

5. The data come from Munnell 2005. Overall replacement rate projections would be worse if earnings were not projected as growing sources of income. Without a projection that most boomers will work more, poverty predictions would be much higher, and preretirement income replacement rates much lower. In other words, more of the elderly are expected to work to avoid poverty and to retain their standard of living.

6. From the president's State of the Union Address, February 2, 2005:

> One of America's most important institutions, a symbol of the trust between generations, is also in need of wise and effective reform. Social Security was a great moral success of the twentieth century, and we must honor its great purposes in this new century. The system, however, on its current path, is headed toward bankruptcy. And so we must join together to strengthen and save Social Security. . . . Here is why personal accounts are a better deal. Your money will grow, over time, at a greater rate than anything the current system can deliver, and your account will provide money for retirement over and above the check you will receive from Social Security. In addition, you'll be able to pass along the money that accumulates in your personal account, if you wish, to your children or grand-children. In addition, best of all, the money in the account is yours, and the government can never take it away.

7. I have not seen a SSA response to Langer's testimony but I would guess that they would defend the practice by saying that their assumption on economic growth is low because their assumptions about mortality are too optimistic—meaning they do not predict that people will live as long as they probably will.

8. American Academy of Actuaries 2004a.

9. The *Business Week* cover story of May 16, 2005, reported that Bush's plan had 38% approval on January 16; approval fell steadily to 31% by April 24.

10. "Using a government filing cabinet as a prop, President Bush yesterday played to fears that the Social Security Trust Fund is little more than a stack of worth-less IOUs. . . . 'There is no trust fund—just IOUs that I saw firsthand, those future generations will pay,' Bush said after inspecting the storage site. 'Imagine—the retire-ment security for future generations is sitting in a filing cabinet' " (Hutcheson 2005).

11. From http://www.polisci.umn.edu/faculty/ljacobs/myths/6.php.

12. It is peculiar that polls taken in the 2000s show that confidence in Social Security is actually increasing among young people (Remez et al. 2004).

13. Burtless 2001.

14. Two think tanks, the liberal Center for Budget Priorities and the conserva-tive Concord Coalition, were among the first organizations to show that the projected deficits in Social Security were far less than the Medicare liabilities, the federal debt, and the Bush administration's tax cuts. The Government Accountability Office also

predicts a $43 trillion liability in the testimony of comptroller and long-time Republican David Walker to Congress in March (Walker 2004).

15. See Langer (2004) and Baker (2005), who argue that the system is not insolvent, rather the projections are overly pessimistic.

16. On August 14, 1995, the Cato Institute inaugurated its Project on Social Security Privatization; its objective is to formulate a plan for privatizing the U.S. Social Security system. The project is co-chaired by José Piñera, architect of Chile's private pension system and labor secretary under General Pinochet. The name of the project was changed to "Social Security Choice" in 2002.

17. Glen Bolger, a Republican pollster, noted that a recent poll that his firm helped conduct for National Public Radio highlighted that effect. When asked, "Do you favor or oppose President Bush's proposal to create voluntary personal retirement accounts as part of the Social Security system?," 41% favored it and 49% opposed it. When asked, "Do you favor or oppose President Bush's proposal to privatize Social Security and divert part of the Social Security system into private accounts?," 34% said they favored it, and 58% were opposed. "Calling it a personal retirement account is stronger across the board," Mr. Bolger said. "Whereas 'privatization' hurts across the board" (Toner 2005).

18. Shiller 2005; Petruno 2005.

19. The 2006 Congressional elections gave the Democrats control of Congress and tabled the privatization of Social Security debate.

20. Lieberman's essay appeared in the March 2005 edition of the *Harvard Alumni Magazine*. I can imagine the difficult editorial decision involved in printing it because another Harvard economist, certainly someone with more of a reputation than young Lieberman in the Social Security debate, Martin Feldstein, is a leading advocate of privatization and would have been a likely choice to write this piece or at least rebut Lieberman.

21. Lazear 2005, 3.

22. Government Accountability Office 2003.

23. Soto 2005.

24. Shiller 2005; Petruno 2005.

25. Baker 2005.

26. CBS News Transcripts 1996.

27. A Social Security privatization plan is predicted to generate over $940 billion over seventy-five years in financial management fees from the industry managing more than 150 million or more new accounts (Goolsbee 2004).

28. Purcell (2005) reviews all the studies that consider the interactions between possible Social Security accounts and the private pension system.

29. In the document "Social Security Personal Account Reform Alternatives," Ferrara (2003) argues for a Senator Paul Ryan and Senator John Sununu plan that pays for the transition with general revenues.

30. Ferrara 2003, 1.

31. Ferarra 2005.

32. Orszag and Diamond give an excellent description of the legacy costs and provide a helpful and extensive metaphor about how multigenerational families make similar decisions. Their description is a narrative version of overlapping generation models (2003, 6–7).

33. Cato Institute 2003.

34. A case could be made, and was made in a more visible way in the 1990s, for tackling the high poverty rates among elderly women by adjusting the survivors' benefits to equal 75% of the beneficiaries' benefits rather than 50% and increasing the welfare portion of the system, the Supplemental Security Income (SSI), by reducing the means test and offset. Social Security comprises 60% of older women's income and, for one in five women, all of their income. The poverty gender gap and race gap is significant: 12% of older women compared to 7% of older men are poor (Smeeding, Estes, and Glasse 1999), and 25% of elderly black women live below the poverty line compared to 11% of elderly white women. Relative to 4% of older married women, 20% of unmarried older women are poor. A new minimum benefit would affect these women most because they rely most heavily on Social Security for retirement income.

35. Peter Orszag of the Brookings Institution and Peter Diamond of MIT proposed to increase payroll tax rates, raise the earnings cap, reduce benefits based on rises in life expectancy, and cover all state and local government workers hired after 2008, in their testimony at the Senate Finance Committee in April 2005.

36. Robert M. Ball was commissioner of Social Security from 1962 to 1973, serving under Presidents Kennedy, Johnson, and Nixon. He was a member of the 1982–83 National Commission on Social Security Reform (the Greenspan Commission), a visiting scholar at the Center for the Study of Social Policy, and senior scholar at the Institute for Medicine. He was a member of the 1989–91 and 1994–96 Advisory Councils on Social Security and has served on many other advisory groups.

37. Altman 2005.

38. The top 1% experienced a 111% increase in their real incomes, while the bottom experienced a 5% gain between the years 1979 and 2002 (Petska and Strudler 2002).

39. The unanticipated large increase in the inequality of income in the late 1980s and 1990s likely caused much of the current shortfall in Social Security (Diamond and Orszag 2004, 67).

40. Carter and Sutch caution us that not all workers in the early part of the century were resigned to the "industrial scrap heap." They reckon that 20% of men were able to retire in relatively good health in the 1910s and 1920s (Carter and Sutch 1995).

41. See Sass (1997, 93–97) for an excellent and efficient discussion of Social Security's legislative origins in the context of developments in employer pensions.

42. The prolonged stagflation in the early 1980s—which was not anticipated in the 1977 actuaries' models—caused the system to head for negative cash flow in two years. The November 29, 1982 copy of *Business Week*—which had a red cover with the tip of a cane crossing the tip of a bayonet—reported that the bipartisan so-called Greenspan Commission would likely propose "no radical surgery, but compromises (in the form of temporary cost of living decreases) and higher taxes." Clearly, the Social Security debate was a guns-and-butter choice of national priorities. Opinion polls showed Americans were willing to pay higher taxes to preserve benefits. Republicans lost by large margins in the midterm November elections primarily because of their negative stand toward the program.

43. The fear of the insurance companies, which were selling individual and group retirement annuities, that Social Security would displace their product soon transformed into delight as Social Security became a complement to these financial products and grew in a demand for retirement and annuity supplements. Social Security legitimizes retirement and encourages people to demand it. In 1935 the Republicans wanted a voluntary system, but the insurance companies wanted a self-serving "pay-or-play" system: employers would have to provide annuity plans as good as the Social Security system. Republicans opposed Medicare in 1965, since Democrats were given electoral credit every time the Democratic Congress raised benefits.

44. The effect of changes in wealth on work effort is beginning to be a popular research topic. Some studies found that the stock market boom and crash in the 1990s and early 2001 affected retirement plans (see Gustman and Steinmeier 2002; Cheng and French 2000; Eschtruth and Gemus 2002; Greene 2002; and Hermes and Ghilarducci 2004); others did not find that support (see Coile and Levine 2005). Retirees who suffer a loss in income mainly reduce consumption (Sevak and Kezdi 2004).

45. Retirement policy was taking shape before the Social Security Act was passed. Company pension plans received tax benefits, but the Treasury Department was always worried that the tax benefits would go only to the elite workers. The IRS so-called anti-discrimination rules required that employers who only wanted to pay for the elite employees had to cover the rank-and-file workers. By integrating Social Security into their promised defined benefit—which would be a percentage of earnings for each year of service—the employer could let the government program (which had higher replacement rates for lower-income workers) pay for the rank and file, and their contributions would compensate managers. Employer responsibility for retirement income was relieved every time Social Security benefits increased and the system expanded.

46. U.S. life expectancy could decline due to the rapid rise in obesity, especially among children. Olshansky et al. (2005) found that obesity reduces average life expectancy by about four to nine months. If child and adolescent rates of obesity continue, life expectancy could be shortened by two to five years in the coming decades.

47. Adams, Hurd, McFadden, Merrill, and Ribeiro (2003) find a link between socioeconomic status and health as reported in Orszag and Diamond 2003, 68.

48. The rate of improvement in the 1990s was largest for the group with the highest longevity—Japanese women—and the least improvement was among U.S. women, the group with the second highest longevity.

49. A recent paper shows that people may adjust their hours of work more than their own consumption in the face of FICA tax hikes or benefit cuts (van de Klaauw and Wolpin 2005). Different economic models of savings—life-cycle and behavioral—conclude that mandatory Social Security taxes distort optimal behavior (Soares 2005).

50. The share of income for the top 5% was 17.5% in 1967 and 22.4% in 2001 (United States Department of the Census 2001).

51. Hurd et al. (2002) and Weller and Wolff (2005) painstakingly measure the level of distribution of all kinds of retirement wealth. Butrica, Iams, and Smith (2004) show that boomers will depend more on earnings than did their parents.

52. "House Speaker J. Dennis Hastert (R-Illinois) and other Republican Congressional representatives stood outside the Capitol with a brown 1935 Ford three-window Coupe making the point that the car was built the same year Franklin D. Roosevelt built Social Security. 'I wouldn't be caught dead in a 1935 automobile,' said Rep. Patrick T. McHenry (North Carolina), vice chairman of the House Republican Conference's PR effort on Social Security. 'And I want to make sure we have an updated system of Social Security, because that's America's investment vehicle'" (Milbank 2005).

53. SSA 2003, table 3.

54. Strudler and Petska 2002.

55. Lazear 2005, 6.

56. Ferrara 2003, 4.

Chapter 6
The Short History of Old Age Leisure in America

1. See Arias 2002.

2. See an especially efficient and refreshing description of Social Security's history in Myles (1988).

3. In April 2000 the U.S. Congress eliminated the earnings test for Social Security beneficiaries between the ages of sixty-five and sixty-nine in the Freedom to Work Act.

4. The Conference Board 2006.

5. Advocates for longer work lives should not be confused with advocates like the National Center for Black Aged, who argue for better working conditions for elderly people forced to work after age sixty-five.

6. Sherrill 2003.

7. In my capacities as trustee of the State of Indiana's public employee pension fund and as advisory board member for the Pension Benefit Guaranty Corporation,

I met the most prominent money managers in the world, who made the profitability of the "worried well" more concrete than the fashion magazines. Trend managers invest according to the "next big thing," for example, information technology and global demographics. In the 1990s their favorite companies included large pharmaceutical firms patenting drugs that cured problems of aging men in affluent nations.

8. There is a rash of economists' work on the rationality of beauty spending and the discrimination against those among us considered less comely (see Harper 2000; Hamermesh et al. 2002; and Hamermesh and Biddle 1993).

9. The Greenspan Commission did not recommend the increase in the retirement age; testimony before the Social Security Trustees suggested that longevity trends did not indicate that the elderly were able to work longer. Congress added the provision in order to gain more revenue and to play it safe by cutting benefits for future retirees.

10. The normal retirement age would rise gradually from age sixty-five to age sixty-seven by 2022.

11. Clark et al. 2004, 21–22.

12. See an excellent resource on the pertinent facts on aging in the United States in Clark et al. 2004, 22.

13. University of Chicago economist and Nobel Laureate Gary Becker's (1965, reprinted in 1998) brilliant reformulation of the definition of time: time is a resource among many that individuals have to sell or use to create value. Time has two functions: we use time to consume things that take a range of time, from a lot to a little. Time can also be sold (to employers for wages) to acquire goods and service that require a range of money, from a lot to a little. Whether we work or not work depends on our preferences for time-laden consumption or money-laden consumption. The details of the struggle for the eight-hour day, sick leave, vacations, retirement, and lunch breaks are all irrelevant because they were the result of personal decisions individuals made about how they spend their endowments of time and saleable skills. After Becker most economists stopped using the word "leisure" (individuals were either producing time-intensive goods or goods-intensive goods) and stopped dealing with leisure as a concept. It was paid work time or nonpaid work time that they analyzed. Leisure was viewed as a nonentity, an irrelevant category.

14. In the case of an emerging nation like India, the aging society came from a rapid decrease in infant mortality, which led to lower fertility, which led to a slower rate of population growth. The population in most nations is growing older; there is a greater share of older people among the working-age population, but the reasons for this shift vary.

15. Weaver (2001) provides a political science review of how aging affects national politics.

16. Clark 2004, 118.

17. Clark 2004, 118.

18. One can think of the elderly rebalancing their portfolio. The elderly have a number of assets—financial wealth, Social Security wealth, housing wealth, and time and human capital. When income is falling in one or more area, a person can make it up by shifting their source of income to other sources; in this case the elderly are receiving more of their income from human capital wealth (meaning they are working more). See Wolff's (2002) excellent study of wealth distribution.

19. Data from the Health and Retirement Survey and from the Current Population Survey show that the retirees in the top quintile obtain about 30% to 33% of their income from pension plans (this does not include lump sums from plans), the second quintile 27% to 30%, the third quintile 16% to 25%, the fourth quintile 7% to 17%, and the bottom quintile 4% to 6% (Munnell, Sundén, and Lidstone 2002).

20. The scheduled reductions of Social Security benefits in 1983 apply to people under the age of thirty-seven—a population that hardly ever pays attention to pensions, so it met little opposition. In contrast, Europeans react with general strikes (millions marched in France and Italy in the summer of 2003) to similar changes.

Chapter 7
The Distribution of Retirement Time

1. Rowe and Kahn 1998.

2. Neuman 2003.

3. The index uses income, wealth, imputed value of government services and insurance, government transfers and taxes, and time to comprehensively measure well-being (Wolff, Zacharias, and Caner 2005).

4. Note here that I am not arguing whether disparity itself is wrong—I am assuming it is.

5. A popular health and fitness book, *Real Age: Are You as Young as You Can Be*, offers a quiz that identifies people's "real" age (Roizen and Stephenson 1999).

6. These economic windfalls from people working a few more years—that is, having more income late in life and perhaps accumulating more retirement savings— are seductive because working longer means that a large problem has a small solution.

7. Older men's retirement behavior between the years 1955 and 1989 suggests that the expansion of employer-provided pensions and Social Security explains one-fourth of the retirement trend; changes in social norms, tastes for leisure, and wealth in general explain the rest (Samwick 1998; Clark and Quinn 1999).

8. Differences in longevity shrink at older ages. Longevity for white males aged sixty-five is 16.3 years and 12.4% longer than black men's longevity; at age seventy-five white men are expected to live only 7.4% longer, or six more months. The trend is the same for women, but the differences are smaller. At age sixty-five, white women are expected to live 10.3% longer and at age seventy-five 8% longer than black women (Arias 2002).

9. For a good literature review, see Gerdtham and Johannesson 2004.

10. A large literature in economics using data from the HRS confirms this commonplace finding (see McGarry 2002; Kerkhofs, Lindeboom, and Theeuwes 1999; Bound, Waidman, and Schoenbaum 1996).

11. See the study by the Social Security Administration (Leonesio, Vaughan, and Wixon 2000).

12. Since the late 1990s, Louis Uchitelle of the *New York Times* has provided excellent reporting on the transition from work to layoff to retirement. In particular, the premature retirements of Midwestern workers was reported in 2003.

13. See Filer and Petri's (1988) excellent study of what explains the many variations in employer-provided pension plans.

14. See the report for the international community on the discrimination against older workers in the banking and auto industries (Quadagno, Hardy, and Hazelrigg 2003).

15. Gustman, Steinmeier, and Goss (2003), and Diamond and Kosezegi (2003) argue that some people have "hyperbolic discounting," a psychological defect enabled by the U.S. retirement system. In a study unrelated to retirement, economist Michael Grossman in 1972 analyzed how people determine their own health by investing in healthy behaviors; he suggested that those with "high discount rates" invest less in health and have worse longevity, which offsets their earlier retirement ages.

16. Gustman and Steinmeier 2002; Government Accountability Office 2000.

17. Coile 2002; Coile and Gruber 2000; Samwick 1998; Stock and Wise 1990.

18. Since 1992 the longitudinal HRS surveys have questioned a nationally representative sample of 27,000 older individuals (biannually, individuals born between 1931 and 1941; other birth cohorts were added later) about their health status, labor market status, family characteristics, wealth, and, remarkably, their assessment of when they will die.

19. A sample of people who are born in a narrow birth cohort reduces the effects of survivor bias; and, therefore, they should have similar health profiles and mortality. The sample includes those who had worked at least fifteen years in order to analyze the leisure decision of career workers and those who retired after the age of forty-nine.

20. Men and women in the sample have similar education levels. But men, predictably, worked more years than women, an average of 38.6 years compared to women's 31.4 years. A higher proportion of men is employed in high-skilled, blue-collar jobs and less in low-skilled, white- and blue-collar jobs.

21. Nonsurvivors are less educated and less likely to work in high-skilled, white-collar occupations, which likely explains the wealth differences between those who died early and those who did not.

22. The variable that captures the idea that people compensate for the predictions of their own death is computed by using a unique question in the HRS survey,

which asks people when they think they will die and compares their guesses to the average life expectancy for persons their age and sex.

23. ADLs—activities of daily living—include eating, dressing, toileting, and getting out of a bed or chair.

24. Neuman and Ghilarducci 2004.

25. Economists James Stock and David Wise in 1990 used the "option value" model exclusively to explain differential retirement behavior.

26. We probed whether mortality considerations affect retirement decisions. Even if dying before age sixty-five has a significant negative coefficient, people may still be accounting for their mortality expectations but cannot do so effectively. As do Hurd, Smith, and Zissimopoulos (2002), our regression asks the individual to rate the probability that he or she will reach the age of seventy-five. Since people were asked this question at different ages (55–61), the variable we use is the ratio of the individual's response and the life table probability given the individual's age and gender. A two-stage least-squares regression is used, where the dependent variable is self-reported re-tirement age, the independent variables are the same controls as for the retirement time regressions, and the key variable of interest is the ratio of self-reported to life table probability of living to age seventy-five, because the self-assessed mortality question was asked in 1992 and some people had already retired by that time. An individual's la-bor force status could affect self-reported life expectancy probability, because retiring reduces the likelihood of a health decline for both men and women, and increases the likelihood of a health improvement for women (Neuman 2003). This effect biases the results away from our prediction that people compensate for predictions of an early death. While the 1992 reported life expectancy would not technically have influenced prior retirement behavior, the 1992 report is a good proxy for previous life expectancy.

The instrumental variables used to predict the probability of death (compared to one's cohort) are the current ages of an individual's parents if alive, parental death ages if deceased, and the number of living siblings. The instruments are proxies for unobservable genetic information and should positively affect the life expectancy of the individual, without affecting one's retirement age. The sample is the same as for the early retirement time regressions, but does not include those who had missing probability of survival or instrument information. The final samples for the regres-sion contain 1,395 men and 1,377 women.

The results are the following: the variable of interest, age-adjusted mortality expectation, has no significant effect on retirement age for both men and women, im-plying that self-assessed mortality does not independently affect retirement decisions. Hurd et al. 2002 found that subjective mortality assessments have small or no effect on consumption or retirement timing.

27. Kingson and Arsenault (2000) and Leonesio et al. (2000) found that 10% to 20% of early retirees are in poor health and nearly half are disabled, implying that these groups would lose income if the Social Security early retirement age was raised.

Burtless and Moffitt (1984) found that retirement decisions were not sensitive to changes in Social Security rules and concluded that a Social Security benefit cut would reduce retirement consumption and not delay retirement.

Chapter 8
Working

1. PRNewswire 2005. JWT Mature Market Group (MMG), in partnership with ThirdAge Inc. recently conducted an online survey of 1,680 adults, forty-plus years of age who currently work full or part time for pay.

2 O'Hara, Brooks, Friedman, Schröder, Morgan, and Kraemer 2006.

3. The Age Discrimination in Employment Act (ADEA) protects you if you are aged forty or over and work for an employer with twenty or more employees. It prohibits hiring and firing decisions based on age. The ADEA also forbids mandatory retirement at a certain age for nearly all employees. Many state laws forbid mandatory retirement for small employers not covered by the ADEA.

4. Greene 2002. The U.S. Department of Labor has sponsored job training programs for impoverished elderly for many years.

5. Mary admitted later that the quip is attributable to Don Keough, retired Coca-Cola chairman, explaining his level of activity postretirement.

6. Technically there are many measures of the magnitude of relationships between variables. I choose to use a simple measure called a Pearson's correlation that essentially determines the extent to which values of the two variables are "proportional" to each other.

7. Labor force participation rates were regressed on the unemployment rate and wage growth, and the S&P 500 for a benchmark time period, between 1994 and 2002 and during the bear financial market and recession of March 2001 to November 2002. In the recession a 10% drop in the S&P 500 caused older men's labor force participation rates to increase from 68.63% to 69.07%, and older women's labor force participation rates increased from 53.90% to 54.44%. The S&P 500 fell 42.47%. In the benchmark period, changes in the S&P 500 had the *opposite* effect; if the stock market fell, older individuals had a slight tendency to retire. These results are corroborated when actual individuals are examined using the HRS: the retirement rates for workers aged sixty-one to sixty-four with only DC plans were much lower in 2002 than in 1998 (the period before the dramatic fall in the stock market starting in January 2000), though the retirement rates for those with DB pensions remained the same (42.84% in 1998 and 42.95% in 2002).

8. Simple two-way correlations reveal that the proportion of the change in older women's labor force participation attributable to the change in the S&P 500 is 0.843 (measured by the square of the Pearson product moment correlation coefficient); the correlation is 0.827 for older men.

9. Zernike 2002, 1.

10. One can't imagine the degree of impoverishment the already poor people of Gary, Indiana, or parts of Detroit would reach without income from both of these sources. However, I know of no published data that can measure and link the income sources to households and the economic activity of the communities the households live and work in at such a small geographical scale. If the data existed, we could establish the connection between household income from these sources and a more than expected stability of the local economy.

11. Employers who are aiming to lay off workers may be wishing they had a way to use the 401(k) plan to manage their labor supply. Pension plans are traditionally used as human-resource tools (Lazear 1991). When product demand falls, early-retirement programs help shrink payroll. Lucent used their DB to manage one of the biggest corporate layoffs in history. It used the DB plan to offer early retirement packages to over 15,000 U.S. managers (Associated Press, "Lucent to Offer Early Retirement," *Toronto Star Newspaper,* June 6, 2001). Generous severance payments have similar effects, but struggling companies often do not have the cash to offer and rely on prefunded pensions to induce the voluntary attrition. Early retirement plans help shrink payroll and are funded by pensions.

12. See Friedberg and Webb 2000.

13. See the Bureau of Labor Statistics series on the how the total cost of hiring changes the Employment Cost Index.

14. There are many studies on how retiree health insurance coverage has fallen for retirees, and many contain excellent surveys of the rising health care costs for elderly people; see Aaron and Schwartz 2005.

15. See the long-standing work of Northwestern economist Brigitte Madrian (1994) and Gruber and Madrian (2002).

16. See the very useful but not widely circulated report by Harvard's James Medoff and lawyer and economist Michael Calabrese (2001, 134).

17. Padgett 2002; Mittelstaedt 2002; Schieber 2002.

18. See the newspaper report about the poll: Jeffrey Jones, "Americans Counting on 401(k)s, Not Social Security: Retirement Savings Tops List of Americans' Financial Worries," *Wall Street Journal,* April 25, 2002.

19. See Burtless (1986) and Anderson, Burkhauser, and Quinn (1986) for particular analyses of the role of Social Security benefit changes in affecting workers' decision to retire during this time period.

20. Imbens, Rubin, and Sacerdote 2001.

21. Without the stock market boom of the 1990s, labor force participation for men over age fifty-five would have been 3.2% higher than that of men aged fifty-five to sixty-four (Cheng and French 2000). Purvi Sevak (2002) found that a $50,000 surprise wealth increase, say a 10% increase, increased work effort by 3.9% for women and 5% for men. Likewise, people work more if they lose money.

22. Purcell 2003.

23. A closer look at women helps make the case that financial need is driving work effort. One stark fact is that women have less DB pension coverage than men. Most comparisons of men's and women's pensions concentrate on coverage rates by type of plan. Data from our sample of the HRS in 1998 and 2002 indicate that older women are more likely not to have any pension coverage at all compared to older men—women have lower coverage rates for both DB and DC-type plans. Moreover, though one cannot observe the difference in employers' pension contributions for men and women, the correlation between the DC share of employers' pension contributions and the percentage of females in an industry is positive, though not large at 0.12. Women are at a higher risk of having lower amounts of employer pension contributions and of working in industries that rely relatively more on DC plans.

24. In 1996, 21.9% of younger workers aged twenty-five to thirty-nine were covered by only 401(k)-type plans, compared to 15% for workers over age fifty-five (author's analysis of the data from the Survey of Income and Program Participation [SIPP], which is a survey that collects information on the amount of income, labor force information, program participation and eligibility data, etc., and is available at the Bureau of the Census <www.sipp.census.gov/sipp>).

Chapter 9
The American Labor Movement

1. The United States is famously exceptional for its reliance on employers to provide many forms of social insurance, such as pensions and health insurance. The private sector's prominent role in providing pensions stands apart from most nations (with some exceptions in Anglo nations). The replacement rate, the ratio of retirement benefits to preretirement earnings, for an average worker after thirty-five to forty-four years of work, ranges in Europe's six largest nations from a low 38% in the United Kingdom to a typical 70% (Peaple 2004, 14). The average U.S. replacement rate is 43% and falling (Munnell 2003a).

2. Economies of scale may help explain the relative growth in employee benefits in union settings. In addition, as defined above, unions provide job protection and "voice," which help employers be somewhat assured that they will reap the benefits from expensive employer-paid on-the-job training. The firm may want to encourage workers to retain pensions and health insurance. Freeman (1981) recognized that the collective bargaining process changes the "relevant preference function" employers must satisfy. Since union members are older, Freeman reasoned, unions will reveal preferences that emphasize older people's concerns—pensions and security compared to cash. I claim that the collective bargaining process has even more complex and enduring effects on compensation.

3. Another way to see unionization's effect on pension coverage is to compare differences in averages by group. Only 33.8% of low-income men are offered a pension at work, but of the small percentage of low-income men who are unionized (6.71%), a full 70.67% have pensions. For all men and women, regardless of income, the union effect is of the same large magnitude. For example, of the high- to middle-income workers (earning between the average wage and 160% of the average wage), 75% of middle-class men and 78.7% of middle-class women are offered a pension at work. If they are unionized, the pension coverage rates rise to 86.9% and 89.8% respectively (Ghilarducci and Lee 2005).

4. Nonunion workers tend to see a higher growth in cash compensation, evinced by a 112% growth in supplemental pay between 1988 and 2003, whereas for union workers the growth rate was much lower—a 58% increase during the same time period. Union members also trade cash wages for time. Union workers saw a paid leave increase from $1.35 per hour to $2.13 per hour compared to a nonunion increase from 89 cents per hour to $1.37 per hour in 2002, which was close to the union level in 1988.

5. Only 17% of low-income men in small firms, compared to 33.8% of low-income men in all firms, are offered a pension at work. A worker's chances of being covered by a pension if working for a small firm is 33% for the lowest-paid earners and 27% for the highest-paid earners, which is half of what a worker's chances are in larger firms. Of middle-class men and women working in small firms, 54% and 58%, respectively, are offered a pension at work; but, if unionized, the pension coverage rates rise to 72.41% and 70.59%, respectively.

6. Interestingly, cutting capital gains taxes and personal income taxes may deeply inhibit employers' willingness to provide pensions, since tax deferral was a main impetus for their formation (Reagan and Turner 2000).

7. Lichtenstein 2003 and the Current Population Survey from the Department of Labor.

8. Sass 1997, 54.

9. EBRI 1998.

10. Multiemployer plans are created by collective bargaining agreements covering more than one employer and are generally operated under the joint trusteeship of labor and management. They provide coverage to almost 10 million of the 45 million participants insured by the Pension Benefit Guaranty Corporation.

11. In the 1930s and 1940s, the UMWA covered a majority (80%) of mineworkers. The union was so wealthy that it helped organize emerging unions in the CIO, which covered workers in the rubber, steel, and auto industries. In the mid-1940s the UMWA directed its bargaining power toward pensions.

12. President Truman delegated his Secretary of Interior to mediate the negotiations in the coal industry, and thus the U.S. government encouraged the relatively weak employers in this vital industry to settle with the powerful union. The result was

a multiemployer pension and a powerful trend and "expectation" setter that unions negotiate pensions (Ghilarducci 1992).

13. Stevens 1986, 17–19.

14. A well-known songwriter dealing with subjects regarding the labor movement, sometimes referred to as "Labor's bard," Joe Glazer recorded a song in 1959 supporting the Chrysler workers' demands that a pension system similar to one offered to management employees be extended to line workers.

15. Jacoby 1997.

16. Lazear 1991.

17. Akerlof 1982.

18. An employee benefit that increases in value with increases in a worker's service with a firm is called "tenure-weighted," and includes DB pensions and vacation periods that increase with seniority.

19. Ghilarducci and Reich 2001; Miller and Mulvey 1992; Freeman 1981.

20. Budd 2004.

21. This poll was conducted by Peter Hart from July 28–31, 2006 for the AFL-CIO. I have a copy of it but the results were not released to the public.

22. It is important to recognize in the analysis of why unions promote model saving behavior that not only do union members have more retirement savings but they are much more likely to direct compensation to their health insurance and more likely to be in a health insurance plan. Forty-nine percent of nonunion workers and 75% of union workers (National Compensation Survey 2002) are covered by health insurance; unionized employers direct more compensation to employment-based social insurance than to cash compensation. If the demand for health insurance arises from risk aversion, union workers may be more averse to risk. Paying health insurance premiums also represents a person saving for future expenditures. If that is a main motivation for health and pensions, then investigating how collective bargaining induces lower discount rates is important.

23. Shiller 2000, 23.

24. This was effected for most private-sector workers in 1935 with the passage of the National Labor Relations Act.

25. Kaufman 1989.

26. Morgan Stanley 2002.

27. Sass 1997.

28. Robertson 1936.

29. Wooten 2001, 2005.

30. Other nations have increasingly promoted the policy that pensions should be advance funded—the pension liabilities are paid for over time and before the pension is due—and that a market standard of investing that includes principles of diversity and of funding for the long term be used.

31. Wright 2000, 981.

32. The key distinction between DB (either the traditional or cash balance) and DC plans is who bears the risk regarding the availability of funds when retirement occurs. Prior to the 1980s, most employer-sponsored pension plans were traditional DB plans. A firm guarantees a monthly or lump sum payment to workers after retirement in DB plans. The company bears the risk of making pension payments. A cash balance plan is technically still a DB plan because the employer completely funds the payments; however, the dollar value of the account is derived from contributions made by the employer (usually a fixed percentage of one's salary) and a guaranteed rate of return on those contributions (either a fixed interest rate or one tied to a given index rate). One benefit of a cash balance plan to an increasingly mobile workforce is that workers can take a lump-sum distribution if they leave the firm prior to retiring. The most common form of a DC plan is the 401(k) plan. Employees make pretax contributions to DCs and employers are not required to contribute.

33. Solomon 2003. Many decades before trade unions in other nations, American unions supported a complementary pension system comprising an employer-based pension and the government-provided pension. Crucially, union movements reject privatizing government pensions and developing pension systems that rely on voluntary individual accounts. Where individual accounts have been implemented—Chile, Argentina, El Salvador, and Mexico—the unions support allowing unions to bring workers in as a group in order to bargain with managers to lower fees and improve the services provided by the financial firms that manage those accounts (a policy option that has never been supported by legislators).

34. Most nations follow the "Bismarckian" design, named after the nineteenth-century German chancellor who oversaw the creation of the first modern social security system that linked entitlement and benefit levels to work histories. For example, only people with work records are entitled to benefits, and the amount of benefit is linked to wages and length of career.

35. Fifty percent of these workers are in plans that are under a union contract or influence. Excluding the monies in individual retirement accounts, like 401(k) plans, there is $1.8 trillion in corporate accounts and over $2 trillion in state and local pension funds; $300 billion are in accounts managed jointly by union and management representatives (Ghilarducci 2001, 166).

36. Jesuit and Smeeding 2002.

37. Davis, Lukomnik, and Watson 2006.

38. Blackburn 2002.

39. Ghilarducci 2003.

40. Hebb and Clark 2002.

41. Minchin 2005.

42. One of the chief features of the AFL-CIO's website is the executive pay watch link http://www.aflcio.org/paywatch/ceou.htm. A worker in a number of large compa-

nies can enter his salary at the website and his hourly wage is compared to that of the bosses. I selected Abbott Laboratories at random and entered $40,000 as my salary. I got this returned: "You would have to work eight years to equal Peter Caswell's 2001 compensation. You'd better get working, because you can't take a vacation until A.D. 2010."

43. Silvers, Patterson, and Mason 2000.

44. *Business Week* 2002.

45. Murray 2007.

46. AFL-CIO Proxy Voting Guidelines (2000, 2). The AFL-CIO's Proxy Voting Guidelines further justify the labor movement's involvement with proxy voters because pension law requires that pension fiduciaries consider proxy votes as trust assets. The AFL-CIO gently warns union trustees that if their pension fund does not have guidelines, and the trustees do not hold managers accountable for voting according to guidelines they eventually might develop, then the trustees could be violating federal pension regulations.

47. Hawley, Williams, and Ghilarducci 1997.

Chapter 10
Rescue Plan for American Workers' Retirement

1. Retirement accounts include traditional and Roth individual retirement accounts, and employer-based DC plans; the 401(k) plan is the most common arrangement and is redesigned so that for-profit private organizations and their employees can make a tax-deductible contribution. Employees can contribute up to $15,000; in 2007 (it is indexed to inflation) and workers aged fifty and over can contribute $5,000. Employer contributions do not count against these limits. A person's employer could contribute up to $20,000 more in 2007 (this is not indexed to inflation) or 100% of earnings, whichever is lower. Employer contributions are optional. Assets in 401(k) plans are not taxed until they are withdrawn, and at that time they are subject to ordinary income tax. If the worker is younger than age 59.5 at the time of withdrawal, an additional 10% is imposed. Separate tax code sections govern plans similar to 401(k) plans in the not-for-profit and government entitles (Section 403(b) and 457 plans). Keogh accounts are for self-employed people.

2. Purcell and Whitman 2005.

3. Tax expenditures for private retirement plans—including revenue not collected because earnings and contributions in traditional employer pensions (defined benefit [DB] plans); in 401(k) plans; in Individual Retirement Accounts (IRAs); and in similar savings vehicles dedicated for disbursement at older ages totaled a full fourth of total annual Social Security contributions—$114 billion in 2004. Federal spending in the form of tax expenditures for 401(k) plans is expected to grow 28% by 2009 while that for traditional plans will fall by 2.1%. The tax expenditures for 401(k)

plans, Keogh plans, and IRAs was $58.9 billion in 2005 and for DB plans it was 61.7 billion (U.S. Budget 2004. Analytical Perspectives, table 18.3).

4. Expanding Social Security is the only practical and effective way to provide retirement income security to lower middle- and low-income workers. Social Security is now the most important source of real pensions. It provides secure income and thus raises the reservation wage—the lowest wage that will induce nonworkers to work for money—for older people.

Expanding the earnings base and raising payroll taxes can secure the base of Social Security. In a very useful 2003 book, *Saving Social Security*, economists Peter Orszag and Peter Diamond have one of the most well thought-out, moderate, and balanced policy proposals, although the provisions could more aggressively tackle poverty. They argue for redistributing income from capital to labor by using dividend and capital gains partially to finance some portion of Social Security benefits, like the cost of living adjustments, with general revenue to recognize the public policy goal of maintaining buying power.

5. Qualified plans meet the standards for tax subsidies, qualified to have the contributions and earnings exempted from personal income taxes.

6. I estimate that over 90% of the new higher limits on 401(k)s will go to the top 5% because only 5% of participants saved amounts that equaled the limit in 2006.

7. Converted into an annuity, the monthly benefit of the earlier retiree will be somewhat lower, because it must cover a longer expected retirement.

8. Burman, Gale, Hall, and Orszag 2004.

9. During most years, TIAA's nominal 3% per year guaranteed return is significantly lower than GDP growth, which has averaged 7% per year in nominal terms in the post–World War II period. Thus, GRAs have a guaranteed rate of return that is higher than the TIAA guaranteed rate. However, the actual TIAA return has been much higher than its guaranteed rate—6.6% per year over the past ten years (TIAA-CREF website, accessed February 2, 2007: http://www.tiaacref.org/performance/retirement/profiles/tiaa_traditional_annuity.html).

10. The Pension Benefit Guarantee Corporation guarantees pension benefits up to $49,500 per year.

11. Kovaleski 2002. At the *Pension and Investments* website (www.pionline .com). I went to the "money manager tab" to compute the shares.

12 Some have proposed that each state could help its employers form such networks and provide pension coverage by offering administrative and investment services for low fees (reflecting costs) through their state and local pension funds. An example is the proposed legislation to allow state residents to have access to the professionals managing the state-employee pension funds in Washington state and Michigan (Watkins 2002).

13. Holzmann and Palmer 2006.

14. A qualified DB plan has employer contributions approximately equal to 5% of payroll. Since we do not want to discourage multiemployer plans—which have favorable effects on productivity and on employee retention in industries and occupations, and create an environment for skill acquisition—but have defined benefit and defined characteristics, plans like TIAA-CREF and others (especially in the public sector) would qualify. These qualifying characteristics include: lower than average management fees, bans workers from spending the assets before retirement, and encourages or requires an annuity option.

15. I calculated these estimates using data from Burman, Gale, Hall, and Orszag 2004.

16. HSBC, The Future of Retirement: What People Want," 2007, at http://a248.e.akamai.net/7/248/3622/7d1c0ed7aa1283/www.img.ghq.hsbc.com/public/groupsite/assets/retirement_future/2006_for_what_people_want.pdf.

17. Samuelson 2005.

18. John Myles (2002) discusses the technical mechanisms by which workers and retirees can share the costs of aging societies.

19. The system is in balance when the costs—determined by the level of benefits, or the benefit "generosity," and number of retirees—in addition to administrative costs, are equal to the revenue, which is composed of taxes on workers, the returns on the assets in the trust funds, and any general revenue devoted to old-age income support. It is politically difficult to increase taxes or decrease benefit generosity rates. Getting general revenues into the system is viewed as a tax increase, and raising the rate of return on pension funds comes with more risk, so the risk-adjusted rate is at its maximum. Reducing administrative costs comes up against the interests of the administrators. These considerations rule out changing anything in the equation but the number of workers, the number of beneficiaries, and the wage rate.

The accounting equation describing the necessary balance between the pension program's revenue stream and the benefit payouts is: $bR + C = t(W) \times t(L) + r(F)$, where

b = benefit generosity rate
R = number of recipients
C = administration costs
t = tax rate
w = wages
L = number of workers
r = annual rate of return on the trust fund
F = \$ in the trust fund
G = General funds

20. Nyce and Schieber 2004.

21. The average retirement age is sixty-three for men and sixty-two for women. Munnell, Webb, and Delorme 2006.

22. Butrica, Smith, and Steuerle 2007.

23. John 2005.

24. Butrica, Johnson, Smith, and Steuerle 2004.

25. Bodie 1988, 2001.

26. Jefford's Pro-Save proposal, President Clinton, U.S.A. accounts; Weller 2005; Baker 2000; Robert Eisner 1998.

27. Johnson 2004.

28. Rotenberg 2006.

29. Greenhouse and Barbaro 2005.

30. Rix 2004.

31. Gale, Gruber, and Orszag 2006.

32. Munnell and Halperin 2005.

33. Quoted in Blackburn 2004, 4.

34. Panis 2003.

35. HSBC, "The Future of Retirement: What People Want" 2007.

Glossary

401(k) plan: Section 401 of the federal tax code specified the terms permitting private employees to save cash or to defer profit-sharing funds or funds from a stock-bonus plan tax-free until the cash or funds are withdrawn. In 1978, part k was added to Section 401. Part k allowed private employers to establish an accounting mechanism to deduct an employee's earnings before taxes, and to accumulate those deductions in an account set up for the employee. The employer chooses the investment vehicles offered in the 401(k); the employee selects those that the employer must invest her or his 401(k) funds. The employer defines what makes an employee eligible (with limitations) to participate in the 401(k) and also specifies and makes known whether or not to contribute to the employee pension accounts. The employee's annual contributions are capped at $15,000 per year, or $20,000 (if over age fifty). Withdrawals for "hardship" (the employer defines "hardship" within IRS guidelines) and withdrawals made prior to age 59½ are charged a tax penalty (because of these restrictions they are sometimes called retirement plans). Many employers match the contribution made by the employee, but do not contribute if the employee does not contribute. For-profit employers provide 401(k) plans.

403(b) plan: Employers that are not-for-profit organizations provide 403(b) plans, which were allowed in the tax code in 1958, and are similar to 401(k)s. The eligible employers are organizations that are tax-exempt under IRC 501(c)(3), and employers in public educational organizations: including colleges and universities, independent schools, research organizations, teaching hospitals, churches, charitable organizations, public teaching institutions, such as state universities and community colleges, and K–12 public school systems. Retirement plans set up under section 403(b) generally operate as defined contribution plans, in which, most of the time, the employer can contribute a percentage of participating employees' compensation each year.

Annuities: A contract between an individual and a financial institution specifying that in exchange for payment (it could be in the form of a single payment, referred to as a lump sum, or it could be a series of payments) to the financial institution, the individual will receive a guaranteed series of payments over a specified period of time, usually until a person's death. The amount of the guaranteed payments the individual will correspond to the amount the financial institution received from the individual.

Average: The average is the sum of values in a set divided by the number of items in the set. For example, the mean of the set of numbers (2,4,6,8,200) is the sum of the numbers, 220, divided by 5, which is 44. If one value in the set is very large or very small compared to the other values, then the average will be correspondingly much higher or much lower than most of the other values in the set. For example, in the example above the median is only 6, which represents the value of most of the members of the set. This simple example should make clear that the mean (the average) is a misleading statistic to describe incomes and wealth in a market society because a few people usually have very large amounts of wealth and income, making the average income and wealth much higher than they are for most people. Medians—the value where half of the sample falls above and half above—are often the preferred way to describe the typical incomes of most people in a market economy.

Boomers, early boomers, late boomers: American baby boomers are the seventy-six million people who were born between 1946 and 1962. The early boomers were born between 1946 and 1955; late boomers were born between 1956 and 1963.

Capital: A large catch-all term that refers to a resource, excluding any form of human resource, needed for production. Physical capital is a store of value, a stock, which helps produce something else of value. Usually capital is valuable because what is produced from it is sold and the result is a flow of income called revenue. For example, a popcorn machine is physical capital used to produce popcorn, which produces a flow of income or sales revenue. Financial capital is money or claims to money that can be used to buy physical capital to make things or provide a service that can be sold.

Cash-out: Refers to the selling of a financial asset in order to consume what can be purchased with the income from that sale. If workers cash-out their retirement accounts before they retire, they will not have anything to cash-out of the account when they will need it most—when they do retire.

Chronological age: The time elapsed from a person's birth. (Not the same as real age; see "real age.")

Complements, complementary good: A complement or complementary good is a *good* that is quite commonly consumed along with the consumption of another good. If the cost of one good goes up and people demand less of it, they also demand less of the goods that complement it.

Contributions to qualified pension plans: The amount of money diverted from wages and salaries to a financial account that qualifies as a retirement account; there are penalties for withdrawing the money from such an account before age 59½ or for hardship. By specifying the conditions that qualify for getting a tax break on the diverted portion of wages or salary, the federal government aims to reward a worker for saving for old age. The income from a qualified plan is taxed when it is disbursed, presumably when tax rates are lower for the retiree. In addition, the earnings accumulated in a qualified plan are tax-free, until disbursed.

Defined benefit (DB): A defined benefit plan is any pension plan that is not a defined contribution plan (see "defined contribution"). A traditional pension plan that *defines* a *benefit* for an employee upon that employee's retirement is a defined benefit plan. The stream of income or the monthly annuity an employee receives in retirement from a DB pension plan is determined by a formula that usually uses the employee's pay, years of employment, age at retirement, among other factors. Defined benefit plans do not require employees to contribute to the plan's account. Defined benefit pensions tend not to be portable except for multiemployer plans—a system where an employee can earn credits in the same plan although changing employment among many employers. The Social Security system is the largest multiemployer DB plan. Defined benefit plans are voluntary. When the benefits are paid as an annuity, retirees do not bear the investment risk of low returns on contributions or of outliving their retirement income. Defined benefit plans are insured by the Pension Benefit Guaranteed Corporation.

Defined contribution (DC): A 401(k) plan is a qualified retirement plan under which an employee covered by this plan can elect to have a *defined*, or specified portion of his or her compensation *contributed* to his or her pension account as a pre-tax reduction in salary. (Some plans also accept after-tax contributions from employees.) The funds in a DC account may be invested in a wide variety of investment vehicles chosen by the employer from which the employee chooses. The pre-tax contributions as well as earnings on the retirement account are taxed only when withdrawn. Employers are not required to make matching contributions to their workers' 401(k) accounts. The plans are named after the section of the Internal Revenue Code in which they appear, and apply to private sector employers. Similar salary-deferral retirement plans are authorized in the tax code for public sector employees (known as 457 retirement plans) and nonprofit-sector employees (known as 403(b) retirement plans).

Deferred wages: This is an economic concept in economic theory and it means income that is owed workers because they had a contract to be paid for certain activities, which they performed, but will be paid at a time in the future. Pensions are viewed as deferred wages; they were promised, and therefore owed to workers because workers deferred consuming a part of their wages until much later in the future, when they are old and presumably retired.

Democratizing: Democratizing anything means making it more available to people regardless of income or ownership of an exclusive claim or right someone might have over it. Removing the prohibition on the right to vote based on sex democratized for everyone the freedom to vote. Having a system of programs that enable people from all income levels to retire is democratizing retirement.

Distribution of retirement readiness: Workers who have enough financial assets to claim a stream of income that will maintain their preretirement standard of living for the rest of their lives are considered ready to retire, or more formally, they have retirement readiness. Retirement readiness is distributed differently across income groups according to income earned while working, i.e., before they retire.

Earnings, in general: Earnings denote all sorts of income, whether from a source of wealth or from wages and salaries.

Entitlement: An enforceable, defined claim a person has to something. For example, people are entitled to Social Security benefits if they are eligible when they meet all the qualifications.

Estate tax: An estate tax is a special tax on inheritances and these rates are usually higher than income tax rates; estate taxes are assessed on very large estates under the theory that: heirs are not entitled to the entire amount of large estates because they didn't earn it; and the revenue from estate taxes help redistribute money from the very rich—applies to less than 1% of estates—to government services for the rest of the population. The arguments against the estate tax are that it induces the growth of wasteful activity around avoiding it.

Funding ratio: In pension economics, funding ratio is the market value of all the financial assets in a DB trust fund divided by the value of all the pensions promised to the workers who have earned entitlement to be paid from that fund in the future.

Home equity: Home equity is the difference between the market value of a home and the amount of money owed on the loan or loans used to purchase the home. There are financial plans whereby the elderly sell their homes to a bank or other financial institution, which pays the owners and permits them to continue to live in the home until they die or move. This financial plan is called a reverse mortgage.

Human capital: A person's ability and potential to sell his or her labor to an employer in return for a stream of income is a form of capital called human capital. The word "capital" used in this sense refers to the capacity of human beings in a market economy to turn their skills and efforts into producing goods and services, with money paid in return. The value of one's skill and pluck is often luck. (For example, my prodigious ability to use Microsoft Excel is a valuable source of human capital where I sit today in South Bend; but I would have less valuable human capital if I were in an octopus's garden under the sea, even though I am the same person.)

Income: A flow of money from any of several sources: to a worker usually obtained by selling her or his labor (human capital) to an employer; a flow of money to the owner of property in the form of rent; or a flow of money from selling a valuable asset (capital gains); or interest received on a loan investment or savings; or a flow of money from a claim to Social Security or a pension. Income is any form of money that is based on a capital asset.

Income distribution: Income distribution is a measure of the income among specified groups in an economy. The income distribution can be measured by the percentage of all the income in a nation received by the poorest 20%, or the income received by the poorest 10%, or any other unit of division so long as it can be compared to income received by the top group of income earners. In the United States, the poorest one-fifth of the population typically has less than 3% of all income while the top 20% has almost 50% of all income.

Individual retirement account (IRA): A financial account in which a person can defer wages and salaries up to a specified amount each year and usually deduct the annual amount deferred, including the interest earned on the accumulating amounts deferred, from taxable income, until retirement. This type of account is a usually called an individual retirement account. The account holder bears the investment risk and financial market risk. In addition, when taking the income out to spend (unless the person buys an annuity product), the account holder—that is, the retiree—takes the risk he or she will live longer than the funds remaining in the account will provide for living expenses—this risk is called longevity risk.

Institutional economics: Institutional economics is different from neoclassical economics. Institutional economics focuses on understanding the role of human-made institutions in shaping behavior regarding work, consumption, and other related economic activity. Institutional economists tend to suspect that power relationships determine outcomes more than the interaction of parties with equal access to information and alternative choices

Labor force participation rate: The labor force participation rate is the ratio of the people that are in the labor force—employed or unemployed but looking for a job—to the total population of people. If people tell government survey takers that they are not working but are retired, going to school full time, too sick or disabled to work, and engaged in other activities that demonstrate they don't want a job, they are not counted as unemployed nor in the labor force. The labor force participation rate for people between the ages of sixteen and sixty-five is much higher than that of the labor force participation rate for people older than sixty-five.

Length of retirement; see retirement leisure

Living standards: The standard of living is a subjective measure of the quality and quantity of material goods and services available to people and affordable to them. The standard of living reflects the ability of people to satisfy their wants. A "standard" is not usually meant to measure the "quality" of life, which takes into account not only material goods but also being able to afford to be educated, or have free time, to be safe, etc. If the value of goods produced with free time could be measured, that value could conceptually be added into a living standard. Usually money income is used as a shortcut to measure standard of living.

Lump sum: A lump sum is a single payment for a total amount due, as opposed to an equivalent series of periodic payments. Annuities may be paid in a lump sum.

Median: The middle value that separates the higher half from the lower half of a list of numbers; see the example in the definition of average.

Money purchase plan: Another kind of DC retirement plan in the form of individual employee accounts. In contrast to 401(k) or 403(b), the employer's contribution rate is fixed. Contributions are usually calculated as a percentage of the worker's earnings.

Neoclassical economics: Neoclassical economics is an approach in economics that focuses on much the same things institutionalist economics focuses on, but within a set of common assumptions about human behavior: individuals and firms seek to get as much claim to valuable rights and goods as possible; people have rational preferences, meaning they know what they like and know what they want, even into the future; people are not influenced to go against their interests by ignoring information, or processing it incorrectly, or being influenced by other people, social norms, customs, and institutions.

Nonqualified pension plan: A nonqualified employer-sponsored retirement plan is any plan that does not meet the requirements of Section 401 of the Internal Revenue Code. Other sections of the Internal Revenue Code provide for special types of retirement savings plans, some of which must meet special requirements. Some of the nonqualified programs can be offered on a discriminatory basis to certain employees; typically, they are offered to key executives in the organization. These plans are used to provide additional income over the limited amount offered by qualified plans, and they are often an effective device for recruiting executive talent. Nonqualified pension plans lack the legislative protections guaranteed by qualified plans, nor do they enjoy the same tax benefits as qualified plans. Nonqualified plans generally must be unfunded arrangements. Unfunded means that the assets held in these plans are not protected from general creditors if the firm experiences financial difficulties. Plan participants have no greater claim to these assets than general creditors of the firm.

Patriarchy: A hierarchy in a society or institution that gives to men more claims to income and entitlements than to women, and gives men the right to control women's behavior and access to valuable goods or rights. Patriarchal-based attitudes and rules partially explain women's subordinate status in the labor market.

Pension assets: The financial capital or claims to income that a person can use in old age to replace wages or salaries.

Pension coverage (rate): Among all the workers for an employer, pension coverage is the percentage of workers offered a pension by that employer.

Pension liabilities: The value of the pensions promised to a group of workers not yet retired.

Pension plan sponsor: A plan sponsor is the employer that offers and administers the retirement account or pension.

Pension security: Pension security is a subjective term that refers to a low probability that what one expects from a claim to income after retirement will disappear.

Poverty level: The U.S. Census determines how much income people—in different kinds of families and at different ages—need to buy enough calories to sustain life for a short period of time (alas, by that measure of calories the meals are not necessarily nutritionally balanced). That number is multiplied by three to get the absolute minimum a person would need to buy clothing and shelter and food. Persons at or below the poverty level are in a chronic state of want.

Pretirement income; see retirement income replacement rate

Profit-sharing plan: Profit-sharing plans in the United States are usually tax-favored incentive plans introduced by firms to provide direct or indirect payments to employees that vary depending on the firm's profitability. These payments can be paid out at the end of a worker's work life and serve as a form of pension.

Qualified pension plans: Qualified pension plans meet the standards for tax subsidies. In other words, they are qualified to have the contributions and earnings exempted from personal income taxes.

Rank-and-file workers: There is no fixed definition of the rank and file. In pension law, it refers to workers who earn less than the "key" employees earn—meaning the people whose earnings put them in the top 5% in the income distribution—and who earn more than the people at the bottom of the income distribution do. Rank-and-file workers can be seen as the middle class.

Real age: Devised by medical experts, real age considers a person's chronological age and adjusts it for expected length of life. If a person is expected to live five years longer than the average person does at the same chronological age, then five years are deducted from that person's chronological age. The concept of real age is meant to take into account the time remaining before a person's death.

Refundable tax credit: A tax credit can be refundable or nonrefundable. A nonrefundable tax credit can reduce the tax owed to the government to zero. A nonrefundable tax credit can reduce the tax owed below zero so that the person filing a declaration of income for tax purposes (a potential taxpayer) will receive a payment from, rather than make a payment to, the tax authorities. Refundable tax credits are ways governments can give money to low-income people based on their income and eligibility for the credit. People who work and earn low wages take the largest refundable tax credit; it is called the earned income tax credit.

Retirement income: Income received by people above the age at which that person retired (in contrast to being unemployed, or disabled).

Retirement income replacement rate: The retirement income replacement rate is strictly the share of retirement income as a percent of income earned in the period before retiring. Retirement income replacement rate is a measure of how much income is needed to enable a retiree to consume the same amount of goods and services consumed while working. The amount of income to maintain the same standard in retirement is usually less because tax rates are lower, and retirees do not pay work-related expenses and are not saving for retirement. However, some experts say that retirees need more than a 100% replacement rate because health care costs are increasing.

Retirement leisure: Retirement leisure is the amount of time between the day a person stops working full or part time and the day that person dies. Sometimes the leisure is spent in nonpaid work, unemployment, or disability. The most meaningful definition of leisure is that it is any time not spent working. For a person to have retirement leisure she must have had a time when she worked for pay. (The term "retirement leisure" is used only by me.)

Retirement savings account (RSA): In 2004, President George W. Bush proposed that "Retirement Savings Accounts" replace all three different types of Individual Retirement Accounts currently used in the United States: traditional IRA, Roth IRA, and Simple IRA. Individuals would contribute to their retirement savings accounts on an after-tax basis. In addition, Employer Retirement Savings Accounts (ERSAs) would consolidate 401(k), Simple 401(k), 403(b), and 457 employer-based DC accounts into a single type of plan.

Retirement wealth portfolio: A retirement wealth portfolio is the total value of the sources that yields or can potentially yield income in retirement. The main sources of retirement wealth include the "net present value," which is the amount of money you would need to pay an insurance company to guarantee the same stream of income that would be due to you according to your Social Security record or defined benefit plan; the stream of income you could get from selling your home equity; your human capital wealth—the value of the income stream you could get by working for pay; and your financial assets. Wealth is a stock; income is a flow.

Social insurance: A social insurance program requires everyone in a society (usually considered the residents in a nation) to belong to a public insurance program that protects against various economic risks (e.g., loss of income due to sickness, old age, or unemployment). The United States lagged behind Europe in developing social insurance programs until 1935, when the Social Security Act was passed. The United States has a wide network of social insurance programs for unemployment, injury or illness sustained on the job, retirement, disability, health care for persons over age sixty-five and for younger poor people. Social insurance contributions are normally compulsory, so that people who have less risk do not exit the system leaving only high-risk individuals in the system. The contributions act like taxes—they are compulsory and may be made by the insured person's employer and the state as well as by the individual. Social insurance is usually self-financing, with contributions being placed in specific funds for that purpose.

Social Security "contributions": Social Security "contributions" are the required payments made by the employer and employee to finance the Social Security system. The Act that allowed the contributions to be deducted from workers' paychecks is the Federal Insurance Contributions Act or FICA.

Substitutes: Substitute goods are goods that can be used to satisfy the same needs, one in the place of another. Apples can substitute for cherries in a pie; they are substitute goods. In neoclassical economics, pensions are viewed as substitutes for wages. This is a key term in economics, and is the opposite of complementary goods, where the use of one complementary good requires the use of another. Piecrust and fruit for pies are complementary goods. In institutional economics, pensions and wages are complements in the primary sector.

Supply-side economics: This was a term first used by conservative and liberal writers to describe the government finance theory that, lowering taxes and regulations for producers would cause the producers to produce more, increasing the number of jobs and increasing the amount of sales; the increased amount of sales would then raise more tax revenue despite the lowered tax rates. This theory favors policies that increase the ability to increase profits.

Tax exemptions, tax favoritism, tax subsidies: Tax expenditure refers to provisions in a tax code that favor a particular activity—usually with a social purpose by somehow lowering the taxes associated with that activity. They take the form of exemptions, exclusions, deductions, credits, deferrals, and preferential tax rates—all of which result in a reduction in government revenues that would otherwise be collected without the special treatment. Thus, tax expenditures for an activity are just as much an expense for the government as if the government spent money to achieve the same outcome. Tax expenditures for retirement income accounts represent hundreds of billions of revenue not collected. They are justified because they advance social obligations to encourage pension savings. The term tax subsidy is often used interchangeably with tax exemption.

Wealth: Although income and wealth are both economic measures of financial security and well-being, there are distinctions between the two. Income is the amount of money received during a period of time in exchange for labor and services, from the sale of goods or property, or as profit from financial investments. Income is critical in meeting a wide range of consumption needs. Wealth encompasses all goods and resources that have value in terms of exchange or use (i.e., a home, business, pension, or investment). Wealth provides a meaningful indication of economic security, as it can gain value over time and provide a cushion during times of unemployment or illness. Wealth is a better gauge than income of the ability of a household to access opportunity and pass on assets to future generations.

Welfare: A welfare program is a government program that gives income or services to people who are poor or have low incomes, or who are in special needy circumstances. The determination of the income levels or circumstances is done by agencies and legislators and is ever changing. The people served are usually disadvantaged by low incomes or stressful circumstance and thus do not have political influence. Therefore the payments are usually low—lower than income from social insurance plans whose entitlement is based on being attached to the labor force and having paid taxes (the terms "contributions" and "premiums" are used interchangeably).

Bibliography

Aaron, Henry J., Barry P. Bosworth, and Gary Burtless. 1989. *Can America Afford to Grow Old? Paying for Social Security.* Washington, D.C: Brookings Institution Press.

Aaron, Henry J., and William B. Schwartz (with Melissa Cox). 2005. *Can We Say No? The Challenge of Rationing Health Care.* Washington, D.C.: The Brookings Institution Press.

Aaronson, Stephanie, and Julia Coronado. 2005. "Are Firms or Workers behind the Shift away from DB Pension Plan?" Board of Governors of the Federal Reserve System (U.S.), Finance and Economics Discussion Series: 2005-17 Working Paper.

Adams, Peter, M. D. Hurd, D. L. McFadden, A. Merrill, and T. Ribeiro. 2003. "Healthy, Wealthy, and Wise? Tests for Direct Causal Paths between Health and Socioeconomic Status." *Journal of Econometrics* 112(1): 3–56.

AEI Public Opinion Study. 2005. "Attitudes about Social Security Reform." American Enterprise Institute, February 4. http://www.aei.org/publications/pubID.21928, filter.all/pub_detail.asp (accessed June 4, 2007).

AFl-CIO Proxy Voting Guidelines. 2000. http://www.aflcio.org/corporateamerica/capital/upload/proxy_voting_guidelines.pdf (accessed on Sept. 27, 2005).

Akerlof, George A. 1982. "Labor Contracts as Partial Gift Exchanges." *Quarterly Journal of Economics* 97: 543–46.

Altman, Nancy J. 2005. *The Battle for Social Security: From FDR's Vision to Bush's Gamble.* New York: John Wiley and Sons.

American Academy of Actuaries. 2004a. "*Assumptions* Used to Project Social Security's Financial Condition." Washington, D.C.: American Academy of Actuaries. January 2004, updates a 2001 issue brief. http://www.actuary.org/pdf/socialsecurity/assumptions_0104.pdf (accessed July 16, 2007).

———. 2004b. "A Balancing Act: Achieving Adequacy and Sustainability in Retirement Income Reform: What Are the Trade-Offs?" Presented by Ron Gebhardtsbauer at the AARP/CEPS Forum, Brussels, March 4. http://www.actuary.org/pdf/pension/tradeoffs_030404.pdf.

Anderson, Gary, and Keith Brainard. 2004. "Profitable Prudence: The Case for Public Employer Defined Benefit Plans." Pension Research Council Working Paper no. PRC WP 2004-6. http://prc.wharton.upenn.edu/prc/prc.html

Anderson, Kathryn H., Richard V. Burkhauser, and Joseph F. Quinn. 1986. "Do Retirement Dreams Come True? The Effect of Unanticipated Events on Retirement Plans." *Industrial and Labor Relations Review* 39(4): 518–56.

Anzick, Michael, and David A. Weaver. 2001. "Reducing Poverty among Elderly Women." ORES Working Paper Series no. 87. Washington, D.C.: Office of Research Economic Statistics, Social Security Administration.

Appell, Douglas. 2004. "Asset Allocation: Defined Benefit Plans Reap Harvest of Equity Markets." *Pensions and Investments* January 26, p. 22.

Arias, E. 2002. "United States Life Tables, 2000." *National Vital Statistics Reports* 51(3).

Bajtelsmit, Vickie, and Alexandra Bernasek. 1999. "Women and Retirement." *Research Dialogue* 61: 1–10. New York: TIAA-CREF Institute.

Baker, Dean. 2000. *Pensions for the Twenty-First Century*. New York: Century Foundation.

———. 2005. "The Council of Economic Advisors Flunk the No Economist Left behind Test: Response to the CEA Memo." Washington, D.C.: Center for Economic and Policy Research. http://www.ourfuture.org/docUploads/05.2.10_cea_response.pdf.

Ball, Robert M. 2004. "How to Fix Social Security? It Doesn't Have to Be Hard." *Aging Today* 25(2).

Bassett, W. F., M. J. Fleming, and A. P. Rodrigues. 1998. "How Workers Use 401(K) Plans: The Participation, Contribution, and Withdrawal Decisions. Staff Report no. 38. New York: Federal Reserve Bank of New York.

Becker, Gary S. 1998. "A Theory of the Allocation of Time." In *Economic demography*, Vol. 1, edited by T. Paul Schultz, 287–311. Elgar Reference Collection. International Library of Critical Writings in Economics, Vol. 86. Cheltenham, U.K. and Northampton, Mass. Previously published 1965.

Béland, Daniel, and Jacob S. Hacker. 2004. "Ideas, Private Institutions and American Welfare State 'Exceptionalism': The Case of Health and Old-Age Insurance, 1915–1965." *International Journal of Social Welfare* 13(1): 42–54.

Bell, Elizabeth, Adam Carasso, and C. Eugene Steuerle. 2005. "Strengthening Private Sources of Retirement Savings for Low-Income Families." Opportunity and Ownership Project Brief no. 5. Washington, D.C.: Urban Institute. http://www.urban.org/url.cfm?ID=311229.

Bellow, Saul. 2000. *Ravelstein*. New York: Penguin.

Bender, Keith A., and Natalia A. Jivan. 2005. "What Makes Retirees Happy?" *An Issue in Brief* no. 28. Boston: Center for Retirement Research at Boston College. http://www.bc.edu/centers/crr/ib_28.shtml.

Bergmann, Barbara. 1986. *The Economic Emergence of Women*. New York: Basic Books.

Bernstein, Merton C., and Joan Brodshaug Bernstein. 1988. *Social Security: The System That Works*. New York: Basic Books.

Blackburn, Robin. 2002. *Banking on Death or Investing in Life: The History and Fututre of Pension Funds*. London: Verso.

———. 2004. "Gray Capital and the Challenge of Pension Finance." Paper presented at Conference on Pension Fund Capitalism and the Crises of Old Age Security, New York.

Blau, Francine D., and Marianne A. Ferber. 1998. *The Economics of Women, Men, and Work*. New York: Prentice-Hall.

Bodie, Zvi. 1988. "Inflation, Index-Linked Bonds, and Asset Allocation." NBER Working Paper no. W2793. Cambridge, Mass.: National Bureau of Economic Research, December. http://ssrn.com/abstract=226853.

———. 2001. "Financial Engineering and Social Security Reform." In *Risk Aspects of Investment-Based Social Security Reform*, edited by John Y. Campbell and Martin Feldstein. Chicago: The University of Chicago Press.

Bound, J., T. Waidman, and M. Schoenbaum. 1996. "Race Differences in Labor Force: Attachment and Disability Status." Working Paper no. 5536. Cambridge, Mass.: National Bureau of Economic Research.

Brown, Clair. 1994. *American Standards of Living 1918–1988*. Cambridge, Mass.: Blackwell.

Brown, Kyle N., Gordon P. Goodfellow, Tomeka Hill, Richard R. Joss, Richard Luss, Lex Miller, and Sylvester J. Schieber. 2000. "The Unfolding of a Predictable Surprise: A Comprehensive Analysis of the Shift from Traditional Pensions to Hybrid Plans." Report. Bethesda, M.D.: Watson Wyatt Worldwide.

Buchmueller, Thomas R., W. Johnson, and Anthony T. Lo Sasso. 2006. "Trends in Retiree Health Insurance, 1997–2003." *Health Affairs* 25(6): 1507–16.

Budd, John. 2004. "Non-Wage Forms of Compensation." *Journal of Labor Research* Fall: 598.

———. 2005. "The Effect of Unions on Employee Benefits: Recent Results from the Employer Costs for Employee Compensation Data." http://www.bls.gov/opub/cwc/cm20050616ar01p1.htm (accessed September 27, 2005).

Burchell, B., S. Deakin, J. Michie, and J. Rubery. 2003. *Systems of Production: Markets, Organisations, and Performance*. London: Routledge.

Bureau of Labor Statistics. 2004. "Employee Tenure in 2004," table 5: "Median Years of Tenure with Current Employer for Employed Wage and Salary Workers by Industry, Selected Years, 2000–06." http://www.bls.gov/news.release/tenure.t05.htm.

Bureau of Labor Statistics, Employment Cost Index. 2002. "Employer Costs for Employee Compensation 1986–2002." Report. Washington, D.C.: Department of Labor, Bureau of Labor Statistics.

Burham, Kimberly. 2003. "401(K)s as Strategic Compensation: Align Pay with Productivity and Enable Optimal Separation." PhD diss., University of Notre Dame.

Burkhauser, Richard V. 2003. "Comments." Paper presented at the 5th Annual Conference of the Retirement Research Consortium, Washington, D.C.

Burkhauser, Richard V., and Kenneth A. Couch. 1996. "Who Takes Early Social Security Benefits? The Economic and Health Characteristics of Early Retirees." *Gerontologist* 36(6): 789–99.

Burman, Leonard E., William G. Gale, Matthew Hall, and Peter R. Orszag. 2004. *Distributional Effects of Defined Contribution Plans and Individual Retirement Accounts.* Washington, D.C.: Urban-Brookings Tax Policy Center.

Burman, Leonard, William G. Gale, and Peter R. Orszag. 2004. "Key Thoughts on RSAs and LSAs." Paper presented at the Urban Institute-Brookings Institution Tax Policy Center, February 4.

Burtless, Gary. 1986. "Social Security, Unanticipated Benefit Increases, and the Timing of Retirement." *Review of Economic Studies* 53(5): 781–805.

———. 2001. "International Evidence on the Desirability of Individual Retirement Accounts in Public Pension Systems." *Testimony before the Subcommittee on Social Security Committee on Ways and Means.* United States Congress, House of Representatives. 105th Cong., 2nd sess., July 31.

Burtless, Gary, and Robert A. Moffitt. 1984. "Effect of Social Security Benefits on Labor Supply." In *Retirement and Economic Behavior*, edited by Gary Burtless and Henry Aaron, 134–50. Washington, D.C.: The Brookings Institution.

Burtless, Gary, and Timothy Smeding. 2007. "Poverty, Work, and Policy: The United States in Comparative Perspective." *Testimony before the Subcommittee on Income Security and Family Support of the House.* United States Congress, House of Representatives, Committee on Ways and Means. 110th Cong., 1st sess., February 13.

Bush, George. 2002. "President Promotes Retirement Security Agenda." Speech given at the 2002 National Summit on Retirement Savings, Washington, D.C.

Butrica, Barbara A., Howard M. Iams, and Karen E. Smith. 2003. "It's All Relative: Understanding the Retirement Prospects of Baby-Boomers." Working Paper no. 2003-21. Boston: Center for Retirement Research at Boston College. http://www.bc.edu/centers/crr/dummy/wp_2003-21.shtml.

———. 2004. "The Changing Impact of Social Security on Retirement Income in the United States." *Social Security Bulletin* 65: 1–13.

Butrica, Barbara A., Richard W. Johnson, Karen E. Smith, and C. Eugene Steuerle. 2004. "Does Work Pay at Older Ages?" Research Report, December 5. Washington, D.C.: Urban Institute.

Butrica, Barbara A., Karen E. Smith, and C. Eugene Steuerle. 2006. "Working for a Good Retirement." Brief, October 26. Washington, D.C.: Urban Institute.

———. 2007. "Working for a Good Retirement." In *Government Spending on the Elderly*, edited by Dimitri B. Papadimitriou. New York: Palgrave Macmillan.

Cappelli, Peter. 2003. "Career Jobs Are Dead." In *Benefits for the Workplace of the Future*, edited by Judith F. Mazo, Olivia S. Mitchell, David S. Blitzstein, and Michael Gordon, 203–25. Philadelphia: University of Pennsylvania Press.

———. 2003a. "Is There Really a Coming Labor Shortage?" *Organizational Dynamics* (August): 221–23.

Carlson, Leah. 2005. "States Continue as Mainstay for DB Pensions." *Employee Benefit News* June 1. http://www.benefitnews.com, http://www.sourcemedia.com.

Carrington, William J., Kristin McCue, and Brooks Pierce. 2002. "Nondiscrimination Rules and the Distribution of Fringe Benefits." *Journal of Labor Economics* 20(2): 5–33.

Carter, S. B., and R. Sutch. 1995. "Myth of the Industrial Scrap Heap: A Revisionist View of Turn-of-the-Century American Retirement." Working Paper no. 73. Cambridge, Mass.: National Bureau of Economic Research.

Cato Institute. 2003. "Social Security Week." Cato Institute Project. Washington, D.C. http://www.socialsecurity.org/sstw/sstw07-14-03.pdf (accessed January 2005).

CBS News Transcripts. 1996. "Poll Finds Americans Opposed to Privatization of Social Security." Anchor Dan Rather. March 12.

Centers for Medicare and Medicaid Services. 2006. "Medicare Premiums and Deductibles for 2007." September 12. Washington, D.C.

CFO Europe. 2004. "Who to Believe?" *CFO Europe* May. http://www.cfoeurope.com/displaystory.cfm/2661813/l_print.

Chamber of Commerce. 2005. *Employee Benefits*, p. 10. Washington, D.C.

Chen, Kathy. 2002. "Fight Looms over Changes to Pension Laws." *Wall Street Journal*, January 22.

Cheng, Ing-Haw, and Eric French. 2000. "The Effect of the Run-Up in the Stock Market on Labor Supply." *Economic Perspectives* 24(4): 48–65.

Chernozhukov, Victor, and Christian Hansen. 2004. "The Effects of 401(K) Participation on Wealth Distribution: An Instrumental Quartile Regression Analysis." *Review of Economics & Statistics* 86(3): 735–51.

Choi, James J., David Laibson, and Brigitte Madrian. 2005. "$100 Bills on the Sidewalk: Suboptimal Saving in 401(K) Plans." Prepared for the 7th Annual Joint Conference of the Retirement Research Consortium, "Creating a Secure Retirement," Washington, D.C., August 11–12, 2005. http://www.bc.edu/centers/crr/papers/Seventh_Paper/Choi2.pdf.

Clark, R., and J. F. Quinn. 1999. "Effects of Pensions on Labor Markets and Retirement." Boston College Working Papers in Economics no. 431. Boston: Boston College Department of Economics.

Clark, Robert L., et al. 2004. *The Economics of an Aging Society.* Oxford: Blackwell Publishing.

Clowes, Mike. 2004. "The Long Road to Extinction." *Pensions and Investments* 32: 8–11.

Coile, Courtney, et al. 2002. "Delays in Claiming Social Security Benefits." *Journal of Public Economics* 84(3): 357–85.

Coile, Courtney, and J. Gruber. 2000a. "Social Security and Retirement." NBER Working Paper no. W7830. Cambridge, Mass.: National Bureau of Economic Research.

———. 2000b. "Social Security Incentives for Retirement." NBER Working Papers no. 7651. Cambridge, Mass.: National Bureau of Economic Research.

Coile, Courtney, and Phillip Levine. 2005. "Bulls, Bears, and Retirement Behavior." NBER Working Papers no. 10779. Cambridge, Mass.: National Bureau of Economic Research.

Congressional Budget Office. 2000. "Federal Spending on Elderly and Children," p. 3. July 28. ftp://ftp.cbo.gov/23xx/doc2300/fsec.pdf.

———. 2004. "Administrative Costs of Private Accounts in Social Security." March. http://www.cbo.gov/showdoc.cfm?index=5277&sequence=0.

———. 2005. "Updated Long-Term Projections for Social Security." Report. Washington, D.C.: Congressional Budget Office.

Coronado, Julia, and Maria Perozek. 2001. "Wealth Effects and the Consumption of Leisure: Retirement Decisions During the Stock Market Boom of the 1990s." Unpublished paper. Washington, D.C.: Federal Reserve Board.

Costa, Dora L. 1998. *The Evolution of Retirement: An American Economic History, 1880–1990.* Chicago: University of Chicago Press.

Creedy, John. 1994. "Pensions and Compensating Wage Variations." *Scottish Journal of Political Economy* 41(4): 454–63.

Currie, Janet. 1993. "Gender Gaps in Benefits Coverage." NBER Working Paper no. 4265. Cambridge, Mass.: National Bureau of Economic Research.

Darlin, Damon. 2007. "O.K. Financial Planners, Grab a Calculator and Let's Get Started." *New York Times*, January 27, C4.

Davis, Stephen, Jon Lukomnik, and David Pitt-Watson. 2006. *The New Capitalists: How Citizen Investors Are Reshaping the Corporate Agenda.* Cambridge, Mass.: Harvard Business School Press.

Deaton, Angus, and Anne Case. 2003. "Broken Down by Work and Sex: How our Health Declines." NBER Working Papers no. 9821. Cambridge, Mass.: National Bureau of Economic Research.

Deloitte Consulting LLP 2005. "Deloitte Consulting LLP 2005 Annual 401(K) Benchmarking Survey." http://www.deloitte.com/dtt/cda/doc/content/Annual_401k_Benchmarking_Survey_2004(1).pdf (accessed August 19, 2006).

Diamond, Peter, and Botond Koszegi. 2003. "Quasi-hyperbolic discounting and retirement." *Journal of public Economics*, Elsevier, vol. 87(9–10), 1839–72.

Diamond, Peter, and Peter R. Orszag. 2004. *Saving Social Security: A Balanced Approach.* Washington, D.C.: Brookings Institution Press.

Dickens, W. T., and K. Lang. 1985. "A Test of Dual Labor Market Theory: A Reconsideration of the Evidence." NBER Working Paper no. 1670. Cambridge, Mass.: National Bureau of Economic Research.

Doeringer, Peter. 2000. "Older Workers: An Essential Resource for Massachusetts." http://www.geront.umb.edu/lit_reports.htm.

Dorsey, Stuart, Christopher Cornwell, and David Macpherson. 1998. *Pensions and Productivity.* Kalamazoo, Mich.: W. E. Upjohn Institute for Employment Research.

Draut, Tamara, and Heether McGhee. 2004. "Retiring in the Red: The Growth of Debt among Older Americans." Briefing Paper. New York: Demos, A Network for Ideas and Action.

Eickelberg, Howard. 2005. *Testimony before the House Ways and Means Subcommittee on Select Revenue Measures on the Administration's Proposal for Single-employer Pension Funding Reform.* March 8.

Ellwood, David. 2000. "Winners and Losers in America: Taking the Measure of the New Economic Realities." In *A Working Nation: Workers, Work and Government in the New Economy,* edited by David Ellwood, Rebecca M. Blank, Joseph Blasi, Douglas Krause, William Niskanen, and Karen Lynn-Dyson, 1–41. New York: Russell Sage Foundation.

Employee Benefits Research Institute (EBRI). 1997. *EBRI Databook on Employee Benefits.* Washington, D.C.: EBRI Publications.

———. 1998. "Public Attitudes on Social Security: The UFO Fallacy. Preparing for Retirement: An Analysis of Personality Types." *EBRI Notes* 19 (3). http://www.ebri.org/notes/0398note.htm (accessed September 6, 2005).

———. 2003 and 2006. *EBRI Databook on Employee Benefits.* http://www.ebri.org/pdf/publications/books/databook (accessed July 23, 2007).

———. 2004a. "Saving and Retiring in America." http://www.ebri.org/pdf/surveys/rcs/2004/04rcsfs2.pdf accessed July 23, 2007.

———. 2004b. "Will Americans Ever Become Savers? The 14th Retirement Confidence Survey, 2004." Issue Brief no. 268. http://www.ebri.org/publications/ib/index.cfm?fa=ibDisp&content_id=496.

———. 2006. "Saving and Retiring in America." http://www.ebri.org/pdf/RCS06_FS_01_Saving_Final.pdf

Engen, E., and W. G. Gale. 2000. "The Effects of 401(K) Plans on Household Wealth: Differences across Earnings Groups." NBER Working Paper no. 8032. Cambridge, Mass.: National Bureau of Economic Research.

Eschtruth, Andrew D., and Jonathan Gemus. 2002. "Are Older Workers Responding to the Bear Market?" *Just the Facts on Retirement Issues,* no. 5. Boston: Center for Retirement Research.

Even, William E., and David A. MacPherson. 1996. "Employer Size and Labor Turnover: The Role of Pensions." *Industrial and Labor Relations Review* 49 (July): 707–28.

———. 2004. "When Will the Gender Gap in Retirement Income Narrow?" *Southern Economic Journal* 71(1): 182–200.

Fernandez, Frank. A., and Kyle L. Brandon. 2006. "Retirement Savings: By the Numbers." Research Reports, Vol. 2 (June 27), 7. New York: Securities Industry Association.

Ferrara, Peter. 2003. "Social Security Personal Account Reform Alternatives." Report. Washington, D.C.: Americans for Tax Reform.

———. 2005. "Social Security Sellout." *Washington Times*, March 9.

Filer, Randall K., and Peter A. Petri. 1988. "A Job Characteristics Theory of Retirement." *Review of Economics and Statistics* 70(1): 123–29.

Fisher, Amy. 2006. "Man's Desire to Go to Prison Is Worrisome." *Columbus Dispatch* October 16, 1C.

Folbre, Nancy. 1994. *Who Pays for the Kids? Gender and the Structures of Constraints.* London: Routledge.

Foster, Kevin, and Paul Cordasco. 2004. "One-Third of Publicly-Traded Companies Do Not Accurately Portray Their True Financial Condition, Rate Financials Study Finds." *Business Wire* June 18.

Freeman, Richard B. 1981. "The Effect of Unionism on Fringe Benefits." *Industrial and Labor Relations Review* 34(4): 489–509.

Freeman, Richard B., and James Medoff. 1982. *What Do Unions Do?* New York: Basic Books.

Friedberg, Leora and Michael Owyang. 2004. "Explaining the Evolution of Pension Structure and Job Tenure." NBER Working Paper no. 10714. Cambridge, Mass.: National Bureau of Economics Research.

Friedberg, Leora, and A. Webb. 2000. "The Impact of 401(K) Plans on Retirement." Discussion Paper no. 2000-30. San Diego: University of California.

Frieswick, Kris. 2002. "Honey, I Shrunk the 401(K)." *CFO Magazine* August.

Galbraith, James. 2005. "The Deficit Trap." *Salon* March 21.

Gale, William G., Jonathan Gruber, and Peter R. Orszag. 2006. "Improving Opportunities and Incentives for Saving by Middle- and Low-Income Households." Hamilton Project Discussion Paper, April.

Gale, William G., and Karen M. Pence. 2006. "Are Successive Generations of Americans Getting Wealthier, and If So, Why? Evidence from the 1990s." Brookings Papers on Economic Activity. Washington, D.C.: The Brookings Institution.

Gebhardtsbauer, Ron. 2004. "A Balancing Act: Achieving Adequacy and Sustainability in Retirement Income Reform: What Are the Tradeoffs?" Appendix A. Presented at the AARP/CEPS Forum, Brussels, March 4. http://www.actuary.org/pdf/pension/tradeoffs_030404.pdf.

Geddes, Lori A., and John S. Heywood. 2003. "Gender and Piece Rates, Commissions, and Bonuses." *Industrial Relations* 42(3): 419–44.

Geisel, Jerry. 2006. "More Employers Likely to Freeze DB Plans: Survey." *Business Insurance* January 10. http://www.businessinsurance.com/cgi-bin/news.pl?newsId=6989.

Gerdtham, Ulf-G., and Magnus Johannesson. 2004. "Absolute Income, Relative Income, Income Inequality, and Mortality." *Journal of Human Resources* 39(1): 228–48.

Ghilarducci, Teresa. 1992. *Labor's Capital: The Economics and Politics of Private Pensions.* Cambridge, Mass.: MIT Press.

———. 1999. "Pensions and Old Age Retirement." In *Elgar Companion to Feminist Economics,* edited by Janice Peterson and Margaret Lewis. London: Edward Elgar.

———. 2001. "Small Benefits, Big Pension Funds, and How Corporate Governance Reforms Can Close the Gap." In *Working Capital: The Power of Labor's Pensions,* edited by Tessa Hub, Archon Fung, and Joel Rogers. Ithaca, N.Y.: Cornell University Press.

———. 2003. "Delinking Employee Benefits from a Single Employer: Alternative Multiemployer Models." In *Benefits for the Workplace of the Future,* edited by Judith F. Mazo et al., 260–84. Philadelphia: University of Pennsylvania Press.

Ghilarducci, Teresa, and M. Lee. 2005. "Small Firm Pension Coverage, Multiemployer Plans, and Middle Class Workers." Presented at the Allied Social Sciences Association Annual National Meeting, Industrial Relations Research Association, Philadelphia.

Ghilarducci, Teresa, and Michael Reich. 2001. "Complementarity of Pensions and Training under Multiemployer Plans." *Journal of Labor Research* 22: 615–34.

Ghilarducci, Teresa, and Wei Sun. 2004. "Latinos' Low Pension Coverage and Disenfranchisement from the U.S. Financial System." Research Reports Vol. 2004.3. Institute for Latino Studies, University of Notre Dame.

———. 2006. "How Defined Contribution Plans and 401(K)s Affect Employer Pension Costs: 1981–1998." *Journal of Pension Economics and Finance* 5(2): 175–96.

Goolsbee, A. 2004. "The Fees of Private Accounts and the Impact of Social Security Privatization on Financial Managers." Unpublished paper. Chicago: University of Chicago.

Gordon, Michael S. 2000. "ERISA at 25: Has the Law Kept Pace with the Evolving Pension and Investment World?" *Testimony before the Subcommittee on Employer-Employee Relations, Committee on Education and the Workforce.* United States Congress, House of Representatives, February 15.

Gordon, Roger H., and Alan S. Blinder. 1980. "Market Wages, Reservation Wages, and Retirement Decisions." *Journal of Public Economics* 14(2): 277–308.

Government Accountability Office (formerly the General Accounting Office). 2000. *Cash Balance Plans: Implications for Retirement Income.* Report no. HEHS-00-185 GAO/HEHS-00-207, September. Washington, D.C.

———. 2001a. "Older Workers: Demographic Trends Pose Challenges for Employers and Workers." GAO Government Accountability Office Report to the Ranking Minority Member, Subcommittee on Employer-Employee Relations, Committee on Education and the Workforce, House of Representatives, November.

———. 2001b. "Private Pensions: Issues of Coverage and Increasing Contribution Limits for Defined Contribution Plans." Report no. GAO-01-846.

———. 2002. "Private Pensions: Improving Worker Coverage and Benefits." Report no. GAO-02-225.

———. 2003a. "Older Workers: Policies of Other Nations to Increase Labor Force Participation." Report no. GAO-03-307, February.

———. 2003b. "Pension Benefit Guaranty Corporation: Single Employer Pension Insurance Program Faces Long-Term Risks." Report no. GAO-04-90.

———. 2003c. "Social Security and Minorities: Earnings, Disability Incidence, and Mortality Are Key Factors That Influence Taxes Paid and Benefits Received." Report no. GAO-03-387, April.

———. 2004. "Private Pensions: Multiemployer Plans Face Short and Long-Term Challenges." Report no. GAO-04-423.

———. 2005a. "Private Pensions: Information on Cash Balance Pension Plans." Report no. GAO-06-42.

———. 2005b. "Private Pensions: Recent Experiences of Large Defined Benefit Plans Illustrate Weaknesses in Funding Rules." Report no. GAO-05-294.

Grabener, William. 1980. *History of Retirement.* New Haven, Conn.: Yale University Press.

Grad, Susan. 2002. "Income of the Population 55 or Older." Social Security Publication no. 13-11871. Washington, D.C.: Social Security Administration.

Greene, Kelly. 2002. "More Older Investors May Delay Retirement as Portfolios Shrink." *Wall Street Journal,* February 14.

Greenhouse, Steven, and Michael Barbaro. 2005. "Wal-Mart Memo Suggests Ways to Cut Employee Benefit Costs." *New York Times*, October 26, Business C1.

Griffin, Gregg. 2004. "United Retirees Perplexed. Airline's Pension Movies Have Some Looking at Lifestyle Changes." *Denver Post*, August 2.

Grossman, Michael. 1972. "On the Concept of Health Capital and the Demand for Health." *Journal of Political Economy* 80(2): 223–25.

Gruber, Jonathan, and Brigitte C. Madrian. 2002. "Health Insurance, Labor Supply, and Job Mobility: A Critical Review of the Literature." NBER Working Paper no. 8817. Cambridge, Mass.: National Bureau of Economic Research.

Guerrera, Francesco, and Christopher Swann. 2006. "US Companies Boost Share of Economic Pie." *Financial Times*, June 5.

Gustman, Alan, and Thomas L. Steinmeier. 1984. "Partial Retirement and the Analysis of Retirement Behavior. *Industrial and Labor Relations Review* 37(3): 403–15.

———. 1985. "The 1983 Social Security Reforms and Labor Supply Adjustments of Older Individuals in the Long Run." *Journal of Labor Economics* 3(2): 237–53.

———. 1992. "The Stampede Toward Defined Contribution Pension Plans: Fact or Fiction." *Industrial Relations* 31: 361–69.

———. 2001. "Retirement and Wealth." NBER Working Paper no. 8229. Cambridge, Mass.: National Bureau of Economic Research.

———. 2002a. "Retirement and the Stock Market Bubble." Working Paper no. 9440. Cambridge, Mass.: National Bureau of Economic Research.

———. 2002b. "The Social Security Early Entitlement Age an a Structural Model of Retirement and Wealth." NBER Working Paper no. 9183. Cambridge, Mass.: National Bureau of Economic Research.

Gustman, Alan, Thomas L. Steinmeier, and S. Goss. 2003. "Retirement Effects of Social Security Reform." Presented at the 5th Annual Conference of the Retirement Research Corporation, Washington, D.C.

Hamermesh, Daniel S. 1999. "Changing Inequality in Markets for Workplace Amenities." *Quarterly Journal of Economics* 114(4): 1085–123.

Hamermesh, Daniel S., and J. E. Biddle. 1993. "Beauty and the Labor Market." NBER Working Paper no. 4518. Cambridge, Mass.: National Bureau of Economic Research.

Hamermesh, Daniel S., Meng Xin, and Zhang Junsen. 2002. "Dress for success—Does Primping Pay?" *Labour Economics* 9(3): 361–73.

Hansen, Fay. 2005. "Rethinking Employee Benefits." *Business Finance* January: 29–37.

Harbrecht, Paul P. 1959. *Pension Funds and Economic Power.* New York: Twentieth Century Fund.

Harper, Barry. 2000. "Beauty, Stature and the Labour Market: A British Cohort Study." *Oxford Bulletin of Economics and Statistics.* Special Issue December 62(s1): 771–800.

Harvard Joint Study on Housing 2004.

Hawley, James, Andrew Williams, and Teresa Ghilarducci. 1997. "Labor's Paradoxical Interests and the Evolution of Corporate Governance." *Journal of Law and Society* 24: 26–43.

Hebb, Tessa, and Gordon L. Clark. 2003. "Understanding Pension Fund Corporate Engagement in a Global Arena." Working Paper. Oxford: University of Oxford, School of Geography and the Environment.

Hermes, S., and Teresa Ghilarducci. 2004. "The Effect of the Stock Market Crash on Retirement Decisions." In *Work Options for Older Americans*, edited by Teresa Ghilarducci and John Turner, 237–66. Notre Dame, Ind.: University of Notre Dame Press.

Hinz, Richard P., and John A. Turner. 1998. "Pension Coverage Initiatives: Why Don't Workers Participate." In *Living with Defined Contribution Pensions*, edited by Olivia S. Mitchell and Sylvester J. Schieber, 17–37. Philadelphia: University of Pennsylvania Press.

Holden, Karen C. 1996. "Social Security and the Economic Security of Women: Is It Fair?" In *Social Security in the 21st Century*, edited by Eric Kingson and James H. Schultz, 91–104. New York: Oxford University Press.

Holden, Sarah, and Jack Vanderhei. 2002. "Can 401(K) Accumulations Generate Significant Income for Future Retirees?" *Investment Company Institute Perspective* 8 (3). http://www.ici.org/pdf/per08-03.pdf (accessed September 27, 2005).

———. 2005. "401(K) Plan Asset Allocation, Account Balances, and Loan Activity in 2004." Issue Brief no. 285. Washington, D.C.: Employee Benefit Research Institute. September

Holtzmann, R., and E. Palmer, editors. 2005. *Non-Financial Defined Contribution (NDC) Pension Schemes: Concept, Issues, Implementation, Prospects.* Washington D.C.: World Bank.

HSBC. 2007. "The Future of Retirement: What People Want." http://a248.e.akamai.net/7/248/3622/7d1c0ed7aa1283/www.img.ghq.hsbc.com/public/groupsite/assets/retirement_future/2006_for_what_people_want.pdf (accessed online February 2, 2007).

Huberman, Gur, and Wei Jiang. 2006. "Offering versus Choice in 401(K) Plans: Equity Exposure and Number of Funds." *Journal of Finance* 61(2): 763–801.

Hunter, Lawrence. "There Are No Transition Costs." www.ipi.org.

Hurd, M., J. P. Smith, and J. M. Zissimopoulos. 2002. "The Effects of Subjective Survival on Retirement and Social Security Claiming." NBER Working Paper no. 9140. Cambridge, Mass.: National Bureau of Economic Research.

Hustead, Edwin C. 1998. "Trends in Retirement Income Plan Administrative Expenses." In *Living with Defined Contribution Pensions: Remaking Responsibility for Retirement,* edited by Olivia S. Mitchell and Sylvester Schieber, 166–77. Philadelphia: The Pension Research Council, the Wharton School of the University of Pennsylvania, and the University of Pennsylvania Press.

Hutchens, Robert M., and Jennjou Chen. 2007. "The Role of Employers in Phased Retirement: Opportunities for Phased Retirement among White Collar Workers." In *Work Options for Older Americans,* edited by Teresa Ghilarducci and John Turner, 95–118. Notre Dame, Ind.: University of Notre Dame Press.

Hutchens, Robert M., and Karen Grace-Martin. 2004 "Who among White Collar Workers Has an Opportunity for Phased Retirement? Establishment Characteristics." IZA Discussion Paper no. 1155. May, SSRN: http://ssrn.com/abstract=554023.

Hutchens, Robert M., and Kerry L. Papps. 2004. "Developments in Phased Retirement." Working Paper no. WP 2004-14. University of Pennsylvania: Pension Research Council. http://rider.wharton.upenn.edu/~prc/PRC/WP/WP2004-14.pdf.

Hutcheson, Ron. 2005. "President Questions Worth of Social Security Fund; Experts Fault Both Sides in Debate Over Retirement Plan." *Pittsburgh Post-Gazette* April 6, p. 1.

Imbens, Guido W., Donald B. Rubin, and Bruce I. Sacerdote. 2001. "Estimating the Effect of Unearned Income on Labor Earnings, Savings, and Consumption: Evidence from a Survey of Lottery Players." *American Economic Review* 91(4): 778–94.

International Labor Organization. 2000. "World Labour Report: Income Security and Social Protection in a Changing World." Washington, D.C., June.

Ippolito, Richard A. 1997. *Pension Plans and Employee Performance: Evidence, Analysis, and Policy.* Chicago: University of Chicago Press.

Jackson, Richard. 2002. "The Global Retirement Crisis—the Threat to World Stability and What to Do about It." Report. Washington, D.C.: Center for Strategic and International Studies and Citigroup.

Jacoby, Sanford. 1997. *Modern Manors: Welfare Capitalism since the New Deal.* Princeton, N.J.: Princeton University Press.

———. 2003. "Career Jobs Are Dead: Reply: Premature Reports of Demise." In *Benefits for the Workplace of the Future,* edited by Judith F. Mazo, et al. Philadelphia: University of Pennsylvania Press.

James, Ralph, and Estelle James. 1965. *Hoffa and the Teamsters: A Study of Union Power.* Princeton, N.J.: Van Nostrand.

Jesuit, David, and Timothy Smeeding. 2002. "Poverty and Income Distribution." Luxembourg Income Study Working Paper no. 293. Syracuse, N.Y.: Syracuse University, Maxwell School of Citizenship and Public Affairs.

John, David C. 2005. "Improving Retirement Security: Three Reforms." Heritage Foundation Study, July 29.

Johnson, Richard. 2004. "Job Demand among Older Workers." *Monthly Labor Review* July, 48–56.

Johnson, Richard W., and Cori E. Uccello. 2002. "Can Cash Balance Pension Plans Improve Retirement Security for Today's Workers?" The Retirement Project Policy Brief no. 14. Washington, D.C.: Urban Institute.

———. 2004. "Cash Balance Plans: What Do They Mean for Retirement Security?" *National Tax Journal* 57(2): 315–28.

Kaiser Family Foundation. 2005. "Prospects for Retiree Health Benefits as Medicare Drug Coverage Begins." Publication no 7439. http://www.kff.org/medicare/retiree.cfm (accessed July 23, 2007).

Kamerman, Sheila B. 2000. "Early Childhood Education and Care: An Overview of Developments in the OECD Countries." *International Journal of Education and Research* 33(1): 7–29.

Kaufman, Bruce E. 1989. "Labor's Inequality of Bargaining Power: Changes over Time and Implications for Public Policy." *Journal of Labor Research* 10: 285–99.

Kerkhofs, Marcel, Maarten Lindeboom, and Jules Theeuwes. 1999. "Retirement, Financial Incentives and Health." *Labour Economics* 6(2): 203–27.

Keynes, John Maynard. [1932] 1963. "Economic Possibilities for Our Grandchildren." In *Essays in Persuasion: The Collected Works,* Vol. 11. London: MacMillian.

Kingson, E. R., and Y. Arsenault. 2000. "The Diversity of Risk among Age-62 Retired Worker Beneficiaries." Working Paper. Center for Retirement Research at Boston College. econpapers.hhs.se/paper/crrcrrwps/2000-08.htm.

Klein, Jennifer. 2003. *For All These Rights: Business, Labor, and the Shaping of America's Public-Private Welfare State*. Princeton, N.J.: Princeton University Press.

Korczyk, Sophie. 1993. "Are Women's Jobs Getting Better or Women Getting Better Jobs?" In *Pensions in a Changing Economy*, edited by Dallas Salisbury and Richard B. Burkhauser. Washington, D.C.: EBRI.

Kotlikoff, Laurence J., and Scott Burns. 2004. *The Coming Generational Storm: What You Need to Know about America's Economic Future*. Cambridge, Mass.: MIT Press.

Kovaleski, Dave. 2002. "Changes: 20 Years Later, It's a Whole New Ballgame; List of Top Managers Reshaped by 401(K) Boom, Bull Market." *Pensions and Investments*, May 27.

Krasner, Jeffrey. 2005. "Polaroid Cuts R & D, Digital Plans: Under New Owner, Firm Is Little More Than Brand Name." *Boston Globe* August 2, C1.

Kruger, Jennifer. 1999. "All Your Eggs?" *CFO: The Magazine for Senior Financial Executives,* December, 69–70, 73.

Kunerth, Jeff. 2002. "Need and Desire Keep Older Workers on the Job." *Orlando Sentinel*, March 2.

Langer, David. 2004. "Scrapping Social Security's Intermediate Cost Projections." Letter to the editor. *Society of Actuaries Journal*, March.

Lazear, Edward P. 1991. Labor economics and the psychology of organizations. *Journal of Economic Perspectives* 5(2): 89–110.

Lazear, Edward P. 2005. "The Virtues of Personal Accounts for Social Security. *Economists' Voice* 2(1): Article 4.

Lee, Ronald. 2003. "The Demographic Transition: Three Centuries of Fundamental Change." *Journal of Economic Perspectives* 17: 167–90.

Leonesio, Michael V., Denton R. Vaughn, and Bernard Wixon. 2000. "Early Retirees under Social Security: Health Status and Economic Resources. *Social Security Bulletin* 63(4): 1–16.

Levine, P., O. Mitchell, and J. Phillips. 2000. "A Benefit of One's Own: Older Women's Retirement Entitlements under Social Security." Working Paper no. WP 2004-6. Philadelphia: University of Pennsylvania Pension Research Council. prc.wharton.upenn.edu/prc/PRC/WP/WP1999-21rev.pdf.

Lichtenstein, Nelson. 2003. *State of the Union: A Century of American Labor*. Princeton, N.J.: Princeton University Press.

Liebman, Jeffrey B. 2005. "Reforming Social Security: Not All Privatization Schemes Are Created Equal." *Harvard Magazine* March/April 104: 4.

Lofgren, Eric, Steven Nyce, and Sylvester Scheiber. 2003. "Designing Total Reward Programs for Tight Labor Markets." In *Benefits for the Workplace of the Future*, edited by Judith F. Mazo, et al., 151–77. Philadelphia: University of Pennsylvania Press.

Madrian, Brigitte C. 1994. "Employment-Based Health Insurance and Job Mobility: Is There Evidence of Job-Lock?" *Quarterly Journal of Economics* 109(1): 27–54.

Madrian, Brigitte C., and Dennis F. Shea. 2000. "The Power of Suggestion: Inertia in 401(K) Participation and Savings Behavior." NBER Working Paper no. 7682. Cambridge, Mass.: National Bureau of Economic Research.

Manning & Napier's Associates, Inc. 2004. "A Solution to Participant Confusion. Help D.C. Plan Participants Make Better Investment Choices Using Tiered Communication and Life Cycle Funds." Fairport, N.Y. http://www.lifecyclefunds.com/pdf/white_paper.pdf (accessed April 19, 2007).

McCaw, Daniel. 2004. "Strengthening Pension Security for All Americans: Are Workers Prepared for a Safe and Secure Retirement?" *Testimony before the House Committee on Education and the Workforce.* United States Congress, House of Representatives. 108th Cong., 1st sess., February 25.

McDonnell, Kenneth J. 2005. "Income of the Elderly Population: 2003." *EBRI Notes* 26(1): 9–14.

McGarry, K. 2002. "Health and Retirement: Do Changes in Health Affect Retirement Expectations?" NBER Working Paper no. 9317. Cambridge, Mass.: National Bureau of Economic Research.

McGill, Dan, et al. 2005. "Defined Contribution Design." In *Fundamentals of Private Pensions*, 8th ed. Oxford: Oxford University Press.

Medoff, J., and M. Calabrese. 2001. "The Impact of Labor Market Trends on Health and Benefit Coverage and Inequality." Report. Pension and Welfare Benefit Agency, U.S. Department of Labor.

Milbank, Diana. 2005. "Driving Points Home on Social Security." *Washington Post*, March 17, A05.

Miller, G. H., and D. R. Gerstein. 1983. "The Life Expectancy of Nonsmoking Men and Women." *Public Health Reports* July–August 98(4): 343–49.

Miller, Paul, and Charles Mulvey. 1992. "Trade Unions, Collective Voice and Fringe Benefits." *Economic Record* 68: 125–41.

Minchin, T. J. 2005. "Organizing a Labor Law Violator: The JP Stevens Campaign and the Struggle to Unionize the US South, 1963–1983." *International Review of Social History* 50: 27–51.

Mishel, Lawrence, Jared Bernstein, and John Schmitt. 2000. *The State of Working America.* Ithaca, N.Y.: Cornell University Press.

Mitchell, Olivia S., and Sylvester J. Schieber. 1998. "Defined Contribution Pensions: New Opportunities, New Risks." In *Living with Defined Contribution Plans*, edited by Olivia Mitchell and Sylvester J. Schieber. Philadelphia: The Pension Research Council, the Wharton School of the University of Pennsylvania, and the University of Pennsylvania Press.

Mitchell, Olivia S., Stephen P. Utkus, and Tongxuan Yang. 2005. "Turning Workers into Savers? Incentives, Liquidity, and Choice in 401(K) Plan Design." NBER Working Paper no. W11726. Cambridge, Mass.: National Bureau of Economic Research.

Mittelstaedt, Fred H. 2002. "Assessing Retiree Health Legacy Costs: Is America Prepared for a Healthy Retirement?" *Testimony before the Committee on Education and the Workforce.* United States Congress, House of Representatives. 106th Cong., 1st sess., May 16.

Morgan Stanley. 2002. "Look for That Union Label and Run the Other Way." *Investment Perspectives,* November 14.

Munnell, Alicia H. 2003. "The Declining Role of Social Security." *Just the Facts on Retirement Issues* 6:1–4. Boston: Center for Retirement Research at Boston College.

———. 2007. "Alicia Munnell Comments." *Work Options for Mature Americans.* Notre Dame, Ind. University of Notre Dame Press.

Munnell, Alicia H., Kevin Cahill, and Natalia Jivan. 2003. "How Has the Shift to 401(K)s Affected the Retirement Age?" *Issues in Brief* no.13. Boston: Center for Retirement Research at Boston College.

Munnell, Alicia H., Francesca Golub-Sass, Mauricio Soto, and Francis Vitagliana. 2006. "Why Are Healthy Employers Freezing Their Pensions?" *Issues in Brief,* no. 44. Boston: Center for Retirement Research at Boston College.

Munnell, Alicia H., Francesca Golub-Sass, and Andrew Varani. 2005. "How Much Are Workers Saving?" *Issues in Brief,* no. 34. Boston: Center for Retirement Research at Boston College. ttp://www.bc.edu/centers/crr/ib_34.shtml.

Munnell, Alicia H., and Daniel Halperin. 2005. "How Should the Private Pension System Be Reformed?" In *The Evolving Pension System,* edited by William G. Gale, John B. Shoven, and Mark Warshawsky. Washington: D.C.: Brookings Institution Press.

Munnell, Alicia H., Jerilyn Libby, John Prinzivalli. 2006. "Investment Returns: Defined Benefit vs. 401(K) Plans." *Issues in Brief,* no. 52. Boston: Center for Retirement Research at Boston College.

Munnell, Alicia H., and Mauricio Soto. 2005. "What Is Progressive Price Indexing?" *Just the Facts on Retirement Issues,* April. Boston: Center for Retirement Research at Boston College.

Munnell, Alicia H., and Annika Sundén. 2003. "Suspending the Employer Match." Boston: Center for Retirement Research at Boston College. http://www.bc.edu/centers/crr/dummy/pr_2003-06-30.shtml.

———. 2004. *Coming Up Short: The Challenge of 401(K) Plans.* Washington, D.C.: Brookings Institution Press.

———. 2006. "Still Coming Up Short." *Issues in Brief.* Boston: Center for Retirement Research at Boston College.

Munnell, Alicia H., Annika Sundén, and Elizabeth Lidstone. 2002. "How Important Are Private Pensions?" *Issues in Brief,* no. 8. Boston: Center for Retirement Research at Boston College.

Munnell, Alicia H., Anthony Webb, and Luke Delorme. 2006. "A New National Retirement Risk Index." *Issues in Brief,* no. 48. Boston, Mass.: Center for Retirement Research at Boston College.

Murray, Alan. 2007. "Labor Leader, Buyout Kings: Speak the Same Language." *Wall Street Journal*, May 30, A2.

Myles, John. 2002. "A New Contract for the Elderly?" In *Why We Need a New Welfare State*, edited by Gosta Esping Andersen, 130–72. Oxford: Oxford University Press.

Myles, John. 1988. "Postwar Capitalism and Social Security." In *The Politics of Social Policy in the United States*, edited by Margaret Weir, Ann Shola Orloff, and Theda Skocpol. Princeton, N.J.: Princeton University Press.

Neuman, K. D. 2003. "The Health Effects of Retirement: A Theoretical and Empirical Investigation." PhD diss., University of Notre Dame.

Neuman, K., and T. Ghilarducci. 2004. "The Distribution of Retirement Leisure: Evidence from the HRS." Working Paper. Notre Dame, Ind.: University of Notre Dame.

Neumark, David, editor. 2000. *On the Job: Is Long-Term Employment a Thing of the Past?* New York: Russell Sage Foundation.

Neumark, David, and M. McLennan. 2003. "Age Discrimination Legislation in the United States." *Contemporary Economic Policy* 21: 297–317.

Nyce, Steven, and Sylvester Schieber. 2004. "Will There Really Be a Labor Shortage?" *Public Policy and Aging Report* 14(3).

O'Hara, Ruth, et al. 2006. "Long-Term Effects of Mnemonic Training in Community-Dwelling Older Adults." *Journal of Psychiatric Research* (41)7: 585–90.

Office of the Management and Budget. 2007. "Analytical Perspectives of the U.S. Budget," chap. 19: "Tax Expenditures." http://www.whitehouse.gov/omb/budget.

Olshansky, S. Jay, et al. 2005. "A Potential Decline in Life Expectancy in the United States in the 21st Century." *New England Journal of Medicine* 352(11): 1138–45.

Olson, Laura Katz. 1982. *The Political Economy of Aging: The State, Private Power, and Social Welfare.* New York: Columbia University Press.

Organization for Economic Cooperation and Development (OECD). 2004. *Reforming Public Pensions: Sharing the Experiences of Transition in OECD Countries.* Paris.

———. 2005. *Pensions at a Glance—Public Policies across OECD Countries.* www.oecd.org/els/social/ageing/PAG.

———. 2006–2007. "OECD in Figures." Paris.

Orszag, Peter R. 2005. "Social Security Reform." *Testimony before the United States Senate Committee on Finance.* April 26.

Orszag, Peter R., and Peter A. Diamond. 2003. "Reforming Social Security: A Balanced Plan." Policy Brief no. 126. Washington, D.C.: Brookings Institution.

Osterman, Paul. 2000. *Securing Prosperity: The American Labor Market: How It Has Changed and What to Do about It.* Princeton, N.J.: Princeton University Press.

Ottawa Citizen. 2006. "GM to Alter Pension Plans." March 8, D3.

Padgett, Thomas O. 2002. "The Enron Collapse and Its Implications for Worker Retirement Security." *Testimony before the Committee on Education and the Workforce.* United States Congress, House of Representatives. 106th Cong., 1st sess., February 7.

Panis, C. 2003. "Annuities and Retirement Satisfaction." Report no. DRU-3021. RAND Labor and Population Program. http://www.rand.org/labor/DRU/DRU-3021.pdf.

Peaple, Nigel. 2004. "European Pension Reform and Private Pensions: An Analysis of the EU's Six Largest Countries." Report. London: Association of British Insurers. http://www.abi.org.uk/BookShop/ResearchReports/.

Pension Rights Center. 2004. "Conversation on Coverage: National Policy Forum Conference Notebook." July 22.

Perun, Pamela. 2001. "The Limits of Saving." Retirement Project, Occasional Paper no. 7. August, http://ssrn.com/abstract=250592"http://ssrn.com/abstract=250592

Petruno, Tom. 2005. "More Companies Increase Dividends." *Los Angeles Times*, January 4, C1.

Petska, Tom, and Mike Strudler. 2002. "Income, Taxes, and Tax Progressivity: An Examination of Recent Trends in the Distribution of Individual Income and Taxes." Washington, D.C.: Internal Revenue Service, Statistics of Income Division.

Phillips, Kevin. 2002. *Wealth and Democracy: A Political History of the American Rich.* New York: Broadway Books.

Plan Sponsor. 2004. "Easy Does It." *Plan Sponsor Magazine*, January 1.

———. 2006. "Michigan's Granholm Announces New 401(K) Plan Proposal," January 26. PLANSPONSOR.com.

Population Resource Center. 2005. "Older Women and Poverty: A Demographic Profile." Washington, D.C. http://www.prcdc.org/summaries/AgingSeries05/women andpoverty.html (accessed July 2007).

PRNewswire. 2005. "Baby Boomers and Aging Midlifers Redefine Retirement. May 5.

Purcell, Patrick. 2003. "Retirement Savings and Household Wealth: A Summary of Recent Data." Report. Washington, D.C.: Congressional Research Service.

———. 2005a. "Pension Sponsorship and Participation: Summary of Recent Trends." CRS Report no. RL30122. Washington, D.C.: Congressional Research Service.

———. 2005b. "Retirement Plan Participation and Contributions: Trends from 1998 to 2003." CRS Report no. RL33116. Washington, D.C.: Congressional Research Service.

———. 2005c. "Retirement Plan Participation and Contributions: Trends from 1998 to 2003." *Journal of Pension Planning and Compliance* 32 (1).

Purcell, Patrick, and Debra Whitman. 2005. "Social Security Individual Accounts and Employer-Sponsored Pensions." *Journal of Pension Planning and Compliance* 31 (2).

Purvi, S., and G. Kezdi. 2004. "Economic Adjustment of Recent Retirees to Adverse Wealth Shocks." Working Paper no. 75. Ann Arbor, Mich.: Michigan Retirement Research Center.

Quadagno, Jill, Melissa Hardy, and Lawrence Hazelrigg. 2003. "Labour Market Transitions and the Erosion of the Fordist Lifecycle: Discarding Older Workers in the Automobile Manufacturing and Banking Industries in the United States." *Geneva Papers on Risk and Insurance: Issues and Practice*, October 28(4): 640–51.

Quinn, Joseph. 1987. "Comment on Moffitt's Life-Cycle Labor Supply and Social Security: A Time Series Analysis." In *Work, Health, and Income among the Aged*, edited by Gary Burtless, 220–28. Washington, D.C.: The Brookings Institution.

———. 1996. "The Role of Bridge Jobs in the Retirement Patterns of Older Americans in the 1990s." Presented at International Association of Research in Income and Wealth Annual Research Conference.

Raab, Lauren. 2005. "UC Nurses Authorize Strike for Pension Plans, Salary: University Health Workers Have Set July 21 as Tentative Date for Action." *Daily Bruin*, July 11.

Ransom, Roger, and Richard Sutch. 1986. "The Labor of Older Men." *Journal of Economic History* 46(1): 1–30.

Rappaport, Anna. 2004. "Retirement Perspective: Exploding the Myth That Employees Always Prefer Defined Contribution Plans." Mercer Human Resource Consulting, 20 May. www.mercerhr.com (accessed October 10, 2005).

Rappaport, Anna, and Monica Dragut. 2004. "Perspectives on Retirement Risk." Mercer Consulting. http://www.nasi.org/usr_doc/Rappaport-Dragut_Paper_2004.pdf (accessed July 23, 2007).

Raskin, A. H. 1980. "The Stevens Settlement." *New York Times*, October 21, p. 19.

Reagan, Patricia B., and John A. Turner. 2000. "Did the Decline in the Marginal Tax Rate in the 1980s Reduce Pension Coverage?" In *Employee Benefits and Labor Markets in Canada and the United States*, edited by Stephen Woodbury and William T. Alpert, 475–96. Kalamazoo, Mich.: W. E. Upjohn Institute.

Remez, S., C. Keegan, S. Gross, and L. Fisher. 2004. "Boomers at Midlife 2002: The AARP Life Stage Study Research Report." November. Washington, D.C.: AARP. http://www.aarp.org/research/reference/boomers/aresearch-import-916.html (accessed July 23, 2007).

Rix, Sara E. 2004. "Aging and Work: A View from the United States." AARP Public Policy Institute Research Report, February. Washington, D.C.

Rix, Sara E., L. Rosenmann, and J. H. Schultz. 1998. "Privatization and Older Women's Financial Needs: Gender Differences in Public/Private Targeting." Presented at the Second International Social Security Association Conference on Social Security, Jerusalem.

Robertson, D. B. 1936. "Railroad Problems in the United States: The Stake of Railroad Labor in the Transportation Problem." *Annals of the American Academy of Political and Social Science, Vol. 187, Railroads and Government* September, 88–94.

Roizen, Michael F., and Elizabeth A. Stephenson. 1999. *Real Age: Are You as Young as You Can Be?* New York: Cliff Street Books.

Rose, Stephen J., and Heidi I. Hartmann. 2004. *Still a Man's Labor Market: The Long-Term Earnings Gap*. Washington, D.C.: Institute for Women's Policy Research.

Rotenberg, J. 2006. "The Retirement Challenge: Expectations vs. Reality." Presentation on McKinsey and Company's 2006 Consumer Retirement Survey at the EBRI/AARP Pension Conference, Washington, D.C., May 15.

Rowe, John W., and Robert Kahn. 1998. *Successful Aging*. New York: Pantheon Books.

Rubery, Jill. 1978. "Structured Labour Markets, Worker Organizations and Low Pay." *Cambridge Journal of Economics* 2(1): 17–36.

Russell, Bertrand. 1935. *In Praise of Idleness*. London: George Allen and Unwin.

Salisbury, Dallas. 2005. "Hearings on Retirement Policy Challenges and Opportunities of an Aging Society." *Testimony before the House Ways and Means Committee*. United States Congress, House of Representatives. May 19.

Samuelson, Robert J. 2005. "Retirement at 70." *Washington Post*. May 18, A17.

Samwick, Andrew A. 1998. "New Evidence on Pensions and Social Security and the Timing of Retirement." *Journal of Public Economics* 70(2): 207–36.

Sass, Steven. A. 1997. *The Promise of Private Pensions: The First Hundred Years*. Cambridge, Mass.: Harvard University Press.

Schieber, Sylvester J. 2002. "Assessing Retiree Health Legacy Costs: Is America Prepared for a Healthy Retirement?" *Testimony before the Committee on Education and the Workforce*. United States Congress, House of Representatives. 106th Cong., 1st sess., May 16.

Schieber, Sylvester J., Richard Dunn, and David L. Wray. 1998. "The Future of the D.C. Revolution." In *Living with Defined Contribution Plans,* edited by Olivia S. Mitchell and Sylvester J. Schieber. Philadelphia: The Pension Research Council, University of Pennsylvania Press.

Scholtz, K., A. Seshadri, and S. Khitatrakun. 2004. "Are Americans Saving 'Optimally' for Retirement?" NBER Working Paper no. 10260, January. Cambridge, Mass.: National Bureau of Economic Research.

Sevak, P. 2002. "Wealth Shocks and Retirement Timing: Evidence from the Nineties." Working Paper no. 27. Ann Arbor, Mich.: Michigan Retirement Research Center.

Sherrill, Martha. 2003. "Walk on the Wild Side." *AARP Magazine*, November/December, 1.

Shiller, Robert J. 2000. *Irrational Exuberance*. Princeton, N.J.: Princeton University Press.

———. 2005. "The Life-Cycle Personal Accounts Proposal for Social Security: A Review." NBER Working Paper no. 11300. Cambridge, Mass.: National Bureau of Economic Research.

Silvers, Damon, William Patterson, and J. W. Mason. 2000. "Challenging Wall Street's Conventional Wisdom: Defining a Worker-Owner View of Value." In *Working Capital: The Power of Labor's Pensions,* edited by Tessa Hub, Archon Fung, and Joel Rogers. Ithaca, N.Y.: Cornell University Press.

Skinner, J. 2007. "Are You Sure You're Saving Enough for Retirement?" NBER Working Paper no. 12981. Cambridge, Mass.: National Bureau of Economic Research.

Sloane, Arthur. 1991. *Hoffa*. Cambridge, Mass.: MIT Press.

Smeeding, T. M., Estes, C. L., and Glasse L. 1999. "Social Security Reform and Older Women: Improving the System." Washington, D.C. Income Security Policy Series Paper no. 22. Syracuse, N.Y.: Center for Policy Research, Maxwell School of Citizenship and Public Affairs, Syracuse University.

Smith, Adam. 1976. *An Inquiry into the Nature and Causes of the Wealth of Nations*. Oxford: Clarendon Press/New York: Oxford University Press. Originally published in 1776

Smith, Paul A., David A. Love, and Lucy C. McNair, 2007. "Do Households Have Enough Retirement Wealth?" (March 2). Available at SSRN: http://ssrn.com/abstract=968412.

Soares, Jorge. 2005. "Social Security Evaluation: A Critique." *Macroeconomic Dynamics* 9: 57–97.

Social Security Administration. 2003. "OASDI Beneficiaries by State and County Table." http://www.ssa.gov/policy/docs/statcomps/oasdi_sc/2003/table3.html (accessed September 6, 2005).

———. 2004. "Income of the Population Aged 55." http://www.ssa.gov/policy/docs/statcomps/income_pop55/2002/index.html#toc.

Solberg, Eric, and Teresa Laughlin. 1995. "The Gender Pay Gap, Fringe Benefits, and Occupational Crowding." *Industrial and Labor Relations Review* 48(4): 692–708.

Solomon, Joel. 2003. "Retirement in the Balance: The Crucial Role of Defined Benefit Pension Plans in Achieving Retirement Security in the United States." Working Paper. Washington, D.C.: AFL-CIO Center for Working Capital.

Soto, Mauricio. 2005. "Will Baby Boomers Drown in Debt?" *Just the Facts on Retirement Issues* 15:1–6. Boston: Center for Retirement Research at Boston College.

Stevens, Beth. 1986. "Complementing the Welfare State: The Development of Private Pensions, Health Insurance and Other Employee Benefits in the United States." Report. Geneva: International Labour Office.

Stewart, Jay. 2002. "Recent Trends in Job Stability and Job Security." Report. Washington, D.C.: U.S. Department of Labor, Bureau of Labor Statistics, Employment Research and Program Development.

Stock, James H. and David A. Wise. 1990. "Pensions, the Option Value of Work, and Retirement." *Econometrica* 58(5): 1151–80.

Strudler, Michael, and Tom Petska. 2002. "Further Analysis of the Distribution of Income and Taxes, 1979–2002." Statistics of Income Division, Internal Revenue Service. http://www.irs.gov/pub/irs-soi/04asastr.pdf (accessed September 6, 2005).

Tasini, Jonathan. 2005. "The Disappearing Pension." *TomPaine.com*, May 31. http://www.tompaine.com/articles/20050531/the_disappearing_pension.php.

Thaler, Richard H. 1991. "Some Empirical Evidence On Dynamic Inconsistency." In *Quasi Rational Economics*, edited by Richard H. Thaler, 127–33. New York: Russell Sage Foundation.

The Conference Board. 2006. "Managing the Mature Workforce." Report no. 369-05-RR, September 19.

Thompson, Larry. 2005. "Paying for Retirement Sharing the Gain." In *In Search of Retirement Security: The Changing Mix of Social Insurance, Employee Benefits and Individual Responsibility*, edited by Teresa Ghilarducci, Van Doorn Oms, John L. Palmer, and Catherine Hill, 115–26. Century Foundation and National Academy of Social Insurance.

Toner, Robin. 2005. "It's 'Private' vs. 'Personal' in Debate over Bush Plan." *New York Times*, March 22.

Turner, J. 2005. "International Comparisons: Administrative Costs for Social Security Private Accounts." Report. Washington, D.C.: AARP Public Policy Institute.

Turner, John. A, 2006. "Designing 401(K) Plans That Encourage Retirement Savings: Lessons from Behavioral Finance Research Report." AARP Public Policy Institute, March. http://www.aarp.org/research/financial/pensions/.

Turner, John, and Dana Muir. 2005. "Longevity and Retirement Age in Defined Benefit Pension Plans." In *Work Options for Older Americans*, edited by John Turner and Teresa Ghilarducci. Notre Dame, Ind.: University of Notre Dame Press.

Uchitelle, Louis. 2003. "lder Workers Are Thriving Despite Recent Hard Times." *New York Times*, September 8, p. 1.

United Nations. 2005. "World Population Prospects: 2002." New York: Population Division.

U.S. Bureau of the Census. 2000. "Statistical Abstract of the United States: 2000. Educational Attainment by Country: 1998." Table 1362, p. 830. Report. Washington, D.C.: U.S. Government Printing Office.

———. 2001. "Statistical Abstract of the United States." Report.

———. 2006. "Older Americans Update 2006: Key Indicators of Well-Being." http://www.agingstats.gov/update2006/default.htm (accessed March 3, 2007).

U.S. Bureau of the Census, Housing and Household Economic Statistics Division. 2005. *Income, Poverty and Health Insurance Coverage in the United States: 2005.*

U.S. Department of Labor. 1998. "Study of 401(K) Plan Fees and Expenses." Report.

———. 2000. "Abstract of 1996 Form 5500 Annual Reports." *Private Pension Plan Bulletin 9.*

———. 2005. *Women in the Labor Force: A Databook.*

U.S. Department of Labor, Bureau of Labor Statistics. 2000. "National Compensation Survey." Washington, D.C.: U.S. Government Printing Office.

———. 2004. "Employee Tenure Summary." Report.

———. 2006. "Current Population Survey." Series ID LFS1603301, LFS21003301, LFS1604901, LFS1604901Q, LFS21004901, LFS1606501, LFS1606501Q, LFS21006501,

LFS1603302, LFS21003302, LFS1604902, LFS1604902Q, LFS21004902, LFS1606502, LFS1606502Q, LFS21006502. http://www.bls.gov/data/home.htm.

Van de Klaauw, Wilbert, and Kenneth Wolpin. 2005. "Social Security and the Retirement and Savings Behavior of Low Income Households." Working Paper no. 05-020. State College, Pa.: Penn Institute for Economic Research.

VanDerhei, Jack, "Defined Benefit Plan Freezes: Who's Affected, How Much, and Replacing Lost Accruals." EBRI Issue Brief no. 291, March 2006. http://ssrn.com/abstract=891170.

Vanguard. 2005. "Vanguard Annuity Options. Create Your Own Personal Pension Plan with an Income Annuity." vanguard.com (accessed October 15, 2005).

Venti, Steven F. 2005. "Choice, Behavior, and Retirement Saving." In *The Oxford Handbook of Pensions and Retirement Income*, edited by Gordon L. Clark, Alicia H. Munnell, and Michael Orszag, 603–17. New York: Oxford University Press.

Vital Statistics of the United States. 1955. Vol. I, introduction, 1957.

Vital Statistics of the United States. 1965. Vol. II, sec. 5, 1968.

Walker, David. 2004. "Airlines Plans' Underfunding Illustrates Broader Problems with the Defined Benefit System." *Testimony before the Committee on Commerce, Science, and Transportation.* United States Congress, Senate. 108th Cong., 1st sess., October 7.

Walsh, Mary Willimas. 2003. "A Lump Sum Threat to Pension Funds." *New York Times*, August 14.

———. 2006. "IBM to Freeze Pension Plans to Trim Costs." *New York Times*, January 6, section A, column 5, Business/Financial Desk, 1.

Washington Post. 2005. "Public Sector Workers under Fire: Schwarzenegger Targets a Last Bastion of Security." June 13.

Watkins, Marilyn. 2002. "Washington Voluntary Accounts: A Proposal Key Elements." Economic Opportunity Institute, January. http://www.econop.org/Policy-WVA.htm-2002 (accessed December 2004).

Watson Wyatt Worldwide. 2004. "Traditional Pension Plans Outperformed 401(K) Plans During Last Bear Market, Watson Wyatt Analysis Finds." Press Release, November 22. http://www.watsonwyatt.com/news/press.asp?ID=13953.

———. 2005. "Recent Funding and Sponsorship Trends among the Fortune 1000." *Watson Wyatt Worldwide Insider*, Washington, D.C. http://www.watsonwyatt.com/us/pubs/insider/showarticle.asp?ArticleID=14750 (accessed July 23, 2007).

Weaver, Kent R. 2001. "International Evidence on the Desirability of Individual Retirement Accounts in Public Pension Systems." *Testimony before the Social Security Subcommittee, House Ways and Means Committee on Social Security Reform.* United States Congerss, House of Representatives. 105th Cong., 1st sess., July 31.

Weller, Christian. 2005. "Ensuring Retirement Income Security with Cash Balance Plans." Center for American Progress, September.

———. 2006. "Presentation on the Immediate Future of Pension Security." Washington, D.C.: Center for American Progress. March.

Weller, Christian, and Jeffrey Wenger. 2003. "The Interaction between Health, Health Insurance, and Retirement." In *Work Options for Older Americans*, edited by Teresa Ghilarducci and John Turner, 227–302. Notre Dame, Ind.: University of Notre Dame Press.

Weller, Christian, and Edward N. Wolff. 2005. *Retirement Income: The Crucial Role of Social Security.* Washington, D.C.: Economic Policy Institute.

Whitehouse, Edward, and Peter Whiteford. 2006. "Reforms in OECD Countries." *Oxford Review of Economic Policy*, Vol. 22, no. 1, 80.

Whitehouse, Kaja. 2002. "Bond Theory Grabs Notice as Pension Debate Swells." *Dow Jones News Service*, December 12, 2002.

———. 2004. "Who to Believe?" *CFO Europe*, May. http://www.cfoeurope.com/displaystory.cfm/2661813/l_print.

Wiatrowski, William J. 2005. "Retirement Plan Design and the Mobile Workforce." Bureau of Labor Statistics, September 28. http://www.bls.gov/opub/cwc/cm20050926ar01p1.htm (accessed July 23, 2007).

Wolfe, John R. 1983. "Perceived Mortality and Early Retirement." *Review of Economics and Statistics* 65(4): 544–551.

Wolff, Edward N. 2002. *Retirement Insecurity: The Income Shortfalls Awaiting the Soon-to-Retire.* Washington, D.C.: Economic Policy Institute.

Wolff, Edward N., Ajit Zacharias, and Asena Caner. 2005. "Household Wealth, Public Consumption and Economic Well-Being in the United States." *Cambridge Journal of Economics* 29(6): 1073–90.

Wooten, James A. 2001. "'The Most Glorious Story of Failure in the Business': The Studebaker-Packard Corporation and the Origins of ERISA." *Buffalo Law Review* 49: 683–739.

———. 2005. *The Employee Retirement Income Security Act of 1974: A Political History.* Berkeley: University of California Press.

Wright, Erik Olin. 2000. "Working-Class Power, Capitalist Class Interests and Class Compromises." *American Sociological Review* 105(4): 957–1002.

Zernike, Kate. 2002. "Stocks' Slide Is Playing Havoc with Older Americans' Dreams." *New York Times*, July 14, p.1.

Zion, David, and Bill Carcache. 2002. "The Magic of Pension Accounting." New York: Credit Suisse/First Boston Equity Research, September 27. http://www.savitz.com/downloads/pension_accounting.pdf (accessed July 23, 2007).

Acknowledgments

I appreciate my colleagues at The New School, the Bernard L. Schwartz Center for Economic Policy Analysis, and the University of Notre Dame and the audiences given me by Harvard University, Oxford University, The Century Foundation, the Levy Institute, University of California at Berkeley and UCLA, Rutgers University, the Government Accountability Office, the W. E. Upjohn Institute, and the Rockefeller Foundation. The Wurf Fellowship at the Labor and Workplace Program at the Harvard School of Law, the Retirement Research Foundation, the Sloan Foundation, the Ford Foundation, and the Heinz Foundation provided generous support.

Beth Almeida, Eileen Appelbaum, Larry Befferman, Paul Booth, Clair Brown, Robert Cirasa, Gordon Clark, Gerald Combs, Charles Craypo, Ross Eisenbrey, Richard Ferlauto, Karen Ferguson, Robert Fishman, Jaime Galbraith, Tessa Hebb, Sharon Hermes, Charles Jeszeck, Daniel Lawson, Mary Lee, Mark Levinson, George Miller, Paul Mishler, Monique Morrissey, Kevin Neuman, Doug Orr, Wei Sun, Chris Tiedemann, John Turner, Lou Uchitelle, Mary Ursu, Michele Varnhagen, David Walker, and Christian Weller provided intellectual insight and information. I was helped by the Anne Zakas and trenchant advice from my editor Peter Dougherty.

My husband William O'Rourke and my son Joseph O'Rourke lovingly and patiently bore the brunt of travel, late nights, and pontificating episodes. I am deeply grateful for the love and distraction provided by my other family members—my mother Marion Ghilarducci, my stepmother Ruth Ghilarducci, my brother David, my sister-in-law Sally, and Ben Mateo, Mia Teresa Ghilarducci, and my late father Harry Ghilarducci. This book would not be possible without the many workers who shared their visions for their retirement and their hope and struggle to secure their pensions.

Index

Note: The letters *b, f, n,* and *t* refer to boxes, figures, notes, or tables on the page indicated. The number following an *n* refers to the note number on that page.

Milton Keynes UK
Ingram Content Group UK Ltd.
UKHW031129290824
447545UK00004B/128